The Nyāya Sūtras of Gotama

The Nyāya Sūtras
of Gotama

Translated by
Satis Chandra Vidyabhusana

Munshiram Manoharlal
Publishers Pvt. Ltd.

ISBN 81-215-1096-1
This edition 2003
Originally published 1913
by Panini Office, Allahabad
© 1993, Munshiram Manoharlal Publishers Pvt. Ltd., New Delhi

Printed in India.
Published by Munshiram Manoharlal Publishers Pvt. Ltd.,
Post Box 5715, 54 Rani Jhansi Road,
New Delhi 110 055.

TABLE OF CONTENTS.

Page.

INTRODUCTION I

BOOK I, CHAPTER I.

The Sixteen categories 1
Release (अपवर्ग) 2
Means of knowledge (प्रमाण) 2
Perception (प्रत्यक्ष) defined 2
Inference (अनुमान) defined 3
Comparison (उपमान) defined 3
Word or verbal testimony (शब्द) defined 4
Objects of knowledge (प्रमेय) 4
Soul (आत्मन्) defined 5
Body (शरीर) defined 5
Sense (इन्द्रिय) defined 5
Element (भूत) defined 5
Qualities (गुण) of earth etc.... 5
Intellect (बुद्धि) defined 6
Mind (मन:) defined 6
Activity (प्रवृत्ति) defined and explained 6
Fault (दोष) defined 7
Transmigration (प्रेत्यभाव) defined 7
Fruit (फल) defined 7
Pain (दुःख) defined 7
Release (अपवर्ग) defined 7
Doubt (संशय) defined and explained 7
Purpose (प्रयोजन) defined 8
Example or familiar instance (दृष्टान्त) 8
Tenet (सिद्धान्त) defined 8
A dogma of all the Schools (सर्वतन्त्रसिद्धान्त) 9
A dogma peculiar to some School (प्रतितन्त्रसिद्धान्त) 9
A hypothetical dogma (अधिकरणसिद्धान्त) 9
An implied dogma (अभ्युपगमसिद्धान्त) 10
Members of a syllogism (अवयव) 10
Proposition (प्रतिज्ञा) 10
Reason (हेतु) 11
Homogeneous or affirmative reason (साधर्म्यहेतु) 11
Heterogeneous or negative reason (वैधर्म्यहेतु) 11

Page.

Example (उदाहरण) 11
Homogeneous or affirmative example (साधर्म्योदाहरण) 11
Heterogeneous or negative example (वैधर्म्योदाहरण) 12
Application, affirmative and negative (उपनय) 12
Conclusion (निगमन) 12
Confutation (तर्क) 13
Ascertainment (निर्णय) 13

BOOK I, CHAPTER II.

Discussion (वाद) 14
Wrangling (जल्प) 15
Cavil (वितण्डा) 15
Fallacies of reason (हेत्वाभास) 15
The erratic (सव्यभिचार) 15
The contradictory (विरुद्ध) 16
The controversial or equal to the question (प्रकरणसम) 16
The reciprocal or unproved (साध्यसम) 16
The mistimed (कालातीत) 17
Quibble (छल) 17
Quibble in respect of a term (वाक्छल) 17
Quibble in respect of a genus (सामान्यछल) 18
Quibble in respect of a metaphor (उपचारछल) 19
Futility (जाति) 19
An occasion for rebuke (निग्रहस्थान) 20

BOOK II, CHAPTER I.

Doubt (संशय) examined 22
The means and objects of knowledge (प्रमाण-प्रमेय) examined 24
Perception (प्रत्यक्ष) examined 29
Special kinds of knowledge (ज्ञानविशेष) 31
The relation of perception and inference (प्रत्यक्षमनुमानम्) 31
The whole (अवयविन्) and its part (अवयव) 32
Inference (अनुमान) examined 33
The time present, past and future (वर्त्तमान, अतीत, अनागत) examined ... 34
Comparison (उपमान) examined 35
Word or verbal testimony (शब्द) examined 36
The Veda (वेद) examined 39
Injunction (विधि) 41
Persuasion (अर्थवाद) 41
Praise (स्तुति) 41
Blame (निन्दा) 41
Warning (परकृति) 41

Page.

Prescription (पुराकल्प) 41
Reinculcation (अनुवाद) 41
Tautology (पुनरुक्त) 42
The Medical Science (आयुर्वेद) 42

BOOK II, CHAPTER II.

Means of knowledge (प्रमाण) examined ... ... - 43
Rumour (ऐतिह्य) 43
Presumption (अर्थापत्ति) 43
Probability (सम्भव) 43
Non-existence (अभाव) 43
The nature of sound (शब्द) examined 46
Otherness (अन्यत्व) 51
Letters, their modifications and substitutes (वर्णविकार) 54
Word (पद) 59
Individual (व्यक्ति) 59
Form (आकृति) 59
Genus (जाति) 59

BOOK III, CHAPTER I.

Sense (इन्द्रिय) is not soul (आत्मन्) 63
Body (शरीर) is not soul (आत्मन्) 63
Duality of the eye (चक्षु:) 65
Remembrance (स्मृति) 66
Mind (मन:) is not soul (आत्मन्) 67
The soul (आत्मन्) established 68
The body (शरीर) is earthy 70
The eye-ball (कृष्णसार) is material 70
The senses (इन्द्रिय) are material (भौतिक) 72
The eye (चक्षु:) and its ray (रश्मि:) 72
The senses (इन्द्रिय) are more than one 75
Touch (त्वक्) 75
The senses are five (पञ्चेन्द्रिय) 77
The qualities of the elements (भूतगुण) 78

BOOK III, CHAPTER II.

Intellect or knowledge (बुद्धि) is not eternal 83
Knowledge is not momentary 86
The nature of knowledge (ज्ञान) 89
Recollection (स्मृति) 92
Desire and aversion (इच्छाद्वेष) 94
The mind (मन:) is not the seat of knowledge 95

Page.

Memory (स्मरण) and its causes 96
Knowledge (ज्ञान) is not a natural quality of the body 99
Non-simultaneousness of knowledge (ज्ञानायौगपद्य) 102
The mind (मन:) is atomic (अणु) 103
Desert (पूर्वकृतफल) producing the body 103

BOOK IV, CHAPTER I.

Activity (प्रवृत्ति) 108
Faults (दोष) 108
Stupidity (मोह) 109
Transmigration (प्रेत्यभाव) 109
Entity does not arise from non-entity (न अभावाद् भावोत्पत्ति:) ... 110
God (ईश्वर:) 112
Production from no-cause (अनिमित्ततो भावोत्पत्ति:) 112
All are not non-eternal (न सर्वमनित्यम्) 113
All are not eternal (न सर्वं नित्यम्) 114
All are not distinct (न सर्वं पृथक्) 115
Self-existence (स्वभावसिद्धि) and relative non-existence (इतरेतराभाव) ... 117
No fixity of number (संख्यैकान्तासिद्धि) 118
Fruit (फल) examined 119
Pain (दु:ख) examined 122
Release (अपवर्ग) examined 123
Debts and troubles (ऋण क्लेश) 123

BOOK IV, CHAPTER II.

The rise of true knowledge (तत्त्वज्ञानोत्पत्ति) 127
The whole and its parts (अवयवावयविन) 127
Atom (अणु) 130
The non-reality of things (भावानां याथात्म्यानुपलब्धि:) 133
False apprehension (मिथ्योपलब्धि:) 135
Meditation (समाधि:) 136
Discussion, wrangling and cavil (वादजल्पवितण्डा:) 138

BOOK V, CHAPTER I.

Futility (जाति) 140
Balancing the homogeneity (साधर्म्यसमा) 141
Balancing the heterogeneity (वैधर्म्यसमा) 141
Balancing an addition (उत्कर्षसमा) 142
Balancing a subtraction (अपकर्षसमा) 143
Balancing the questionable (वर्ण्यसमा) 143
Balancing the unquestionable (अवर्ण्यसमा) 144
Balancing the alternative (विकल्पसमा) 144

Page.

Balancing the reciprocity (साधर्म्यसमा) 145
Balancing the co-presence (प्राप्तिसमा) 147
Balancing the mutual absence (अप्राप्तिसमा) 148
Balancing the infinite regression (प्रसङ्गसमा) ... ..., 149
Balancing the counter-example (प्रतिदृष्टान्तसमा) 149
Balancing the non-produced (अनुत्पत्तिसमा) 150
Balancing the doubt (संशयसमा) 152
Balancing the controversy (प्रकरणसमा) 153
Balancing the non-reason (अहेतुसमा) 153
Balancing the presumption (अर्थापत्तिसमा) 155
Balancing the non-difference (अविशेषसमा) 156
Balancing the demonstration (उपपत्तिसमा) 157
Balancing the perception (उपलब्धिसमा) 158
Balancing the non-perception (अनुपलब्धिसमा) 159
Balancing the non-eternal (अनित्यसमा) 160
Balancing the eternal (नित्यसमा) 161
Balancing the effect (कार्य्यसमा) 162
Admission of an opinion (मतानुज्ञा) 164
Six-winged disputation (षट्पक्षीकथा) 165

BOOK V, CHAPTER II.

Occasions for rebuke (निग्रहस्थान) 167
Hurting the proposition (प्रतिज्ञाहानि) 167
Shifting the proposition (प्रतिज्ञान्तर) 168
Opposing the proposition (प्रतिज्ञाविरोध) 169
Renouncing the proposition (प्रतिज्ञासन्न्यास) 169
Shifting the reason (हेत्वन्तर) 169
Shifting the topic (अर्थान्तर) 170
The meaningless (निरर्थक) 170
The unintelligible (अविज्ञातार्थ) 171
The inopportune (अप्राप्तकाल) 171
Saying too little (न्यून) 172
Saying too much (अधिक) 172
Repetition (पुनरुक्त) 172
Silence (अननुभाषण) 173
Ignorance (अज्ञान) 173
Non-ingenuity (अप्रतिभा) 174
Evasion (विक्षेप) 174
Admission of an opinion (मतानुज्ञा) 174
Overlooking the censurable (पर्य्यनुयोज्योपेक्षण) 174
Censuring the non-censurable (निरनुयोज्यानुयोग) 175
Fallacies of a reason (हेत्वाभास) 175

INTRODUCTION

I.—GOTAMA THE FOUNDER OF NYAYA PHILOSOPHY.

Pâṇini, the celebrated Sanskrit grammarian, who is supposed to have flourished about 350 B. C.,[*] derives the word "Nyâya"[†] from the root "i" which conveys the same meaning as "gam"—to go. "Nyâya" as signifying logic is therefore etymologically identical with "nigama" the conclusion of a syllogism. Logic is designated in Sanskrit not only by the word "Nyâya" but also by various other words which indicate diverse aspects of the science. For instance, it is called "Hetu-vidyâ"[‡] or "Hetu-Śâstra" the science of causes, "Ânvîkṣikî"[§] the science of inquiry, "Pramâṇa-Śâstra" the science of correct knowledge, "Tattva-Śâstra" the science of categories, "Tarka-vidyâ" the science of reasoning, "Vâdârtha" the science of discussion and "Phakkikâ-Śâstra" the science of sophism. Nyâya-sûtra is the earliest work extant on Nyâya Philosophy.

The word "Nyâya explained.

---

[*] Paṇini is said to have been a disciple of Upavarṣa, minister of a King of the Nanda dynasty about 350 B. C., as is evident from the following :—

अथ कालेन वर्षस्य शिष्यवर्गो महानभूत् ।
तत्र एकः पाणिनिनाम जडबुद्धितरोऽभवत् ॥

(Kathâsarit-sâgara, Chapter IV., verse 20).

Dr. Otto Bœhtlingk observes :—
"We need therefore only make a space of fifty years between each couple of them, in order to arrive at the year 350, into the neighbourhood of which date our grammarian is to be placed, according to the Kathâsarit-sâgara."—Goldstucker's Panini, p. 85.

[†] अध्यायन्यायोद्यावसंहाराश्च ।
(Panini's Aṣṭâdhyâyî 3-3-122.)

[‡] निर्घण्टौ निगमे पुराणे इतिहासे वेदे व्याकरणे निरुक्ते शिक्षायां छन्दसि यज्ञकल्पे ज्योतिषि सांख्ये योगे क्रियाकल्पे वैशेषिके वैशिके अर्थविद्यायां बार्हस्पत्ये आश्चर्य्ये आसुरे मृगपक्षिरुते हेतुविद्यायां जतुयन्त्रे......सर्वत्र बोधिसत्त्व एव विशिष्यते स्म ॥

(Lalitavistara, Chapter XII., p. 179, Dr. Rajendra Lal Mitra's edition).

[§] आन्वीचिकी दण्डनीतिस्तर्कविद्यार्थशास्त्रयोः ।
(Amarakosa, svargavarga, verse, 155).

The Nyâya or logic is said to have been founded by a sage named Gotama.* He is also known as Gautama, Akṣapâda† and Dìrghatapas.‡ The names Gotama and Gautama point to the family to which he belonged while the names Akṣapâda and Dìrghatapas refer respectively to his meditative habit and practice of long penance.

The founder of Nyâya called Gotama, Gautama, Akṣapâda or Dìrghatapas.

In the Rigveda-saṁhitâ as well as the Śathapatha-Brâhmaṇa of the white Yajurveda we find mention of one Gotama who was son of Rahûgaṇa § and priest of the Royal family of Kuru-sṛñjaya for whose victory in battle he prayed to Indra. Nodhâḥ, ‖ son of Gotama, was also called Gotama who composed several new hymns in honour of Indra. The sages sprung from the family of Gotama are designated Gotamâsaḥ ¶ who were very intelligent ; and Agni,

The family of Gotama.

मुक्तये यः शिलात्त्वाय शास्त्रमूचे महामुनिः ।
गोतमं तमवेतेव यथा वित्थ तथैव सः ॥

(Naiṣadhacharitam 17-75.)

कणादेन तु सम्प्रोक्तं शास्त्रं वैशेषिकं महत् ।
गोतमेन तथा न्यायं सांख्यं तु कपिलेन वै ॥

(Padmapurâṇa, Uttarakhaṇḍa, Chapter 263.)

गोतमः स्वेन तर्केण खण्डयन् तत्र तत्र हि ।

(Skanda-purâṇa, Kâlikâ Khaṇḍa, Chapter XVII.)

†*यदक्षपादः प्रवरो मुनीनाम् शमाय शास्त्रं जगतो जगाद ।*
कुतार्किकाज्ञाननिवृत्तिहेतुः करिष्यते तत्र मया निबन्धः ॥

(Udyotakara's Nyâyavârtika, opening lines).

In the Sarvadarśanasaṁgraha Nyâya philosophy is called the Akṣapâda system.
‡ Kâlidâsa's Raghuvamsam 11-33.

§*अत्रेदमाख्यानम् । रहूगणपुत्रो गोतमः कुरु सृञ्जयानां राज्ञां पुरोहित आसीत् । तेषां राज्ञां परैः सह युद्धे सति स ऋषिरनेन सूक्तेनेन्द्रं स्तुत्वा स्वकीयानां जयं प्रार्थयामासेति । तस्य च तत्पुरोहितत्वं वाजसनेयिभिराम्नातम् । गोतमो ह वै राहूगण उभयेषां कुरु सृञ्जयानां पुरोहित आसीत् ॥*

(Rigveda-saṁhitâ, Maṇḍala 1, Sûkta 81, mantra 3, Sâyaṇa's commentary).

विदेघो ह माधवोऽग्निं वैश्वानरं मुखे बभार ।
तस्य गोतमो राहूगण ऋषिः पुरोहित आस ॥

(Satapatha Brâhmaṇa of the white Yajurveda, Kâṇḍa 1, Adhyâya 4, Mâdhyandinîya recension.)

‖ *सनायते गोतम इन्द्र नव्यमतद्ब्रह्म हरियोजनाय ।*
सुनीथाय नः शवसान नोधाः प्रातर्मक्षू धिया वसुर्जगम्यात् ॥

(Rigveda-samhitâ, Maṇḍala 1, Sûkta 63, Mantra 13.)

¶ *एवा ते हरियोजना सुवृक्तीन्द्र ब्रह्माणि गोतमासो अक्रन् ।*

(Rigveda-samhitâ, Maṇḍala 1, Sûkta 61, Mantra 16).

एवाग्निर्गोतमेभिर्ऋतावा विप्रेभिरस्तोष्ट जातवेदाः ।
स एषु द्युम्नं पीपयत् स वाजं स पुष्टिं याति जोषमाचिक्विान् ॥

(Rigveda-samhitâ, Maṇḍala 1, Sûkta 77, Mantra 5).

pleased with their adoration, gave them cattle and rice in abundance.
It is related that Gotama, once pinched with thirst, prayed for water of the
Marut-Gods, who out of mercy, placed a well* before him transplanted
from elsewhere. The water gushing out copiously from the well not only
quenched his thirst but formed itself into a river, the source of which
was the seat of the original well.

In the Rigveda-saṁhitâ the descendants of Gotama as already
noticed are also called Gotama while in later Vedic
literature they are called Gautama. The Vaṁsa-
Brâhmaṇa of the Sâmaveda mentions four members
of the Gotama family† among the teachers who transmitted that Veda to
posterity, viz., the Râdha-Gautama, Gâtṛ-Gautama, Sumanta-bâbhrava-
Gautama and Saṁkara-Gautama ; and the Chândogya Upaniṣad of the
same Veda mentions another teacher named Hâridrumata-Gautama‡ who
was approached by Satya-Kâma Jâvâla to be his teacher. The Gobhila
Gṛhya Sûtra of the Sâmaveda cites the opinion of a Gautama § who held
that during the winter season there should be three oblations offered to the

The teachers called Gautama.

---

*जिह्वां नुनुद्रेऽवत तया दिशासि चन्नुस्सं गोतमाय तृष्णाजे ।
आगच्छ तीमवसा चित्रभानवः कामं विप्रस्य तर्पयंत धामभिः ॥

(Rigveda-saṁhitâ, Maṇḍala 1, Sûkta 85, Mantra 11.)

Sâyaṇa in commenting on Rigveda saṁhitâ, Maṇḍala 1, Sûkta 77, Mantra 10,
observes :—

अत्रेयमाख्यायिका । गौतम ऋषिः पिपासया पीड़ितः सन् मरुत उदकं ययाचे । तदनंतरं
मरुतोऽद्रस्थं कृपमुद्धृत्य यत्र स गौतम ऋषिस्तिष्ठति तां दिशं नीत्वा ऋषिसमीपे कृपमवस्थाप्य तत्पार्श्व
आहावं च कृत्वा तस्मिन्नाहावे कृपमुरसिञ्च तमृषिं तेनोदकेन तर्पयांचक्रुः । अगमशोऽनया उत्तरया
च प्रतिपद्यते ।

The well (utsadhi) is alluded to in the Rigveda, Maṇḍala 1, Sûkta 88, Mantra
4, thus :—

आहानि गृध्राः पर्या व आगुरिमां धियं वार्कार्थां च देवीं ।
ब्रह्म कृणवंतो गोतमासो अकैर्ऊर्ध्वं नुनुद्र उत्सधिं पिबध्वै ॥

†राधाच्च गौतमाद्राधो गौतमो गातुर्गौतमात् पितुर्गाता गौतमः ।

Sâmavedîya Vaṁśa-Brâhmaṇa, Khaṇḍa 2, Satyavrata Sâmaśvamiś edition p. 7.)

सुमन्ताद् बाभ्रवाद् गौतमात् सुमन्तो बाभ्रवो गौतमः ।

(Sâmavedîya Vaṁśa-Brâhmaṇa, Khaṇḍa 2).

संकराद् गौतमात् संकरो गौतमः ।

(Sâmavedîya Vaṁśa-Brâhmaṇa, Khaṇḍa 3.)

‡ स ह हारिद्रुमतं गौतममेत्योवाच ब्रह्मचर्यं भगवति वत्स्याम्युपेयां भगवन्तमिति ॥ १ ॥

(Chândogya Upaniṣad, Adhyâya 4, Khaṇḍa 4).

§चतुरष्टको हेमन्तः ॥ ४ ॥
अष्टक इत्यौद्गाहमानिः ॥ ७ ॥
तथा गौतमवार्केखण्डी ॥ ८ ॥

(Gobhila Gṛhya Sûtra 3-10.)

dead ancestors. Another Gautama was the author of the Pitṛmedha Sûtra*
which perhaps belongs to the Sâmaveda. The Bṛhadâraṇyaka † of the
white Yajurveda mentions a teacher named Gautama, while in the Kaṭhopaniṣad of the Black Yajurveda the sage Nâciketas‡ who conversed with
Yama on the mystery of life, is called Gautama which evidently is a
generic name as his father is also called Gautama in the same work. A
Gautama§ is mentioned as a teacher in the Kauśika sûtra of the
Atharvaveda while to another Gautama is attributed the authorship of
the Gautama Dharma sûtra‖ an authoritative work on the sacred law.

We need not take any notice of one Gautama ¶ who, at the bidding
of his mother as stated in the Mahâbhârata, cast into the Ganges his old
and blind father Dìrghatamas who was however miraculously saved.

The Râmâyaṇa mentions a Gautama** who had his hermitage in a
grove at the outskirts of the city of Mithilâ where
Gautama, husband he lived with his wife Ahalyâ. It is well-known how
of Ahalyâ. Ahalyâ for her flirtation with Indra, was cursed by
her lord to undergo penance and mortification until

---

* An incomplete manuscript of the Pitṛmedha Sûtra is contained in the Library of the
Calcutta Sanskrit College, but the work was printed in America several years ago.

† गौतमाद् गौतमः ॥ १ । २ । ३ ॥
(Bṛhadâvaṇyaka, Adhyâya 4.)

‡हन्त त इदं प्रवद्यामि गुह्यं ब्रह्म सनातनम् ।
यथा च मरणं प्राप्य आत्मा भवति गौतम ॥ ६ ॥
(Kaṭhopaniṣad, Valli 5).

शान्तसंकल्पः सुमना यथा स्याद्वीतमन्युगौ तमो माभिमृत्यो ।
त्वत् प्रसृष्टं माभिवदेत् प्रतीत एतत् त्रयाणां प्रथमं वरं वृणे ।
(Kaṭhopaniṣad, Valli 5.)

§Vide Weber's History of Indian Literature, p. 153.

‖The text of the Gautama Dharma-sûtra has been printed several times in India
while an English translation of it by Dr. G. Bûhler has appeared in the Sacred Books of
the East Series.

¶स वै दीर्घतमा नाम शापादृषिरजायत ॥ २२ ॥
जात्यन्धो वेदवित् प्राज्ञः पत्नीं लेभे स विद्यया ॥ २३ ॥
तरुणीं रूपसम्पन्नां प्रद्वेषीं नाम ब्राह्मणीम् ।
स पुत्रान् जनयामास गौतमादीन् महायशाः ॥ २४ ॥
(Mahâbhârata, Âdiparva Adhyâya 104).

**मिथिलोपवने तत्र आश्रमं दृश्य राघवः ।
पुराणं निर्जनं रम्यं पप्रच्छ मुनिपुङ्गवम् ॥ ११ ॥
इदमाश्रमसंकाशं किं न्विदं मुनिवर्जितम् ।
श्रोतुमिच्छामि भगवन् कस्यायम्पूर्वे आश्रमः ॥ १२ ॥
गौतमस्य नरश्रेष्ठ पूर्वमासीन्महात्मनः ।
आश्रमो दिव्यसंकाशः सुरैरपि सुपूजितः ॥ १४ ॥
(Râmâyaṇa, Adikâṇḍa, Sarga 48).

her emancipation at the happy advent of Râma. The Adhyâtma Râmâ-yaṇa, while repeating the same account, places the hermitage of Gautama* on the banks of the Ganges; and our great poet Kâlidâsa follows the Râmâyaṇic legend describing Gautama† as Dîrghatapas, a sage who prac-tised long penance.

The Vâyupurâṇa describes a sage named Akṣapâda‡ as the disciple of a Brâhmaṇa named Soma Sarmâ who was Śiva incarnate and well-known for his practice of austerities at the shrine of Prabhâsa during the time of Jâtûkarṇya Vyâsa. This Akṣapâda mentioned along with Kanâda is evidently no other person than Gotama or Gautama who founded the Nyâya philosophy. As to the origin of the name Akṣapâda ("having eyes in the feet") as applied to Gautama, legend has it that Gautama was so deeply absorbed in philosophical contemplation that one day during his walks he fell unwittingly into a well out of which he was rescued with great difficulty. God therefore mercifully provided him with a second pair of eyes in his feet to protect the sage from further mishaps. Another legend§ which

Akṣapâda.

---

* इत्युक्त्वा मुनिभिस्ताभ्यां ययौ गङ्गासमीपगम् ।
गौतमस्याश्रमं पुण्यं यत्राहल्या शिलामयी ॥ १४ ॥

     (Adhyâtma Râmâyaṇa, âdikâṇḍa, adhyâya 6).

† तैः शिवेषु वसतिर्गंताध्वभिः ।
सायमाश्रमतरुष्वगृह्यत ।
येषु दीर्घंतपसः परिग्रहो
बासवच्चणकलत्रतां ययौ ॥ ३३ ॥
प्रलपयत चिराय यत् पुन-
श्चारुगौतमबधूः शिलामयी ।
स्वं वपुः स किल किल्विषच्छिदां
रामपादरजसामनुग्रहः ॥ ३४ ॥

     (Raghuvaṁśa, Sarga 11).

‡ सप्तविंशति मे प्राप्ते परिवर्त्ते क्रमागते ।
जातुकर्ण्यो यदा व्यासो भविष्यति तपोधनः ॥ २०१ ॥
तदाहं संभविष्यामि सोमशर्म्मा द्विजोत्तमः ।
प्रभासतीर्थमासाद्य योगात्मा लोकविश्रुतः ॥ २०२ ॥
तत्रापि मम ते पुत्रा भविष्यन्ति तपोधनाः ।
अक्षपादः कणादश्च उलूको वत्स एव च ॥ २०३ ॥

     (Vâyupurâṇa, Adhyâya 23).

§ गौतमो हि स्वमतदूषकस्य व्यासस्य मुखदर्शनं चक्षुषा न कर्त्तव्यमिति प्रतिज्ञाय पश्चात् व्यासेन प्रसादितः पादे नेत्रं प्रकाश्य तं दृष्टवान् इति पौराणिकी कथा ।
(Nyâyakoṣa, 2nd edition, by M. M. Bhîmâcârya Jhâlakîkar, Bombay).

represents Vyâsa, a disciple of Gautama, lying prostrate before his master until the latter condescended to look upon him, not with his natural eyes, but with a new pair of eyes in his feet, may be dismissed with scanty ceremony as being the invention of a later generation of logicians, anxious to humiliate Vyâsa for vilification of the Nyâya system in his Mahâbhârata and Vedânta sûtra.

The people of Mithilâ (modern Darbhanga in North Behar) ascribe the foundation of Nyâya philosophy to Gautama, husband of Ahalyâ, and point out as the place of his birth a village named Gautamasthâna where a fair is held

Local tradition.

every year on the 9th day of the lunar month of Chaitra (March-April). It is situated 28 miles north-east of Darbhanga and has a mud-hill of considerable height (supposed to be the hermitage of Gautama) at the base of which lies the celebrated "Gautama-kunda" or Gautama's well the water whereof is like milk to the taste and feeds a perennial rivulet called on this account Kṣirodadhi or Khiroi (literally the sea of milk). Two miles to the east of the village there is another village named Ahalyâ-sthâna where between a pair of trees lies a slab of stone identified with Ahalyâ in her accursed state. In its vicinity there is a temple which commemorates the emancipation of Ahalyâ by Râma Chandra. The Gautama-kunda and the Kṣirodadhi river, which are still extant at Gautama-sthâna verify the account of Gotama given above from the Rigveda while the stone slab and the temple of Râma at Ahalyâ-sthâna are evidences corroborative of the story of Ahalyâ as given in the Râmâyana. There is another tradition prevalent in the town of Chapra that Gautama, husband of Ahalyâ and founder of the Nyâya philosophy, resided in a village now called Godná at the confluence of the rivers Ganges and Sarayû where a Sanskrit academy called Gautama Thomson Pâthasâlâ has been established to commemorate the great sage.

It seems to me that Goutama, son of Rahûgaṇa, as mentioned in the Rigveda, was the founder of the Gautama family from which sprang Gautama, husband of Ahalyâ, as narrated

The founder of Nyâya philosophy identified.

in the Râmâyana. It is interesting to note that Śatânanda* son of Gautama by Ahalyâ, is a priest in the royal family of Janaka much in the same way as Goutama, son of

---

*शतानन्दं पुरस्कृत्य पुरोहितमनिन्दितः ।
प्रतिगृह्य तु तां पूजां जनकस्य महात्मनः ।
(Râmâyana, âdikâṇḍa, Sarga 50).

गौतमश्च शतानन्दो जनकानां पुरोहितः ।
(Uttara Râma charitam).

Rahûgaṇa is a priest in the royal family of Kuruśṛñjaya. The fields waving with paddy plants which greet the eyes of a modern traveller near and round Gautama-sthâna bear testimony to Agni's gift of rice and cattle in abundance to the family of Gautama. The Nyâya philosophy was, on the authority of the tradition prevalent in Mithilâ, founded by Gautama husband of Ahalyâ. The same Gautama has been designated as Akṣapâda in the Vâyu Purâṇa already referred to. Akṣapada has been identified by Anantayajvan* with the author of the Pitṛmedha Sûtra as well as with that of the Gautama Dharma sûtra, and it is possible that he is not other than the Gautama referred to in the Kauśika sûtra of the Atharva Veda. The other Gautamas mentioned in the Brâhmaṇas, Upaniṣads etc., appear to be the kinsmen of their illustrious name-sake.

The Râmâyaṇa, as we have found, places the hermitage of Gautama, husband of Ahalyâ, at Gautama-sthâna twenty-eight

His residence.

miles north-east of Darbhâṅgâ while the Adhyâtma Râmâyaṇa places it on the banks of the Ganges at its confluence with the Sarayû off the town of Châprâ. The Vâyupurâṇa fixes the residence of Akṣapâda, supposed to be identical with Gautama, at Prabhâsa† beyond Girnar in Kathiawar on the sea-coast. To reconcile these conflicting statements it has been suggested that Akṣapâda otherwise known as Gotama or Gautama was the founder of the Nyâya philosophy, that he was born at Gautama-sthâna in Mithilâ on the river Kṣîrodadhi, lived for some years at the village now called Godnâ at the confluence of the Ganges and Sarayû until his retirement into Prabhâsa the well-known sacred place of pilgrimage in Kathiawar on the sea-coast.

---

*To the Gṛhya Sûtras of the Sâmaveda probably belong also Gautama's Pitṛmedha-sûtra (Cf. Burnell, p. 57 ; the commentator Anantayajvan identifies the author with Akṣapâda the author of the Nyâya-sûtra), and the Gautama-dharma-sûtra.—Weber's History of Indian Literature, p. 85.

† Prabhâsa washed on its western side by the river Sarasvati and reputed as the residence of Kṛiṣṇa, is mentioned in the Srimad Bhâgavata thus :—

न वस्तव्यमिहास्माभिर्जिजीविषुभिरार्थ्यकाः ।

प्रभासं सुमहत्पुण्यं यास्यामोऽद्यैव माचिरम् ॥ ३५ ॥

(Bhâgavata, Skandha II, adhyaya 6.)

स्त्रियो बालाश्च वृद्धाश्च शंखोद्धारं व्रजन्तिवतः ।

वयं प्रभासं यास्यामो यत्र प्रत्यक् सरस्वती ॥ ६ ॥

(Bhâgavata, Skandha II, adhyâya 30.)

Prabhâsa was situated beyond the rock of Girnar in Kathiawar where we come across all the edicts of Asoka as well as an inscription of Rudradâma supposed to be the first inscription in Sanskrit dated about 100 A. D. which mentions Chandra Gupta and Asoka by names. There are also some inscriptions in Gupta characters, and there is no doubt that Prabhâsa situated on the Sarasvati acquired celebrity in very old times.

This Prabhâsa is not to be confounded with another town called Prabhâsa in Kausâmbi near Allahabad on the Jumna where there is an inscription, dated about the 2nd century B. C., of Aṣadasena, a descendant of Sonakâyana of Adhicchatra, (vide Dr. Fuhrer's Pabhosa inscriptions in Epigraphia Indica, Vol. II, pp. 242-243.)

The Śatapatha Brâhmaṇa mentions Gautama along with Âsurâyaṇa and the Vâyupurâṇa (already quoted) states that Akṣapâda, *alias* Gotama or Gautama, flourished during the time of Jâtûkarṇya Vyâsa. Now, Jâtûkarṇya, according to the Madhukâṇḍa and Yâjñavalkya Kâṇḍa of the Śatapatha Brâhmaṇa* (Kânva recension) was a pupil of Âsurâyaṇa and Yâska who are supposed to have lived about 550 B. C. This date tallies well with the time of another Gautama who, together with Araṇemi, is described in the Divyâvadâna†, a Buddhist Sanskrit work translated into Chinese in the 2nd century A. D., as having transmitted the Vedas to posterity before they were classified by Vyâsa. It does not conflict with the view that Akṣapâda is identical with Gautama author of the Gautama Dharma-Sûtra which is "declared to be the oldest of the existing works on the sacred law‡." Akṣapâda-Gautama, founder of the Nyâya Philosophy, was almost a contemporary of Buddha-Gautama who founded Buddhism and Indrabhûti Gautama who was a disciple of Mahâvîra the reputed founder of Jainism.

His age about 550 B. C.

The fourfold division of the means of knowledge (Pramâṇa) into perception, inference, comparison and word found in the Jaina Prâkṛta scriptures such as the Nandî-Sûtra, Sthânâṅga-Sûtra§ and Bhagavatî-

---

* *Vide* Weber's History of Indian Literature, p. 140.

In the Mâdhyandinîya recension of the Śatapatha Brâhmaṇa a teacher intervenes between Yâska and Jâtûkarṇya, *viz*. Bhâradvâja. Cf.

जातुकर्ण्याज्जातुकर्ण्यो भारद्वाजाद् भारद्वाजो भारद्वाजाच्चासुरायणाच्च गौतमाच्च गौतमो
.........पाराशर्य्यात् पाराशर्य्यो जातुकर्ण्याज्जातुकर्ण्यो भारद्वाजाद् भारद्वाजो भारद्वाजाच्चासुरायणाच्च
यास्काच्चासुरायणः ।

(Śatapatha Brâhmaṇa, Mâdhyandinîya recension, Kâṇḍa 14, adhyâya 5.)

† The 33rd chapter of the Divyâvadâna called Mâtanga Sûtra, in Chinese Mo-tan-nu-cin, was translated into Chinese by An-shi-kao-cie of the Eastern Han dynasty in A. D. 148-170. (*Vide* Bunjiu Nanjio's Catalogue of the Chinese Tripitaka). In it we read :—

ब्रह्मा देवानां परमतापसः इन्द्रस्य कौशिकस्य वेदार्थान् वाचयति स्म । इन्द्रः कौशिकोऽरण्य-
मीगौतमे वेदान् वाचयति । अरण्येमीगौतमौ श्वेतकेतुं वेदान् वाचयतः । श्वेतकेतुः शुकं पण्डितं वेदान्
वाचयति । शुकः पण्डितश्चतुर्धा वेदान् विभजति स्म ।

(Divyâvadâna, Chap. XXXIII).

‡ Buhler observes :—These arguments which allow us to place Gautama before both Baudhâyana and Vâsiṣṭha are, that both these authors quote Gautama as an authority on law............ These facts will, I think suffice to show that the Gautama Dharma Sûtra may be safely declared to be the oldest of the existing works on the sacred law." (Buhler's Gautama, Introduction, pp. XLIX and LIV, S. B. E. series).

§ अथवा हेऊ चउव्विहे पन्नत्तं तं जहा

पच्चक्खे अनुमाणे उवमे आगमे ।

(Sthânâṅga-Sûtra, Page 309, published by Dhanapat Sing).

Sûtra compiled by Indrabhûti-Gautama finds its parallel in the Nyâya-Sûtra of Akṣapâda-Gautama leading to the conclusion that this particular doctrine was either borrowed by Indrabhûti from Akṣapâda or was the common property of both. In the Pâli and Prâkṛta scriptures Gautama is called Gotama, and a Pâli Sutta mentions a sect called "Gotamakâ,* who were followers of Gautama, identified perhaps with the founder of the Nyâya Philosophy. The Pâli Canonical scriptures such as the Brahmajâla Sutta,† Udâna etc., which embody the teachings of Buddha, mention a class of Śramaṇas and Brâhmaṇas who were "takkî" or "takkika" (logicians, and "vîmamsî" (casuists) and indulged in "takka" (logic) and vîmamsâ (casuistry), alluding perhaps to the followers of Akṣapâda-Gautama described as "Gotamakâ."

The Kathâvatthuppakaraṇa ‡, a Pâli work of the Abhidhammapiṭaka, composed by Moggaliputta Tissa at the third Buddhist Council during the reign of Aśoka about 255 B. C., mentions "paṭiññâ" (in Sanskrit: "pratijña," proposition), "Upanaya" (application of reasons), "Niggaha" (in Sanskrit: "Nigraha," humiliation or defeat) etc., which are the technical terms of Nyâya philosophy or Logic. Though Moggaliputta Tissa has not made any actual reference to Logic or Nyâya, his mention of some of its technical terms warrants us to suppose that, that philosophy existed in some shape in India in his time about 255 B. C. These facts lead us to conclude that Gotama, Gautama or Akṣapâda, the founder of Nyâya Philosophy, lived about the year 550 B. C.

---

* *Vide* Prof. T. W. Rhys David's Introduction to the Kassapa-Sîhanâda Sutta, pp. 220-222. It is observed :—

"The only alternative is that some Brâhmaṇa, belonging to the Gotama Gotra, is here referred to as having had a community of Bhikṣus named after him."

† इध, भिक्खवे, एकच्चो समणो वा ब्राह्मणो वा तक्की होति वीमंसी । सो तक्कपरियाहतं वीमंसानुचरितं सयं पटिभानं एवं आह "अधिच्चसमुप्पन्नो अत्ता च लोको चाति" ।

(Brahmajâla Sutta 1-32, edited by Rhys Davids and carpenter).

याव सम्मासम्बुद्धा लोके नुप्पज्जन्ति, न तक्किका सुज्झन्ति न चापि सावका, दुद्दिट्ठी न मुक्खा पमुच्चरेति ।

(Udâna, p. 10. edited by Paul Steinthal, P. T. S. edition).

‡ The terms "Paṭiññâ" (pratijñâ, proposition) and "niggaha" (nigraha, defeat) occur in the following passages :—

न च मय तया तत्थ हेताय पटिज्जाय हेवं पटिजानन्ता हेवं निग्गहेतब्बो ।

(Kathâvatthuppakaraṇa, Siamese edition, p. 3).

"Niggaha-Catukkam" is the name of a section of the first chapter of the Kathâvatthuppakaraṇa while "Upanaya-Catukkam" is the name of another section of that work.

II. NYÂYASÛTRA THE FIRST WORK ON NYÂYA PHILOSOPHY.

To Gotama, Gautama or Akṣapâda, of whom a short account has
been given above, is attributed the authorship of
the Nyâya-Sûtra the earliest work on Nyâya
Philosophy. Sanskrit literature in the Sûtra or
aphoristic style was presumably inaugurated at about 550 B. C., and the
Nyâya-Sûtra the author of which lived, as already stated, at about that
time, must have been the first[*] contribution to that literature. The
" Sutta" or Sûtra section of the Pâli literature reads very much like a body
of sermons bearing no affinity with the Sûtra works of the Brâhmaṇas.

The earliest contribution to the Sûtra literature.

The Nyâya-Sûtra is divided into five books, each containing two
chapters called âhnikas or Diurnal portions. It is
believed that Akṣapâda finished his work on Nyâya
in ten lectures corresponding to the âhnikas referred
to above. We do not know whether the whole of the Nyâya-Sûtra, as it
exists at present, was the work of Akṣapâda, nor do we know for certain
whether his teachings were committed to writing by himself or transmitted by oral tradition only. It seems to me that it is only the first book
of the Nyâya Sûtra containing a brief explanation of the 16 categories
that we are justified in ascribing to Akṣapâda, while the second, third
and fourth books which discuss particular doctrines of the Vaiśeṣika, Yoga,
Mîmâmsâ, Vedânta and Buddhist Philosophy bear marks of different
hands and ages. In these books there are passages quoted almost *verbatim*
from the Laṅkâvatara-Sûtra[†], a Sanskrit work of the Yogâcâra Buddhist
Philosophy, from the Mâdhyamika Sûtra of Nâgârjuna[‡] and from the
Sataka[§] of Ârya Deva—works which were composed in the early
centuries of Christ. The fifth book treating of the varieties of futile
rejoinders and occasions for rebuke was evidently not the production of
Akṣapâda who dismissed those topics without entering into their details.
The last and most considerable additions were made by Vâtsyâyana otherwise known as Pakṣila Svâmi, who about 450 A D, wrote the first regular
commentary, "Bhâṣya", on the Nyâya Sûtra, and harmonised the
different and at times conflicting, additions and interpolations by the
ingenious introduction of Sûtras of his own making fathered upon Akṣapâda.

*The gradual develop-
ment of the Nyâya-
Sûtra.*

* Kapila is stated in the Sâmkhya-Kârikâ, verse 70, to have taught his philosophy
to Âsuri who is mentioned in the Satapatha Brâhmaṇa as a teacher. Âsurâyaṇa and
Yâska who followed Âsuri were the teachers of Jâtûkarnya, a contemporary of Akṣapâda-
Gautama. Kapila therefore proceeded Akṣapâda by at least three generations. Kapila's
Philosophy is believed to have come down by oral traditions and was not perhaps
committed to writing in his life-time. Hence the Nyâya-Sûtra has been stated to be
the first work of the Sûtra period.
† *Vide* Nyâya Sûtra 4-2-26, which quotes the Laṅkâvatâra Sûtra (dated about 300 A.D.)
‡ *Vide* Nyâya-Sûtra 2-1-39, 4-1-39, and 4-1-48, which criticise the Mâdhyamika Sûtra.
§ *Vide* Nyâya-Sutra 4-1-48 which criticises Sataka of Aryadeva.

The Nyâya-Sûtra has, since its composition, enjoyed a very great popularity as is evident from the numerous commenta-ries that have from time to time, centred round it. A few of the commentaries are mentioned below :—

Commentaries on the Nyâya-Sûtra.

TEXT.

1. Nyâya-Sûtra by Gotama or Akṣapâda (550 B. C.)

Commentaries.

2. Nyâya-Bhâṣya by Vâtsyâyana (450 A D.)
3. Nyâya-Vârtika by Udyotakara.
4. Nyâya-Vârtika tatparya-tika by Vâcaspati Miśra.
5. Nyâya-Vartika-tatparyatika-pariśuddhi by Udayana.
6. Pariśuddiprakâsâ by Vardhamâna.
7. Vardhamânendu by Padmanâbha Misra.
8. Nyâyâlankâra by Śrîkaṇṭha.
9. Nyâyâlankâra Vṛtti by Jayanta.
10. Nyâya mañjari by Jayanta.
11. Nyâya-Vṛtti by Abhayatilakopâdhyâya.
12. Nyâya-Vṛtti by Visvanâtha,
13. Mitâbhâṣiṇî Vṛtti by Mahâdeva Vedânti.
14. Nyâyaprakâsa by Kesava Miśra.
15. Nyâyabodhinî by Govardhana.
16. Nyâya Sûtra Vyâkhyâ by Mathurânâtha.

III. RECEPTION ACCORDED TO THE NYAYA PHILOSOPHY.

It appears from the Chândogya-upaniṣad, Bṛhadâraṇyaka-upaniṣad and Kauṣîtikî Brâhmaṇa * that Philosophy (Adhyât-ma-Vidyâ) received its first impetus from the Kṣatriyas (members of the military caste) who carried it to great perfection. King Ajâtasâtru in an assembly of the Kuru-Pâñcâlas consoled a Brâhmaṇa named Śvetaketu,

Philosophy inaugur-ated by members of the military caste.

---

* Kauṣitakî-Brâhmaṇa 2-1, 2; 16, 4.
Brihadâraṇyaka 2-1-20, 2-3-6.
(Chândogya 3-14-1 ; 5-11, 24 ; 1-8, 9 ; 1-9-3, 7-1-3, and 5-11.

मा त्वं गौतमावदो यथेयं न प्राक् त्वत्तः पुरा विद्या ब्राह्मणान् गच्छति तस्मादु सर्वेषु लोकेषु क्षत्रस्यैव प्रशासनमभूदिति तस्मै होवाच ॥ ७ ॥

(Chândogya-upaniṣad 5-3).

Professor P. Deussen observes :—
In this narrative, preserved by two different Vedic schools, it is expressly declared that the knowledge of the Brahman as âtman, the central doctrine of the entire Vedânta, is possessed by the King ; but, on the contrary, is not possessed by the Brâhmaṇa "famed as a Vedic scholar."—Philosophy of the Upanishads, pp. 17—18.
Again, he remarks :—We are forced to conclude, if not with absolute certainty, yet with a very high degree of probability, that as a matter of fact the doctrine of the âtman standing as it did in such sharp contrast to all the principles of the Vedic ritual, though the original conception may have been due to Brâhmaṇas, was taken up and cultivated primarily not in Brâhmaṇa but in Kṣatriya circles, and was first adopted by the former in later times—Philosophy of the Upanishads, p. 19.

सत्यं ज्ञानमनन्तं ब्रह्म । विज्ञानमानन्दं ब्रह्म । तत्त्वमसि श्वेतकेतो । सोऽहं ब्रह्म ।

These four pregnant expressions (Mahâvâkya) originated from the Brâhmaṇas, whenje it may be concluded Nirguṇa-Brahma-Vidyâ or knowledge of absolute Brahma was confined among them. It was the Saguṇa-Brahma-Vidyâ or knowledge of Brahma limited by form and attributes that is said to have been introducted by the Kṣatriyas.

son of Âruṇi of the Gautama family, that he had no cause of being sorry
for his inability to explain certain doctrines of Adhyâtma-Vidyâ which
were known only to the Kṣatriyas. It may be observed that Mahâvîra
and Buddha who founded respectively Jainism and Buddhism—two
universal religions based on philosophy or Adhyâtma-Vidyâ—were also
Kṣatriyas. Kapila is reputed to be the first Brâhmana who propounded
a sytem of philosophy called Sâṁkhya, but his work on the subject not
having come down to us in its original form we are not in a position to
ascertain what relation it bore to the Vedas or what kind of reception was
given to it by the orthodox Brâhmaṇas. We know for certain that the
most powerful Brâhmaṇa who undertook to study and teach philosophy
openly was Gotama, Gautama or Akṣapâda the renouned author of the
Nyâya-Sûtra. He founded a rational system of philosophy called "Nyâya"
which at its inception had no relation with the topics of the Vedic Saṁhita
and Brâhmaṇa. At this stage the Nyâya was pure Logic unconnected with
the scriptural dogmas. Akṣapâda recognised four means of valid
knowledge, viz., perception, inference, comparison and word of which the
last signified knowledge derived through any reliable assertion.

This being the nature of Nyâya or Logic at its early stage it was not
received with favour by the orthodox community of

Nyâya (Logic) not received with favour. Brâhmaṇas who anxious to establish an organised society, paid their sole attention to the Saṁhitâs and Brâh-
maṇas which treated of rituals, ignoring altogether the portions which had
nothing to do with them. The sage Jaimini * in his Mîmâmsa-Sûtra distinctly says that the Veda having for its sole purpose the prescription of
actions, those parts of it which do not serve that purpose are useless."
We are therefore not surprised to find Manu † enjoining ex-communication
upon those members of the twice-born caste who disregarded the Vedas and
Dharma-Sûtras relying upon the support of Hetu-Śâstra or Logic. Similarly
Vâlmîki in his Râmâyana ‡ discredits those persons of perverse intellect
who indulge in the frivolities of Ânvîkṣikî the science of Logic regardless
of the works of sacred law (Dharma-sâstra) which they should follow as

---

*आम्नायस्य क्रियार्थकत्वात् आनर्थक्यम् अतदर्थानाम् ॥ १ ॥ २ ॥ १ ॥

(Mîmâmsâ-Sûtra).

†योऽवमन्येत ते मूले हेतुशास्त्राश्रयाद् द्विजः ।
स साधुभिर्बहिष्कार्यो नास्तिको वेदनिन्दकः ॥

(Manu, adhyâya 2, verse II).

‡धर्मशास्त्रेषु मुख्येषु विद्यमानेषु दुबुधाः ।
बुद्धिमान्वीचिकीं प्राप्य निरर्थं प्रवदन्ति ते ॥ ३६ ॥

(Râmâyaṇa, Ayodhyâ Kânda, Sarga 100).

their guide. Vyâsa in the Mahâbhârata,* Sântiparva, relates the doleful
story of a repentant Brâhmaṇa who, addicted to Tarkavidyâ (Logic)
carried on debates divorced from all faith in the Vedas and was on
that account, turned into a jackal in his next birth as a penalty. In
another passage of the Sântiparva,† Vyâsa warns the followers of the
Vedânta Philosophy against communicating their doctrines to a Naiyâyika
or Logician. Vyâsa‡ does not care even to review the Nyâya system
in the Brahma-sûtra seeing that it has not been recognised by any
worthy sage. Stories of infliction of penalties on those given to the study
of Nyâya are related in the Śkanda Purâṇa,§ and other works; and in the
Naiṣadha-carita‖ we find Kali satirising the founder of Nyâya Philosophy
as " Gotama " the " most bovine " among sages.

*ब्रह्मासं पण्डितको हैतुको वेदनिन्दकः ।

ग्रान्वीचिकीं तर्कविद्यामनुरक्तो निरर्थकाम् ॥ ४७ ॥

हेतुवादान् प्रवदिता वक्ता संसत्सु हेतुमत् ।

ग्राक्रोष्टा चाभिवक्ता च ब्रह्मवाक्येषु च द्विजान् ॥ ४८ ॥

ना स्तिकः सर्वशङ्की च मूर्खः पण्डितमानिकः ।

तस्येयं फलनिर्वृत्तिः श्रृगालत्वं मम द्विज ॥ ४६ ॥

(Mahâbhârata, Sântiparva, adhyâya 180.)

In the Gandharva tantra we find :—

गोतमप्रोक्तशास्त्रार्थनिरताः सर्वे एव हि ।

शार्गालीं योनिमापन्नाः सन्दिग्धाः सर्वकर्मसु ॥

(Quoted in Prâṇatoṣiṇitantra).

†स्त्रातकानामिदं शास्त्रं वाच्यं पुत्रानुशासनम् ।

   ×   ×   ×   ×

न तर्कशास्त्रदग्धाय तथैव पिशुनाय च ॥ १८ ॥

(Mahâbhârata, Sântiparva adhyâya 246).

‡अपरिग्रहाच्चालन्तमनपेच्चा ॥ १७ ॥

(Vedânta-sûtra 2-2).

§गोतमः स्वेन तर्केण खण्डयन् तत्र तत्र हि ।

शासोऽथ मुनिभिस्तत्र शार्गालीं योनिमृच्छति ।

पुनश्चानुगृहीतोऽसौ श्रुतिसिद्धान्ततर्कतः ।

सर्वलोकोपकाराय तव शास्त्रं भविष्यति ॥

(Skanda Purâṇa, Kâlikâkhaṇḍa, adhyâya 17;

‖मुक्तये यः शिलात्वाय शास्त्रमूचे महामुनिः ।

गोतमं तमवेतैव यथा विरथ तथैव सः ॥

Gradually however this system of philosophy instead of relying entirely upon reasoning came to attach due weight to the authority of the Vedas, and later on after its reconciliation with them, the principles of Nyâya were assimilated in other systems of philosophy such as the Vaiśeṣika,[*] Yoga, Mîmâmsâ,[†] Sâmkhya[‡] etc.

Nyâya reconciled with scriptural dogmas.

Henceforth the Nyâya was regarded as an approved branch of learning. Thus the Gautama-Dharma-sûtra,[§] prescribes a course of training in Logic (Nyâya) for the King and acknowledges the utility of *Tarka* or Logic in the administration of justice though in the case of conclusions proving incompatible ultimate decision is directed to be made by reference to persons versed in the Vedas. Manu[||] says that *dharma* or duty is to be ascertained by logical reasoning not opposed to the injunctions of the Vedas. He recommends Logic (Nyâya) as a necessary study for a King and a logician to be an indispensable member of a legal assembly Yâjña-valkya[¶] counts "Nyâya" or Logic among the fourteen principal sciences while Vyâsa[||] admits that he was able to arrange and classify the

Nyâya as an approved branch of knowledge.

---

[*] Vaiśeṣika-sûtra 1-1-4, 2-1-15, 2-1-16-. 2-1-17, 2-2-17, 2-2-32, 3-1-15, 9-2-3, 9-2-4.

(Jayanârâyaṇa Tarkapancânan's edition).

[†] Mîmâmsâ-sûtra 1-1-4, 1-3-1, 1-3-2, 1-3-3, 1-4-14, 1-4-35, 1-5-8, 3-1-17, 3-1 20, 4-3-18, 5-1-6, 10-3-35.

[‡] Sâmkhyâ-sûtra 1-60, 1-101, 1-106, 5-10, 5-11, 5-12.

Yoga-sûtra 1-5, 6.

[§]राजा सर्वस्येष्टे ब्राह्मणवर्जं, साधुकारी स्यात् साधुवादी, त्रय्याम् आन्वीचिक्याञ्चाभिविनीतः । न्यायाधिगमे तर्कोऽभ्युपायः । तेनाभ्युह्य यथास्थानं गमयेत् । विप्रतिपत्तौ त्रैविद्यवृद्धे भ्यः प्रत्यवह्य निष्ठां गमयेत् ।

(Gautamadharma-sûtra, adhyâya 11),

आर्षं धर्मोपदेशं च वेदशास्त्राविरोधिना ।
यस्तर्केणानुसंधत्ते स धर्मं वेद नेतरः ॥

(Manu, adhyâya 12, verse 106).

|| त्रैविद्येभ्यस्त्रयीं विद्याद् दण्डनीतिञ्च शाश्वतीम् ।
आन्वीचिकीञ्चात्मविद्यां वार्त्तारम्भांश्च लोकतः ॥

(Manu, adhyâya 7, verse 43).

त्रैविद्यो हैतुकस्तर्की नैरुक्तो धर्म्मपाठकः ।
त्र्यश्चाश्रमिणः पूर्व्वे परिषत् स्यादृशावरा ॥

(Manu, adhyâya 12, verse 111).

¶ पुराण्यायमीमांसा धर्म्मशास्त्राङ्गमिश्रिताः ।
वेदाः स्थानानि विद्यानां धर्म्मस्य च चतुर्द्दश ॥

(Yâjnâvalkya samhitâ, adhyâya 1, verse 3).

|| तन्त्रोपनिषदं तात परिशेषं तु पार्थिव ।
मन्थामि मनसा तात दृष्ट्वा चान्वीचिकिं पराम् ॥

(Mahâbhârata quoted by Visvanâtha in his Vṛitti on Nyâya-sûtra 1 1-1).

Upaniṣads with the help of the 'Ânvîkṣikî' or Logic. In the Padma-purâna*
Logic is included among the fourteen principal branches of learning
promulgated by God Viṣṇu, while in the Matsya-purâna,† Nyâya-vidyâ
together with the Vedas is said to have emanated from the mouth of
Brahma himself. In fact so wide-spread was the study of Nyâya that
the Mahâbhârata is full of references to that science.

In the Âdiparva of the Mahâbhârata Nyâya‡ or Logic is mentioned
along with the Veda and Cikitsâ (the science of medicine), and the
hermitage of Kâśyapa is described as being filled with sages who were
versed in the Nyâya-tattva (logical truths) and knew the true meaning of
a proposition, objection and conclusion. The Sânti-parva§ refers to
numerous tenets of Nyâya supported by reason and scripture while the
Asvamedha-parva‖ describes the sacrificial ground as being resounded
by logicians (Hetu-vâdin) who employed arguments and counter-argu-

---

* अज्ञानि चतुरो वेदान् पुराण्यायविस्तरान् ।

मीमांसां धर्म्मशास्त्रञ्च परिगृह्याथ साम्प्रतम् ॥

मत्स्यरूपेण च पुनः कल्पादावुदकान्तरे ।

(Padma-purâna, *vide* Muir's Sanskrit text Vol. III, p. 27).

† अनन्तरञ्च वक्त्रेभ्यो वेदास्तस्य विनिःसृताः ।

मीमांसा न्यायविद्या च प्रमाणाष्टकसंयुता ॥

(Matsya-purâna 3-2).

‡ न्यायशिक्षा चिकित्सा च दानं पाशुपतं तथा ।

हेतुनैव समं जन्म दिव्यमानुषसंज्ञितम् ॥ ६७ ॥

(Mahâbhârata, Âdiparva, adhyâya 1).

न्यायतत्त्वात्मविज्ञानसम्पन्नैर् वेदपारगैः ॥ ४२ ॥

नानावाक्यसमाहारसमवायविशारदैः ।

विशेषकार्यविद्विद्भिश्च मोक्षधर्म्मपरायणैः ॥ ४३ ॥

स्थापनाक्षेपसिद्धान्त परमार्थज्ञतां गतैः ।

शब्दच्छन्दोनिरुक्तज्ञैः कालज्ञानविशारदैः ॥ ४४ ॥

द्रव्यकर्म्मगुणज्ञैश्च कार्य्यकारणवेदिभिः ॥

(Mahâbhârata, Âdiparva, adhyâya 70).

§ न्यायतन्त्रीण्यनेकानि तैस्तैरुक्तानि वादिभिः ।

हेत्वागमसमाचारैर्यदुक्तं तदुपास्यताम् ॥ २२ ॥

(Mahâbhârata, Sântiparva, adhyâya 210).

‖ तस्मिन् यज्ञे प्रवृत्ते तु वाग्मिनो हेतुवादिनः ।

हेतुवादान् बहूनाहुः परस्परजिगीषवः ॥ २७ ॥

(Mahâbhârata, Aśvamedhaparva, adhyâya, 85).

ments to vanquish one another. In the Sabhâ-parva* the sage Nârada is described as being versed in Logic (Nyâyavid) and skilful in distinguishing unity and plurality (" aikya " and "nânâtva ") conjunction and co-existence (" samyoga " and "samavâya "), genus and species (" parâ-para ") etc·, capable of deciding questions by evidences (Pramâna) and ascertaining the validity and invalidity of a five-membered syllogism (Pañcâvayava-vâkya).

In fact the Nyâya (Logic) was in course of time deservedly **The course of Nyâya.** held in very high esteem. If it were allowed to follow its original course unimpeded by religious dogmas it would have risen to the very height of perfection. Nevertheless the principles of Nyâya entering into the different systems of philosophy gave them each its proper compactness and cogency just as Bacon's Inductive Method shaped the sciences and philosophies of a later age in a different country. It is however to be regretted that during the last five hundred years the Nyâya has been mixed up with Law (smriti), Rhetoric (alankâra), Vedânta, etc., and thereby has hampered the growth of those branches of knowledge upon which it has grown up as a sort of parasite.

SANSKRIT COLLEGE, CALCUTTA. } SATIS CHANDRA VIDYABHUSANA.
 The 7th November, 1913.

---

* न्यायविद् धर्म्मतत्त्वज्ञः षडङ्गविदनुत्तमः ।
ऐक्यसंयोगनानात्व समवायविशारदः ॥ ३ ॥
वक्ता प्रगल्भो मेधावी स्मृतिमान्नयवित् कविः ।
परापरविभागज्ञः प्रमाणकृतनिश्चयः ॥ ४ ॥
पञ्चावयवयुक्तस्य वाक्यस्थ गुणदोषवित् ।
उत्तरोत्तरवक्ता च वदतोऽपि बृहस्पतेः ॥ ५ ॥

(Mahâbhârata, Sabhâparva, adhyâya 5).

THE NYÂYA-SÛTRAS.

BOOK I.—CHAPTER I.

प्रमाणप्रमेयसंशयप्रयोजनदृष्टान्तसिद्धान्तावयवतर्कनिर्णय-
वादजल्पवितण्डाहेत्वाभासच्छलजातिनिग्रहस्थानानां तत्त्वज्ञाना-
न्निश्श्रेयसाधिगमः ॥१।१।१॥

1. **Supreme felicity** is attained by the knowledge about the true nature of sixteen categories, *viz.*, means of right knowledge (pramâṇa), object of right knowledge (prameya), doubt (saṁśaya), purpose (prayojana), familiar instance (dṛṣṭânta), established tenet (siddhânta), members (avayava), confutation (tarka*), ascertainment (nirṇaya), discussion (vâda), wrangling (jalpa), cavil (vitaṇḍâ), fallacy (hetvâbhâsa), quibble (chala), futility (jâti), and occasion for rebuke (nigrahasthâna).

Knowledge about the true nature of sixteen categories† means true knowledge of the " enunciation," " definition " and " critical examination " of the categories. Book I (of the Nyâya-Sûtra) treats of " enunciation " and " definition," while the remaining four Books are reserved for " critical examination." The attainment of supreme felicity is preceded by the knowledge of four things, *viz.*, (1) that which is fit to be abandoned (*viz.*,

---

* The English equivalent for "tarka" is variously given as "confutation," "argumentation," "reductio ad absurdum," "hypothetical reasoning," etc.

† Vâtsyâyana observes :—

त्रिविधा चास्य शास्त्रस्य प्रवृत्तिः । उद्देशोलक्षणं परीच्चाचेति ।

—(Nyâyadarśana, p. 9, Bibliotheca Indica Series).

pain), (2) that which produces what is fit to be abandoned (*viz.*, misapprehension, etc.), (3) complete destruction of what is fit to be abandoned and (4) the means of destroying what is fit to be abandoned (*viz.*, true knowledge*).

दुःखजन्मप्रवृत्तिदोषमिथ्याज्ञानानामुत्तरोत्तरापाये तदनन्तरापा-
यादपवर्गः ॥१।१।२॥

2. ⌐Pain, birth, activity, faults and misapprehension—on the successive annihilation of these in the reverse order, there follows **release**.

Misapprehension, faults, activity, birth and pain, these in their uninterrupted course constitute the "world." Release, which consists in the soul's getting rid of the world, is the condition of supreme felicity marked by perfect tranquillity and not tainted by any defilement. A person, by the true knowledge of the sixteen categories, is able to remove his misapprehensions. When this is done, his faults, *viz.*, affection, aversion and stupidity, disappear. He is then no longer subject to any activity and is consequently freed from transmigration and pains. This is the way in which his release is effected and supreme felicity secured.

प्रत्यक्षानुमानोपमानशब्दाः "प्रमाणानि" ॥१।१।३॥

3. Perception, inference, comparison and word (verbal testimony)—these are the **means of right knowledge**.

[The Cârvâkas admit only one means of right knowledge, *viz.*, perception (pratyakṣa), the Vaiśeṣikas and Bauddhas admit two, *viz.*, perception and inference (anumâna), the Sânkhyas admit three, *viz.*, perception, inference and verbal testimony (âgama or śabda) while the Naiyâyikas whose fundamental work is the Nyâya-sûtra admit four, *viz.*, perception, inference, verbal testimony and comparison (upamâna). The Prâbhâkaras admit a fifth means of right knowledge called presumption arthâpatti), the Bhâṭṭas and Vedântins admit a sixth, *viz.*, non-existence (abhâva) and the Paurâṇikas recognise a seventh and eighth means of right knowledge, named probability (sambhava) and rumour (aitihya)].

इन्द्रियार्थसन्निकर्षोत्पन्नं ज्ञानमव्यपदेश्यमव्यभिचारि व्यव-
सायात्मकं "प्रत्यक्षम्" ॥१।१।४॥

---

*इदं तस्य निवर्त्तकं ज्ञानमात्यन्तिकं तस्योपायोऽधिगन्तव्य इत्येतानि चत्वारि अर्थ पदानि सम्यक् बुद्ध्वा निःश्रेयसमधिगच्छति ।

4. **Perception** is that knowledge which arises from the contact of a sense with its object and which is determinate, unnameable and non-erratic.

Determinate.—This epithet distinguishes perception from indeterminate knowledge; as for instance, a man looking from a distance cannot ascertain whether there is smoke or dust.

Unnameable.—Signifies that the knowledge of a thing derived through perception has no connection with the name which the thing bears.

Non-erratic.—In summer the sun's rays coming in contact with earthly heat quiver and appear to the eyes of men as water. The knowledge of water derived in this way is not perception. To eliminate such cases the epithet non-erratic has been used.

[This aphorism may also be translated as follows:—**Perception** is knowledge and which arises from the contact of a sense with its object and which is non-erratic being either indeterminate (nirvikalpaka as "this is something") or determinate (savikalpaka as "this is a Brâhmaṇa")].

अथ तत्पूर्व्वकं "त्रिविधमनुमानं" पूर्ववच्छेषवत्सामान्यतो दृष्टं च ॥१।१।५॥

5. **Inference** is knowledge which is preceded by perception, and is of three kinds, *viz.*, â priori, â posteriori and 'commonly seen.'

Â *priori* is the knowledge of effect derived from the perception of its cause, *e. g.*, one seeing clouds infers that there will be rain.

Â *posteriori* is the knowledge of cause derived from the perception of its effect, *e. g.*, one seeing a river swollen infers that there was rain.

['*Commonly seen*' is the knowledge of one thing derived from the perception of another thing with which it is commonly seen, *e. g.*, one seeing a beast possessing horns, infers that it possesses also a tail, or one seeing smoke on a hill infers that there is fire on it].

Vâtsyâyana takes the last to be "*not commonly seen*" which he interprets as the knowledge of a thing which is not commonly seen, *e. g.*, observing affection, aversion and other qualities one infers that there is a substance called soul.

प्रसिद्धसाधर्म्यात्साध्यसाधनम् "उपमानम्" ॥१।१।६॥

6. **Comparison** is the knowledge of a thing through its similarity to another thing previously well known.

A man hearing from a forester that a *bos gavaeus* is like a cow resorts to a forest where he sees an animal like a cow. Having recollected what he heard he institutes a comparison, by which he arrives at the conviction that the animal which he sees is *bos gavaeus*. This is knowledge derived through comparison. Some hold that comparison is not a separate means of knowledge, for when one notices the likeness of a cow in a strange animal one really performs an act of perception. In reply it is urged that we cannot deny comparison as a separate means of knowledge, for how does otherwise the name *bos gavaeus* signify the general notion of the animal called *bos gavaeus*. That the name *bos gavaeus* signifies one and all members of the *bos gavaeus* class is not a result of perception but the consequence of a distinct knowledge called comparison.

आप्तोपदेशः "शब्दः" ॥१।१।१।७॥

7. Word (verbal testimony) is the instructive assertion of a reliable person.

A *reliable person* is one—may be a ṛiṣi, ârya or mleccha, who as an expert in a certain matter is willing to communicate his experiences of it.

[Suppose a young man coming to the side of a river cannot ascertain whether the river is fordable or not, and immediately an old experienced man of the locality, who has no enmity against him, comes and tells him that the river is easily fordable : the word of the old man is to be accepted as a means of right knowledge called verbal testimony].

"स द्विविधो" दृष्टाऽदृष्टार्थत्वात् ॥ १।१।८ ॥

8. It is of two kinds, *viz.*, that which refers to *matter which is seen* and that which refers to *matter which is not seen*.

The first kind involves matter which can be actually verified. Though we are incapable of verifiying the matter involved in the second kind, we can somehow ascertain it by means of inference.

[*Matter which is seen, e.g.,* a physician's assertion that physical strength is gained by taking butter].

[*Matter which is not seen, e.g.,* a religious teacher's assertion that one conquers heaven by performing horse-sacrifices].

आत्मशरीरेन्द्रियार्थबुद्धिमनःप्रवृत्तिदोषप्रेत्यभावफलदुःखा-पवर्गास्तु "प्रमेयम्" ॥१।१।९॥

9. Soul, body, senses, objects of sense, intellect, mind, activity, fault, transmigration, fruit, pain and release— are the **objects of right knowledge.**

The objects of right knowledge are also enumerated as substance, quality, action, generality, particularity, intimate relation [and non-existence which are the technicalities of the Vaiśeṣika philosophy].

इच्छाद्वेषप्रयत्नसुखदुःखज्ञानानि "आत्मनो लिङ्गम्" इति ॥१।१।१०॥

10. Desire, aversion, volition, pleasure, pain and intelligence are the marks of the soul.

[These abide in the soul or rather are the qualities of the substance called soul].

चेष्टेन्द्रियार्थाश्रयः "शरीरम्" ॥१।१।११॥

11. **Body** is the site of gesture, senses and sentiments.

Body is the site of *gesture* inasmuch as it strives to reach what is desirable and to avoid what is hateful. It is also the site of *senses* for the latter act well or ill, according as the former is in good or bad order. *Sentiments* which comprise pleasure and pain are also located in the body which experiences them.

घ्राणरसनचक्षुस्त्वक्श्रोत्राणि "इन्द्रियाणि" भूतेभ्यः ॥१।१।१२॥

12. Nose, tongue, eye, skin and ear are the **senses** produced from elements.

Nose is of the same nature as earth, tongue as water, eye as light, skin as air and ear as ether.

पृथिव्यापस्तेजो वायुराकाशमिति "भूतानि" ॥ १।१।१३ ॥

13. Earth, water, light, air and ether—these are the **elements.**

गन्धरसरूपस्पर्शशब्दाः "पृथिव्यादिगुणाः" तदर्थाः ॥१।१।१४॥

14. Smell, taste, colour, touch and sound are **objects of the senses** and qualities of the earth, etc.

Smell is the object of nose and the prominent quality of earth, taste is the object of tongue and quality of water, colour is the object of eye and quality of light, touch is the object of skin and quality of air, and sound is the object of ear and quality of ether.

"बुद्धिः" उपलब्धिर्ज्ञानमित्यनर्थान्तरम् ॥१॥१॥१५॥

15. Intellect, apprehension and knowledge—these are not different from one another.

[The term apprehension (*upalabdhi*) is generally used in the sense of perception (*pratyakṣa*). According to the Sânkhya philosophy, intellect (*buddhi*), which is the first thing evolved out of primordial matter (*prakṛiti*), is altogether different from knowledge (*jñâna*), which consists in the reflection of external objects on the soul (*puruṣa*) the abode of transparent consciousness.]

युगपज्ज्ञानानुत्पत्तिः "मनसो लिङ्गम्" ॥१॥१॥१६॥

16. The mark of the mind is that there do not arise (in the soul) more acts of knowledge than one at a time.

It is impossible to perceive two things simultaneously. Perception does not arise merely from the contact of a sense-organ on its object, but it requires also a conjunction of the mind. Now, the mind, which is an atomic substance, cannot be conjoined with more than one sense-organ at a time, hence there cannot occur more acts of perception than one at one time.

"प्रवृत्तिः" वाग्बुद्धिशरीरारम्भ इति ॥१॥१॥१७॥

17. **Activity** is that which makes the voice, mind and body begin their action.

There are three kinds of action, *viz.*, *vocal*, *mental* and *bodily*, each of which may be sub-divided as good or bad.

Bodily actions which are *bad* are :—(1) killing, (2) stealing, and (3) committing adultery.

Bodily actions which are *good* are :—(1) giving, (2) protecting, and (3) serving.

Vocal actions which are *bad* are :—(1) telling a lie, (2) using harsh language, (3) slandering, and (4) indulging in frivolous talk.

Vocal actions which are *good* are :—(1) speaking the truth, (2) speaking what is useful, (3) speaking what is pleasant, and (4) reading sacred books.

Mental actions which are *bad* are :—(1) malice, (2) covetousness, and (3) scepticism.

Mental actions which are *good* are :—(1) compassion, (2) refraining from covetousness, and (3) devotion.

प्रवर्त्तनालच्चणा "दोषाः" ॥१।१।१८॥

18. Faults have the characteristic of causing activity.

The faults are affection, aversion, and stupidity.

पुनरुत्पत्तिः "प्रेत्यभावः" ॥१।१।१९॥

19. Transmigration means re-births.

Transmigration is the series of births and deaths. Birth is the connection of soul with body, sense-organs, mind, intellect, and sentiments, while death is the soul's separation from them.

प्रवृत्तिदोषजनितोऽर्थः "फलम्" ॥१।१।२०॥

20. Fruit is the thing produced by activity and faults.

Fruit consists in the enjoyment of pleasure or suffering of pain. All activity and faults end in producing pleasure, which is acceptable, and pain, which is fit only to be avoided.

बाधनालच्चणं "दुःखम्" इति ॥१।१।२१॥

21. Pain has the characteristic of causing uneasiness.

Pain is affliction which every one desires to avoid. The aphorism may also be translated as follows:—

Pain is the mark of hindrance to the soul.

तदत्यन्तविमोच्चः "अपवर्गः" ॥१।१।२२॥

22. Release is the absolute deliverance from pain.

A soul which is no longer subject to transmigration is freed from all pains. Transmigration, which consists in the soul's leaving one body and taking another, is the cause of its undergoing pleasure and pain. The soul attains release as soon as there is an end of the body, and, consequently, of pleasure and pain. Those are mistaken who maintain that release enables the soul not only to get rid of all pains but also to attain eternal pleasure, for pleasure is as impermanent as pain and the body.

समानानेकधम्मौपपत्तेर्विप्रतिपत्तेरुपलब्ध्यनुपलब्धिव्यवस्थात-
श्र विशेषापेच्चो विमर्शः "संशयः" ॥१।१।२३॥

23. Doubt, which is a conflicting judgment about the precise character of an object, arises from the recognition of properties common to many objects, or of properties not

common to any of the objects, from conflicting testimony, and from irregularity of perception and non-perception.

Doubt is of five kinds according as it arises from—

(1) *Recognition of common properties*—e.g., seeing in the twilight a tall object we cannot decide whether it is a man or a post, for the property of tallness belongs to both.

(2) *Recognition of properties not common*—e.g., hearing a sound, one questions whether it is eternal or not, for the property of soundness abides neither in man, beast, etc., that are non-eternal nor in atoms which are eternal.

(3) *Conflicting testimony,* e.g., merely by study one cannot decide whether the soul exists, for one system of philosophy affirms that it does, while another system states that it does not.

(4) *Irregularity of perception,* e.g., we perceive water in the tank where it really exists, but water appears also to exist in the mirage where it really does not exist.

A question arises whether water is perceived only when it actually exists or even when it does not exist.

(5) *Irregularity of non-perception,* e.g., we do not perceive water in the radish where it really exists, or on dry land where it does not exist.

A question arises, whether water is not perceived only when it does not exist, or also when it does exist.

यमर्थमधिकृत्य प्रवर्त्तते तत् "प्रयोजनम्" ॥१॥१॥२४॥

24. Purpose is that with an eye to which one proceeds to act.

Purpose refers to the thing which one endeavours to attain or avoid. [A man collects fuel for the purpose of cooking his food].

लौकिकपरीक्षकाणां यस्मिन्नर्थे बुद्धिसाम्यं स "दृष्टान्तः" ॥ १ । १ । २५ ॥

25. A familiar instance is the thing about which an ordinary man and an expert entertain the same opinion.

[With regard to the general proposition " wherever there is smoke there is fire " the familiar instance is a kitchen in which fire and smoke abide together, to the satisfaction of an ordinary man as well as an acute investigator.]

तन्त्राधिकरणाभ्युपगमसंस्थितिः "सिद्धान्तः" ॥ १ । १ । २६ ॥

26. An established tenet is a dogma resting on the authority of a certain school, hypothesis, or implication.

सर्वतन्त्रप्रतितन्त्राधिकरणाभ्युपगमसंस्थित्यर्थान्तरभा-
वात् ॥ १ । १ । २७ ॥

27. The tenet is of four kinds owing to the distinction between *a dogma of all the schools, a dogma peculiar to some school, a hypothetical dogma,* and *an implied dogma.*

सर्वतन्त्राविरुद्धस्तन्त्रेऽधिकृतोऽर्थः "सर्वतन्त्रसिद्धान्तः"
॥ १ । १ । २८ ॥

28. A dogma of all the schools is a tenet which is not opposed by any school and is claimed by at least one school.

The five elements (*viz.*, earth, water, light, air and ether), the five objects of sense (*viz.*, smell, taste, colour, touch and sound), etc., are tenets which are accepted by all the schools.

समानतन्त्रसिद्धः परतन्त्रासिद्धः प्रतितन्त्रसिद्धान्तः
॥ १ । १ । २६ ॥

29. A dogma peculiar to some school is a tenet which is accepted by similar schools but rejected by opposite schools.

"A thing cannot come into existence out of nothing"—this is a peculiar dogma of the Sânkhyas. [The eternity of sound is a peculiar dogma of the Mîmâmsakas].

यत्सिद्धावन्यप्रकरणसिद्धिस्स "अधिकरणसिद्धान्तः"-
॥ १ । १ । ३० ॥

30. A hypothetical dogma is a tenet which if accepted leads to the acceptance of another tenet.

"There is a soul apart from the senses, because it can recognise one and the some object by seeing and touching." If you accept this tenet you must also have accepted the following :—(1) That the senses are more than one, (2) that each of the senses has its particular object, (3) that the soul derives its knowledge through the channels of the senses, (4) that a substance which is distinct from its qualities is the abode of them, etc.

2

अपरीचिताभ्युपगमात्तद्विशेषपरीचणम् "अभ्युपगमसिद्धान्तः"
॥ १ । १ । ३१ ॥

31. **An implied dogma** is a tenet which is not explicitly declared as such, but which follows from the examination of particulars concerning it.

The discussion whether sound is eternal or non-eternal presupposes that it is a substance. "That sound is a substance" is here an implied dogma. [The mind has nowhere been stated in the Nyâya-sûtra to be a sense-organ, but it follows from the particulars examined concerning it that it is so].

प्रतिज्ञाहेतूदाहरणोपनयनिगमनानि "अवयवाः" ॥ ९ । ९ । ३२ ॥

32. The **members** (of a syllogism) are proposition, reason, example, application, and conclusion.

[1.   Proposition.—This hill is fiery,
2.   Reason.—Because it is smoky,
3.   Example.—Whatever is smoky is fiery, as a kitchen,
4.   Application.—So is this hill (smoky),
5.   Conclusion.—Therefore this hill is fiery].

Some lay down *five more members* as follows :—

1 (*a*) Inquiry as to the proposition (jijñâsâ).—Is this hill fiery in all its parts, or in a particular part ?

2 (*a*) Questioning the reason (samsaya).—That which you call smoke may be nothing but vapour.

3 (*a*) Capacity of the example to warrant the conclusion (sakya-prâpti). Is it true that smoke is always a concomitant of fire? In a kitchen there are of course both smoke and fire, but in a red-hot iron-ball there is no smoke.

4 (*a*) Purpose for drawing the conclusion (prayojana).—Purpose consists in the determination of the true conditions of the hill, in order to ascertain whether it is such that one can approach it, or such that one should avoid it, or such that one should maintain an attitude of indifference towards it.

4 (*b*) Dispelling all questions (samsayavyudâsa).—It is beyond all questions that the hill is smoky, and that smoke is an invariable concomitant of fire.

साध्यनिर्देशः "प्रतिज्ञा" ॥ १ । १ । ३३ ॥

33. A **proposition** is the declaration of what is to be established.

Sound is non-eternal—this is a proposition.

उदाहरणसाधर्म्यात्साध्यसाधनं "हेतुः" ॥ १ । १ । ३४ ॥

34. The **reason** is the means for establishing what is to be established through the *homogeneous* or affirmative character of the example.

Proposition.—Sound is non-eternal,

Reason —Because it is produced,

Example (homogeneous).—Whatever is produced is non-eternal, as a pot.

The example "pot" possesses the same character as is implied in the reason, *viz.*, " being produced," inasmuch as both are non-eternal.

"तथा" वैधर्म्यात् ॥ १ । १ । ३५ ॥

35. Likewise through *heterogeneous* or *negative* character.

Proposition.—Sound is non-eternal,

Reason.—Because it is produced,

Example (heterogeneous).—Whatever is not non-eternal is not produced, as the soul.

The example "soul" possesses a character heterogeneous to that which is implied in the reason, *viz.*, " being produced," inasmuch as one is eternal and the other non-eternal.

साध्यसाधर्म्यात्तद्धर्म्मभावी दृष्टान्त "उदाहरणम्" ॥ १ । १ । ३६ ॥

36. A **homogeneous** (or affirmative) example is a familiar instance which is known to possess the property to be established and which implies that this property is invariably contained in the reason given.

Proposition—Sound is non-eternal,

Reason—Because it is produced,

Homogeneous example—Whatever is produced is non-eternal, as a pot.

Here "pot" is a familiar instance which possesses the property of non-eternality and implies that whatever is "produced" is attended by the same property (non-eternality).

तद्विपर्य्ययाद्वा "विपरीतम्" ॥ १ । १ । ३७ ॥

37. A heterogeneous (or negative) example is a familiar instance which is known to be devoid of the property to be established and which implies that the absence of this property is invariably rejected in the reason given.

Proposition—Sound is non-eternal,

Reason—Because it is produced,

Heterogeneous example—Whatever is not non-eternal is not produced, as the soul.

Here the soul is a familiar instance which is known to be devoid of the property of non-eternality and implies that if anything were produced, it would necessarily be deprived of the quality of eternality, *i.e.*, 'being produced' and 'eternal' are imcompatible epithets.

उदाहरणापेचत्तस्तथेत्युपसंहारो न तथेति वा साध्यस्य "उपनयः" ॥ १ । १ । ३८ ॥

38. Application is a winding up, with reference to the example, of what is to be established as being so or not so.

Application is of two kinds : (1) *affirmative* and (2) *negative*. The affirmative application, which is expressed by the word "so," occurs when the example is of an affirmative character. The negative application, which is expressed by the phrase "not so," occurs when the example is of a negative character.

Proposition—Sound is non-eternal,

Reason—Because it is produced,

Example—Whatever is produced is non-eternal, as a pot,

Affirmative application.—So is sound (produced),

Conclusion.—Therefore sound is non-eternal.

Or :

Proposition—Sound is not eternal,

Reason—Because it is produced,

Example—Whatever is eternal is not produced, as the soul,

Negative application.—Sound is not so (*i.e.*, sound is not produced),

Conclusion.—Therefore sound is not eternal.

हेत्वपदेशात्प्रतिज्ञायाः पुनर्वचनं "निगमनम्" ॥ १ । १ । ३९ ॥

39. **Conclusion** is the re-stating of the proposition after the reason has been mentioned.

Conclusion is the confirmation of the proposition after the reason and the example have been mentioned.

    Proposition—Sound is non-eternal,

    Reason—Because it is produced,

    Example—Whatever is produced is non-eternal, as a pot,

    Application—So is sound (produced),

    Conclusion.—Therefore sound is produced.

अविज्ञाततत्त्वेऽर्थे कारणोपपतितस्तत्त्वज्ञानार्थमूहः "तर्कः"

॥ १ । १ । ४० ॥

40. **Confutation**, which is carried on for ascertaining the real character of a thing of which the character is not known, is reasoning which reveals the character by showing the absurdity of all contrary characters.

Is the soul eternal or non-eternal ? Here the real character of the soul, *viz.*, whether it is eternal or non-eternal, is not known. In ascertaining the character we reason as follows:—If the soul were non-eternal it would be impossible for it to enjoy the fruits of its own actions, to undergo transmigration, and to attain final release. But such a conclusion is absurd: such possibilities are known to belong to the soul: therefore, we must admit that the soul is eternal.

विमृश्यपक्षप्रतिपक्षाभ्यामर्थावधारणं "निर्णयः" ॥ १ । १ । ४१ ॥

41. **Ascertainment** is the removal of doubt, and the determination of a question, by hearing two opposite sides.

A person wavers and doubts if certain statements are advanced to him by one of two parties, but opposed by the other party. His doubt is not removed until by the application of reasons he can vindicate either of the parties. The process by which the vindication is effected is called ascertainment. Ascertainment is not, however, in all cases preceded by doubt, for instance, in the case of perception things are ascertained directly. So also we ascertain things directly by the authority of scriptures, or through discussion. But in the case of investigation, doubt must precede ascertainment.

इति श्रीगौतममहर्षिप्रणीते न्यायदर्शने प्रथमस्याध्यायस्य प्रथममाह्निकम् ॥ १ । १ ॥

Book I.—Chapter II.

प्रमाणतर्कसाधनोपालम्भसिद्धान्ताविरुद्धः पञ्चावयवोपपन्नः
पक्षप्रतिपक्षपरिग्रहो "वादः" ॥ १ । २ । १ ॥

1. **Discussion** is the adoption of one of two opposing sides. What is adopted is analysed in the form of five
members, and defended by the aid of any of the means of
right knowledge, while its opposite is assailed by confutation, without deviation from the established tenets.

[A *dialogue* or *disputation* (kathā) is the adoption of a side by a disputant and its opposite by his opponent. It is of three kinds, *viz.,*
discussion which aims at ascertaining the truth, *wrangling* which aims at
gaining victory, and *cavil* which aims at finding mere faults. A *discutient*
is one who engages himself in a disputation as a means of seeking the
truth].

An instance of discussion is given below :—
Discutient—There is soul.
Opponent—There is no soul.
Discutient—Soul is existent (proposition).

Because it is an abode of consciousness (reason).

Whatever is not existent is not an abode of consciousness,
as a hare's horn (negative example).

Soul is not so, that is, soul is an abode of consciousness
(negative application).

Therefore soul is existent (conclusion).
Opponent—Soul is non-existent (proposition).
Because, etc.
Discutient—The scripture which is a verbal testimony declares the
existence of soul.
Opponent   ...   .
Discutient—If there were no soul, it would not be possible to appre-
hend one and the same object through sight and touch.
Opponent   ...   .
Discutient—The doctrine of soul harmonises well with the various
tenets which we hold, *viz.,* that there are eternal things, that everybody
enjoys pleasure or suffers pain according to his own actions, etc. Therefore there is soul.

[The discussion will be considerably lengthened if the opponent happens to be a Buddhist who does not admit the authority of scripture, and holds that there are no eternal things, etc.].

यथोक्तोपपन्नश्छलजातिनिग्रहस्थानसाधनोपालम्भो "जल्पः" ॥ १ । २ । २ ॥

2. **Wrangling**, which aims at gaining victory, is the defence or attack of a proposition in the manner aforesaid by quibbles, futilities, and other processes which deserve rebuke.

A *wrangler* is one who, engaged in a disputation, aims only at victory, being indifferent whether the arguments which he employs support his own contention or that of his opponent, provided that he can make out a pretext for bragging that he has taken an active part in the disputation.

स्वप्रतिपक्षस्थापनाहीनो "वितराडा" ॥ १ । २ । ३ ॥

3. **Cavil** is a kind of wrangling which consists in mere attacks on the opposite side.

A *caviller* does not endeavour to establish anything, but confines himself to mere carping at the arguments of his opponent.

सव्यभिचारविरुद्धप्रकरणसमसाध्यसमातीतकाला "हेत्वा- भासाः" ॥ १ । २ । ४ ॥

4. **Fallacies of a reason** are the erratic, the contradictory, the equal to the question, the unproved, and the mistimed.

अनैकान्तिकः "सव्यभिचारः" ॥ १ । २ । ५ ॥

5. **The erratic** is the reason which leads to more conclusions than one.

An instance of the *erratic* is given below :—
Proposition—sound is eternal,
Erratic reason—Because it is intangible,
Example—Whatever is intangible is eternal as atoms,
Application—So is sound (intangible),
Conclusion.—Therefore sound is eternal.

Again :

Proposition—Sound is non-eternal,

Erratic reason.—Because it is intangible,

Example.—Whatever is intangible is non-eternal, as intellect,

Application.—So is sound (intangible),

Conclusion.—Therefore sound is non-eternal (intangible).

Here from the reason there have been drawn two opposite conclusions, *viz.* : that sound is eternal, and that sound is non-eternal. The reason or middle term is erratic when it is not pervaded by the major term, that is, when there is no universal connection between the major term and middle term, as pervader and pervaded. Intangible is pervaded neither by 'eternal' nor by 'non eternal.' In fact there is no universal connection between 'intangible' and "eternal' or 'non-eternal.'

सिद्धान्तमभ्युपेत्य तद्विरोधी "विरुद्धः" ॥ १ । २ । ६ ॥

6. The **contradictory** is the reason which opposes what is to be established.

Proposition.—A pot is produced,

Contradictory reason.—Because it is eternal.

Here the reason is contradictory because that which is eternal is never produced.

यस्मात्प्रकरणचिन्ता स निर्णयार्थमपदिष्ट: "प्रकरणसमः ॥ १ । २ । ७ ॥

7. **Equal to the question** is the reason which provokes the very question for the solution of which it was employed.

Proposition.—Sound is non-eternal,

Reason which is *equal to the question*—Because it is not possessed of the attribute of eternality.

'Non-eternal' is the same as 'not possessed of the attribute of eternality.' In determining the question whether sound is non-eternal the reason given is that sound is non-eternal, or in other words the reason begs the question.

साध्याविशिष्टस्साध्यत्वात् "साध्यसमः" ॥ १ । २ । ८ ॥

8. The **unproved** is the reason which stands in need of proof in the same way as the proposition does.

Proposition—Shadow is a substance.

Unproved reason.—Because it possesses motion.

Here unless it is actually proved that shadow possesses motion, we cannot accept it as the reason for the proposition that shadow is a substance. Just as the proposition stands in need of proof so does the reason itself. It is possible that the motion belongs to the person who causes that obstruction of light which is called shadow.

कालात्ययापदिष्टः "कालातीतः" ॥ १ । २ । ९ ॥

50. The **mistimed** is the reason which is adduced when the time is past in which it might hold good.—9.

Proposition—Sound is durable.

Mistimed reason—Because it is manifested by union, as a colour.

The colour of a jar is manifested when the jar comes into union with a lamp, but the colour existed before the union took place, and will continue to exist after the union has ceased. Similarly, the sound of a drum is manifested when the drum comes into union with a rod, and the sound must, after the analogy of the colour, be presumed to have existed before the union took place, and to continue to exist after the union has ceased. Hence sound is durable. The reason adduced here is mistimed, because the manifestation of sound does not take place at the time when the drum comes into union with the rod, but at a subsequent moment when the union has ceased. In the case of colour, however, the manifestation takes place just at the time when the jar comes into union with the lamp. Because the time of their manifestation is different, the analogy between colour and sound is not complete, therefore, the reason is mistimed.

Some interpret the aphorism as follows:—The *mistimed* is the reason which is adduced in a wrong order among the five members, for instance, as, if the reason is stated before the proposition. But this interpretation, according to Vâtsyâyana, is wrong for a word bears its legitimate connection with another word (in a Sanskrit sentence) even if they are placed at a distance from each other, and, on the other hand, even the closest proximity is of no use if the words are disconnected in their sense.* Moreover, the placing of members in a wrong order is noticed in the Nyâya-sûtra as a *nigrahasthâna* (occasion for rebuke) called *aprâpta-kâla* (inopportune).

वचनविघातोऽर्थविकल्पोपपत्त्या "छलम्" ॥ १ । २ । १० ॥

51. Quibble is the opposition offered to a proposition by the assumption of an alternative meaning.—10.

---

* (Quoted by Vâtasyâyana in the Nyâya-bhâṣya, p. 250).

"तत्त्रिविधं" वाक्छलं सामान्यच्छलमुपचारच्छलं चेति-
॥ १ । २ । ११ ॥

52.   It is of *three* kinds, *viz.*, quibble in respect of
a term, quibble in respect of a genus, and quibble in respect of a metaphor.—11.

अविशेषाभिहितेऽर्थे वक्तुरभिप्रायादर्थान्तरकल्पना "वाक्छ-
लम्" ॥ १ । २ । १२ ॥

53.   Quibble in respect of a term consists in wilfully taking the term in a sense other than that intended
by a speaker who has happened to use it ambiguously.—12.

A speaker says : "this boy is *nava-kambala* (possessed of a new
blanket)."

A quibbler replies : "this boy is not certainly *nava-kambala*
(possessed of nine blankets) for he has only one blanket.

Here the word *nava* which is ambiguous was used by the speaker
in the sense of "new," but has been wilfully taken by the quibbler in
the sense of "nine."

सम्भवतोऽर्थस्यातिसामान्ययोगादसम्भूतार्थिकल्पना "सामा-
न्यच्छलम्" ॥ १ । २ । १३ ॥

54.   Quibble in respect of a genus consists in asserting the impossibility of a thing which is really possible,
on the ground that it belongs to a certain genus which is
very wide.—13.

A speaker says : "this Brâhmaṇa is possessed of learning and
conduct."

An objector replies : "it is impossible, for how can it be inferred
that this person is possessed of learning and conduct because he is a
Brâhmaṇa.   There are little boys who are Brâhmaṇas, yet not possessed
of learning and conduct.

Here the objector is a quibbler, for he knows well that possession
of learning and conduct was not meant to be an attribute of the whole
class of Brâhmaṇas, but it was ascribed to "this" particular Brâhmaṇa

who lived long enough in the world to render it possible for him to pursue studies and acquire good morals.

धर्मविकल्पनिर्देशेऽर्थसद्भावप्रतिषेध "उपचारच्छलम्"

॥ १ । २ । १४ ॥

55. Quibble in respect of a metaphor consists in denying the proper meaning of a word by taking it literally while it was used metaphorically, and *vice versa.*—14.

A speaker says : " the scaffolds cry out."

An objector replies: " it is impossible for scaffolds to cry out for they are inanimate objects."

Here the objector is a quibbler, for he knew well that the word *scaffold* was used to signify those standing on the scaffolds.

वाक्छलमेवोपचारच्छलं तदविशेषात् ॥ १ । २ । १५ ॥

56. It may be said that, quibble in respect of a metaphor is in reality quibble in respect of a term, for the first is not different from the second.—15.

न तदर्थान्तरभावात् ॥ १ । २ । १६ ॥

57. But it is not so, for there is a distinction between them.—16.

Words are taken in their direct (literal) meanings in the case of ' quibble in respect of a term ' while they are taken in their direct (literal) as well as indirect (secondary) meanings in the case of ' quibble in respect of a metaphor.'

अविशेषे वा किञ्चित्साधर्म्यादेकच्छलप्रसङ्गः ॥ १ । २ । १७ ॥

58. If you do not admit that one is different from another simply because there is some similarity between them, then we should have only one kind of quibble.—17.

If ' quibble in respect of a metaphor ' were not different from ' quibble in respect of a term,' then these two also would not be different from ' quibble in respect of a genus ' because there is some similarity among all of them. This is absurd, hence the three kinds of quibble are different from one another.

साधर्म्यवैधर्म्याभ्यां प्रत्यवस्थानं "जातिः" ॥ १ । २ । १८ ॥

59. **Futility** consists in offering objections founded on mere similarity or dissimilarity.— 18.

A disputant says : " the soul is inactive because it is all-pervading as ether."

His opponent replies : "if the soul is inactive because it bears similarity to ether as being all-pervading, why is it, not active because it bears similarity to a pot as being a seat of union ?"

The reply is futile, because it overlooks the universal connection between the middle term and the major term which is existent in the arguments of the disputant, but wanting in the arguments of the opponent. Whatever is all-pervading is inactive, but whatever is a seat of union is not necessarily active.

Or again :

Disputant—Sound is non-eternal because unlike ether it is a product.

Opponent—If sound is non-eternal because as a product it is dissimilar to ether, why it is not eternal because as an object of auditory perception it is dissimilar to a pot ?

The reply is futile because it overlooks the universal disconnection between the middle term and the absence of the major term. There is a universal disconnection between " a product " and " not non-eternal," but there is no such disconnection between " an object of auditory perception " and " not eternal."

विप्रतिपत्तिरप्रातिपत्तिश्च "निग्रहस्थानम्" ॥ १ । २ । १९ ॥

60. **An occasion for rebuke** arises when one misunderstands or does not understand at all.—19.

If a person begins to argue in a way which betrays his utter ignorance, or wilfully misunderstands and yet persists in showing that he understands well, it is of no avail to employ counter arguments. He is quite unfit to be argued with, and there is nothing left for his opponent but to turn him out or quit his company, rebuking him as a blockhead or a knave.

An instance of *occasion for rebuke* :—

Whatever is not quality is substance.

Because there is nothing except colour, etc. (quality).

A person who argues in the above way is to be rebuked as a fool, for his reason (which admits only quality) opposes his proposition (which admits both quality and substance).

Another instance:

Disputant—Fire is not hot.

Opponent—But the evidence of touch disproves such a statement.

Disputant, in order to gain the confidence of the assembled people, says—"O learned audience, listen, I do not say that fire is not hot," etc.

It is only meet that the opponent should quit the company of a man who argues in this way.

तद्विकल्पाज्जातिनिग्रहस्थानबहुत्वम् ॥ १ । २ । २० ॥

61. Owing to the variety of kinds, there is multiplicity of futilities and occasions for rebuke.—20.

There are 24 kinds of futility and 22 kinds of occasion for rebuke which will be treated respectively in Chapter I and Chapter II of Book V.

इति श्रीगौतममहर्षिप्रणीते न्यायदर्शने प्रथमस्याध्यायस्य द्वितीयमाह्निकम् ॥ १ । २ ॥

Book II.—Chapter I.

समानानेकधर्म्माध्यवसायादन्यतरधर्म्माध्यवसायाद्वा न संशयः
॥ २ । १ । १ ॥

62.   Some say that **doubt** cannot arise from the recognition of common and uncommon properties whether
conjointly or separately.—1.

Conjointly.—It is said that doubt about an object is never produced if *both* the common and uncommon properties of the object are
recognised.   For instance, if we see in the twilight a tall object which
moves we do not doubt whether it is a man or a post.   We at once decide
that it is a man, for though tallness is a property possessed in common
by man and post, locomotion is a property which distinguishes a man from
a post.

Separately.—Likewise doubt about an object is said never to be produced if *only* the common or the uncommon properties are recognised.   For
instance, if we see a tall object in the twilight, we have no reason to doubt
whether it is a man or a post.   Tallness is certainly a property possessed
in common by man and post, but the tallness of a man is not identical
with that of a post: it merely resembles it.   Now the knowledge of similarity between the tallness of a man and that of a post presupposes a
knowledge of the man and the post, of which the two kinds of tallness are
attributes.   If there is already a knowledge of the man and the post,
there cannot be any doubt about them, for knowledge is the vanquisher
of doubt.

विप्रतिपत्त्यव्यवस्थाध्यवसायाच्च ॥ २ । १ । २ ॥

63.   It is further said that doubt cannot arise either
from conflicting testimony or from the irregularity of perception and non-perception.—2.

विप्रतिपत्तौ च सम्प्रतिपत्तेः ॥ २ । १ । ३ ॥

64.   In the case of conflicting testimony there is,
according to them, a strong conviction (on each side).—3.

Suppose a disputant (Naiyâyika) says: there is soul.   His opponent
(Buddhist) replies: there is no soul.

The disputant and his opponent are quite sure that their respective
statements are correct.   Hence there is no doubt, but on the contrary
there is conviction, in the minds of both.

अव्यवस्थात्मनि व्यवस्थितत्वाच्चाव्यवस्थायाः ॥ २ । १ । ४ ॥

65. Doubt, they say, does not arise from the irregularity of perception and non-perception, because in the irregularity itself there is regularity.—4.

An irregularity may be designated as such with reference to something else, but with reference to itself it is a settled fact. If the irregularity is settled in itself, it is regular and cannot cause doubt. On the other hand, if the irregularity is not settled in itself, it is devoid of its own character and cannot cause doubt.

तथाऽत्यन्तसंशयस्तद्धर्म्मसातत्योपपत्तेः ॥ २ । १ । ५ ॥

66. Likewise there is, they say, the chance of an endless doubt owing to the continuity of its cause.—5.

Recognition of properties common to many objects is, for instance, a cause of doubt. The common properties continue to exist and hence there will, they say, be no cessation of doubt.

यथोक्ताध्यवसायादेव तद्विशेषापेच्चात्संशयेनासंशयो नात्यन्त-संशयो वा ॥ २ । १ । ६ ॥

67. In reply, it is stated that the recognition of properties common to many objects, etc., are certainly causes of doubt if there is no reference to the precise characters of the objects: there is no chance of no-doubt or of *endless-doubt*.—6.

It is admitted that doubt does not arise from the recognition of common and uncommon properties conjointly. Aphorism 2-1-1 brings forth the objection that doubt is not produced even by the recognition of common or uncommon properties alone. It is said that while we see a tall object in the twilight, we at once think of a man and a post, both of which are tall. Thus there is knowledge rather than doubt about the man and post suggested by the tall object. The present aphorism dismisses the objection by stating that there is certainly a common (non-distinctive) knowledge about a man and a post suggested by the tall object, but there is no precise (distinctive) knowledge about them. Precise knowledge (that is, knowledge of the precise character which distinguishes a man from a post) being absent, doubt must arise. Similar arguments will apply to doubt arising from the recognition of non-common properties alone.

Aphorisms 2-1-2 and 2-1-3 raise the objection that doubt does not arise from conflicting testimony, as the disputant and his opponent are both confident of their respective contentions. The present aphorism disposes of the objection by pointing out that in the case of conflicting statements one is led to believe that both statements are worth consideration, but is unable to penetrate into the precise characters of the statements. Hence though the disputant and his opponent remain fixed, the umpire and the audience are thrown into doubt by their conflicting statements.

Aphorism 2-1-4 raises the objection that doubt cannot arise from the irregularity of perception and non-perception as the irregularity is settled in itself. The present aphorism meets the objection by stating that the irregularity cannot be concealed by mere verbal tricks. The irregularity though settled in itself does not lose its own character until the objects which cause it are removed.

Aphorism 2-1-5 gives rise to the fear that there is the possibility of an endless doubt inasmuch as the cause is continuous. The present aphorism removes the fear by stating that though materials of doubt, such as common properties, etc., continue to exist, we do not always recognise them. Unless there is recognition of the common properties, etc , there cannot be doubt.

यत्र संशयस्तत्रैवमुत्तरोत्तरप्रसङ्गः ॥ २ । १ । ७ ॥

68. **Examination** should be made of each case where there is room for doubt.—7.

It has been stated that knowledge about the true nature of the categories consists in the true knowledge of their enunciation, definition, and examination. In case of well-known facts admitted by all, there should be no examination. We are to examine only those cases where there is room for doubt. The author explains, therefore, first the nature of doubt, and then proceeds to examine the other categories, lest there should be any room for doubt in them.

प्रत्यक्षादीनामप्रामाण्यं त्रैकाल्यासिद्धेः ॥ २ । १ । ८ ॥

69. **Perception** and other means of knowledge, says an objector, are invalid as they are impossible at all the three times.—8.

According to the objector, perception is impossible at the present, past and future times, or in other words, perception can neither be prior to, nor posterior to, nor simultaneous with, the objects of sense.

पूर्वं हि प्रमाणसिद्धौ नेन्द्रियार्थसन्निकर्षात्प्रत्यक्षोत्पत्तिः ॥ २ । १ । ६ ॥

70. If perception occurred anteriorly it could not, he says, have arisen from the contact of a sense with its object. —9.

With reference to the perception of colour, for instance, it is asked whether the colour precedes perception or the perception precedes colour. If you say that perception occurred anteriorly or preceded the colour, you must give up your definition of perception, *viz.*, that perception arises from the contact of a sense with its object.

पश्चात्सिद्धौ न प्रमाणेभ्यः प्रमेयासिद्धिः २ । १ । १० ॥

71. If perception is supposed to occur posteriorly you cannot, he continues, maintain the conclusion that objects of sense are established by perception.—10.

The objection stands thus :—The means of right knowledge are stated by you to be perception, inference, comparison and verbal testimony. All objects of right knowledge are said to be established by them. The objects of sense, for instance, are supposed to be established by perception; colour is said to be established by visual perception. This conclusion will have to be abandoned if you say that perception occurs posteriorly to the objects.

युगपत्सिद्धौ प्रत्यर्थनियतत्वात्क्रमवृत्तित्वाभावो बुद्धीनाम् ॥ २ । १ । ११ ॥

72. If perception were simultaneous with its object there would not, says the objector, be any order of succession in our cognitions as there is no such order in their corresponding objects.—11.

Various objects of sense can exist at one time, *e.g.*, colour and smell exist in a flower at the same time. If we hold that perception is simultaneous with its object we must admit that the colour and the smell can be perceived at the same time, that is, our perception of colour must be admitted to be simultaneous with our perception of smell. This is absurd because two acts of perception, nay, two cognitions cannot take place

4

at the same time. As there is an order of succession in our cognitions, perception cannot be simultaneous with its object. The aphorism may also be explained as follows :—

In knowing a colour we perform, we may say, two kinds of knowledge simultaneously, *viz.*, perception and inference. As soon as our eye comes in contact with the colour, perception results which does not, however, enable us to be aware of the colour. The colour is brought home to us by inference which, we may say, is performed simultaneously with the perception. Now, says the objector, perception and inference being two different kinds of knowledge cannot be simultaneous, as the mind which is an atomic substance cannot be instrumental in producing more than one kind of knowledge at a time.—11.

त्रैकाल्यासिद्धेः प्रतिषेधानुपपत्तिः ॥ २ । १ । १२ ॥

73. In reply, it is stated that if perception and other means of right knowledge are impossible, the denial of them is also impossible.—12.

Owing to absence of the matter to be denied, the denial is inoperative.

सर्वप्रमाणप्रतिषेधाच्च प्रतिषेधासिद्धिः ॥ २ । १ । १३ ॥

74. Moreover, the denial itself cannot be established, if you deny all means of right knowledge.—13.

If you are to establish anything (*e.g.*, denial), you can do so only by one or more of the means of right knowledge, *viz.*, perception, inference, comparison, etc. If you deny them there will be left nothing which will lead you to the establishment of the thing. Hence you will not be able to establish the denial itself.

तत्प्रामायये वा न सर्वप्रमाणप्रतिषेधः ॥ २ । १ । १४ ॥

75. If you say that your denial is based on a certain means of right knowledge, you do thereby acknowledge the validity of the means.—14.

Suppose you deny a thing because it is not perceived. You do thereby acknowledge that perception is a means of right knowledge. Similarly inference, etc., are also to be acknowledged as means of right knowledge.

त्रैकाल्याप्रतिषेधश्च शब्दादातोद्यसिद्धिवत्तत्सिद्धेः ॥ २ । १ । १५ ॥

76. The means of right knowledge cannot, therefore, be denied. They are established in the manner that a drum is proved by its sound.—15.

There is, says Vâtsyâyana, no fixed rule that the means of right knowledge should precede the objects of right knowledge or should succeed them or be simultaneous with them. The order of precedence is never · uniform. Look at the analogous cases : a drum precedes its sound, and illumination succeeds the sun, while smoke is synchronous with fire.

प्रमेयता च तुलाप्रामाएयवत् ॥ २ । १ । १६ ॥

77. The character of an object of right knowledge resembles that of a balance by which a thing is weighed.—16.

Just as a balance is an instrument for measuring weight but is a measured object when it is itself weighed in another balance, so the senses, etc., are said to be instruments of right knowledge from one point of view, and objects of right knowledge from another point of view. The eye, for instance, is an instrument of perception as well as an object of perception. So also the means of right knowledge may, if occasion arises, be also regarded as objects of right knowledge.

प्रमाणतस्सिद्धेः प्रमाणानां प्रमाणान्तरसिद्धिप्रसङ्गः ॥ २ । १ । १७ ॥

78. If an object of right knowledge, continues the objector, is to be established by a means of right knowledge, this latter needs also to be established by another means of right knowledge.—17.

The objection stands thus : —

You say that an object of right knowledge is to be established by a means of right knowledge. I admit this and ask how you establish the means of right knowledge itself. Since a means of right knowledge may also be regarded as an object of right knowledge, you are required to establish the so-called means of right knowledge by another means of right knowledge and so on.

तद्विनिवृत्तेर्वा प्रमाणसिद्धिवत्तत्सिद्धिः ॥ २ । १ । १८ ॥

79. Or, he continues, if a means of right knowledge does not require another means of right knowledge for its establishment, let an object of right knowledge

be also established without any means of right knowledge.
—18.

A means of right knowledge stands in the same category as an
object of right knowledge, if you are to establish either of them.
If the means of right knowledge is accepted as self-established,
the object of right knowledge must also, according to the objector, be
accepted as self-established. In such a contingency perception, inference,
etc., will be superfluous.

न प्रदीपप्रकाशवत्तत्सिद्धेः ॥ २ । १ । १६ ॥

80. It is not so: the means of right knowledge are
established like the illumination of a lamp.—-19.

A lamp illumines a jar and our eye illumines the lamp. Though
it is sometimes the lamp, and sometimes the eye, that illumines, you are
bound to admit a general notion of illuminator. Similarly you must admit
a general notion of the means of right knowledge as distinguished from
that of the objects of right knowledge. The means will not, of course,
be regarded as such when included under the category of an object.

[The aphorism is also interpreted as follows:—Just as a lamp
illumines itself and the other objects, the means of right knowledge
establish themselves and the objects of right knowledge. Hence perception establishes itself and the objects of sense].

Note.—Objections raised in aphorisms 8, 9, 10, 11, 16, 17 and 18 emanated from the
Buddhist philosophy. The reply given in aphorisms 12, 13, 14, 15 and 19, represents the
views of Brâhmanic philosophers who regard perception as a real act and objects as
self-existent entities. According to the Buddhist philosophers, however, neither perception nor objects have any self-existence. They acquire an apparent or conditional
existence in virtue of a certain relation which exists between them. Cause and effect,
long and short, prior and posterior, etc., are all relative terms. The whole world is a
network of relations. The relations themselves are illusory as the objects which are
related have no self-existence. Hence the world is an illusion or has a mere conditional
existence. But where there is conditionality there is no truth. Truth and conditionality
are incompatible terms. That which neutralises all relations is the void or absolute
which lies beyond the conditional world. To speak the truth, the world is an absolute
nothing though it has a conditional existence. Vide my Translation of the Madhyamika
aphorisms in the Journal of the Buddhist Text Society, Calcutta, for 1895, 1896, 1897, 1898
and 1899.

प्रत्यक्षलक्षणानुपपत्तिरसमग्रवचनात् ॥ २ । १ । २० ॥

81. An objector may say that the definition of perception as given before is untenable because incomplete.
—20.

Perception has been defined as knowledge which arises from the contact of a sense with its object. This definition is said to be defective because it does not notice the conjunction of soul with mind, and of mind with sense, which are causes of perception.

नात्ममनसोस्सन्निकर्षाभावे प्रत्यक्षोत्पत्तिः ॥ २ । १ । २१ ॥

82. Perception, it is said, cannot arise unless there is conjunction of soul with mind.—21.

From the contact of a sense with its object no knowledge arises unless, it is said, there is also conjunction of soul with mind. A sense coming in contact with its object produces knowledge in our soul only if the sense is conjoined with the mind. Hence the conjunction of soul with mind should be mentioned as a necessary element in the definition of perception.

दिग्देशकालाकाशेष्वप्येवं प्रसङ्गः ॥ २ । १ । २२ ॥

83. Were it so, we reply, then direction, space, time and ether, should also be enumerated among the causes of perception.—22.

Direction, space, time and ether are also indispensable conditions in the production of knowledge. But even the objector does not feel the necessity of enumerating these among the causes of perception.

ज्ञानलिङ्गत्वादात्मनो नानवरोधः ॥ २ । १ । २३ ॥

84. The soul, we point out, has not been excluded from our definition inasmuch as knowledge is a mark of the soul.—23.

Perception has been described as knowledge, and knowledge implies the soul which is its abode. Consequently in speaking of knowledge the soul has, by implication, been mentioned as a condition in the production of perception.

तदयौगपद्यलिङ्गत्वाच्च मनसः ॥ २ । १ । २४ ॥

85. The mind too has not been omitted from our definition inasmuch as we have spoken of the non-simultaneity of acts of knowledge.—24.

Perception has been defined as knowledge. An essential characteristic of knowledge is that more than one act of knowing cannot take place at a time. This characteristic is due to the mind, an atomic substance, which is conjoined with the sense, when knowledge is produced. Hence in speaking of knowledge we have by implication mentioned the mind as a condition of perception.

प्रत्यक्षनिमित्तत्वाचेन्द्रियार्थयोस्सन्निकर्षस्य पृथग्वचनम्

॥ २ । १ । २५ ॥

86. The contact of a sense with its object is mentioned as the special cause of perception.—25.

There are many kinds of knowledge, such as perception, recollection, etc. Conjunction of soul with mind is a cause which operates in the production of all kinds of knowledge, while the contact of a sense with its object is the cause which operates only in perception. In our definition of perception we have mentioned only the special cause, and have omitted the common causes which precede not only perception but also other kinds of knowledge.

सुप्तव्यासक्तमनसाञ्चेन्द्रियार्थस्सन्निकर्षनिमित्तत्वात्॥ २ । १ । २६ ॥

87. The contact of a sense with its object is certainly the main cause as perception is produced even when one is asleep or inattentive.—26.

Even a sleeping person hears the thundering of a cloud if his ear is open to it, and a careless person experiences heat if his skin is exposed to it.

[Aphorisms 25 and 26 are omitted by Vâtsyâyana, the earliest commentator, but are noticed by Udyotakara, Vâchaspati, Viśvanâtha and other subsequent annotators].

तैश्चापदेशो ज्ञानविशेषाणाम् ॥ २ । १ । २७ ॥

88. By the senses and their objects are also distinguished the special kinds of knowledge.—27.

The special kinds of knowledge are the five varieties of perception, viz., by sight, hearing, smell, taste and touch. These are distinguished by the senses in whose spheres they lie or by the objects which they illumine. Thus the visual perception is called eye-knowledge or colour-knowledge, the auditory perception is called ear-knowledge or sound-knowledge, the olfactory perception is called nose-knowledge or smell-knowledge, the gustatory perception is called tongue-knowledge or taste-knowledge and the tactual perception is called skin-knowledge or touch-knowledge,

व्याहृतत्वादहेतुः ॥ २ । १ । २८ ॥

89. It may be objected that the contact of a sense with its object is not the cause of perception, as it is inefficient in some instances.—28.

An objector may say that the contact of a sense with its object is not the cause of perception, as we find that a person listening to a song may not see colour though it comes in contact with his eye.

[Vâtsyâyana interprets the aphorism as follows :—If the conjunction of soul with mind is not accepted as the cause of perception, a well-known conclusion will be debarred, viz., the mark of the mind is that only one act of knowledge is possible at a time. This interpretation, here inappropriate, is based on the Bhâṣya-commentary published by the Asiatic Society of Bengal in 1865. I fully agree with those who hold that the real Bhâṣya-commentary of Vâtsyâyana is not yet available to us.]

नार्थविशेषप्राबल्यात् ॥ २ । १ । २९ ॥

90. It is not so because there is pre-eminence of some particular object.—29.

It is admitted that a person while listening to a song may not see colour though it comes in contact with his eye. Yet the instance does not prove that the contact of a sense with its object is not the cause of perception, for it is to be understood that his intent listening prevents him from seeing the colour. In other words, the auditory perception supersedes the visual perception, because the song is more attractive than the colour.

[Vâtsyâyana interprets the aphorism thus :—The conjunction of soul with mind is not rendered useless, even if there is predominance of the senses and their objects. If perception is produced when a person is asleep or inattentive, it is because there is then the predominance of his sense and its object though even then there is a faint conjunction of soul with mind. This interpretation is based on the Bhâṣya-commentary as available to us. It is ingenious but out of place here].

प्रत्यक्षमनुमानमेकदेशग्रहणादुपलब्धेः ॥ २ । १ । ३० ॥

91. Perception, it may be urged, is inference because it illumines only a part as a mark of the whole.—30.

We are said to perceive a tree while we really perceive only a part of it. This knowledge of the tree, as a whole, derived from the knowledge of a part of it is, according to the objectors, a case of inference.

न प्रत्यक्षेण यावत्तावदप्युपलम्भात् ॥ २ । १ । ३१ ॥

92. But this is not so, for perception is admitted of
at least that portion which it actually illumines.—31.

The objectors themselves admit that a part is actually perceived.
Hence perception as a means of knowledge is not altogether denied and it
is accepted as different from inference.

न चैकदेशोपलब्धिरवयविसद्भावात् ॥ २ । १ । ३२ ॥

93. Moreover, the perception is not merely of a part,
for there is a whole behind the part.—32.

The perception of a part does not exclude perception of the whole
of which it is a part. If you touch the hand, leg or any other limb of a
person you are said to touch the person. Similarly, if you perceive a part
of a thing you are said to perceive the thing. A part implies the whole,
and perception of a part implies perception of the whole.

साध्यत्वादवयविनि सन्देहः ॥ २ । १ । ३३ ॥

94. There is, some say, doubt about the **whole**,
because the whole has yet to be established.—33.

The objectors say that parts alone are realities and that there is no
whole behind them. A tree, for instance, is yellow in some parts and
green in other parts. If the tree was one whole, then the contradictory
qualities of yellowness and greenness could not have belonged to it
simultaneously. Hence the parts alone must, according to them, be
regarded as real.

सर्वाग्रहणमवयव्यसिद्धेः ॥ २ । १ । ३४ ॥

95. If there were no whole there would, it is replied,
be non-perception of all.—34.

All signifies substance, quality, action, generality, particularity and
intimate relation. None of these would be perceptible if the whole were
denied. Suppose that the parts alone are real. Then since a part is not
of fixed dimension, it may itself be divided into parts, these latter again
into further parts and so on until we reach the atoms which are the
ultimate parts. Now the atoms which possess no bulk are not perceptible.
Similarly, the quality, action, etc., which inhere in the atoms are also not
perceptible. Consequently if we deny that there is a 'whole' neither the
substance nor quality, etc., would be perceptible.

धारणाकर्षणोपपत्तेश्च ॥ २ । १ । ३५ ॥

96. There is a *whole* because we can hold, pull, etc.—35.

If there were no whole we could not have held or pulled an entire thing by holding or pulling a part of it. We say, 'one jar,' 'one man,' etc. This use of 'one' would vanish if there were no whole.

सेनावनवदिति चेन्नातीन्द्रियत्वादणूनाम् ॥ २ । १ । ३६ ॥

97. The illustration from an army or a forest does not hold good, for atoms cannot be detected by the senses. —36.

If any one were to say that just as a single soldier or a single tree may not be seen from a distance but an army consisting of numerous soldiers or a forest consisting of numerous trees is seen, so a single atom may not be perceptible but a jar consisting of numerous atoms will be perceptible, and these atoms being called 'one jar,' the use of 'one' will not vanish. The analogy, we reply, does not hold good because the soldiers and trees possess bulk and so are perceptible, whereas the atoms do not possess bulk and are individually not perceptible. It is absurd to argue that because soldiers and trees are perceptible in the mass, atoms are perceptible in the mass also : to avoid this conclusion we must admit the existence of a whole beyond the parts.

रोधोपघातसादृश्येभ्यो व्यभिचारादनुमानमप्रमाणम् ॥ २ । १ । ३७ ॥

98. Inference, some say, is not a means of right knowledge as it errs in certain cases, *e.g.*, when a river is banked, when something is damaged and when similarity misleads, &c.—37.

If we see a river swollen we infer that there has been rain, if we see the ants carrying off their eggs, we infer that there will be rain and if we hear a peacock scream, we infer that clouds are gathering. These inferences, says an objector, are not necessarily correct, for a river may be swollen because embanked, the ants may carry off their eggs because their nests have been damaged, and the so-called screaming of a peacock may be nothing but the voice of a man.

नैकदेशत्राससादृश्येभ्योऽर्थान्तरभावात् ॥ २ । १ । ३८ ॥

99. It is not so, because our inference is based on something else than the part, fear and likeness.—38.

The swelling of a river caused by rain is different from that which results from the embankment of a part of it; the former is attended by a great rapidity of currents, an abundance of foam, a mass of fruits, leaves, wood, etc. The manner in which ants carry off their eggs just before rain is quite different from the manner in which they do so when their nests are damaged. The ants run away quickly in a steady line when rain is imminent but fear makes them fly in disorder when their nests are damaged. The screaming of a peacock which suggests gathering clouds is quite different from a man's imitation of it, for the latter is not natural. If in such cases any wrong inference is drawn, the fault is in the person, not in the process.

वर्त्तमानाभावः पनतः पतितपतितव्यकालोपपत्तेः ॥२।१।३९॥

100. There is, some say, no present time—because when a thing falls we can know only the time through which it has fallen and the time through which it will yet fall.—39.

Inference has reference to three times. In the *a priori* inference we pass from the past to the present, in the *a posteriori* from the present to the past and in the 'commonly seen' from the present to the present. It is, therefore, proper that we should examine the three times. The reason which leads some people to deny the present time is that when a fruit, for instance, falls from a tree we recognise only the past time taken up by the fruit in traversing a certain distance and the future time which will yet be taken up by the fruit in traversing the remaining distance. There is no intervening distance which the fruit can traverse at the so-called present time. Hence they say there is no present time.

तयोरप्यभावो वर्त्तमानाभावे तदपेच्चत्वात् ॥२।१।४०॥

101. If there is no present time there will, it is replied, be no past and future times because they are related to it.—40.

The past is that which precedes the present and the future is that which succeeds it. Hence if there is no present time there cannot be any past or future time.

नातीतानागतयोरितरेतरापेच्चासिद्धिः ॥२।१।४१॥

102. The past and future cannot be established by a mere mutual reference.—41.

If the past is defined as that which is not the future and the future is defined as that which is not the past, the definition would involve a fallacy of mutual dependency. Hence we must admit the present time to which the past and future are related.

वर्त्तमानाभावे सर्व्वाग्रहणम्प्रत्यच्चानुपपत्ते: ॥२।१।४२॥

103. If there were no present time, sense perception would be impossible, knowledge would be impossible.—42.

If you deny the present time there cannot be any perception which illumines only what is present in time ; and in the absence of perception all kinds of knowledge would be impossible. Hence the present time is established by confutation or the principle of *reductio ad absurdum*.

कृततार्कर्तव्यतोपपत्तेरुभयथा ग्रहणम् ॥२।१।४३॥

104. We can know both the past and the future for we can conceive of a thing as made and as about to be made.—43.

The present time is indicated by what continues, the past by what has been finished and the future by what has not yet begun.

अत्यन्तप्रायैकदेशसाधर्म्यादुपमानासिद्धि: ॥२।१।४४॥

105. Comparison, some say, is not a means of right knowledge as it cannot be established either through complete or considerable or partial similarity.—44.

On the ground of complete similarity we never say "a cow is like a cow," on the ground of considerable similarity we do not say that "a buffalo is like a cow," and on the ground of partial similarity we do not say that "a mustard seed is like Mount Meru." Hence comparison is regarded by some as not a means of right knowledge, for it has no precise standard.

प्रसिद्धसाधर्म्यादुपमानसिद्धेर्यथोक्तदोषानुपपत्ति: ॥२।१।४५॥

106. This objection does not hold good, for comparison is established through similarity in a high degree.—45.

The similarity in a high degree exists between such well known objects as a cow and a bos gavaeus, etc.

प्रत्यक्षेणाप्रत्यक्षसिद्धेः ॥ २ । १ । ४६ ॥

107. Comparison, some say, is not different from inference, for both seek to establish the unperceived by means of the perceived.—46.

We recognise a bos gavaeus at first sight through its special similarity to a cow which we have often perceived. This knowledge of a previously unperceived object derived through its similarity to a perceived object is, it has been said, nothing but a case of inference.

नाप्रत्यक्षे गवये प्रमाणार्थमुपमानस्य पश्याम इति ॥ २ । १ । ४७ ॥

108. It is not in a bos gavaeus *unperceived* that we find the real matter of comparison.—47.

The matter of comparison is similarity, *e.g.*, between a cow and a bos gavaeus. The bos gavaeus in which we notice the similarity is first perceived, that is, on perceiving a bos gavaeus we notice its similarity to a cow. Hence comparison supplies us with knowledge of a *perceived* thing through its similarity to another thing also *perceived*. This characteristic distinguishes it from inference which furnishes us with knowledge of an *unperceived* thing through that of a thing *perceived*.

तथेत्युपसंहाराद्रुपमानसिद्धेर्नाविशेषः ॥ २ । १ । ४८ ॥

109. There is no non-difference inasmuch as comparison is established through the compendious expression "so."—48.

It is not true that comparison is identical with inference because the former is established through the compendious expression "so." 'As is a cow, *so* is a bos gavaeus'—this is an instance of comparison. This use of 'so' makes it clear that comparison is a distinct means of right knowledge.

शब्दोऽनुमानमर्थस्यानुपलब्धेरनुमेयत्वात् ॥ २ । १ । ४९ ॥

110. Verbal testimony, say some, is inference because the object revealed by it is not perceived but inferred.—49.

Inference gives us the knowledge of an unperceived object through the knowledge of an object which is perceived. Similarly, verbal testimony enables us to acquire the knowledge of an unperceived object through the knowledge of a word which is perceived. The verbal testimony is, therefore, supposed by some to be inference, as the object revealed by both is unperceived.

उपलब्धेरद्विपूर्ववृत्तित्वात् ॥२।१।५०॥

111. In respect of perceptibility the two cases are not, continues the objector, different.—50.

In inference as well as in verbal testimony we pass to an unperceived object through an object which is perceived. In respect of perceptibility of the object through which we pass, the inference does not, continues the objector, differ from the verbal testimony.

सम्बन्धाच्च ॥२।१।५१॥

112. There is moreover, adds the objector, the same connection.—51.

Just as in inference there is a certain connection between a sign (e.g., smoke) and the thing signified by it (e. g., fire), so in verbal testimony there is connection between a word and the object signified by it. So inference, says the objector, is not different from verbal testimony.

आप्तोपदेशसामर्थ्याच्छब्दादर्थे सम्प्रत्ययः ॥२।१।५२॥

113. In reply we say that there is reliance on the matter signified by a word because the word has been used by a reliable person.—52.

In reference to the objections raised in aphorisms 49 and 50 we say that we rely on unseen matter not simply because it is signified by words but because they are spoken by a reliable person. There are, some say, paradise, nymphs, Uttarakurus, seven islands, ocean, human settlements, etc. We accept them as realities not because they are known through words, but because they are spoken of by persons who are reliable. Hence verbal testimony is not inference. The two agree in conveying knowledge of an object through its sign, but the sign in one is different from the sign in the other. In the case of verbal testimony the special point is to decide whether the sign (word) comes from a reliable person.

Aphorism 51 speaks of a certain connection between a word and the object signified by it. The present aphorism points out that the connection is not a natural one. We acknowledge that a word indicates a certain object, but we deny that the object is naturally or necessarily connected with the word. Hearing, for instance, the word " cow," we think of the animal signified by it, nevertheless the word and the animal are not connected with each other by nature or necessity. In the case of inference, however, the connection between a sign (*e. g.*, smoke) and the thing signified (*e. g.*, fire) is natural and necessary. Therefore the connection involved in inference is not of the same kind as that involved in verbal testimony.

प्रमाणतोऽनुपलब्धेः ॥ २ । १ । ५३ ॥

114. There is, in the case of verbal testimony, no perception of the connection.—53.

The connection between a sign and the thing signified, which is the basis of inference, is obvious to perception. For instance, the inference that " the hill is fiery because it is smoky" is based on a certain connection between smoke and fire which is actually perceived in a kitchen or elsewhere. The connection between a word and the objects signified by it, which is the basis of verbal testimony, is not obvious to perception. The word Uttarakuru, for instance, signifies the country of that name, but the connection between the word and the country is not perceived, as the latter lies beyond our observation. Hence verbal testimony is not inference.

पूरणप्रदाहपाटनानुपलब्धेश्च सम्बन्धाभावः ॥ २ । १ । ५४ ॥

115. There is no natural connection between a word and the object signified by it, as we do not find that the words food, fire and hatchet, are accompanied by the actions filling, burning and splitting.—54

If a word were naturally connected with the object signified by it, then by uttering the words food, fire and hatchet we should have found our mouth filled up (with food), burnt (with fire) and split (by a hatchet). But such is never the case. Hence there is no natural connection between a word and the object signified by it, and consequently verbal testimony is not inference.

शब्दार्थव्यवस्थानादप्रतिषेधः ॥ २ । १ । ५५ ॥

116. It cannot, says an objector, be denied that there is a fixed connection between words and their meanings.—55.

A particular word denotes a particular meaning, *e.g.*, the word ' cow ' denotes the animal of that name, but it does not denote a horse, a jar or any other thing. There is, therefore, in the case of verbal testimony, a fixed connection between a word and its meaning as there is in the case of inference a fixed connection between a sign and the thing signified. Hence verbal testimony is considered by the objector to be a case of inference.

न सामयिकत्वाच्छब्दार्थसम्प्रत्ययस्य ॥२।१।५६॥

117. We reply it is through convention that the meaning of a word is understood.—56.

The connection between a word and its meaning is conventional and not natural. The connection though fixed by man is not inseparable and connot therefore be the basis of an inference.

जातिविशेषे चानियमात् ॥२।१।५७॥

118. There is no universal uniformity of connection between a word and its meaning.—57.

The riṣis, âryas and mlecchas use the same word in different senses, e.g., the word "yava" is used by the âryas to denote a long-awned grain but by the mlecchas to denote a panic-seed. So the connection between a word and its meaning is not everywhere uniform and consequently verbal testimony cannot be considered as inference.

तदप्रामाण्यमनृतव्याघातपुनरुक्तदोषेभ्यः ॥२।१।५८॥

119. The Veda, some say, is unreliable as it involves the faults of untruth, contradiction and tautology.—58.

The Veda, which is a kind of verbal testimony, is not, some say, a means of right knowledge. It is supposed by them to be tainted with the faults of untruth, contradiction and tautology. For instance, the Veda affirms that a son is produced when the sacrifice for the sake of a son is performed.

It often happens that the son is not produced though the sacrifice has been performed.

There are many contradictory injunctions in the Veda, e.g., it declares "let one sacrifice when the sun has risen," also "let one sacrifice when the sun has not risen," etc. There is such tautology as "let the first hymn be recited thrice," "let the last hymn be recited thrice," etc.

न कर्मकर्तृसाधनवैगुण्यात् ॥२।१।५९॥

120. The so-called untruth in the Veda comes from some defect in the act, operator or materials of sacrifice.—59.

Defect in the act consists in sacrificing not according to rules, defect in the operator (officiating priest) consists in his not being a learned man, and defect in the materials consists in the fuel being wet, butter being not fresh, remuneration (to the officiating priest) being small, etc. A son is sure to be produced as a result of performing the sacrifice if these defects are avoided. Therefore there is no untruth in the Veda.

अभ्युपेत्य कालभेदे दोषवचनात् ॥२।१।६०॥

121. Contradiction would occur if there were alteration of the time agreed upon.—60.

Let a person perform sacrifice before sunrise or after sunrise if he has agreed upon doing it at either of the times. Two alternative courses being open to him he can perform the sacrifice before sunrise or after sun-rise according to his agreement or desire. The Veda cannot be charged with the fault of contradiction if it enjoins such alternative courses.

अनुवादोपपत्तेश्च ॥ २ । १ । ६१ ॥

122. There is no tautology, because re-inculcation is of advantage.—61.

Tautology means a useless repetition, which never occurs in the Veda. If there is any repetition there it is either for completing a certain number of syllables, or for explaining a matter briefly expressed, etc. "Let the first hymn be recited thrice," "let the last hymn be recited thrice,"————such instances embody a useful repetition.

वाक्यविभागस्य चार्थग्रहणात् ॥ २ । १ । ६२ ॥

123. And because there is necessity for the classification of Vedic speech.—62.

It is necessary to divide the Vedic speech into classes based on special characters.

विध्यर्थवादानुवादवचनविनियोगात् ॥ २ । १ । ६३ ॥

124. The Vedic speech being divided on the principle of injunction, persuasion and re-inculcation.—63.

The two main divisions of the Veda are (1) hymn and (2) ritual. The ritual portion admits of three sub-divisions, viz., injunctive, persuasive and re-inculcative.

(विधिः) विधायकः ॥ २ । १ । ६४ ॥

125. An injunction is that which exhorts us to adopt a certain course of action [as the means of attaining good].—64.

The following is an injunction :—"Let him who desires paradise perform the fire-sacrifice." This is a direct command.

स्तुतिर्निन्दा परकृतिः पुराकल्प इति (अर्थवादः) ॥ २ । १ । ६५ ॥

126. Persuasion is effected through praise, blame, warning, and prescription.—65.

Praise is speech which persuades to a certain course of action by extolling its consequences, *e.g.*, "By the Sarvajit sacrifice gods conquered all, there is nothing like Sarvajit sacrifice, it enables us to obtain everything and to vanquish every one, etc." Here there is no direct command but the Sarvajit sacrifice is extolled in such a way that we are persuaded to perform it.

Blame is speech which persuades us to adopt a certain course of action by acquainting us with the undesirable consequences of neglecting it, *e. g.*, "One who performs any other sacrifice neglecting the Jyotiṣṭoma falls into a pit and decays there." Here one is persuaded to perform the Jyotiṣṭoma sacrifice the neglect of which brings about evil consequences.

Warning is the mentioning of a course of action the obstruction of which by some particular person led to bad consequences, *e.g.*, on presenting oblation one is to take the fat first and the sprinkled butter afterwards, but alas ! the Charaka priests first took the sprinkled butter which was, as it were, the life of fire, etc. Here the foolish course of action adopted by the Charaka priests should serve as a warning to other priests who ought to avoid the course.

Prescription implies the mention of some thing as commendable on account of its antiquity, *e.g.*, "By this the Brâhmanas recited the Sâma hymn, etc."

विधिविहितस्यानुवचनम् (अनुवादः) ॥ २ । १ । ६६ ॥

127. Re-inculcation is the repetition of that which has been enjoined by an injunction.—66.

Re-inculcation may consist of (1) the repetition of an *injunction*, or (2) the repetition of that which has been *enjoined*. The first is called verbal re-inculcation and the second objective re-inculcation. In the Veda

there is re-inculcation as in ordinary use there is repetition. "Non-eternal,
not eternal"—this is a verbal repetition. "Non-eternal, possessing the
character of extinction"—this is objective repetition.

नानुवादपुनरुक्तयोर्विशेषः शब्दाभ्यासोपपत्तेः ॥ २ । १ । ६७ ॥

128. There is, some say, no difference between re-inculcation and tautology, as there is in either case a repetition
of some expression already used.—67.

Re-inculcation is supposed by some to be a fault inasmuch as it
does not, according to them, differ from tautology.

शीघ्रतरगमनोपदेशवदभ्यासान्नाविशेषः ॥ २ । १ । ६८ ॥

129. There is a difference, because re-inculcation
serves some useful purpose, e.g., a command to go faster.—68.

Tautology consists of a useless repetition but the re-petition in the
case of re-inculcation is useful, e. g., "go on, go on"—signifies "go faster."

मन्त्रायुर्वेदप्रामाण्यवच्च तत्प्रामाण्यमाप्तप्रामाण्यात् ॥२।१।६९॥

130. The Veda is reliable like the spell and medical
science, because of the reliability of their authors.—69.

The spell counteracts poison, etc., and the medical science prescribes
correct remedies. The authority which belongs to them is derived from
their authors, the sages, who were reliable persons. The sages themselves were reliable because (1) they had an intuitive perception of truths,
(2) they had great kindness for living beings and (3) they had the desire
of communicating their knowledge of the truths. The authors (lit., the
seers and speakers) of the Veda were also the authors of the spell and
medical science. Hence like the spell and medical science the Veda must
be accepted as authoritative. The view that the Veda is authoritative
because eternal, is untenable.

इति गौतममहर्षिप्रणीते न्यायदर्शने द्वितीयस्याध्यायस्य प्रथममाह्निकम् ॥२।१॥

BOOK II—CHAPTER II.

न चतुष्ट्वमैतिह्यार्थापत्तिसम्भवाभावप्रामाण्यात् ॥ २ । १ । १ ॥

131. Some say that the means of right knowledge are more than four, because **rumour, presumption, probability** and **non-existence** are also valid,—1.

In Book I, chapter I, aphorism 3, the means of right knowledge have been stated to be four, *viz.*, perception, inference, comparison and verbal testimony. Some say that there are other means of right knowledge such as rumour, presumption, probability and non-existence.

Rumour is an assertion which has come from one to another without any indication of the source from which it first originated, *e.g.*, in this fig tree there live goblins.

Presumption is the deduction of one thing from the declaration of another thing: *e.g.*, from the declaration that 'unless there is cloud there is no rain' we deduce that 'there is rain if there is cloud.' [A more familiar instance of presumption is this: the fat Devadatta does not eat during the day time. Here the presumption is that he eats in the night for it is impossible for a person to be fat if he does not eat at all].

Probability consists in cognising the existence of a thing from that of another thing in which it is included, *e.g.*, cognising the measure of an *âḍhaka* from that of a *droṇa* of which it is a fourth part, and cognising the measure of a *prastha* from that of an *âḍhaka* of which it is a quarter.

Of two opposite things the *non-existence* of one establishes the existence of the other, *e.g.*, the non-existence of rain establishes the combination of wind and cloud. When there is a combination of wind and cloud, drops of water cannot fall in spite of their weight.

शब्द ऐतिह्यानर्थान्तरभावादनुमानेऽर्थापत्तिसम्भवाभावाना-
मनर्थान्तरभावाच्चाप्रतिषेधः ॥ २ । १ । २ ॥

132. This, we reply, is no contradiction since rumour is included in verbal testimony, and presumption, probability and non-existence are included in inference.—2.

Those who maintain that rumour, presumption, probability and non-existence are valid, do not really oppose our division of the means of right knowledge into four, *viz.*, perception, inference, comparison and verbal testimony.

Rumour partakes of the general characteristics of verbal testimony and is a special kind of it.

Presumption is explained as the knowledge of a thing derived through the consideration of it from the opposite standpoint. For instance, the fat Devadatta does not eat during the day time : here the presumption is that he eats in the night. The fact of his eating in the night has not been expressly stated but is ascertained from this consideration that a person who does not eat during the day cannot be strong unless he eats in the night. It is evident that presumption like inference passes from a perceived thing to an unperceived one because they are in some way connected.

Probability is inference because it is the cognizance of a part from knowledge of a whole with which it is inseparably connected.

Non-existence is inference inasmuch as it really infers the obstruction of a cause from the non-existence of its effect through a certain connection, viz., if the obstruction occurs the effect cannot occur.

Hence rumour, etc., are not independent means of right knowledge but are included in the four enumerated in Book I, Chapter I, aphorism 3.

अर्थापत्तिरप्रमाणमनैकान्तिकत्वात् ॥ २ ॥ १ ॥ ३ ॥

133. **Presumption,** some say, is not valid because it leads to uncertainty.—3.

"If there is no cloud there will be no rain"—from this we are said to presume that if there is a cloud there will be rain. But it often happens that a cloud is not followed by rain. So presumption does not always lead to certainty.

अनर्थापत्तावर्थापत्त्यभिमानात् ॥ २ ॥ १ ॥ ४ ॥

134. **We reply:** if there is any uncertainty it is due to your supposing that to be a presumption which is not really so.—4.

"If there is no cloud there will be no rain." From this we are entitled to presume that if there is rain there must have been cloud. But if you pretend to presume that "if there is a cloud there will be rain" your so-called presumption will be an invalid one.

प्रतिषेधाप्रामाण्यञ्चानैकान्तिकत्वात् ॥ २ ॥ १ ॥ ५ ॥

135. The objection itself, we say, is invalid because it leads to uncertainty.—5.

"Presumption is not valid because it leads to uncertainty "—this is your objection. In it there are two points for consideration, *viz.*, (1) the validity of presumption and (2) the existence of presumption. Your objection refers to one of the points, *viz.*, the validity of presumption. So you do not deny the existence of presumption. In some instances, however, your objection may refer to more points than one. In fact the nature of your objection is not definite in itself, or in other words, it leads to uncertainty. Hence your objection is invalid.

तत्प्रामाण्ये वा नार्थापत्त्यप्रामाण्यम् ॥ २ । १ । ६ ॥

136. Or, if that be valid, then our presumption is not invalid.—6.

Perhaps you will say that your objection is valid because you can ascertain in each case whether one or more points are referred to by the objection. Similarly, we shall say that our presumption is not invalid because we can ascertain in each case whether the presumption is capable of leading to more conclusions than one. Hence if you say that your objection is valid, we shall say that our presumption is also valid.

नाभावप्रामाण्यं प्रमेयासिद्धेः ॥ २ । १ । ७ ॥

137. Some say that non-existence is not a means of right knowledge because there is no object which is known by it.—7.

लच्चितेष्वलच्चणलच्चितत्वादलच्चितानां तत्प्रमेयसिद्धिः ॥२।१।८॥

138. Non-existence, we reply, serves to mark out an object unmarked by the mark which characterises other objects.— 8.

Suppose a person wants to bring a pot which is not blue. The absence of blueness is a mark which will enable him to mark out the particular pot he wants to bring and to exclude the other pots which are blue. Thus an object may be known through the non-existence (absence) of its mark.

असत्यर्थे नाभाव इति चेन्नान्यलच्चणोपपत्तेः ॥ २ । १ । ६ ॥

139. If you say that the non-existence (absence) of a mark is impossible where there was no mark at all, it is, we reply, not so, because the non-existence (absence) is possible in reference to a mark elsewhere.—9.

We can, says an objector, talk of a mark being non-existent (absent) if it was previously existent (present). A pot is said to be not blue only in reference to its being blue previously. In reply we say that it is not so. "Not-blue" is no doubt possible only in reference to "blue" but that blueness may exist elsewhere. For instance, we can talk of this pot being not-blue, in contrast to that pot which is blue.

तत्सिद्धेरलचितेष्वहेतुः ॥ २ । १ । १० ॥

140. Though a mark may distinguish the object which is marked, the non-existence (absence) of the mark cannot, some say, distinguish the object which is not marked.—10.

A blue pot is distinguished by the blueness which is its mark. But how can we, says the objector, distinguish an unmarked object by the non-existence (absence) of the mark which it does not possess?

न लचणावस्थितापेचासिद्धेः॥ २ । १ । ११ ॥

141. This is not so, because the non-existence (absence) of a mark serves as a mark in relation to the presence of the mark.—11.

We can speak of a pot being not blue in relation to one which is blue. Hence though not-blueness is not a positive mark it serves as a (negative) mark in relation to blueness.

प्रागुत्पत्तेरभावोपपत्तेश्च ॥ २ । १ । १२ ॥

142. Moreover we perceive non-existence, as a mark antecedent to the production of a thing.—12.

There are two kinds of non-existence, viz., antecedent non-existence and subsequent non-existence. When we say that there will be a jar, we perceive the mark of non-existence of the jar in the halves which are destined to compose it. This is antecedent non-existence. Similarly, when we say that a jar has broken, we perceive the mark of non-existence of the jar in the parts which composed it. This is subsequent non-existence.

विमर्शहेत्वनुयोगे च विप्रतिपत्तेः संशयः ॥ २ । १ । ३ ॥

143. There is doubt about the nature of sound because there are conflicting opinions supported by conflicting reasons.—13.

Some say that sound is a quality of ether and that it is all-pervading, eternal, and capable of being manifested. Others say that sound like smell, etc., is a quality of the substance in which it abides, and is capable of being manifested. Sound is said by others to be a quality of ether and to be subject to production and destruction like knowledge. Others again say that sound arises from the concussion of elements, requires no abode, and is subject to production and destruction. Hence there arises doubt about the true nature of sound.

आदिमत्त्वादैन्द्रियकत्वात् कृतकवदुपचाराच्च ॥ २ । १ । १४ ॥

144. Sound is not eternal because it has a beginning and is cognised by our sense and is spoken of as artificial.—14.

Sound is non-eternal because it begins or arises from the concussion of two hard substances *e. g.* an axe and a tree, etc. Another ground for the non-eternality of sound is that it is cognised by our sense. Moreover we attribute to sound the properties of an artificial object, *e.g.*, we speak of a sound being grave, acute, etc. This would be impossible if it had been eternal.

Some say that the so-called beginning of a sound is merely a manifestation of it, that is, sound does not really begin but is merely manifested by the concussion of two hard substances. In reply we say that the concussion does not manifest but produces sound. You cannot suppose the concussion to be the manifester and sound the manifested unless you can prove that the concussion and sound are simultaneous. But the proof is impossible as a sound is heard at a great distance even after the concussion of the substances has ceased. So sound is not manifested by the concussion. It is, however, legitimate to suppose that sound is produced by the concussion, and that one sound produces another sound and so on until the last sound is heard at a great distance.

न घटाभावसामान्यनित्यत्वान्नित्येष्वप्यनित्यवदुपचाराच्च

॥ २ । १ । १५ ॥

145. Some will not accept this argument because the non-existence of a jar and the genus of it are eternal, and eternal things are also spoken of as if they were artificial.—15.

Some say that it is not true that whatever has a beginning is non-eternal. Look! the non-existence (destruction) of a jar which began when the jar was broken is eternal (indestructible). Whatever is cognised by our sense is non-eternal : this is also said to be an unsound argument. When, for instance, we perceive a jar we perceive also its genus (*i.e.*, jar-ness) which is eternal. It is further said that we often attribute to eternal things the properties of an artificial object, *e.g.*, we speak of the extension of ether as we speak of the extension of a blanket.

तत्त्वभाक्तयोर्नानात्वस्य विभागादव्यभिचारः ॥ २ । १ । १६ ॥

146. There is, we reply, no opposition because there is distinction between what is really eternal and what is partially eternal.—16.

That which is really eternal belongs to the three times. But the non-existence (destruction) of a jar does not belong to three times as it was impossible before the jar was broken. Hence the non-existence (destruction) of a jar which has a beginning is not really eternal.

सन्तानानुमानविशेषणा (षा) तु ॥ २ । १ । १७ ॥

147. It is only the things cognised by our sense as belonging to a certain genus that must, we say, be inferred to be non-eternal.—17.

The objectors have said that things cognised by our sense are not necessarily non-eternal, *e.g.*, as we perceive a jar we also perceive its genus jar-ness which is eternal. In reply we say that not all things cognised by our sense are non-eternal, but only those that belong to a certain genus. A jar, for instance, is non-eternal because we perceive it as belonging to the genus jar-ness. But jar-ness which is cognised by our sense is not non-eternal because it does not belong to a further genus named jar-ness-ness. Similarly, sound is non-eternal because it is cognised by our sense as belonging to the genus called sound-ness.

The aphorism may also be interpreted as follows :—Sound is non-eternal because it is inferred to advance in a series.

We do not say that whatever is cognised by our sense is non-eternal : our intention is to say that things cognised by our sense as advancing in a series are non-eternal. Sound is cognised in that manner (*i.e.*, sound advances like a wave) and hence sound is non-eternal.

कारणद्रव्यस्य प्रदेशशब्देनाभिधानात्(नित्येष्वप्यव्यभिचार इति) ॥ २ । १ । १८ ॥

148. We further say, that only artificial things are designated by the term extension.—18.

When we speak of the extension of ether we really mean that the extension belongs to an artificial thing which has for its substratum the ether. Hence we do not in reality attribute to eternal things the properties of artificial objects.

प्रागुच्चारणादनुपलब्धेरावरणाद्यनुपलब्धेः ॥ २ । १ । १९ ॥

149. Sound is non-eternal because neither do we perceive it before pronunciation nor do we notice any veil which covers it.—19.

If sound were eternal it would be perceived before pronunciation. You cannot say that sound really existed before pronunciation but was covered by some veil, for we do not notice any such veil.

तदनुपलब्धेरनुपलम्भादावरणोपलब्धिः ॥ २ । १ । २० ॥

150. The veil, some say, really exists because we do not perceive the non-perception thereof.—20.

The objectors say :—If you deny the veil because it is not perceived, we deny the non-perception of the veil because it is also not perceived. The denial of non-perception is the same as the acknowledgment of perception, or in other words, the veil is acknowledged to be existent.

अनुपलम्भादप्यनुपलब्धिसद्भाववतावरणानुपपत्तिरनुपलम्भात् ॥ २ । १ । २१ ॥

151. If you assert non-perception of the veil though the non-perception is not perceived we, continue the objectors, assert the existence of the veil though it is not perceived.—21.

You admit non-perception of the veil though you do not perceive it (non-perception). Similarly, we, the objectors admit the existence of the veil though we do not perceive it.

अनुपलम्भात्मकत्वादनुपलब्धेरहेतुः ॥ २ । १ । २२ ॥

152. This, we reply, is no reason, because non-perception consists of absence of perception.—22.

A veil is a thing fit to be perceived. Our non-perception of it indicates its absence. On the other hand, the non-perception of a veil is not a thing fit to be perceived. Hence non-perception of the non-perception leads us to nothing real.

7

अस्पर्शत्वात् ॥ २ । १ । २३ ॥

153. Some say that sound is eternal because it is intangible.—23.

Ether which is intangible is eternal. Sound must similarly, according to some, be eternal because it is intangible.

न कर्मानित्यत्वात् ॥ २ । १ । २४ ॥

154. This we deny, because action is non-eternal.—24.

Action is non-eternal though it is intangible. Hence intangibility does not establish eternality.

नाणु नित्यत्वात् ॥ २ । १ । २५ ॥

155. An atom, on the other hand, is eternal though not intangible.—25.

Tangibility is not incompatible with eternality, *e.g.*, atoms are tangible yet eternal.

सम्प्रदानात् ॥ २ । १ । २६ ॥

156. Sound, some say, is eternal because of the traditionary teaching.—26.

A preceptor could not have imparted knowledge to his pupils by means of sounds if these were perishable (non-eternal). In fact the traditionary teaching would, according to the objectors, be impossible if the sounds were non-eternal.

तदन्तरालानुपलब्धेरहेतुः ॥ २ । १ । २७ ॥

157. This is, we reply, no reason because sound is not perceived in the interval.—27.

Suppose a preceptor delivers certain sounds (in the form of lecture) which are received by his pupil. The sounds are not audible in the interval between the preceptor giving them and the pupil receiving them. They would never be inaudible if they were eternal.

अध्यापनादप्रतिषेधः ॥ २ । १ । २८ ॥

158. This, say the objectors, is no argument because there is the teaching.—28.

The objectors say :—If the sounds as soon as they came out of the preceptor were destoyed and did not reach the pupil, there could not be any teaching carried on. But there is the teaching, hence sound does not perish or in other words it is eternal.

उभयोः पक्षयोरन्यतरस्याध्यापनादप्रतिषेधः ॥ २ । २ । २९ ॥

159. In whichever of the two senses it is accepted the teaching does not offer any opposition.—29.

The word "teaching" may be interpreted either as (1) the pupil's receiving the sounds given by his preceptor, or as (2) the pupil's imitating the sounds of his preceptor as one imitates dancing. Neither of these interpretations would support the eternality of sound. In consonance with the first interpretation we shall say that the sound coming out of the preceptor produces another sound and so on until the last sound reaches the pupil. This would make sound non-eternal. It is obvious that the second interpretation similarly proves the non-eternality of sound.

अभ्यासात् ॥ २ । २ । ३० ॥

160. Sound, continue the objectors, is eternal because it is capable of repetition.—30.

That which is capable of repetition is persistent or not perishable, e.g., one and the same colour can be repeatedly looked at because it is persistent. One and the same sound can similarly be repeatedly uttered, hence it is persistent or not perishable.

नान्यत्वेऽप्यभ्यासस्योपचारात् ॥ २ । २ । ३१ ॥

161. It is, we reply, not so because even if sounds were "other" (different), repetition could take place.—31.

Repetition does not prevent perishableness because repetition is possible even if the things repeated are "other" or different, e.g., he sacrifices twice, he dances thrice, etc. Here the two sacrifices are different and yet we use the repetitive word twice, similarly the three dancings are different and yet we use the repetitive word 'thrice.'

अन्यादन्यस्मादनन्यत्वादनन्यदित्यन्यताऽभावः ॥ २ । २ । ३२ ॥

162. Some say that there is no such thing as otherness because what is called "other" in reference to some other is not other in reference to itself.—32.

We maintain that repetition is possible even if the things repeated are "other" or different. Our position is said to be untenable: the term "other" is described as unmeaning, as nothing is other than itself.

तदभावे नास्त्यनन्यता तयोरितरेतरापेच्चासिद्धे: ॥ २ । १ । ३ ॥

163. In the absence of otherness there would, we reply, be no sameness because the two exist in reference to each other.—33.

If there was no otherness there would be no sameness. This would lead us to absurdity as it would disprove both persistency and perishableness. Hence we must admit otherness, and if there is "other" there will be no flaw in our expression, *viz.*, repetition is possible even if things were "other" or different.

विनाशकारणानुपलब्धे: ॥ २ । २ । ३४ ॥

164. Sound, some say, is eternal because we perceive no cause why it should perish.—34.

Whatever is non-eternal is destroyed by some cause. Sound is said to have no cause of destruction, hence sound is held by some to be not non-eternal, (*i.e.*, is regarded as eternal).

अश्रवणकारणानुपलब्धेस्सततश्रवणप्रसङ्ग: ॥ २ । २ । ३५ ॥

165. But by the same argument we are afraid that non-perception of the cause of inaudition would mean constant audition.—35.

If non-perception is to establish non-existence we should not cease to hear because we do not perceive any cause of our not hearing. But such a conclusion is absurd.

उपलभ्यमाने चानुपलब्धेरसत्त्वादनपदेश: ॥ २ । २ । ३६ ॥

166. Your position, we further say, is untenable because there is no non-perception, on the contrary there is perception, of the cause of inaudition.—36.

Suppose that a sound is produced by an axe striking against a tree. This sound will perish after producing another sound which will again perish giving rise to another and so on until the last sound is destroyed by some obstacle. In fact every sound that is produced is destined to perish. Hence there is no non-perception of the cause of inaudition, on the contrary there is perception of such a cause. Consequently sound is not eternal.

पाणिनिमित्तप्रश्लेषाच्छब्दाभावे नानुपलब्धिः ॥२।२।३७॥

167. There is, we again say, no non-perception because the sound [of a gong] ceases on the contact of our
hand [with the gong].—37.

You cannot say that there is non-perception of the cause of cessation
of sound, because we actually perceive that by the contact of our hand
we can stop the sound of a gong.

विनाशकारणानुपलब्धेश्चावस्थाने तन्नित्यत्वप्रसङ्गः ॥२।२।३८॥

168. We call a thing eternal (persistent) if it continues to exist, and if we cannot perceive any cause why it
should cease.—38.

Sound does not continue to exist and its cause of cessation is also
perceived. Hence sound is not eternal.

अस्पर्शत्वादप्रतिषेधः ॥ २।२।३९ ॥

169. That the substratum of sound is intangible is no
counter-argument.—39.

Sound has not for its substratum any of the tangible substances,
viz., earth, water, fire and air, for it is found to be produced even where
these do no exist. For instance, sound is produced in a vacuum which
is devoid of smell, taste, colour and touch which are the qualities of
tangible substances. The reason why the sound produced in a vacuum
does not reach our ears is that there is no air to carry it. Hence the
substratum of sound is an intangible substance, *viz.*, ether.

It is a peculiarity of sound that it cannot co-abide with colour, etc.
A tangible substance (*e.g.*, earth) which is the abode of smell may also
be the abode of colour, taste or touch. But the substance, in which
sound abides, cannot be the abode of any other qualities. This distinguishes the substratum of sound from the subtrata of other qualities.
This peculiar substratum is called ether.

The fact of having an intangible substratum is no bar to the non-
eternality of sound. Sound, though its substratum is the intangible ether,
is produced by the contact of two hard substances. One sound produces
another sound (or a certain vibration) which again causes another sound
(or vibration) and so on until the last sound (or vibration) ceases owing
to some obstacle. Sound is therefore non-eternal.

विभक्त्यन्तरोपपत्तेश्च समासे ॥ २ । २ । ४० ॥

170. Sound cannot be supposed to co-abide with other qualities, for there are varieties of it.—40.

In each tangible substance there is only one kind of smell, taste, touch or colour. If we suppose that sound abides with one or more of these qualities in a tangible substance, we must admit that sound is of one kind only. But sound is of various kinds such as grave, acute, etc. ; and even the same sound may vary in degrees according to the nature of the obstruction it meets. This proves that sound does not abide with other qualities in a tangible substance. It further proves that sound is not unalterable or eternal.

Also signifies that this aphorism is to be considered along with aphorism 2–2–86 in which a reason for the non-eternality of sound is given.

विकारादेशोपदेशात् संशयः ॥ २ । २ । ४१ ॥

171. From the injunction about modification and substitute there arises doubt.—41.

The word ʻdadhi' conjoined with the word ʻatra' becomes ʻdadhyatra' by the rule of Sanskrit grammar. Looking at ʻdadhi-atra' and ʻdadhyatra' we notice that there is *i* in the former and *y* in the latter. Here some say that *i* undergoes modification as *y* while others say that *y* comes as substitute for *i*. Consequently we are thrown into doubt whether letters really undergo modifications or take up substitutes.

प्रकृतिविवृद्धौ विकारविवृद्धेः ॥ २ । २ । ४२ ॥

172. If letters underwent modification an increase of bulk in the original material would be attended by an increase of bulk in the modification.—42.

If we accept the theory of modification the letter *y* which originated from the short *i* must be supposed to be less in bulk than the *y* which originated from the long *ī*. But in reality the *y* in both the cases is of the same bulk. Hence it is concluded that letters do not undergo modification but take up other letters as substitutes.

न्यूनसमाधिकोपलब्धेर्विकाराणामहेतुः ॥ २ । २ । ४३ ॥

173. The foregoing argument, some say, is futile because we find modifications less than, equal to, and greater than, the original material.—43.

The bulk of the modification does not, in all cases, correspond to the bulk of the original material, e.g., thread is of less bulk than cotton which is its original material, a bracelet is equal in bulk to the gold of which it is made, and a banyan tree is greater in bulk than the seed from which it springs. Hence the argument against the theory of modification is, according to the objectors, baseless.

नातुल्यप्रकृतीनां विकारविकल्पात् ॥ २ । २ । ४४ ॥

174. It is, I reply, not so because I spoke of those modifications which originated from different materials.—44.

A modification may not correspond in bulk to its original material. But if the original materials are different their modifications are expected to be different. Here i being different from $\hat{i}$ their modifications are expected to be different. But y issues from i as well as $\hat{i}$. Hence y is not a modification of i or $\hat{i}$.

द्रव्यविकारे वैषम्यवद्वर्णविकारविकल्पः ॥ २ । २ । ४५ ॥

175. There is, says an objector, difference between a letter and its modification as there is between a substance and its modification.—45.

According to the objector there is difference between the letter i (or $\hat{i}$) and its modification y as there is difference between the substance cotton and its modification thread.

न विकारधर्मानुपपत्तेः ॥ २ । २ । ४६ ॥

176. In reply I say that it is not so because the character of a modification does not exist here.—46.

A modification must be of the same nature with its original material, though the former may not correspond in bulk to the latter. A bracelet is no doubt a modification of gold or silver but a horse is not a modification of a bull. Similarly y which is a semi-vowel is not a modification of i (or $\hat{i}$) which is a full vowel.

विकारप्राप्तानामपुनरावृत्तेः ॥ २ । २ । ४७ ॥

177. A thing which has undergone modification does not again return to its original form.—47.

Milk modified into curd does not again attain the state of milk. But i having reached the condition of y may again revert to its original from. Hence y is not a modification of i.

सुवर्णादीनां पुनरापत्तेरहेतुः ॥ २ । २ । ४८ ॥

178.   Some say that this is untenable because golden ornaments may again be converted into their original forms. —48.

A golden bracelet is converted into a mass of gross gold which again may be modified into a bracelet. The objector relying on the analogy of golden ornaments says that in the case of letters the theory of modification does not suffer by *i* reaching the condition of *y* and again returning to its original form.

तद्विकाराणां सुवर्णभावाव्यतिरेकात् ॥ २ । २ । ४९ ॥

179.   The analogy, we say, is inapt because the modifications of gold (called ornaments) do not relinquish the nature of gold.—49.

A mass of gold when made into ornaments does not relinquish its own nature. But *i* when converted into *y* loses its own nature. Hence the analogy is unsuitable.

वर्णत्वाव्यतिरेकाद्वर्णविकाराणामप्रतिषेधः ॥ २ । २ । ५० ॥

180.   There is, according to the objector, no inaptness in the analogy as the modification of a letter does not relinquish the general notion of letters.—50.

Just as gold is modified into a bracelet without relinquishing the general notion of gold, so the letter *i* undergoes modification as *y* without relinquishing the general notion of letters.

सामान्यवतो धर्म्मयोगो न सामान्यस्य ॥ २ । २ । ५१ ॥

181.   A quality belongs, we reply, to a thing possessing a general notion but not to the general notion itself.—51.

A bracelet is a modification of a ring inasmuch as both of them are gold which possesses the general notion of goldness. The letter *y* cannot be a modification of the letter *i* because they have not as their common basis another letter which possesses the general notion of letterness.

नित्यत्वे विकारादनित्यत्वे चानवस्थानात् ॥ २ । २ । ५२ ॥

182.   If the letter were eternal it could not be modified, and if it were impermanent it could not abide ong enough to fhurnis the material for modification.—52

On the supposition of the letters being eternal *i* cannot be modified into *y*, and on the supposition of their being impermanent *i* must perish before it can be modified into *y*.

नित्यानामतीन्द्रियत्वात्तद्धर्म्मविकल्पाच्च वर्णविकाराणाम-प्रतिषेधः ॥ २ । २ । ५३ ॥

183. Though the letters be eternal their modification, says an objector, cannot be denied, as some of the eternal things are beyond the grasp of the senses while others possess a different character.—53.

Just as some eternal things (as ether) are supersensuous while others (such as cowhood) are cognisable by the sense, so some eternal things as ether may be unmodifiable while others as letters may be susceptible to modification.

अनवस्थायित्वे च वर्णोपलब्धिवत्तद्विकारोपपत्तिः ॥ २ । २ । ५४ ॥

184. Even if the letters are impermanent their modification, like their perception, is, according to the objector, possible.—54.

Even if you say that letters are impermanent you admit that they abide long enough to be capable of being perceived. Why then cannot they abide long enough to be capable of being modified?

विकारधर्म्मित्वे नित्यत्वाभावात्कालान्तरे विकारोपपत्तेश्चा-प्रतिषेधः ॥ २ । २ । ५५ ॥

185. In reply we say that our position is unassailable because there is no eternalness where there is the character of modification and because your so-called modification presents itself at a time subsequent to the destruction of the original material.—55.

The letters cannot be modified if you say that they are eternal because modification is the reverse of eternalness. When a thing is modified it assumes another nature, abandoning its own. Again, the letters cannot be modified if you say that they are impermanent because there is no time for *i* (of dadhi) to be modified into *y* when *a* (of atra) follows. The sound 'dadhi' is produced (pronounced) at the first moment, exists (continuously) during the second moment and perishes at the third moment. The sound (atra) is produced (pronounced) at the second moment, exists (continues) during the third moment and perishes at the fourth moment. Now, *i* (of dadhi) cannot be modified into *y* until *a* (of atra) has come into existence. But *a* comes into existence at the third moment when *i* has already perished. So on the supposition of impermanency of letters, modification is impossible.

प्रकृत्यनियमाद्वर्णविकाराणाम् ॥ २ । २ । ५६ ॥

186. Letters are not modified because there is no fixity as to the original material of their modification.—56.

In the case of real modifications there is a fixity as regards their original materials, *e.g.*, milk is the original material of curd but not *vice versa*. In the case of letters, however, there is no fixed rule, *e.g.*, *i* is the original material of *y* in dadhyatra (dadhi+atra) but *y* is the original material of *i* in vidhyati (vyadh+ya+ti). Hence the operation of modification is not really applicable to letters.

अनियमे नियमान्नानियमः ॥ २ । २ । ५७ ॥

187. Some say that there is no lack of fixity because the absence of fixity itself is fixed.—57.

I is sometimes modified into *y* and *y* sometimes into *i*. So in respect of letters there is no fixity as to the original materials of their modification. This much, however, is fixed that there is no fixity, or in other words, the absence of fixity is fixed. Hence the objector, who is a quibbler, contends that there is fixity at least as to the negative aspect of modification.

नियमानियमविरोधादनियमे नियमाच्चाप्रतिषेधः ॥ २ । २ । ५८ ॥

188. By saying that the absence of fixity is fixed you cannot set aside our reason, because the fixity and its absence are contradictory terms.—58.

Our reason is that in respect of letters there is no fixity as to their modification. You contend that though there is no fixity, the absence of fixity is fixed. Our reply is that though the absence of fixity is fixed it does not establish fixity as a positive fact, because fixity is incompatible with the absence of fixity.

गुणान्तरापत्युपमर्दह्रासवृद्धिलेशश्लेषेभ्यस्तु विकारोपपत्ते-र्वर्णविकारः ॥ २ । २ । ५९ ॥

189. There is an apparent modification of letters in the case of their attaining a different quality, taking up substitutes, becoming short or long and undergoing diminution or augmentation.—59.

A letter is said to attain a different quality when, for instance, the grave accentuation is given to what was acutely accented. As an instance of a letter accepting a substitute we may mention *gam* as becoming *gacch.* A long vowel is sometimes shortened, *e.g.,* nadî (in the vocative case) becomes nadi. A short vowel is lengthened, *e.g.,* 'muni'(in the vocative case) becomes 'mune.' Diminution occurs in such cases as 'as+tas' becoming 'stas.' In 'devânâm' (deva+âm) *na* is an augment.

ते विभक्त्यन्ताः पदम् ॥ २ । २ । ६० ॥

190. The letters ended with an affix form a word.—60.

Words are of two kinds : *nouns* and *verbs.* A noun ends in a *sup* affix, *e. g.* Râmas (Râma+su) while a verb ends in a *tiñ* affix, *e.g.,* bhavati (bhû+ti).

तदर्थे व्यक्त्याकृतिजातिसन्निधावुपचारात् संशयः ॥२।२।६१॥

191. There is doubt what a word (noun) really means as it invariably presents to us an individual, form and genus.—61.

The word 'cow' reminds us of an individual (a four-footed animal), its form (limbs) and its genus (cowhood). Now, it is asked what is the real signification of a word (noun)—an individual, form or genus?

याशब्दसमूहत्यागपरिग्रहसंख्यावृद्ध्युपचयवर्षसमासानु-बन्धानां व्यवस्तावुपचाराद्व्यक्तिः ॥ २ । २ । ६२ ॥

192. Some say that the word (noun) denotes individual because it is only in respect of individuals that we can use "that," "collection," "giving," "taking," "number," "waxing," "waning," "colour," "compound" and "propagation."—62.

"That cow is going"—here the term "that" can be used only in reference to an individual cow. Similarly it is only in respect of individuals that we can use the expressions "collection of cows" "he gives the cow," "he takes the cow," "ten cows," "cow waxes," "cow wanes," "red cow," "cow-legs" and "cow gives birth to cow,"

न तदनवस्थानात् ॥ २ । २ । ६३ ॥

193. A word (noun) does not denote an individual
because there is no fixation of the latter.—63.

Unless we take genus into consideration, the word cow will denote
any individual of any kind. Individuals are infinite. They cannot be
distinguished from one another unless we refer some of them to a certain
genus and others to another genus and so on. In order to distinguish a
cow-individual from a horse-individual, we must admit a genus called
cow distinguished from a genus called horse.

सहचरणस्थानतादर्थ्यवृत्तमानधारणसामीप्ययोगसाधना-
धिपत्येभ्यो ब्राह्मणमञ्चकटराजशक्तुचन्दनगङ्गा शाटकान्न पुरुषे-
ष्वतद्भावेऽपि तदुपचारः ॥ २ । २ । ६४ ॥

194. Though a word does not literally bear a certain
meaning it is used figuratively to convey the same as in
the case of Brahmana, scaffold, mat, king, flour, sandal-
wood, Ganges, cart, food and man in consideration of
association, place, design, function, measure, containing,
vicinity, conjunction, sustenance and supremacy.—64.

If the word does not denote an individual how is it that we refer to
an individual cow by the expression "that cow is feeding"? The answer
is that though the word cow may not literally mean an individual we may
refer to the same figuratively. There are such instances as :—'Feed the
staff' means 'feed the Brahmaṇa holding a staff,' 'the scaffolds shout'
means "men on the scaffolds shout ,' 'he makes a mat' means 'he aims at
making a mat,' 'Yama' (chastiser) means 'a king,' a bushel of 'flour' means
flour measured by a bushel, 'a vessel of sandal-wood' means 'sandal-
wood placed in a vessel,' 'cows are grazing on the Ganges' means ' 'cows
are grazing in the vicinity of the Ganges,' 'a black cart' means a cart
marked with blackness, 'food' means 'life' and 'this person (Bharadvâja)
is a clan' means 'this person is the head of a clan.'

आकृतिस्तदपेचत्वात् सत्वव्यवस्थानसिद्धेः ॥ २ । ६५ ॥

195. Some say that the word (noun) denotes form by
which an entity is recognised.—65.

We use such expressions as 'this is a cow' and 'this is a horse'
only with reference to the forms of the cow and the horse. Hence it is
alleged by some that the word denotes form.

व्यक्त्याकृतियुक्तेप्यप्रसङ्गात्प्रोचणादीनां मृद्ववके जाति:
॥ २ । २ । ६६ ॥

196. Others say that the word (noun) must denote genus, otherwise why in an earthenware cow possessed of individuality and form do we not find immolation, etc.—66.

We can immolate a real cow but not an earthenware cow though the latter possesses individuality and form. The distinction between a real cow and an earthenware one is that the former comes under the genus cow but the latter does not. Hence it is urged by some that a word (noun) denotes genus.

नाकृतिव्यक्त्यपेचत्वाजात्यभिव्यक्ते: ॥ २ । २ । ६७ ॥

197. In reply we say that it is not genus alone that is meant by a word (noun) because the manifestation of genus depends on the form and individuality.—67.

The genus abides in the individual and the individual cannot be recognised except by its form. Hence genus has reference both to the form and individual, or in other words, the genus alone is not the significa-tion of a word.

व्यक्त्याकृतिजातयस्तु पदार्थ: ॥ २ । २ । ६८ ॥

198. The meaning of a word (noun) is, according to us, the genus, form and individual.—69.

The word (noun) signifies all the three though prominence is given to one of them. For the purpose of distinction the individual is pro-minent. In order to convey a general notion, pre-eminence is given to the genus. In practical concerns much importance is attached to the form. As a fact the word (noun) ordinarily presents to us the form, denotes the individual and connotes the genus.

व्यक्तिर्गुणविशेषाश्रयो मूर्त्ति: ॥ २ । २ । ६६ ॥

199. An individual is that which has a definite form and is the abode of particular qualities.—69.

An individual is any substance which is cognised by the senses as a limited abode of colour, taste, smell, touch, weight, solidity, tremulousness, velocity or elasticity.

आकृतिर्जातिलिङ्गाख्या ॥ २ । २ । ७० ॥

200. The **form** is that which is called the token of
the genus.—79.

The genus, cowhood for instance, is recognised by a certain collocation of the dewlap which is a form. We cannot recognise the genus of a
formless substance.

समानप्रसवात्मिका जातिः ॥ २ । २ । ७१ ॥

201. **Genus** is that whose nature is to produce the
same conception.—71.

Cowhood is a genus which underlies all cows. Seeing a cow some-
where we acquire a general notion of cows (*i.e.*, derive knowledge of
cowhood). This general notion enables us on all subsequent occasions to
recognise individual cows.

BOOK III.—CHAPTER I.

दर्शनस्पर्शनाभ्यामेकार्थग्रहणात् ॥ ३ । १ । १ ॥

1.   A sense is not soul because we can apprehend an object through both sight and touch.

"Previously I saw the jar and now I touch it:" such expressions will be meaningless if "I" is not different from eye which cannot touch and from skin which cannot see. In other words, the "I" or soul is distinct from the senses.

न विषयव्यवस्थानात् ॥ ३ । १ । २ ॥

2.   This is, some say, not so because there is a fixed relation between the senses and their objects.

Colour, for instance, is an exclusive object of the eye, sound of the ear, smell of the nose, and so on. It is the eye that, according to the objectors, apprehends colour, and there is no necessity for assuming a soul distinct from the eye for the purpose of explaining the apprehension of colour.

तद्व्यवस्थानादेवात्मसद्भावा ऽप्रतिषेधः ॥ ३ । १ । ३ ॥

3.   This is, we reply, no opposition because the existence of soul is inferred from that very fixed relation.

There is a fixed relation between the senses and their objects, e.g., between the eye and colour, the ear and sound, and so on. It is the eye and not the ear that can apprehend colour, and it is the ear and not the eye that can apprehend sound. If a sense were the soul it could apprehend only one object, but "I" can apprehend many objects, that is, "I" can see colour, hear sound, and so on. Hence the "I" or soul which confers unity on the various kinds of apprehension is different from the senses each of which can apprehend only one object.

शरीरदाहे पातकाभावात् ॥ ३ । १ । ४ ॥

4.   If the body were soul there should be release from sins as soon as the body was burnt.

If a person has no soul beyond his body he should be freed from sins when the body is destroyed. But in reality sins pursue him in his subsequent lives. Hence the body is not soul.

9

The aphorism admits of another interpretation :—

If the **body** were soul there could arise no sin from killing living beings.

Our body varies in dimension and character with every moment. The body which exists at the present moment is not responsible for the sin which was committed at a previous moment inasmuch as the body which committed the sin is now non-existent. In other words, no sin would attach to the person who killed living beings if the soul were identical with our transient body.

तदभावः सात्मकप्रदाहेऽपि तन्निवृत्त्वात् ॥ ३ । १ । ५ ॥

5. There would, says an objector, be no sin even if the body endowed with a soul were burnt for the soul is eternal.

In the previous aphorism it was shown that the commission of sins would be impossible if we supposed the body to be the soul. In the present aphorism it is argued by an objector that we should be incapable of committing sins even on the supposition of the soul being distinct from our body, for such a soul is eternal and cannot be killed.

न काय्योश्रयकर्तृबधात् ॥ ३ । १ । ६ ॥

6. In reply we say that it is not so because we are capable of killing the body which is the site of operations of the soul.

Though the soul is indestructible we can kill the body which is the seat of its sensations. Hence we are not incapable of committing sins by killing or murder. Moreover, if we do not admit a permanent soul beyond our frail body we shall be confronted by many absurdities such as "loss of merited action" (krita hâni) and "gain of unmerited action" (akritâbhyâgama). A man who has committed a certain sin may not suffer its consequences in this life and unless there is a soul continuing to his next life he will not suffer them at all. This is a "loss of merited action." Again, we often find a man suffering the consequences of action which he never did in this life. This would be a "gain of unmerited action" unless we believed that his soul did the action in his previous life.

सव्यदृष्टस्येतरेण प्रत्यभिज्ञानात् ॥ ३ । १ । ७ ॥

7. [There is a soul beyond the sense] because what is seen by the left eye is recognised by the right.

A thing perceived previously by the left eye is recognised now by the right eye. This would have been impossible if the soul were identical with the left eye or the right eye on the principle that the seat of recognition must be the same as the seat of perception. Consequently we must admit that there is a soul which is distinct from the left and right eyes and which is the common seat of perception and recognition.

नैकस्मिन्नासास्थिव्यवहिते द्वित्वाभिमानात् ॥ ३ । १ । ८ ॥

8. Some say that the eyes are not two : the conceit of duality arises from the single organ of vision being divided by the bone of the nose.

The objectors argue as follows :—

If the eyes were really two, viz., right and left, we would have been bound to admit a soul distinct from the senses as the common seat of perception and recognition. But there is only one eye which is divided by the bridge of the nose and which performs the two functions of perception and recognition. Hence there is, according to the objectors, no soul beyond the eye.

एकाविनाशे द्वितीयाविनाशान्नैकत्वम् ॥ ३ । १ । ६ ॥

9. The eyes, we reply, are really two because the destruction of one does not cause the destruction of the other.

If the organ of vision was only one, then on the destruction of that one (i.e., one eye) there would be total blindness.

अवयवनाशेप्यवयव्युपलब्धेरहेतुः ॥ ३ । १ । १० ॥

10. This is, some say, no argument for the destruction of a part does not cause the destruction of the whole.

The objectors say :—Just as a tree does not perish though a branch of it has been destroyed, so there may not be total blindness though one eye (a part of the organ of vision) has been destroyed.

दृष्टान्तविरोधादप्रतिषेधः ॥ ३ । १ । ११ ॥

11. This is, we reply, no opposition to our argument inasmuch as your illustration is inapt.

The illustration of a tree and its branch is not quite apt for a tree does not exist in its entirety but assumes a mutilated condition when a branch of it is cut off. The right eye, on the other hand, remains in a perfect condition and performs the full function of an eye even when the left eye is destroyed.

इन्द्रियान्तरविकारात् ॥ ३ । १ । १२ ॥

12. The soul is distinct from the senses because there is an excitement of one sense through the operation of another sense.

When we see an acid substance, water overflows our tongue. In other words, in virtue of the operation of our visual sense there is an excitement in the sense of taste. This would be impossible unless there was a soul distinct from the senses. The soul seeing the acid substance remembers its properties; and the remembrance of the acid properties excites the sense of taste.

न स्मृतेः स्मर्त्तव्यविषयत्वात् ॥ ३ । १ । १३ ॥

13. It is, some say, not so because remembrance is lodged in the object remembered.

Remembrance, according to the objectors, is lodged in the thing remembered and does not necessarily presuppose a soul.

तदात्मगुणसद्भावादप्रतिषेधः ॥ ३ । १ । १४ ॥

14. This is, we reply, no opposition because remembrance is really a quality of the soul.

Remembrance is based on perception, that is, one can remember only that thing which one has perceived. It often happens that seeing the colour of a thing we remember its smell. This would be impossible if remembrance was a quality of a sense, e.g., the eye which has never smelt the thing. Hence remembrance must be admitted to be a quality of a distinct substance called soul which is the common seat of perceptions of colour and smell.

अपरिसङ्ख्यानाच्च स्मृतिविषयस्य ॥ ३ । १ । १५ ॥

15. Also because the things remembered are innumerable.

If memory were lodged in things, we could remember innumerable things at a time. But none can remember more things than one at a time. Hence memory must be supposed to be a quality of a separate substance called soul (endowed with a mind).

नात्मप्रतिपत्तिहेतूनां मनसि सम्भवात् ॥ ३ । १ । १६ ॥

16. There is, some say, no soul other than the mind because the arguments which are adduced to establish the "soul" are applicable to the mind.

The substance of the objection is this :—

We can apprehend an object by both the eye and the skin. It is true that the acts of seeing and touching the object by one agent cannot be explained unless we suppose the agent to be distinct from both the eye and the skin (*i.e.*, from the senses), let however the agent be identified with the mind.

ज्ञातुर्ज्ञानसाधनोपपत्तेः संज्ञाभेदमात्रम् ॥ ३ । १ । १७ ॥

17. Since there is a knower endowed with an instrument of knowledge it is, we reply, a mere verbal trick to apply the name " mind" to that which is really the " soul."

To explain the acts of seeing, touching, etc., you admit an agent distinct from the senses which are called its instruments. The sense or instrument by which the act of thinking is performed is called the " mind." The agent sees by the eye, hears by the ear, smells by the nose, tastes by the tongue, touches by the skin and thinks by the " mind." Hence we must admit the agent (soul) over and above the mind. If you call the agent as " mind," you will have to invent another name to designate the instrument. This verbal trick will not, after all, affect our position. Moreover, the mind cannot be the agent as it is atomic in nature. An atomic agent cannot perform the acts of seeing, hearing, knowing, feeling, etc.

नियमश्च निरनुमानः ॥ ३ । १ । १८ ॥

18. Your conclusion is moreover opposed to inference.

We admit a mind apart from the soul. If you deny any one of them or identify one with the other, an absurd conclusion will follow. Unless you admit the mind you will not be able to explain the internal perception. By the eye you can see, by the ear you can hear, by the nose you can smell, by the tongue you can taste and by the skin you can touch. By what sense do you carry on internal perception, *viz.*, thinking, imagining, etc. ? Unless you admit the mind for that purpose your conclusion will be opposed to inference.

पूर्वाभ्यस्तस्मृत्यनुबन्धाज्जातस्य हर्षभयशोकसंप्रतिपत्ते:॥३।१।१६॥

19. (The soul is to be admitted) on account of joy, fear and grief arising in a child from the memory of things previously experienced.

A new-born child manifests marks of joy, fear and grief. This is inexplicable unless we suppose that the child perceiving certain things in this life remembers the corresponding things of the past life. The things which used to excite joy, fear and grief in the past life continue to do so in this life. The memory of the past proves the previous birth as well as the existence of the soul.

पद्मादिषु प्रबोधसंमीलनविकारवत्तद्विकार: ॥ ३ । १ । २० ॥

20. It is objected that the changes of countenance in a child are like those of expanding and closing up in a lotus.

The objection stands thus:—

Just as a lotus which is devoid of memory expands and closes up by itself, so a child expresses joy, fear and grief even without the recollection of the things with which these were associated in the previous life.

नोष्णशीतवर्षकालानिमित्तत्वात् पञ्चात्मकविकाराणाम् ॥३।१।२१॥

21. This is, we reply, not so because the changes in inanimate things are caused by heat, cold, rain and season.

The changes of expansion and contraction in a lotus are caused by heat and cold. Similarly the changes of countenance in a child must be caused by something. What is that thing? It is the recollection of pleasure and pain associated with the things which are perceived.

प्रेत्याहाराभ्यासकृतात् स्तन्याभिलाषात् ३ । १ । २२ ॥

22. A child's desire for milk in this life is caused by the practice of his having drunk it in the previous life.

A child just born drinks the breast of his mother through the remembrance that he did so in the previous life as a means of satisfying hunger. The child's desire for milk in this life is caused by the remembrance of his experience in the previous life. This proves that the child's soul, though it has abandoned a previous body and has accepted a new one, remembers the experiences of the previous body.

अयसोऽयस्कान्ताभिगमनवत्तदुपसर्पणम् ॥ ३ । १ । २३ ॥

23. Some deny the above by saying that a new-born child approaches the breast of his mother just as an iron approaches a loadstone (without any cause).

The objection runs thus :—

Just as an iron approaches a loadstone by itself, so does a child approach the breast of his mother without any cause.

नान्यत्र प्रवृत्त्यभावात् ॥ ३ । १ । २४ ॥

24. This is, we reply, not so because there is no approach towards any other thing.

You say that there is no cause which makes an iron approach a loadstone, or a child the breast of his mother. How do you then explain that an iron approaches only a loadstone but not a clod of earth and a child approaches only the breast of his mother and not any other thing ? Evidently there is some cause to regulate these fixed relations.

वीतरागजन्मादर्शनात् ॥ ३ । १ । २५ ॥

25. We find that none is born without desire.

Every creature is born with some desires which are associated with the things enjoyed by him in the past life. In other words, the desire proves the existence of the creature or rather of his soul in the previous lives. Hence the soul is eternal.

सगुणद्रव्योत्पत्तिवत्तदुत्पत्तिः ॥ ३ । १ । २६ ॥

26. Some say that the soul is not eternal because it may be produced along with desire as other things are produced along with their qualities.

The objection stands thus :—

Just as a jar, when it is produced, is distinguished by its colour, etc., so the soul when it is produced is marked by its desire, etc. Hence the desires do not pre-suppose the soul in the previous lives or, in other words, the soul is not eternal.

न संकल्पनिमित्तत्वाद्रागादीनाम् ॥ ३ । १ । २७ ॥

27. This is, we reply, not so because the desire in a new-born child is caused by the ideas left in his soul by the things he enjoyed in his previous lives.

The desire implies that the soul existed in the previous lives or, in other words, the soul is eternal.

पार्थिवं गुणान्तरोपलब्धेः ॥ ३ । १ । २८ ॥

28. Our body is earthy because it possesses the special qualities of earth.

In other worlds there are beings whose bodies are watery, fiery, airy or ethereal. Though our body is composed of all the five elements we call it earthy owing to the preponderance of earth in it.

श्रुतिप्रामाण्याच ॥ ३ । १ । २९ ॥

29. In virtue of the authority of scripture too.

That our body is earthy is proved by our scripture. In the section on "Dissolution into the primordial matter," there are such texts as : May the eye be absorbed into the sun, may the body be absorbed into the earth, etc. The sun is evidently the source of the eye and the earth of the body.

कृष्णसारे सत्युपलम्भात्क्षतिरिच्य चोपलम्भात्संशयः ॥ ३ । १ । ३० ॥

30. It is doubtful as to whether a sense is material or all-pervading because there is perception when there is (contact with) the eye-ball and there is perception even when the eye-ball is far off.

The eye-ball is said by some to be a material (elemental) substance inasmuch as its function is limited by its contact. A thing is seen when it has contact with the eye-ball but it is not seen when the eye-ball is not connected. In other words, the eye-ball, like any other material substance, exercises its function only in virtue of its contact with things. Others hold that the eye-ball is a non-material all-pervading substance in as much as it can perceive things with which it has not come in contact. The eye-ball does not touch the things which it sees from a distance. Hence the question arises as to whether the eye-ball is a material or an all-pervading substance.

महदणुग्रहणात् ॥ ३ । १ । ३१ ॥

31. It is contended that the eye-ball is not a material substance because it can apprehend the great and the small.

If the eye-ball had been a material substance it could have apprehended only those things which coincided with itself in bulk. But we find it can apprehend things of greater and smaller bulk. So it is contended that the eye-ball is not a material substance.

रश्म्यर्थसन्निकर्षविशेषात्तद्ग्रहणम् ॥ ३ । २ । ३२ ॥

32. (The Naiyâyika's reply to the above is that) it is by the contact of the ray that the things, great and small, are apprehended.

The Naiyâyikas say that· even on the supposition of the eye-ball being a material substance the apprehension by it of the great and the small will not be impossible. Their· explanation is that though the eye-ball itself does not coincide with 'things which are greater or smaller in bulk, yet the rays issuing from the eye-ball reach the things in their entire extent. Hence in spite of the eye-ball being a material substance there is no impóssibility for it to apprehend the great and the small.

तदनुपलब्धेरहेतुः ॥ ३ । १ । ३३ ॥

33. Contact is not the cause because we do not perceive the ray.

The contact of a ray with a thing is not the cause of apprehension of the thing because we perceive no ray issuing from the eye-ball.

नानुमीयमानस्य प्रत्यक्षतोऽनुपलब्धिरभावहेतुः ॥ ३ । १ । ३४॥

34. That we do not apprehend a thing through perception is no proof of non-existence of the thing because we may yet apprehend it through inference.

The ray issuing from the eye is not perceived as it is supersensuous. But it is established by inference like the lower half of the earth or the other side of the moon.

द्रव्यगुणधर्मभेदाच्चोपलब्धिनियमः ॥ ३ । १ । ३५ ॥

35. And perception depends upon the special character of the substance and its qualities.

A substance unless it possesses magnitude, or a quality unless it possesses obviousness is not perceived. From the absence of magnitude and obvious colour the ray of the eye-ball is not perceived.

अनेकद्रव्यसमवायात् रूपविशेषाच्च रूपोपलब्धिः ॥ ३ । १ । ३६ ॥

36. A colour is perceived only when it abides in many things intimately and possesses obviousness.

The sun's ray is perceived as it possesses an obviousness in respect of colour and touch. But the ray of the eye-ball is not perceived as it is obvious neither in respect of colour nor in respect of touch.

10

कर्मकारितश्रेन्द्रियाणां व्यूहः पुरुषार्थतन्त्रः ॥ ३।१।३७ ॥

37. And the senses subservient to the purposes of man have been set in order by his deserts.

The order referred to is as follows :—

The eye emits ray which does not possess the quality of obviousness and cannot consequently burn the thing it touches. Moreover, had there been obviousness in the ray it would have obstructed our vision by standing as a screen between the eye and the thing. This sort of arrangement of the senses was made to enable man to attain his purposes according to his merits and demerits.

अव्यभिचाराच्च प्रतीघातो भौतिकधर्म्मः ॥ ३।१।३८ ॥

38. The senses are material substances inasmuch as they invariably receive obstruction.*

Nothing can offer obstruction to a non-material all-pervading substance. The senses receive obstruction from wall, etc., and are therefore material substances.

मध्यन्दिनोल्काप्रकाशानुपलब्धिवत्तदनुपलब्धिः ॥३।१।३९॥

39. Some say that the ray of the eye (possesses obviousness of colour but it) is not perceived just as the light of a meteor at midday is not perceived.

The light of a meteor though possessing obviousness of colour is not perceived at midday because it is then overpowered by the light of the sun. Similarly, some say, the ray of the eye possesses obviousness of colour but it is not perceived during the day time on account of its being overpowered by the light of the sun.

न रात्रावप्यनुपलब्धेः ॥ ३।१।४० ॥

40. It is, we reply, not so because even in the night the ray of the eye is not perceived.

Had the ray of the eye possessed obviousness of colour it would have been perceived during the night when it cannot be overpowered by the light of the sun. As the ray of the eye is not perceived even during the night we must conclude that it does not possess obviousness of colour.

---

* No. 38 appears to be a part of the commentary of Vâtsyâyana.

बाह्यप्रकाशानुग्रहाद्दिषयोपलब्धेरनभिव्यक्तितोऽनुपलब्धिः

॥ ३।१।४१ ॥

41. The ray of the eye is not perceived in consequence of its unobviousness but not on account of its total
absence because it reaches objects through the aid of external light.

In the eye there is ray which does not however possess an obvious
colour. Had the eye possessed no ray it could not have perceived any
object. Since the eye perceives objects, it possesses ray in it, and since it
requires the aid of external light (such as the light of the sun) to perceive
them it follows that the ray does not possess the quality of obviousness.
This aphorism answers the objection raised in 3-1-33.

अभिव्यक्तौ चाभिभवात् ॥ ३।१।४२ ॥

42. And the invisibility of the ray of the eye cannot
be due to its being overpowered (by an external light such
as the light of the sun) because the overpowering is possible
only of a thing which possessed obviousness.

It is only a thing which possesses obviousness or manifestation that
can be overpowered or obscured. But how can we throw a thing into
obscurity which never possessed manifestation ? We cannot therefore say
that the ray of the eye is not perceived on account of its having been
overpowered by an external light.

नक्तंचरनयनरश्मिदर्शनाच्च ॥ ३।१।४३ ॥

43. There must be ray in the eye of man as we see
it in the eye of animals that move about in the night.

We see that animals wandering by night, such as cats, possess ray
in their eyes. By this we can conjecture that there is ray in the eye of
man.

अप्राप्य ग्रहणं काचाभ्रपटलस्फटिकान्तरितोपलब्धेः ॥३।१।४४॥

44. Some say that the eye can perceive a thing even
without coming in contact with it by means of its rays just
as things screened from us by glass, mica, membrane or
crystal are seen.

The objection raised in this aphorism controverts the Nyâya theory of contact (in pratyakṣa) and seeks to prove that the senses are not material substances.

न कुड्यान्तरितानुपलब्धेरप्रतिषेधः ॥ ३।१।४५ ॥

45. The foregoing objection is not valid because we cannot perceive what is screened from us by walls.

The eye cannot really perceive a thing without coming in contact with it by means of its rays. For instance, a thing which is screened from us by a wall is not perceived by our eyes.

अप्रतिघातात् सन्निकर्षोपपत्तिः ॥ ३।१।४६ ॥

46. There is a real contact because there is no actual obstruction (caused by glass, mica, membrane or crystal).

The ray issuing from the eye can reach an external object through glass, mica, etc., which are transparent substances. There being no obstruction caused by these substances, the eye comes really in contact with the external object.

आदित्यरश्मेः स्फटिकान्तरेऽपि दाह्येऽविघातात् ॥ ३।१।४७ ॥

47. A ray of the sun is not prevented from reaching a combustible substance though the latter is screened by a crystal.

This is an example which supports the theory of contact, viz., a ray issuing from the eye passes actually through a crystal to an object lying beyond it.

नेतरेतरधर्म्मप्रसङ्गात् ॥ ३।१।४८ ॥

48. It is, some say, not so because the character of one presents itself in the other.

The objection stands thus :—

If a ray issuing from the eye can reach an object screened by a crystal, why can it not reach another object which is screened by a wall? According to the objector the property of the crystal presents itself in the wall.

आदर्शोदकयोः प्रसादस्वाभाव्याद्रूपोपलब्धिवत्तदुपलब्धिः ॥ ३।१।४९ ॥

49. In reply we say that the perception of a thing screened by a crystal takes place in the same manner as that

of a form in a mirror or water owing to the possession of the character of transparency.

The form of a face is reflected on a mirror because the latter possesses transparency. Similarly, a thing is reflected on a crystal inasmuch as the latter is transparent. A wall which does not possess transparency can reflect nothing. It is therefore entirely due to the nature of the screens that we can or cannot perceive things through them.

दृष्टानुमितानां नियोगप्रतिषेधानुपपत्ति:॥३।१।५०॥

50. It is not possible to impose injunctions and prohibitions on facts which are perceived or inferred to be of some fixed character.

A crystal and a wall are found respectively to be transparent and non-transparent. It is not possible to alter their character by saying " let the crystal be non-transparent " and " let the wall be transparent." Likewise, a ray of the eye in passing to a thing is obstructed by a wall but not by a crystal. This is a perceived fact which cannot be altered by our words. Hence the theory of contact remains intact.

स्थानान्यत्वेनानात्वादवयविनानात्वादवयविनानास्थानत्वाच्च संशय:॥३।१।५१॥

51. Since many things occupy many places and since also one thing possessing different parts occupies many places, there arises doubt as to whether the senses are more than one.

There is doubt as to whether there are as many senses as there are sensuous functions or whether all the functions belong to one sense possessing different parts.

त्वग्व्यतिरेकात् ॥३।१।५२॥

52. Some say that the senses are not many as none of them is independent of touch (skin).

The eye, ear, nose and tongue are said to be mere modifications of touch (skin) which pervades them, that is, there is only one sense, viz., touch (skin), all others being merely its parts.

नेन्द्रियान्तरार्थानुपलब्धेः॥३।१।५३॥

53.   It is, we reply, not so because the objects of other senses are not perceived by touch (skin).*

If there had been only one sense, *viz.*, touch (skin) then it could have seen colour, heard sound and so on. But a blind man possessing the sense of touch cannot see colour. Hence it is concluded that senses are many.

त्वगवयवविशेषेण धूमोपलब्धिवत्तदुपलब्धिः॥३।१।५४॥

54.   Perception of various objects of sense is comparable to that of smoke by a special part of touch.*

Just as smoke is perceived by a special part of touch located in the eye, so sound, smell etc., are perceived by special parts of touch specially located.

व्याहतत्वादहेतुः॥३।१।५५॥

55.   This is, according to us, absurd as it involves contradiction.*

It has been said that touch is the only sense by the special parts of which special functions are performed. Now it is asked whether the special parts of touch do not partake of the nature of senses. If they do, then the senses are many. If on the other hand they do not partake of the nature of senses, then it is to be admitted that colour, sound, etc., are not cognisable by the senses.

न युगपदर्थानुपलब्धेः॥३।१।५६॥

56.   Touch is not the only sense because objects are not perceived simultaneously.

Had there been only one sense, *viz.*, touch, it would have in conjunction with the mind produced the functions of seeing, hearing, smelling, tasting etc., simultaneously But we cannot perform different functions at once. This proves that the senses are many : the mind which is an atomic substance being unable to come in contact with the different senses at a time cannot produce different functions simultaneously.

विप्रतिषेधाच्च नत्वगेका ॥३।१।५७॥

57.   Touch cannot be the only sense prohibiting the functions of other senses.†

---

* This is not really an aphorism but a part of the commentary of Vâtsyâyana.
† This seems to be a part of the commentary of Vâtsyâyana.

Touch can perceive only those objects which are near (contaguous) but it cannot perceive objects which are far off. As a fact we can perceive colour and sound from a great distance. This is certainly not the function of touch but of some other sense which can reach distant objects.

इन्द्रियार्थपञ्चत्वात् ॥३।१।५८॥

58. Senses are five because there are five objects.

There are five objects, viz., colour, sound, smell (odour), taste (savour) and touch which are cognised respectively by the eye, ear, nose, tongue and skin. There are therefore five senses corresponding to the five objects.

न तदर्थबहुत्वात् ॥३।१।५९॥

59. Some say that the senses are not five because there are more than five objects.

The objects of sense are said to be many such as good smell, bad smell, white colour, yellow colour, bitter taste, sweet taste, pungent taste, warm touch, cold touch etc. According to the objector there must be senses corresponding to all these objects.

गन्धत्वाद्व्यतिरेकाद्गन्धादीनामप्रतिषेधः ॥३।१।६०॥

60. There is, we reply, no objection because odour (smell) etc. are never devoid of the nature of odour (smell) etc.

Good odour, bad odour, etc. are not different objects of sense but they all come under the genus odour. It is the nose alone that cognises all sorts of odour—good or bad. Similarly all colours—white, yellow, blue or green—are cognised by the eye. In fact there are only five objects which are cognised by the five senses.

विषयत्वाव्यतिरेकादेकत्वम् ॥३।१।६१॥

61. Some say that there is only one sense as the so-called different objects of sense are not devoid of the character of an object.

The objection raised in this aphorism is as follows :—

The so-called different objects, viz., colour, sound, smell (odour), taste (savour) and touch agree with one another in each of them being an object of sense. As they all possess the common characteristic of being an object of sense, it is much simpler to say that the object of sense is only one. If there is only one object of sense, the sense must also be one only.

न बुद्धिलक्षणाधिष्ठानगत्याकृतिजातिपञ्चत्वेभ्यः ॥३।१।६२॥

62. It is, we reply, not so because the senses possess a five-fold character corresponding to the characters of knowledge, sites, processes, forms and materials

The senses must be admitted to be five on the following grounds :—

(a) The characters of knowledge—There are five senses corresponding to the five characters of knowledge, viz., visual, auditory, olfactory, gustatory and tactual.

(b) The sites—The senses are five on account of the various sites they occupy. The visual sense rests on the eyeball, the auditory sense on the ear-hole, olfactory sense on the nose, the gustatory sense on the tongue, while the tactual sense occupies the whole body.

(c) The processes—There are five senses involving five different processes, e. g., the visual sense apprehends a colour by approaching it through the (ocular) ray while the tactual sense apprehends an object which is in association with the body, and so on.

(d) The forms—The senses are of different forms, e. g., the eye partakes of the nature of a blue ball, and the ear is not different from ether, etc.

(e) The materials—The senses are made up of different materials : the eye is fiery, the ear is ethereal, the nose is earthy, the tongue is watery, and the skin (touch) is airy.

भूतगुणविशेषोपलब्धेस्तादात्म्यम् ॥३।१।६३॥

63. The senses are essentially identical with the elements in consequence of the possession of their special qualities.

The five senses, viz., the eye, ear, nose, tongue and skin (touch) are essentially identical with the five elements, viz., fire, ether, earth, water and air whose special qualities, viz., colour, sound, smell (odour), savour (taste) and tangibility are exhibited by them.

गन्धरसरूपस्पर्शशब्दानां स्पर्शपर्य्यन्ताः पृथिव्याः
अतेजोवायूनां पूर्व्वं पूर्व्वमपोह्याकास्योत्तरः ॥३।१।६४॥

64. Of odour (smell), savour (taste), colour, tangibility (touch) and sound those ending with tangibility belong to earth, rejecting each preceding one in succession they

belong respectively to water, fire and air ; the last (sound) belongs to ether.

The earth possesses four qualities, viz., odour (smell), savour (taste), colour and tangibility. In water there are three qualities, viz., savour, colour and tangibility ; colour and tangibility are known to be the qualities of fire while tangibility and sound belong respectively to air and ether.

न सर्व्वगुणानुपलब्धेः ॥३।१।६५॥

65. An objector says that it is not so because an element is not apparently found to possess more than one quality.

The substance of the objection is that the earth does not possess four qualities but only one quality, viz., odour (smell) which is apprehended by the nose. Water does not possess three qualities but possesses only one quality, viz., savour (taste) which is apprehended by the tongue. Similarly the other elements do, each of them, possess only one quality.

एकैकस्यैवोत्तरोत्तरगुणसद्भावादुत्तरोत्तराणां तदनुपलब्धिः ॥३।१।६६॥

66. The objector further says that the qualities belong to the elements, one to one, in their respective order so that there is non-perception of other qualities in them.

The substance of the objection is this :—

Odour (smell) is the only quality of the earth. Consequently the other three qualities, viz., savour (taste), colour and tangibility alleged to belong to the earth, are not found in it. Savour (taste) is the only quality of water, hence the other two qualities, viz., colour and tangibility alleged to belong to water are not found in it. Colour is the only quality of fire, and hence the other quality, viz., tangibility alleged to belong to fire is not found in it. Tangibility is of course the quality of air and sound of ether.

संसर्गाच्चानेकगुणग्रहणम् ॥३।१।६७॥

67. And it is through their commixture, continues the objector, that there is the apprehension of more than one quality.

The objector further says as follows :—

The earth possesses only odour (smell), and if sometimes savour (taste) is also found there it is because the earth is then mixed with water.

Similarly if there is odour (smell) in water it is because the earth is mixed with it.

विष्टं ह्यपरम्परेण ॥३।१।६८॥

68.   Of the elements one is, according to the objector, often interpenetrated by others.

The objection is explained as follows :—

The earth is often interpenetrated by water,, fire and air and is consequently found to possess savour (taste), colour and tangibility besides odour (smell).   Similar is the case with water etc.

न पार्थिवाप्ययोः प्रत्यक्त्वात् ॥३।१।६९॥

69.   It is, we reply, not so because there is visual perception of the earthy and the watery.

The Naiyâyikas meet the foregoing objections by saying that the earth really possesses four qualities, water three, fire two, air one, and ether one.   Had the earth possessed only odour (smell) and the water only savour (taste) then it would have been impossible for us to see the earthy and watery things.   We are competent to see only those things which possess colour, and if the earth and water had not possessed colour how could we have seen them?   Since we can see the earthy and the watery it follows that they possess colour.   If you say that the earth and water are visible because they are mixed with the fiery things which possess colour, why then the air and ether are also not visible?   There is no rule that it is only the earth and water that can be mixed with fiery things but that the air and ether cannot be so mixed.   Proceeding in this way we find that the earth etc. do not each possess only one quality.

पूर्व्वपूर्व्वगुणोत्कर्षात्तत्तत्प्रधानम् ॥३।१।७०॥

70.   Owing to the predominance of one quality in an element a sense is characterised by the quality which predominates in its corresponding element.

The nose is characterised by odour (smell) which predominates in its corresponding element the earth; the tongue is characterised by savour (taste) which predominates in its corresponding element the water; the eye is characterised by colour which predominates in its corresponding element the fire; the skin (touch) is characterised by tangibility which abides in its corresponding element the air while the ear is characterised by sound which is the special quality of its corresponding element the ether.

तद्व्यवस्थानन्तु भूयस्त्वात् ॥३।१।७१॥

71. A sense as distinguished from its corresponding element is determined by its fineness.

A sense (e. g., the nose) which is the fine part of an element (e. g., the earth) is able to perceive a special object (e. g., odour) owing to the act-force (sanskâra, karma) of the person possessing the sense. A sense cannot perceive more than one object because it possesses the predominant quality of an element, e. g., the nose possesses only odour which is the predominant quality of the earth, the tongue the savour of water, the eye the colour of fire, and so on.

सगुणानामिन्द्रियभावात् ॥३।१।७२॥

72. A sense is really called as such when it is attended by its quality.

Some may say why a sense (the nose for instance) cannot perceive its own quality (odour). The reply is that a sense consists of an element endowed with its quality. It is only when a sense is attended by the quality that it can see an object. Now in perceiving an object the sense is attended by the quality but in perceiving its own quality it is not so attended. Consequently a sense cannot perceive its own quality.

तेनैव तस्याग्रहणाच्च ॥३।१।७३॥

73. Moreover an object is never perceived by itself.

An eye can see an external object but it cannot see itself. On the same principle a sense cannot perceive its own quality.

न शब्दगुणोपलब्धेः ॥३।१।७४॥

74. It is, some say, not so because the quality of sound is perceived by the ear.

The objection stands thus :—

It is not true that a sense cannot perceive its own quality. The ear, for instance, can perceive sound which is its own quality.

तदुपलब्धिरितरेतरद्रव्यगुणवैधर्म्यात् ॥३।१।७५॥

75. The perception of sound furnishes a contrast to that of other qualities and their corresponding substrata.

The nose, tongue, eye and skin can respectively smell earth, taste water, see colour and touch air only when they are attended by their own qualities, *viz*, odour (smell), savour (taste), colour and tangibility. But an ear when it hears sound is not attended by any quality. In fact the ear is identical with the ether and hears sound by itself. By indirect inference we can prove that sound is the special quality of the ether: Odour is the predominant quality of the earth, savour of water, colour of the eye, and tangibility of the skin (touch): Sound must therefore be the quality of the remaining element, *viz.*, the ether.

BOOK III, CHAPTER II.

कर्म्माकाशसाधर्म्यात् संशयः ॥ ३ । २ । १ ॥

76. Since the intellect resembles both action and
ether there is doubt as to whether it is transitory or permanent.—1.

Inasmuch as the intellect bears likeness to both action and ether
in respect of intangibility, there arises the question whether it is transitory like an action or permanent like the ether. We find in the intellect
the function of origination and decay which marks transitory things as
well as the function of recognition which marks permanent things. "I
knew the tree," "I know it" and "I shall know it"—these are expressions which involving the ideas of origination and decay indicate our
knowledge to be transitory. "I who knew the tree yesterday am knowing
it again to-day"—this is an expression which involving the idea of
continuity indicates our knowledge to be permanent. Hence there is
doubt as to whether the intellect which exhibits both kinds of knowledge
is really transitory or permanent.

विषयप्रत्यभिज्ञानात् ॥ ३ । २ । २ ॥

77. Some say that the intellect is permanent because
there is recognition of objects.—2.

The Sâmkhyas maintain the permanency of the intellect on the ground
of its capacity for the recognition of objects. A thing which was known
before is known again now—this sort of knowledge is called recognition.
It is possible only if knowledge which existed in the past continues also
at the present, that is, if knowledge is persistent or permanent. Recognition would have been impossible if knowledge had been transitory. Hence
the Sâmkhyas conclude that the intellect which recognises objects is
permanent.

साध्यसमत्वादहेतुः ॥ ३ ।२ । ३ ॥

78. The foregoing reason is not, we say, valid inasmuch as it requires proof like the very subject in dispute.—3.

Whether the intellect is permanent or not—this is the subject
in dispute. The Sâmkhyas affirm that it is permanent and the reason
adduced by them is that it can recognise objects. The Naiyâyikas dispute
not only the conclusion of the Sâmkhyas but also their reason. They

say that the intellect does not recognise objects but it is the soul that does
so. Knowledge cannot be attributed to an unconscious instrument, the
intellect, but it must be admitted to be a quality of a conscious agent,
the soul. If knowledge is not a quality of the soul, what else can be its
quality? How is the soul to be defined? There is therefore no proof as
to the validity of the reason, *viz.*, that the intellect recognises objects.

न युगपद्ग्रहणात् ॥ ३ । २ । ४ ॥

79. Knowledge is neither a mode of the permanent
intellect nor identical with it because various sorts of knowledge do not occur simultaneously.—4.

The Sâmkhyas affirm that knowledge is a mode of the permanent
intellect from which it is not different. Knowledge, according to them,
is nothing but the permanent intellect modified in the shape of an object
which is reflected on it through the senses. The Naiyâyikas oppose this
view by saying that if knowledge as a mode of the permanent intellect is
not different from it, then we must admit various sorts of knowledge to be
permanent. But as a fact various sorts of knowledge are not permanent,
that is, we cannot receive various sorts of knowledge simultaneously.
Hence knowledge is not identical with the permanent intellect.

अप्रत्यभिज्ञाने च विनाशप्रसङ्गः ॥ ३ । २ । ५ ॥

80. And in the cessation of recognition there arises
the contingency of cessation of the intellect.—5.

If knowledge as a mode of the intellect is not different from it, then
the cessation of recognition which is a kind of knowledge should be
followed by the cessation of the intellect. This will upset the conclusion
of the Sâmkhyas that the intellect is permanent. Hence knowledge is not
identical with the intellect.

क्रमवृत्तित्वादयुगपद्ग्रहणम् ॥ ३ । २ । ६ ॥

81. The reception of different sorts of knowledge is
non-simultaneous owing, according to us, to our mind coming in contact with different senses in succession.—6.

The Naiyâyikas say that if knowledge as a mode of the permanent
intellect had been identical with it, then there would have been neither a
variety of knowledge nor origination and cessation of it. The different
sorts of knowledge do not occur simultaneously because they are produced,

according to the Naiyâyikas, by the mind which is atomic in dimension coming in contact with the senses in due succession.

अप्रत्यभिज्ञानञ्च विषयान्तरव्यासङ्गात् ॥ ३ । २ । ७ ॥

82. The recognition (or knowledge) of an object cannot take place when the mind is drawn away by another object.—7.

We cannot hear a sound by our ear when the mind conjoined with the eye is drawn away by a colour. This shows that knowledge is different from the intellect, and that the mind which is atomic in dimension serves as an instrument for the production of knowledge.

न गत्यभावात् ॥ ३ । २ । ८ ॥

83. The intellect cannot be conjoined with the senses in succession because there is no motion in it.—8.

The mind which, according to the Naiyâyikas, is atomic in dimension can move from one sense-organ to another in succession to produce different kinds of knowledge. This is impossible in the case of the intellect which, according to the Sâmkhyas, is not only permanent but also all-pervading and as such cannot change its place, that is, does not possess the tendency to be conjoined with the different sense-organs in succession. In fact there is only one internal sense called the mind, the other two so-called internal senses—intellect (Buddhi) and self-conceit (Ahaṃkâra)—being superfluous. It is not all-pervading, and knowledge is not its mode. Knowledge classified as visual, olfactory etc. is of different kinds which belong to the soul.

स्फटिकान्यत्वाभिमानवत्तदन्यत्वाभिमानः ॥ ३ । २ । ९ ॥

84. A conceit of difference is said to arise in the intellect in the same way as the appearance of difference in a crystal.—9.

As a single crystal appears to assume the different colours of different objects which are reflected on it, so the intellect though one appears, according to the Sâmkhya, to be modified into different sorts of knowledge under the influence of different objects reflected on it through the senses.

न हेत्वभावात् ॥ ३ । २ । १० ॥

85. It is, we reply, not so because there is no proof.—10.

The Sâmkhya says that the variety of knowledge arises from the same intellect appearing to be modified by the various objects which are reflected on it through the senses. The various modes which the intellect undergoes, that is, the various kinds of knowledge are not real but only apparent. The Naiyâyikas dispose of this view by saying that there is no proof as to the unreality of the modes, that is, the various kinds of knowledge inasmuch as they are found to originate and cease in due order in consequence of the contact of senses and their objects and *vice versa*.

स्फटिकेऽप्यपरापरोत्पत्ते: क्षाणिकत्वादुव्यक्तीनामहेतु: ॥३।२।११॥

86. It is said to be absurd even in the case of a crystal being replaced by newer and newer ones which grow up owing to all individuals being momentary—11.

The Sâmkhya says that as a crystal seems to be modified by the colours which are reflected on it, so the intellect seems to be modified by the objects which are reflected on it through the senses. In reality there is, according to the Sâmkhya, neither any modification of the crystal nor that of the intellect. This theory has in the preceding aphorism been controverted by the Naiyâyikas and is in the present aphorism opposed by the Buddhists. According to the latter all things, including even our body, are momentary. A thing which exists at the present moment grows up into another thing at the next moment so that there is no wonder that in the course of moments there should grow up crystals of different colours or intellects of different modes. Hence the conclusion of the Sâmkhyas that a crystal remains unaltered is, according to the Buddhists, untenable.

नियमहेत्वभावाद्यथादर्शनमभ्यनुज्ञा ॥ ३ । २ । १२ ॥

87. Owing to the absence of any absolute rule we shall give our assent according to the nature of each occurrence—12.

It is not true that in every case there are at each moment newer growths. Our body no doubt undergoes increase and decrease but a piece of stone or a crystal does not, so that the doctrine of growth applies to the first case but not to the second. Hence there is no general rule that a thing at the lapse of a moment should be replaced by another thing which grows up in its place.

नोत्पत्तिविनाशकारणोपलब्धेः ॥ ३ । २ । १३ ॥

88. There is no absence of link as we perceive the cause of growth and decay—13.

The growth of a thing is the increase of its parts while the decay is the decrease of them. An ant-hill gradually increases in dimension before it attains its full growth while a pot decreases in dimension before it reaches its final decay. We never find an instance in which a thing decays without leaving any connecting link for another thing which grows in its place. There is in fact no linkless growth or linkless decay.

क्षीरविनाशे कारणानुपलब्धिवद्द्युत्पत्तिवच्च
तदुपपत्तिः ॥ ३ । २ । १४ ॥

89. The growth of newer crystals in the place of an old one is comparable, according to some, to the growth of curd in the place of milk the cause of whose decay is not perceived—14.

The Buddhist says that there are things which grow and decay without the gradual increase and decrease of their parts. Of such things we do not find the cause of the first growth (origination) and the last decay (cessation), that is, there is no link between the thing which ceases and another thing which grows in its place. The milk, for instance, ceases without leaving any connecting link for the curd which grows in its place. Similarly new crystals grow to take the place of an old one which decays without leaving any mark. The crystal which exists at the present moment is not the same one that existed at the previous moment. There is no connection whatsoever between them.

लिङ्गतोग्रहणान्नानुपलब्धिः ॥ ३ । २ । १५ ॥

90. There is no non-perception of the cause of final decay as it is cognisable by its mark—15.

The Naiyâyikas say that it is not true that we do not perceive the final decay of the milk which is the cause of the first growth of the curd. The mark attending the final decay of milk (that is, the disappearance of sweet flavour) is the cause of the destruction of the milk, and that attending the first growth of curd (that is, the appearance of acid flavour) is the cause of its production. So through the mark we really perceive

12

the cause of decay of milk and growth of curd. But there is no such mark perceptible in the case of a crystal which at the lapse of a moment is said to be replaced by another crystal of a different character.

न पयसः परिणामगुणान्तरप्रादुर्भावात् ॥ ३ । २ । १६ ॥

91.   There is, it is alleged, no destruction of the milk but only a change of its quality—16.

The Sâmkhya says that the milk as a substance is not destroyed to produce another substance called curd. In reality a quality of the milk, *viz.*, sweet flavour, is changed into another quality, *viz.*, acid flavour.

व्यूहान्तराद्द्रव्यान्तरोत्पात्तिदर्शनं पूर्व्वद्रव्यनि- वृत्तेरनुमानम् ॥ ३ । २ । १७ ॥

92.   Seeing that a thing grows from another thing whose parts are disjoined, we infer that the latter thing is destroyed—17.

Seeing that a thing grows after the component parts of another thing have been disjoined, we infer that the latter thing has really been destroyed. The curd, for instance, is not produced until the component parts of the milk have been destroyed. This shows that the growth of curd follows the decay of milk.

क्वचिद्विनाशकारणानुपलब्धेः क्वचिच्चोप- लब्धेरनेकान्तः ॥ ३ । २ । १८ ॥

93.   There will be an uncertainty of conclusion on the assumption that the cause of destruction is perceived in some cases and not perceived in others—18.

In the case of a jar being produced out of a piece of clay you say you perceive the cause of destruction of the clay and production of the jar, but in the case of the curd growing out of milk you say that you do not perceive the cause of destruction of the milk and production of the curd. This sort of perception in certain cases and non-perception in others will lead to an uncertainty of conclusion. As a fact in every case there is perception of the cause of destruction. Milk, for instance, is destroyed when there is the contact of an acid substance.

नेन्द्रियार्थयोस्तद्विनाशेऽपि ज्ञानावस्थानात् ॥३।२।१९ ॥

94. Knowledge belongs neither to the sense nor to the object because it continues even on the destruction thereof.—19.

If knowledge had been a quality of the sense, it could not continue after the sense has been destroyed. But knowledge in the form of memory is found actually to abide even after the sense has perished. Hence the sense is not the abode of knowledge. Similarly it may be proved that knowledge does not abide in the object.

युगपज्ज्ञेयानुपलब्धेश्च न मनसः ॥३।२।२० ॥

95. It does not also belong to the mind the existence of which is inferred from the knowables not being perceived simultaneously.—20.

As two or more things cannot be known (perceived) simultaneously, it is to be concluded that the mind which is an instrument of our knowledge is atomic in dimension. If we supposed this mind to be the abode of knowledge we could not call it an instrument in the acquisition of the same; and knowledge as a quality of an atom would in that case become imperceptible. An atomic mind as the abode of our knowledge would stand moreover in the way of a *yogi* perceiving many things simultaneously through many sensuous bodies formed by his magical power.

तदात्मगुणत्वेऽपि तुल्यम् ॥३।२।२१॥

96. Even if knowledge were a quality of the soul it would, says some one, give rise to similar absurdities.—21.

The objection stands thus:—If the soul which is all-pervading were the abode of knowledge, there would be the simultaneous perceptions of many things in virtue of different sense-organs coming in contact with the soul simultaneously. But two or more things are never perceived simultaneously: the soul cannot therefore be the abode of knowledge, that is, knowledge cannot be a quality of the soul.

इन्द्रियैर्मनसः सन्निकर्षाभावात् तदनुत्पत्तिः ॥३।२।२२॥

97. There is, we reply, non-production of simultaneous cognitions on account of the absence of contact of the mind with many sense-organs at a time.—22.

The Naiyâyikas say that the soul cannot perceive an object unless the latter comes in contact with a sense which is conjoined with the mind. Though many objects can come in proximity with their corresponding senses simultaneously, the mind which is atomic in dimension can come in conjunction with only one sense at a time. Hence two or more things are not perceived simultaneously although the soul which perceives them is all-pervading.

नोत्पत्तिकारणानपदेशात् ॥३।२।२३ ॥

98. This is held by some to be untenable as there is no ground for the production of knowledge.—23.

The objection stands thus :—It has been argued by the Naiyâyikas that there is absence of production of simultaneous cognitions on account of the lack of contact of the senses with the mind. An opponent takes exception to the word " production " and says that knowledge cannot be said to be produced if it is regarded as a quality of the soul which is eternal.

विनाशकारणानुपलब्धेश्चावस्थाने तन्नित्यत्वप्रसङ्गः ॥३।२।२४॥

99. If knowledge is supposed to abide in the soul there is the contingency of its being eternal as there is perceived no cause of its destruction.—24.

Knowledge can never be destroyed if it is supposed to be a quality of the soul. A quality may be destroyed in two ways—(1) either by the destruction of its abode, (2) or by the production of an opposite quality in its place. In the case of knowledge neither of these is possible as the soul which is its abode is eternal and as we find no opposite quality taking its place. Hence it follows that if knowledge is a quality of the soul it is eternal. But as knowledge is not eternal it is not a quality of the soul.

अनित्यत्वग्रहादबुद्धेर्बुद्ध्यन्तराद्विनाशः शब्दवत् ॥३।२।२५॥

100. Cognitions being found to be non-eternal there is, we reply, destruction of one cognition by another like that of a sound.—25.

We realize that cognition (knowledge) is not eternal when we observe that at one time there arises in us a certain kind of cognition (knowledge) and at the next time that cognition (knowledge) vanishes giving rise to another kind of cognition (knowledge). It has been asked how cognitions undergo destruction. Our reply is that one cognition vanishes as soon as it is replaced by another cognition which is opposed to it just as a sound-wave is destroyed by another sound-wave which takes its place.

ज्ञानसमवेतात्मप्रदेशसन्निकर्षान्मनसः स्मृत्युत्पत्तेर्न
युगपदुत्पत्तिः ॥३।२।२६॥

101. Since recollection (memory) is produced, according to some, by the conjunction of the mind with a certain part of the soul in which knowledge (impression) inheres, there is no simultaneous production of many recollections. —26.

If knowledge be a quality of the soul there is the possibility of many recollections being produced simultaneously inasmuch as the many impressions deposited in our soul by our past perceptions are liable at once to be revived and developed into recollections by the mind whose contact with the soul always remains constant. Some say that there is no such possibility of simultaneousness because recollections are produced according to them, by the mind coming in contact with particular parts of the soul in which particular impressions inhere. As the mind cannot come in contact with all parts of the soul simultaneously, the many impressions deposited in different parts of the soul are not revived and developed into recollections at once.

नान्तः शरीरवृत्तित्वान्मनसः ॥३।२।२७॥

102. This is, we reply, not so because it is within the body that the mind has its function.—27.

It has been said in the preceding aphorism that recollections are produced by the mind coming in due order in conjunction with particular parts of the soul in which impressions inhere. This is, according to the Naiyâyikas, untenable because the mind cannot come in conjunction with the soul except in the body, and if the conjunction takes place in the body then there remains the possibility of simultaneous recollections.

साध्यत्वादहेतुः ॥३।२।२८॥

103. This is, some say, no reason because it requires to be proved.—28.

The Naiyâyikas say that the mind comes in conjunction with the soul only within the limit of the body. Some oppose this by saying that until they receive sufficient proof they cannot admit that the conjunction takes place only in the body.

स्मरतः शरीरधारणोपपत्तेरप्रतिषेधः ॥३।२।२९॥

104. It is, we reply, not unreasonable because a person is found to sustain his body even while he performs an act of recollection.—29.

If we suppose that a recollection is produced by the mind coming in conjunction with a particular part of the soul outside the body, we cannot account for the body being sustained during the time when the recollection is performed. The body in order that it may be sustained requires an effort which is supplied by the mind coming in conjunction with the soul. Now the effort which arises from the conjunction is of two kinds, viz., (1) the effort for sustaining, and (2) that for impelling (setting in motion). The body will be devoid of the first kind of effort if we suppose the mind to wander away from it for conjunction with the soul.

न तदाशुगतित्वान्मनसः ॥३।२।३०॥

105. This is, some say, not so because the mind moves swiftly.—30.

Some meet the objection raised in the preceding aphorism by saying that the mind while producing a recollection by its conjunction with the soul outside the body can, on account of its swift motion, come back at once to the body to produce the effort required for the sustenance of the same.

न स्मरणकालानियमात् ॥ ३।२।३१॥

106. It is, we reply, not so because there is no fixed rule as to the duration of recollection.—31.

The Naiyâyikas oppose the view expressed in the foregoing aphorism on the ground that the mind, if it is to be conjoined with the soul outside the body, may take a pretty long time to produce a recollection there, so that it may not come back to the body with sufficient quickness to produce the effort required for the sustenance of it.

आत्मप्रेरणयदृच्छाज्ञताभिश्च न संयोगविशेषः ॥३।२।३२॥

107. There is no peculiar conjunction of the soul with the mind either in virtue of the former sending the latter in search of what it wishes to recollect or through the latter being cognizant of what is to be recollected or through arbitrariness.—32.

If we suppose the soul to send the mind to recollect a particular thing we encounter the absurdity of admitting that the soul already possesses the memory of what it is going to recollect. If on the other hand we suppose the mind to move out of its own accord for a particular recollection, we shall have to assume that the mind is the knower but in reality it is not so. We cannot even hold that the mind comes in conjunction with the soul arbitrarily for in that case there will remain no order then as to the occurrence of the objects of recollection.

व्यासक्तमनसः पादव्यथनेन संयोगविशेषेण समानम् ॥३।२।३३॥

108. This is, some say, parallel to the particular conjunction which occurs in a man who while rapt in mind hurts his foot.—33.

If a man while looking eagerly at dancing hurts his foot with a thorn, he feels pain because his mind comes instantly in conjunction with his soul at the foot which has been hurt. Similarly the peculiar conjunction referred to in the foregoing aphorism takes place, according to some, through the mind being cognizant of what is to be recollected.

प्रणिधानलिङ्गादिज्ञानानामयुगपद्भावाद्युगपदस्मरणम् ॥३।२।३४॥

109. Recollections are not simultaneous owing to the non-simultaneousness of the efforts of attention, operations of stimuli etc.—34.

A recollection is produced by the mind coming in conjunction with the soul in which impressions inhere. The production of recollection also presupposes efforts of attention, operations of stimuli etc. As these do not occur simultaneously there is no simultaneousness of recollections.

प्रातिभवत्तु प्रणिधानायनपेच्चे स्मार्त्तं यौगपद्यप्रसङ्गः ॥३।२।३५॥

110. [It is not true that] there is possibility of simultaneousness in the case of recollections which are independent of the efforts of attention etc., just as in the case of cognitions derived from impressions of equal vividness not dependent on stimuli.—35.

Some say that recollections which are not dependent on the efforts of attention etc., may be simultaneous like several cognitions or acts of knowledge that are produced from impressions of equal vividness without the aid of external stimuli. But this view is untenable because neither the recollections nor the several acts of knowledge are simultaneous. The acts of knowledge though derived from impressions of equal vividness, will appear in succession according to the amount of attention paid to them, and the recollections though not dependent on the efforts of attention will appear one after another in proportion to the strength of stimuli that revive them.

ज्ञस्येच्छाद्वेषनिमित्तत्वादारम्भनिवृत्त्योः ॥३।२।३६॥

111. Desire and aversion belong to the soul inasmuch as they are the causes of its doing an act or forbearing from doing the same.—36.

The Sâmkhyas say that knowledge is a quality of the soul (Puruṣa) while desire aversion, volition, pleasure and pain are the qualities of the internal sense (the mind). This is, according to the Naiyâyikas, unreasonable because a person does an act or forbears from doing it on account of a certain desire for or aversion against the same. The desire and aversion again are caused by the knowledge of pleasure and pain respectively. Hence it is established that knowledge, desire, aversion, volition, pleasure and pain have all of them a single abode, that is, they are the qualities of a single substance called the soul.

तल्लिङ्गत्वादिच्छाद्वेषयोः पार्थिवाद्येष्वप्रतिषेधः ॥३।२।३७॥

112. It cannot, some say, be denied that desire and aversion belong to the body inasmuch as they are indicated by activity and forbearance from activity.—37.

The Cârvâkas say that activity and forbearance from activity are the marks respectively of desire and aversion which again are the effects of knowledge. Now the body which is made of earth etc., is the abode (field) of activity and forbearance from activity. Hence it is also the abode of knowledge, desire, aversion etc.

परश्वादिष्वारम्भनिवृत्तिदर्शनात् ॥३।२।३८॥

113. This is, we reply, unreasonable because activity and forbearance from activity are found in the axes and the like.—38.

Just as an axe, which is found sometimes to split a tree and at other times not to split it, is not a receptacle of knowledge, desire and aversion, so the body which is made of earth etc., is not an abode of knowledge etc., though we may find activity and forbearance from activity in it.

कुम्भादिष्यनुपलब्धेरहेतुः ॥३।२।३९॥

114. It is unreasonable also on account of the non-perception of knowledge in pots and the like.—39.

In a pot there is activity indicated by the conglomeration of different earthy parts while in sands there is forbearance from activity indicated by the disruption of the parts from one another. Yet there is no knowledge, desire or aversion in a pot or sand. Hence the body is not the seat of knowledge, desire or aversion.

नियमानियमौ तु तद्विशेषकौ ॥३।२।४०॥

115. The regularity and irregularity of possession demarcate the soul and matter.—40.

A material thing is by nature inactive but becomes endowed with activity when it is moved by a conscious agent. There is no such irregularity or uncertainty as to the possession of activity etc., by the soul. Knowledge, desire, aversion, etc., abide in the soul through an intimate connection, while these belong to matter through a mediate connection. We cannot account for the function of recognition etc., if we assume knowledge to abide in the material atoms a conglomeration of which forms the body. Those who suppose the body to be the seat of knowledge cannot admit the efficacy of deserts and can offer no consolation to sufferers.

यथोक्तहेतुत्वात् पारतन्त्र्यादकृताभ्यागमाच्च न मनसः ॥३।२।४१॥

116. The mind is not the seat of knowledge on account of reasons already given, on account of its being subject to an agent and owing to its incapacity to reap the fruits of another's deeds.—41.

The mind cannot be the seat of knowledge because it has already been shown in aphorism I.1.10 that desire, aversion, volition, pleasure and pain are the marks of the soul. Had the mind been the abode of knowledge it could have come in contact with the objects of sense independent of any agent. Since it cannot do so it is to be admitted to be a material thing serving the purpose of an instrument in the acquisition of knowledge. If you say that the mind itself is the agent you will have to admit that it is not an atom but possessed of magnitude like the soul so that it can apprehend knowledge etc., which are its qualities. In order to avoid the simultaneousness of many perceptions it will further be necessary to assume an internal sense of an atomic dimension like the mind as we understand it. These assumptions will lead you to accept in some shape

13

the tenets of the Naiyâyikas. On the supposition of the mind (or body)
being the seat of knowledge and consequently of merits and demerits,
it will be possibe for work done by a person not to produce its effects on
him after death and it may even necessitate a person to suffer for work
not done by him. Hence the mind is not the seat of knowledge, desire,
aversion, volition, pleasure and pain.

परिशेषाद्यथोक्तहेतूपपत्तेश्च ॥३।२।४२॥

117. Knowledge etc., must be admitted to be
qualities of the soul by the principle of exclusion and on
account of arguments already adduced.—42.

Knowledge is a quality which inheres in a substance. That substance is neither the body nor the sense nor the mind. It must therefore
be the soul. The body cannot be the abode of knowledge because it is a
material substance like a pot, cloth etc. Knowledge cannot belong to the
sense as the latter is an instrument like an axe. Had the sense been the
abode of knowledge there could not be any recollection of things which
were experienced by the sense before it was destroyed. If knowledge
were a quality of the mind many perceptions could be simultaneous.
But this is impossible. Hence the abode of knowledge is not the mind,
but it is the soul which is permanent so that it can perceive a thing now
as well as remember one perceived in the past.

स्मरणन्त्वात्मनोज्ञस्वाभाव्यात् ॥३।२।४३॥

118. Memory belongs to the soul which possesses
the character of a knower.—43.

The soul is competent to recollect a thing because it possesses the
knowledge of the past, present and future.

प्रणिधाननिबन्धाभ्यासलिङ्गलक्षणसादृश्यपरिग्रहाश्रयाश्रि-
तसम्बन्धानन्तर्य्यवियोगैककार्य्यविरोधातिशयप्राप्तिव्यवधानसुख
दुःखेच्छाद्वेषभयार्थित्वक्रियारागधर्म्माधर्म्मनिमित्तेभ्यः॥३।२।४४॥

119. Memory is awakened by such causes as attention, context, exercise, signs, marks, likeness, possession,
relation of refuge and refugee, immediate subsequency,
separation, similar employment, opposition, excess, receipt,
intervention, pleasure and pain, desire and aversion, fear,
entreaty, action, affection and merit and demerit.—44.

Attention—enables us to fix the mind on one object by checking it from wandering away to any other object.

Context—is the connection of subjects such as proof, that which is to be proved etc.

Exercise—is the constant repetition which confirms an impression.

Sign—may be (1) connected, (2) inseparable (intimate), (3) correlated, or (4) opposite *e. g.*, smoke is a sign of fire with which it is connected ; horn is a sign of a cow from which it is inseparable ; an arm is a sign of a leg with which it is correlated ; and the non-existent is a sign of the existent by the relation of opposition.

Mark—a mark on the body of a horse awakens the memory of the stable in which it was kept.

Likeness—as the image of Devadatta drawn on a board reminds us of the real person.

Possession—such as a property awakens the memory of the owner and *vice versa*.

Refuge and refugee—such as a king and his attendants.

Immediate subsequency—as sprinkling the rice and pounding it in a wooden mortar.

Separation—as of husband and wife.

Similar employment—as of fellow-disciples.

Opposition—as between a snake and ichneumon.

Excess—awakening the memory of that which exceeded.

Receipt—reminding us of one from whom something has been or will be received.

Intervention—such as a sheath reminding us of the sword.

Pleasure and pain—reminding us of that which caused them.

Desire and aversion—reminding us of one whom we liked or hated.

Fear—reminding us of that which caused it, *e. g.*, death.

Entreaty—reminding us of that which was wanted or prayed for.

Action—such as a chariot reminding us of the charioteer.

Affection—as recollecting a son or wife.

Merit and demerit—through which there is recollection of the causes of joy and sorrow experienced in a previous life.

कर्म्मानवस्थायिग्रहणात् ॥३।२।४५॥

120.   Knowledge perishes instantly because all actions are found to be transitory.—45.

Does knowledge perish instantly like a sound or does it continue like a pot? Knowledge perishes as soon as it is produced in virtue of its being an action.   In analysing an action, such as the falling of an arrow, we find that the arrow undergoes a series of movements in the course of its falling on the ground.   Similarly in examining an act of knowledge we find that a series of steps are undergone by the act in the course of its production.   These steps perish one after another in due succession.   Hence it is clear that knowledge is transitory.   If knowledge were permanent we could say,   "I am preceiving a pot" even after the pot has been removed from our sight.   Since we cannot use such an expression we must admit that knowledge is not permanent but transitory.

बुद्ध्यवस्थानात् प्रत्यक्तत्वे स्मृत्यभावः ॥३।२।४६॥

121.   If knowledge were permanent it would always be perceptible so that there would be no recollection.—46.

If there is knowledge it is perceptible and as long as there is perception there is no recollection.   Hence on the supposition of knowledge being permanent there would be a total absence of recollection.

अव्यक्तग्रहणमनवस्थायित्वात् विद्युत्सम्पाते रूपाव्यक्त- ग्रहणवत् ॥३।२।४७॥

122.   An opponent fears that if knowledge were transitory no object could be known distinctly just as there is no distinct apprehension of colour during a flash of lightning.—47.

The fear of the opponent arises thus :—If knowledge were transitory it could not at a moment apprehend an object in its entirety, that is, could not apprehend the infinite number of its properties at once.   Hence the object could only be known indistinctly.   As a fact, however, we can know things distinctly.   Hence knowledge is not transitory.

हेतूपादानात् प्रतिषेद्धव्याभ्यनुज्ञा ॥३।२।४८॥

123.   From the argument advanced you have, we reply, to admit that which you went to disprove.—48.

In the previous aphorism the opponent feared that if knowledge were transitory no object could be apprehended distinctly. The Naiyâyika removes the fear by saying that objects are apprehended indistinctly not owing to the transitoriness of knowledge but on account of our apprehending only their general qualities. The knowledge which takes cognizance of objects as possessed of both the general and special qualities is distinct but that which concerns itself only with the general qualities is indistinct.

The aphorism may be explained in another way :—The very illustration cited by you, *viz.*, that there is indistinct apprehension during a flash of lightning leads you to admit the transitoriness of knowledge which you went to disprove.

प्रदीपार्चिः सन्तत्यभिव्यक्तग्रहणवत्तद्ग्रहणम् ॥३।२।४६॥

124. Although knowledge is transitory there is distinct apprehension through it as there is one through the series of momentary rays of a lamp.—49.

Though the series of rays emitted by a lamp are transitory the apprehension through them is distinct. Similarly though our knowledge is transitory there is no obstacle to our apprehension being distinct.

द्रव्ये स्वगुणपरगुणोपलब्धेः संशयः ॥३।२।५०॥

125. From our perceiving in a substance the qualities of itself as well as of others there arises, says an opponent, a doubt as to whether the knowledge perceived in our body is a quality of its own.—50.

In water we perceive liquidity which is one of its natural qualities as well as warmth which is an adventitious one. One may therefore ask as to whether the knowledge perceived in our body is a natural quality of the latter or is a mere adventitious one.

यावच्छरीरभावित्वाद्रूपादीनाम् ॥३।२।५१॥

126. [Knowledge is not a natural quality of the body because it furnishes a contrast to] colour etc. which as natural qualities of the body do exist as long as the latter continues.—51.

Knowledge, according to the Naiyâyika, is not a natural quality of the body because it may not continue quite as long as the body does. But such is not the case with colour etc. which as natural qualities of the body do always exist with it. Hence knowledge is merely an adventitious quality of the body.

न पाकजगुणान्तरोत्पत्ते: ॥३।२।५२॥

127. It is, says an opponent, not so because other qualities produced by maturation do arise.—52.

It has been stated that a substance and its natural qualities co-exist with each other and that knowledge not being always co-existent with the body is not a natural quality of the latter. An opponent in order to maintain that a substance and its natural qualities are not necessarily co-existent cites the instance of a jar whose natural colour is blue but which assumes a red colour through maturation in fire.

प्रतिद्वन्द्विसिद्धे: पाकजानामप्रतिषेध: ॥३।२।५३॥ ।

128. This is, we reply, no opposition because maturation occurs if there is production of opposite qualities.—53.

A jar which was blue may through maturation become red but it is never totally deprived of colour which is its natural quality. But a body (dead) may be totally devoid of knowledge which is therefore not a natural quality of it. In the case of maturation moreover a quality is replaced by an opposite one with which it cannot co-abide e. g., the blueness of a jar may through maturation assume redness but cannot co-abide with the same. In the case of the body however knowledge is not replaced by an opposite quality. Hence knowledge is not a natural quality of the body.

शरीरव्यापित्वात् ॥३।२।५४॥

129. [Knowledge, says an opponent, is a natural quality] because it pervades the whole body.—54.

The opponent tries to prove that knowledge is a natural quality of the body because it pervades, according to him, the whole body and the numerous parts of it. But this, according to the Naiyâyika, is unreasonable as it leads to the assumption of numerous seats of knowledge, that is, souls in the body destructive of all order and system as to the feeling of pleasure, pain etc.

केशनखादिष्वनुपलब्धे: ॥३।२।५५॥

130. [Knowledge does not pervade the whole body] as it is not found in the hair, nails etc.—55.

Knowledge does not pervade the whole body, *e. g.*, it is not found in the hair, nails etc. It cannot therefore be a natural quality of the body.

This aphorism may also be explained as follows :—

It is not true that a substance should be entirely pervaded by its natural qualities. Colour, for instance, is a natural quality of the body but it does not pervade the hair, nails etc.

त्वक्पर्य्यन्तत्वाच्छरीरस्य केशनखादिष्वप्रसङ्गः ॥३।२।५६॥

131. The body being bounded by touch (cuticle) there is, says an opponent, no possibility of knowledge abiding in the hair, nails etc.—56.

The hair, nails etc. are not, according to the opponent, parts of the body as they are not bounded by touch (cuticle). Knowledge cannot consequently abide in them.

The aphorism may also be interpreted as follows :—

The body being bounded by touch (cuticle) there is no possibility of colour abiding in the hair, nails etc.

शरीरगुणवैधर्म्यात् ॥३।२।५७॥

132. Knowledge, we reply, is not a quality of the body because of its difference from the well known qualities of the same.—57.

The Naiyâyika says :—

The qualities of the body are of two kinds, *viz* : (1) those which are cognised by the external senses, *e.g.*, colour, and (2) those which are not cognised by them, *e.g.*, gravity. Knowledge does not come under either of the categories as it is uncognizable by the external senses and is at the same time cognizable on account of our being aware of the same.

The aphorism may also be explained as follows :—

The qualities of the body are cognized by the external senses but knowledge is not so cognized. Consequently knowledge cannot be a quality of the body.

न रूपादीनामितरेतरवैधर्म्यात् ॥३।२।५८॥

133. This is, says the opponent, not so because of the mutual difference in character of the colour, etc.—58.

The opponent argues :—

If you say that knowledge is not a quality of the body because it differs in character from other well known qualities of the same, I should say that the weil known qualites themselves differ from each other, *e.g.*, the colour is cognized by the eye but the touch is not. You cannot on this ground say that colour is a quality of the body but touch is not.

ऐन्द्रियकत्वाद्रूपादीनामप्रतिषेधः ॥३।२।५६॥

134. There is, we reply no objection to colour, etc., being qualities of the body because these are cognized by the senses.— 59.

The colour, etc., may differ from touch etc. in respect of certain aspects of their character but they all agree in one respect, *viz.*, that they are all cognizable by one or another of the external senses. But knowledge is not so cognized and cannot therefore be a quality of the body.

ज्ञानायौगपद्यादेकं मनः ॥ ३ । २ । ६० ॥

135. The mind is one on account of the non-simultaneousness of cognitions.—60.

If there were more minds than one, they could come in contact with many senses at a time so that many cognitions could be produced simultaneously. As many cognitions are never produced at once the mind must be admitted to be one.

न युगपदनेकक्रियोपलब्धेः ॥ ३ । २ । ६१ ॥

136. It is, says an opponent, not so because we do cognize many acts simultaneously.—61.

The objection stands thus :--A certain teacher while walking on a road holds a waterpot in his hand. Hearing wild sounds he, out of fear, looks at the road, recites a sacred text and thinks of the nearest place of safety. The teacher is supposed in this instance to perform visual perception, auditory perception, recollection, etc., simultaneously. This would be impossible if there were only one mind.

अलातचक्रदर्शनवत्तदुपलब्धिराशुसञ्चारात् ॥ ३ । २ । ६२ ॥

137. The appearance of simultaneousness is, we reply, due to the mind coming in contact with different senses in rapid succession like the appearance of a circle of firebrand.—62.

Just as a firebrand while whirling quickly appears to form a continuous circle, so the mind moving from one sense to another in rapid succession appears to come in contact with them simultaneously. Hence the cognitions produced by the contact appear to be simultaneous though in reality they are successive.

यथोक्तहेतुत्वाच्चाणु ॥ ३ । २ । ६३ ॥

138. And on account of the aforesaid reasons the mind is an atom.—63.

If the mind were possessed of magnitude it could come in contact with many senses at a time so that many cognitions could take place simultaneously. Since this has been found to be impossible the mind is an atom.

पूर्वकृतफलानुबन्धाच्चदुत्पत्तिः ॥ ३ । २ । ६४ ॥

139. The body is produced as the fruit of our previous deeds (deserts) —64.

Our present body has been made up of elements endowed with the fruits of merit and demerit of our previous lives.

भूतेभ्यो मूर्त्युपादानवत् तदुपादानम् ॥ ३ । २ । ६५ ॥

140. The formation of our body of elements, says an opponent, resembles that of a statue of stone, etc.—65.

The objection stands thus :—Just as a statue is formed of stone, clay, etc., which are deviod of deserts, our body has been made up of elements which are not endowed with the fruits of our previous merits and demerits.

न साध्यसमत्वात् ॥ ३ । २ । ६६ ॥

141. It is, we reply, not so because the statement requires proof —66.

To prove that our body is formed of elements which are devoid of deserts, the opponent cites the instance of a statue made up of clay or stone, which is supposed to bear no connection whatsoever with deserts. The Naiyâyika replies that the very example cited requires to be verified for clay etc. are made of atoms which have actually a reference to desert as they comport themselves in such a way as to work out the designs of Retributive Justice.

नोत्पत्तिनिमित्तत्वान्मातापित्रोः ॥ ३ । २ । ६७ ॥

142. Not so because father and mother are the cause of its production.—67.

14

The formation of our body cannot be compared to that of a clay-statue because the body owes its origin to the sperm and blood of our father and mother while the statue is produced without any seed at all.

तथाहारस्य ॥ ३ । २ । ६८ ॥

143.   So too eating is a cause.—68.

The food and drink taken by the mother turns into blood which develops the embryo (made up of the sperm of the father) through the various stages of formation of the *arbuda* (a long round mass) *mâmsa-peśî* (a piece of flesh), *kalala* (a round lump), *kaṇḍarâ* (sinews), *śiraḥ* (head), *pâṇi* (hands), *pâdu* (legs), etc.   Eating is therefore a cause of production of our body but not of a clay-statue.

प्रात्तौ चानियमात् ॥ ३ । २ । ६९ ॥

144.   And there is desert because of uncertainty even in the case of union.—69.

All unions between husband and wife are not followed by the production of a child (body).   Hence we must acknowledge the desert of the child to be a co-operative cause of its birth.

शरीरोत्पत्तिनिमित्तवत् संयोगोत्पत्तिनिमित्तं कर्म्म ॥ ३।२।७० ॥

145.   Desert is the cause not only of the production of the body but also of its conjunction with a soul.—70.

Just as the earth, etc., independent of a person's desert are unable to produce his body, so the body itself as a seat of particular pleasures and pains is unable to be connected with a soul without the intervention of the desert of the latter.

एतेनानियमः प्रत्युक्तः ॥ ३ । २ । ७१ ॥

146.   By this the charge against inequality is answered.—71.

Some persons are found to possess a healthy body while others an unhealthy one; a certain body is beautiful while another ugly.   This inequality in the formation of the body is due to the desert acquired by the persons in their previous lives.

The aphorism may also be interpreted as follows:—

146.   By this the charge against uncertainty is answered.—71.

It is due entirely to the interference of the desert that the union between husband and wife is not always followed by the production of a child (body).

उपपन्नश्च तद्वियोगः कंर्म्मक्षयोपपत्तेः ॥ ३ । २ । ७२ ॥

147. And the separation between the soul and the body is effected by the termination of the deserts.—72.

It is in virtue of its deserts that a soul is joined with a particular body and it is by the exhaustion of the deserts that the separation between the two takes place. The soul cannot be separated from the body until it attains perfect knowledge through the cessation of ignorance and lust.

तदृष्टकारितमिति चेत् पुनस्तत्प्रसङ्गोऽपवर्गे ॥ ३ । २ । ७३ ॥

148. If the body was attached to a soul only to remove the inexperience of the latter, then the same inexperience would recur after the soul had been emancipated (released).—73.

An opponent says that there is no necessity for admitting the desert and that the body which is made up of elements is connected with a soul only to enable the latter to experience objects and realize its distinction from matter (prakṛiti). As soon as the soul satisfies itself by the experience and attains emancipation (release) it is separated from the body for ever. The Naiyâyika asks: "Why is not the soul, even after emancipation (release), again connected with a body to regain its experiential power?" Since the opponent does not admit desert there is nothing else to stop the connection.

न करणाकरणयोरारम्भदर्शनात् ॥ ३ । २ । ७४ ॥

149. It is not reasonable, because the body is found to be produced in case of both fulfilment and non-fulfilment of its ends.—74.

In the previous aphorism it was stated that the body was produced only to enable the soul to experience objects and to realize its distinction from matter (prakṛiti). In the present aphorism the Naiyâyika points out the worthlessness of the statement by showing that the body is produced irrespective of the fulfilment or non-fulfilment of its ends, that is, it is produced in case of the soul experiencing objects and realizing its distinction from matter as well as in the case when the soul remains enchained on account of its failure to realize its distinction from matter.

In a certain school of philosophy the desert is supposed to be a quality of the atoms and not of the soul. In virtue of the desert atoms are said to combine together into a body (endowed with a mind) to enable the soul to experience objects, and realize its distinction from matter. This school of philosophy fails to explain why the soul after it has attained emancipation (release) is not again connected with a body inasmuch as the atoms composing the body are never devoid of deserts.

मनः कर्मनिमित्तत्वाच्च संयोगानुच्छेदः ॥ ३ । २ । ७५ ॥

150. And there will be no cessation of the conjunction if it is caused by the desert of the mind.—75.

Those who maintain that the desert is a quality of the mind cannot explain why there should at all be a separation of the body from the mind which is eternal. If it is said that the very desert which connected the body with the mind does also separate it therefrom, we shall be constrained to admit an absurd conclusion that one and the same thing is the cause of life and death.

नित्यत्वप्रसङ्गश्च प्रायणानुपपत्तेः ॥ ३ । २ । ७६ ॥

151. Owing to there being no reason for destruction we should find the body to be eternal.—76.

If the body is supposed to be produced from elements independent of deserts, we should not find any thing the absence of which will cause its destruction. In the event of the destruction being arbitrary, there will be no fixed cause to effect emancipation or rebirth thereafter as the elements will always remain the same.

अणुश्यामतानित्यत्ववदेतत् स्यात् ॥ ३ । २ । ७७ ॥

152. The disappearance of the body in emancipation (release) is, according to an opponent, eternal like the blackness of an atom.—77.

The opponent says :—Just as the blackness of an atom suppressed by redness through contact with fire does not reappear, so the body which has once attained emancipation (release) will not reappear.

नाकृताभ्यागमप्रसङ्गात् ॥ ३ । २ । ७८ ॥

153. This is, we reply, not so because it would lead us to admit what was undemonstrable.—78.

The argument employed in the previous aphorism is, according to the Naiyâyika, futile for it cannot be proved that the blackness of an atom is suppressed by redness through contact with fire for it is possible that the blackness is altogether destroyed,

The aphorism may also be interpreted as follows :—

153.   This is, we reply, not so, because it would lead us to acknow-ledge the consequence of actions not done by us.—78.

Unless we acknowledge deserts there will be no principle governing the enjoyment of pleasure and suffering of pain.   The absence of such a principle will be repugnant to all evidences—perception, inference and scripture.

BOOK IV.—CHAPTER I.

प्रवृत्तिर्यथोक्ता ॥ ४ । १ । १ ॥

1. Activity, as it is, has been explained.—1.

The definition of activity is to be found in aphorism 1-1-17.

तथा दोषाः ॥ ४ । १ । २ ॥

2. So the faults.—2.

The definition of faults has been given in aphorism 1-1-18. The faults which co-abide with intellect in the soul are caused by activity, produce rebirths and do not end until the attainment of final release (apavarga).

तत्त्रैराश्यं रागद्वेषमोहार्थान्तरभावात् ॥ ४ । १ । ३ ॥

3. The faults are divisible in three groups, as all of them are included in affection, aversion and stupidity.—3.

The faults are divided in three groups, viz., affection, aversion and stupidity. Affection includes lust, avarice, avidity and covetousness. Aversion includes anger, envy, malignity, hatred and implacability. Stupidity includes misapprehension, suspicion, arrogance and carelessness.

नैकप्रत्यनीकभावात् ॥ ४ । १ । ४ ॥

4. It is, some say, not so, because they are the opposites of one single thing.—4.

The objection stands thus:—There is no distinction between affection, aversion and stupidity, as all of them are destructible by one single thing, viz., perfect knowledge. The three, in so far as they are destructible by one single thing, are of a uniform character.

व्यभिचारादहेतुः ॥ ४ । १ । ५ ॥

5. This reason, we reply, is not good, because it is erratic. —5.

To prove that there is no distinction between affection, aversion and stupidity, the opponent has advanced the reason that all the three are destructible by one single thing. This reason is declared by the Naiyâyika to be erratic, because it does not apply to all cases, e. g., the blue, black, green, yellow, brown and other colours, although they are different from one another, are destructible by one single thing, viz., contact with fire.

तेषां मोहः पापीयान्नामूढस्येतरोत्पत्तेः ॥ ४ । १ । ६ ॥

6 Of the three, stupidity is the worst, because in the case of a person who is not stupid, the other two do not come into existence.—6.

There are three faults, *viz.*, affection, aversion and stupidity, of which the last is the worst, because it is only a stupid person who may be influenced by affection and aversion.

प्राप्तस्तर्हि निमित्तनैमित्तिकभावादर्थान्तरभावो दोषेभ्यः॥४।१।७॥

7. There is then, says an opponent, a difference between stupidity and other faults owing to their inter-relation of cause and effect.—7.

The opponent argues as follows:—Since stupidity is the cause of the other two faults, it must be different from them. In fact there cannot be the relation of cause and effect between two things which are not different from each other.

न दोषलक्षणावरोधान्मोहस्य ॥ ४ । १ । ८ ॥

8. It is, we reply, not so, because faults as already defined include stupidity.—8.

Stupidity is indeed a fault because it is homogeneous with or possesses the character of the same as defined in aphorism 1-1-18.

निमित्तनैमित्तिकोपपत्तेश्च तुल्यजातीयानामप्रतिषेधः ॥ ४ । १ । ९ ॥

9. And there is, we reply, no prohibition for homogeneous things to stand in the relation of cause and effect.—9.

It is not proper to exclude stupidity from the faults on the mere ground that they stand to each other in the relation of cause and effect. In fact the homogeneous things such as two substances or two qualities may stand to each other in the relation of cause and effect, *e. g.*, in the case of a jar being produced from its two halves we notice the relation of cause and effect between the jar and the halves which are homogeneous with each other.

आत्मनित्यत्वे प्रेत्यभावासिद्धिः ॥ ४ । १ । १० ॥

10. Transmigration is possible if the soul is eternal.—10.

Transmigration defined in 1-1-19 belongs to the soul and not to the body. The series of births and deaths included in it is possible only if the soul is eternal. If the soul were destructible, it would meet with two unexpected chances, viz., destruction of actions done by it (krita-hâni) and suffering from actions not done by it (akritâbhyâgama).

व्यक्ताव्यक्तकानां प्रत्यक्षप्रामाण्यात् ॥ ४ । १ । ११ ॥

11. There is evidence of perception as to the production of the distinct from the distinct.—11.

It is found that jars, etc., which are distinct are produced from earth, etc., which are also distinct. Similarly our body is produced from the elements.

न घटाद् घटानिष्पत्तेः ॥ ४ । १ । १२ ॥

12. It is, some say, not so, because a jar is not produced from another jar.—12.

The objection stands thus:—You cannot say that there is the production of a distinct thing from another distinct thing, e. g., a jar is not produced from another jar.

व्यक्ताद्घटनिष्पत्तेरप्रतिषेधः ॥ ४ । १ । १३ ॥

13. There is, we reply, no prohibition for a jar being produced from a distinct thing.—13.

A jar may not be produced from another jar but it is certainly produced from another distinct thing, viz., from its bowl-shaped halves. There is therefore no bar against the production of the distinct from the distinct.

अभावाद्भावोत्पत्तिर्ननुपमृद्य प्रादुर्भावात् ॥ ४ । १ । १४॥

14.—Some say that entity arises from non-entity, as there is no manifestation unless there has been destruction.—14.

A sprout cannot come into existence, unless the seed from which it comes has been destroyed. This shows that there is no manifestation of effect without the destruction of its cause.

व्याघातादप्रयोगः ॥ ४ । १ । १५ ॥

15. It is, we reply, not so, because such an expression, inconsistent as it is, cannot be employed.—15.

To say that a thing comes into existence by destroying another thing which is its cause, is a contradiction in terms, for if that which, according to you, destroys the cause and takes the place thereof, was not existent prior to the destruction, then it cannot be said to be a destroyer, and if it existed prior to the cause, then it cannot be said to come into existence on the destruction thereof.

नातातानागतयोः कारकशब्दप्रयोगात् ॥ ४ । १ । १६ ॥

16. There is, says the objector, no inconsistency, because terms expressive of action are figuratively applied to the past and future.—16.

The objector says as follows:—There is no impropriety in the statement that a thing comes into existence by destroying another thing which is its cause, for terms expressive of action are figuratively employed to denote that which is not existent now but which existed in the past or will exist in the future, e. g., he congratulates himself on the son that is to be born. In the sentence " a sprout comes into existence by destroying its cause "—the term expressive of destruction is figuratively applied to the sprout that will come into existence in the future.

न विनष्टेभ्योऽनिष्पत्तेः ॥ ४ । १ । १७ ॥

17. It is, we reply, not so, because nothing is produced from things destroyed.—17.

A sprout does not spring from a seed already destroyed. Hence, we can lay down the general rule that entity does not arise from non-entity.

क्रमनिर्देशादप्रतिषेधः ॥ ४ । १ । १८ ॥

18. There is no objection if destruction is pointed out only as a step in the processes of manifestation.—18.

In connection with earth, water, heat etc., a seed undergoes destruction of its old structure and is endowed with a new structure. A sprout cannot grow from a seed, unless the old structure of the seed is destroyed and a new structure is formed. It is in this sense allowable to say that manifestation is preceded by destruction. This does not preclude a seed from being the cause of a sprout. But we do not admit an unqualified assertion that production springs from destruction or entity arises from non-entity.

15

ईश्वरः कारणं पुरुषकर्म्माफल्यदर्शनात् ॥ ४ । १ । १६ ॥

19. God, says some one, is the sole cause of fruits, because man's acts are found occasionally to be unattended by them.—19.

Seeing that man does not often attain success proportionate to his exertions, some one infers that these are entirely subservient to God who alone can provide them with fruits.

न पुरुषकर्म्माभावे फलानिष्पत्तेः ॥ ४ । १ । २० ॥

20. This is, some are afraid, not so, because in the absence of man's acts there is no production of fruits.—20.

The fear referred to arises thus :—If God were the only source of fruits, man could attain them even without any exertions.

तत्कारितत्वादहेतुः ॥ ४ । १ । २१ ॥

21. Since fruits are awarded by God, man's acts, we conclude, are not the sole cause thereof.—21.

Man performs acts which are endowed with fruits by God. The acts become fruitless without His grace. Hence it is not true that man's acts produce fruits by themselves.

God is a soul specially endowed with qualities. He is freed from misapprehension, carelessness, etc., and is enriched with merit, knowledge and concentration. He possesses eight supernatural powers (such as the power of becoming as small as an atom) which are the consequences of his merit and concentration. His merit, which conforms to his will, produces merit and demerit in each person and sets the earth and other elements in action. God is, as it were, the father of all beings. Who can demonstrate the existence of Him who transcends the evidences of perception, inference and scripture?

अनिमित्तो भावोत्पत्तिः कण्टकतैक्ष्ण्यादिदर्शनात् ॥ ४।१।२२ ॥

22. From an observation of the sharpness of thorn, etc., some say that entities are produced from no cause. —22.

The objectors argue as follows :—Thorns are by nature sharp, hills beautiful, and stones smooth. None has made them so. Similarly our bodies, etc., are fortuitous effects which did not spring from a cause, that is, were not made by God.

अनिमित्तनिमित्तत्वान्नानिमित्ततः ४ । १ । २३ ॥

23. Entities cannot be said to be produced from no-cause, because the no-cause is, according to some, the cause of the production.—23.

An opponent has said that entities are produced from no-cause. Some critics point out that the use of the fifth case-affix in connection with no-cause indicates that it is the cause.

निमित्तानिमित्तयोरर्थान्तरभावादप्रतिषेधः ॥ ४ । १ । २४ ॥

24. The aforesaid reason presents no opposition, because cause and no-cause are two entirely different things. —24.

Cause and no-cause cannot be identical, e. g., a jar which is water-less cannot at the same time be full of water. The doctrine involved in this aphorism does not differ from the one explained in 3-2-70 according to which our body cannot be made up independent of our desert (Karma).

सर्व्वमनित्यमुत्पत्तिविनाशधर्म्मकत्वात् ॥ ४ । १ । २५ ॥

25. All, says some one, are non-eternal, because they possess the character of being produced and destroyed. —25.

All things including our body which is material and our intellect which is immaterial are non-eternal inasmuch as they are subject to the law of production and destruction. All things which are produced and destroyed are non-eternal.

नानित्यतानित्यत्वात् ॥ ४ । १ । २६ ॥

26. These are, we reply, not so, because of the non-eternalness being eternal.—26.

If non-eternalness pervades all things you must admit it to be eternal. Hence, all are not non-eternal, for there is at least one thing, viz., non-eternalness which is eternal.

तदनित्यत्वमग्नेर्दाहं विनाश्यानुविनाशवत् ॥ ४ । १ । २७ ॥

27. Some hold non-eternalness to be not eternal on the analogy of a fire which dies out after the combustibles have perished.—27.

The objection is explained as follows :—Just as a fire dies out as soon as the things which caught it have perished, so the non-eternalness disappears as soon as all non-eternal things have passed away. Hence, non-eternalness is not eternal.

नित्यस्याप्रत्याख्यानं यथोपलब्धिव्यवस्थानात् ॥ ४ । १ । २८ ॥

28.　There is no denial of the eternal, as there is a regulation as to the character of our perception.—28.

Whatever is perceived to be produced or destroyed is non-eternal and that which is not so is eternal, e. g., there is no perceptual evidence as to the production or destruction of ether, time, space, soul, mind, generality, particularity and intimate relation. Consequently these are eternal.

सर्वं नित्यम्पञ्चभूतनित्यत्वात् ॥ ४ । १ । २९ ॥

29.　Some say that all are eternal, because the five elements are so.—29.

The elements which are the material causes of all things are eternal, consequently the things themselves are eternal.

नोत्पत्तिविनाशकारणोपलब्धेः ॥ ४ । १ । ३० ॥

30.　These are, we reply, not so, because we perceive the causes of production and destruction.—30.

All things are non-eternal because we find them to be produced and destroyed. Whatever is produced or destroyed is non-eternal.

तल्लक्षणावरोधादप्रतिषेधः ॥ ४ । १ । ३१ ॥

31.　This is, some say, no refutation, because the character of the elements is possessed by the things which are produced or destroyed.—31.

The objector says as follows :—A thing which is made up of an element, possesses the character of the element. Since the element is eternal, the thing also must be so.

नोत्पत्तितत्कारणोपलब्धेः ॥ ४ । १ । ३२ ॥

32.　This is, we reply, no opposition, because we perceive production and the cause thereof.—32.

An effect inherits the character of its cause but the two are not identical, e. g., ether is the cause of sound, although the former is eternal and the latter non-eternal.

Moreover, we actually perceive that things are produced which convince us of their non-eternalness. If production is regarded as a mere vision of a dream, then the whole world is no better than an illusion which can serve no practical purpose.

If all things were eternal there could be no effort or activity on our part to attain any object. Hence all are not eternal.

न व्यवस्थानुपपत्ते: ॥ ४ । १ । ३३ ॥

33. If all things were eternal there would be no regulation of time.—33.

Some say that things are eternal, because they existed even before they were produced and will continue even after they are destroyed. But this view, contends the Naiyâyika, is absurd. It destroys all regulations with regard to time, for if all things were perpetually existent, there could not be any use of such expression as " was produced" and " will be destroyed," which presuppose a thing which was non-existent to come into existence or one which is existent to lose its existence.

सर्वं पृथग्भावलच्चणपृथक्त्वात् ॥४।१।३४॥

34. Some say that all are aggregates because each consists of several marks.—34.

A jar, for instance, is an aggregate consisting of several parts, such as bottom, sides, back, etc., and several qualities, such as, sound, smell, taste, colour, touch, etc. There is not a single entity devoid of its several parts or qualities.

[This refers to the Buddhist doctrine which denies a substance apart from its qualities and a whole apart from its parts as is evident from the writings of Nâgârjuna*, Ârya Deva † and others.]

---

* लच्याल्लच्चणमन्यच्चेत् स्यात्तल्लच्यमलच्चणम् ।
तयोरभावोऽनन्यत्वे विष्पष्टं कथितं त्वया ॥
(Mâdhyamika Sûtra. Chap. I, page 64 ; Prof. Poussin's, edition.)
रूपादिव्यतिरेकेण यथा कुम्भो न विद्यते ।
वाख्वादिव्यतिरेकेण तथा रूपो न विद्यते ॥ इति ॥
(Mâdhyamika Sûtra, Chap. I, page 71 ; Poussin's edition.)
† सर्व एव घटोऽद्दष्टो रूपे द्दष्टे हि जायते ।
ब्रूयात् कस्तच्चविन्नाम घटः प्रलच्च इत्यपि ॥
एतेनैव विचारेण सुगन्धि मधुरं मृदु ।
प्रतिषेधयितव्यानि सर्वाण्युत्तमबुद्धिना ॥
(Śataka quoted in the Mâdhyamikâ Vritti, p. 71.)

नानेकलच्चगैरेकभावनिष्पच्चे: ॥४॥१॥३५॥

35. These are, we reply, not so because by several marks one single entity is constituted.—35.

The Naiyâyika says that there is certainly a substance apart from its qualities and a whole apart from its parts, *e.g.*, we must admit an entity called jar as the substratum of its several qualities, such as colour, smell, etc., and its several parts such as bottom, sides, back, etc.

[The Buddhists* oppose this view by saying that the substance independent of its qualities and the whole independent of its parts admitted by the Naiyâyikas are opposed to reason and cannot be accepted as realities though there is no harm in acknowledging them as "appearances"† for the fulfilment of our practical purposes.]

लच्चण्व्यवस्थानादेवाप्रतिषेध: ॥४॥१॥३६॥

36. There is, moreover, no opposition on account of the very distribution of the marks.—36.

The Naiyâyika says as follows:—Our conclusion is unassailable owing to the marks abiding in one single entity. A jar, for instance, possesses two marks, *viz.*, tangibility and colour, by each of which it can be identified.

If there were no jar beyond its tangibility and colour we could not use such expression as "I see the jar which I touched yesterday." To enable us to ascertain the identity there must be a substance called jar beyond its tangibility and colour which are two distinct qualities belonging to the same substance.

The opponent has said that "all are aggregates." Whence, we ask, does the aggregate arise if there are no units? The very reason given that "each consists of several marks" presupposes an "each" or unity or entity beyond the marks or aggregate.

---

*इह तु काठिन्यादिव्यतिरिक्तपृथिव्याद्यसम्भवे सति न युक्तो विशेषणविशेष्यभावः । तिथि कैन्र्यति-
रिक्तलच्चयाभ्युपगमात्तदनुरोधेन विशेषणाभिधानमदुष्टमितिचेत् । नैतदेवं नहि तिथि कपरिकल्पिता
युक्तिविधुराः पदार्थाः स्वसमयेऽभ्युपगन्तु न्याय्याः । प्रमाणान्तरादेरप्यभ्युपगमप्रसङ्गात् ।

(Mâdhyamikâ Vṛitti, Chap. I. p. 66; Poussin's edition.)

†घटः प्रत्यच्च इत्यत्र तु नहि घटो नाम कश्चिद्योऽप्रलच्चः पृथगुपलब्धो यस्योपचारात्प्रलच्चत्वं स्यात् ॥
नीलादिव्यतिरिक्तस्य घटस्याभावादौपचारिकं प्रलच्चत्वमिति चेत् । एवमपि सुतरामुपचारो न युक्त
उपचर्यमायस्याश्रयस्याभावात् । नहि खरविषारणे तैच्णयमुपचर्यते ।

(Mâdhyamikâ Vṛitti, p. 70, Chap. I; Poussin's edition.)

सर्वमभावो भावेष्वितरेतराभावसिद्धेः ॥४॥१।३७॥

37. All are non-entities because the entities are non-existent in relation to one another.—37.

In the expression " a horse is not a cow " there is the non-existence of " cow " in the " horse " and in the expression " a cow is not a horse " there is the non-existence of " horse " in the " cow." As a fact every thing is non-existent in so far as it is not identical with another thing.

न स्वभावसिद्धेर्भावानाम् ॥४॥१।३८॥

38. It is, we reply, not so because the entities are existent in reference to themselves.—38.

A cow is a cow though it is not a horse : a thing is existent in reference to itself though it is non-existent in so far as it is not another thing.

न स्वभावसिद्धिरापेक्षिकत्वात् ॥४॥१।३९॥

39. Some say, that entities are not self-existent inasmuch as they exist in relation to one another.—39.

The objection is explained as follows :—

A thing is called short only in relation to another thing which is long, and *vice versa* ; the long and short are inter-related.

[This refers to the Mâdhyamikâ Buddhist doctrine*of " relation " according to which all things are inter-dependent and nothing is self-existent.]

व्याहतत्वादयुक्तम् ॥४॥१।४०॥

40. The doctrine, we reply, is unreasonable because it hurts itself.—40.

If the long and short are inter-dependent then neither of them can be established in the absence of the other ; if neither of them is self-existent, then it will be impossible to establish the inter-relation ; and in the absence of all relations the doctrine of the opponent will fall to the ground.

[The Mâdhyamikas say that there is no reality† underlying any

---

*न सम्भवः स्वभावस्य युक्तः प्रलयहेतुभिः ।
स्वभावः कृतको नाम भविष्यति पुनः कथम् ॥
(Mâdhyamikâ Sûtra, Chap. XV, p. 93 ; B. T. Society's edition.)

† शून्यविद'ं नहि विद्यते क्वचित् अन्तरिच्चि शकुनस्य वा पदम् ॥
यन्न विद्यति स्वभावतः क्वचित् सा न जातु परहेतु भविष्यति ॥

(Ârya Ratnâkara Sûtra quoted in Mâdhyamikâ Vṛitti, Chap. I. 24 ; B. T. Society's edition.)

entity, and that the entities exist only by virtue of their mutual relations which are mere illusions. Viewed from the standpoint of absolute truth the world is void, Śûnya,* but measured by the standard of "relation" or "condition" it possesses an apparent existence which serves all our practical purposes.]

सङ्ख्यैकान्तासिद्धिः कारणानुपपत्त्युपपत्तिभ्याम् ॥४।१।४१॥

41. Neither through the reason being given nor through the reason being omitted there is the establishment of the fixity of number.—41.

Some say, that there is only *one* thing (Brahma) pervading all the so-called varieties. Others say, that things are of *two* kinds, viz, the eternal and the non-eternal. Certain philosophers find *three* things viz., the knower, knowledge and the knowable, while others treat of *four* things, viz., the agent of knowledge, means of knowledge, object of knowledge and act of knowledge. In this way the philosophers indulge themselves in a fixed number of things. The Naiyâyikas oppose them by saying that there is no reason to establish the fixity of number. The fixed number is the *Sâdhya* or that which is to be proved and the reason is that which is to prove it. Now is the reason included in the *Sâdhya* or excluded from it? In either case the fixity of number will be unfixed. If, on the other hand, the reason is not different from the *Sâdhya*, there is no means to establish the *Sâdhya*.

न कारणावयवभावात् ॥४।१।४२॥

42. This is, some say, not so, because the reason is a part of the number.—42.

The objection is this :—

The number of things is fixed, and there is no disturbance of the fixity on the score of the reason being included in, excluded from, or identical with, the number for the reason is a part of the number and as such is not different from it.

निरवयवत्वादहेतुः ॥४।१।४३॥

43. The reason, we reply, is not valid because there is no part available for the purpose.—43.

* स्वभावं परभावञ्च भावाभावमेव च ।
ये पश्यन्ति न पश्यन्ते तत्त्वं हि बुद्धशासने ॥
(Mâdhyamika Sûtra, Chap. XV, p. 96 ; B. T. Society's edition.)

The opponent has argued that the number is fixed and that the reason is only a part of it. The Naiyâyika counterargues that the number cannot be fixed until the reason is fixed and it will be absurd to fix the number with an unfixed reason. The reason which is asserted by the opponent to be a part of the number will remain unfixed until the number itself is fixed.

The doctrine of the fixity of number, opposed as it is to the evidences of perception, inference and scripture, is a false doctrine which cannot refute the variety of things established through the speciality of their characters. If there is an agreement as to the number of things on the ground of their general characters, and difference on the ground of their special characters, then the doctrine of fixity is admittedly to be abandoned.

सद्यः कालान्तरे च फलनिष्पत्तेःसंशय : ॥ ४। १। ४४ ॥

44. There arises doubt as to the fruit which is produced either instantly or after a long interval.—44.

Seeing that some action such as *cooking* produces its effect immediately while another action such as *ploughing* does not bring about any effect until sometime has passed away, a certain person asks whether the fruit of maintaining the sacred fire will be produced immediately or after a considerable lapse of time.

न सद्यः कालान्तरोपभोग्यत्वात् ॥४।१।४५॥

45. The fruit, we reply, is not immediate because it is enjoyable after a lapse of time.—45.

The fruit of maintaining the sacred fire is the attainment of heaven which is not possible until the time of death when the soul departs from our body.

कालान्तरेणानिष्पत्तिर्हेतुविनाशात् ॥४।१।४६॥

46. It cannot, says some one, be produced after a lapse of time because the cause has disappeared.—46.

The objection is this :—

The fruit (*viz.*, the attainment of heaven) cannot be produced after our death because the action (*viz.*, maintaining the sacred fire) calculated to produce the fruit was destroyed before our death.

प्राङ्निष्पत्तेर्वृक्षफलवत्तत् स्यात् ॥४।१।४७॥

47. This fruit, before it is produced, bears analogy to the fruit of a tree.—47.

16

Just as a tree, whose roots are now nourished with water, will be able to produce fruits in the future, so the sacred fire which is maintained now will enable the maintainer to attain heaven after death. The doctrine involved here has been explained in aphorism 3-2-64.

नासन्नसन्नसदसदसत्सतोर्वैधर्म्यात् ॥४॥१॥४८॥

48. Some say that the fruit, anterior to its production, is neither existent nor non-existent nor both, because existence and non-existence are incongruous.—48.

The fruit (or any effect) anterior to its production was not non-existent because the material causes are so regulated that each one thing is not produced from each other thing promiscuously. We cannot suppose the fruit to have been existent prior to its production because a thing cannot be said to come into existence if it had already an existence. The fruit was not both existent and non-existent prior to its production because existence and non-existence are incompatible with each other.

[This aphorism refers to the Mâdhyamika Buddhist philosophy which maintains that the effect, before it is produced, is neither existent nor non-existent nor both, as is evident from the writings of Nāgārjuna* and Ârya Deva†.]

उत्पादव्ययदर्शनात् ॥४॥१॥४९॥

49. It is, we reply, a fact that the fruit before it was produced was non-existent because we witness the production and destruction.—49.

When a jar is produced we find that it was non-existent prior to the production.

---

*सतश्च ताबदुत्पत्तिरसतश्च न युज्यसे ।
न सतश्चासतश्चेति पूर्वमेवोपपादितम् ॥
नैवासतो नैव सतः प्रलयार्थस्य युज्यते ।
न सन्नासन्न सदसन् धर्मो निर्वत्ते ते सदा ॥

(Nâgârjuna's Mâdhyamika Sûtra, Chap. VII, p. 51 ; B. T. Society's edition.)

†सदसत्सदसच्चेति यस्य पक्षो न विद्यते ।
उपारम्भश्चिरेणापि तस्य वक्तुञ्च शक्यते ॥

(Ârya Deva's Śataka quoted in the Mâdhyamikâ Vṛitti, Chap. I, p. 4 ; B. T. Society's edition.)

बुद्धिसिद्धन्तु तदसत् ॥४।१।५०॥

50. That it was non-existent, |is established by our understanding.—50.

It is only when a thing is non-existent that we can apply ourselves to the production of it by means of suitable materials. A weaver, for instance, sets himself to work for a web which is non-existent but which, he knows, he can make by means of threads.

आश्रयव्यतिरेकादुब्बृत्तफलोत्पत्तिवदित्यहेतुः॥४।१।५१॥

51. Some say that the analogy to the fruit of a tree is ill-founded because a receptacle is awanting.—51.

It has been stated that the fruit obtainable from maintaining the sacred fire bears analogy to the fruit of a tree. An opponent finds fault with the analogy by showing that the tree which produces fruits now is the same tree which was previously nourished with water, but the body which is alleged to attain heaven after death is not the same body which maintained the sacred fire. The two bodies being different their analogy to the tree is ill-founded.

प्रीतेरात्माश्रयत्वादप्रतिषेधः ॥४।१।५२॥

52. The foregoing objection, we reply, is unreasonable because the soul is the receptacle of happiness.—52.

It is not our body that maintains the sacred fire or attains heaven. In reality the soul is the receptacle for both these acts. The soul which maintained the sacred fire is identical with the soul which enjoys happiness in heaven. Consequently a receptacle is not awanting and the analogy to the tree is not ill-founded.

पुत्रपशुस्त्रीपरिच्छदहिरएयान्नादिफलनिर्देशात् ॥४।१।५३॥

53.—The soul, some say, cannot be the receptacle for the fruits which are mentioned, viz., a son, a wife, cattle, attendants, gold, food, etc.

The objection is this :—

If the fruit consists merely of happiness it can be lodged in the soul. But the soul cannot be the receptacle for such fruits as a son, a wife, cattle, etc. which are mentioned in the scripture.

तत्सम्बन्धात् फलनिष्पत्तेस्तेषु फलवदुपचारः ॥४।१।५४॥

54. The fruit, we reply, is attributed to them because it is produced through their conjunction.—54.

In reality the fruit is happiness. We attribute the name fruit to a son, a wife, etc., because happiness is produced through them.

विविधबाधनायोगाद्दुःखमेव जन्मोत्पत्तिः ॥४।१।५५॥

55. Birth is a pain because it is connected with various distresses.—55.

Birth is stated to be a pain because it signifies our connection with the body, the senses and the intellect which bring us various distresses. The body is the abode in which pain resides, the senses are the instruments by which pain is experienced, and the intellect is the agent which produces in us the feeling of pain. Our birth as connected with the body, the senses and the intellect is necessarily a source of pain.

न सुखस्यान्तरालनिष्पत्तेः ॥४।१।५६॥

56. Pleasure is not denied because it is produced at intervals.—56.

We cannot altogether deny the existence of pleasure which often arises amidst pains.

बाधनाऽनिवृत्तेर्वेदयतः पर्य्येषणदोषादप्रतिषेधः ॥४।१।५७॥

57. This is, we reply, no opposition because distresses do not disappear from a person who enjoys one pleasure and seeks another.—57.

The substance of the Naiyâyika's reply is this :—Pleasure itself is to be regarded as pain because even a person who enjoys pleasure is tormented by various distresses. His objects may be completely frustrated or fulfilled only partially, and while he attains one object he cannot resist the temptation of pursuing another which causes him uneasiness.

दुःखविकल्पे सुखाभिमानाच्च ॥ ४ । १ । ५८ ॥

58. And because there is conceit of pleasure in what is only another name for pain.—58.

Some persons thinking that pleasure is the *summum bonum* are addicted to the world which causes them various distresses through birth, infirmity, disease, death, connection with the undesirable, separation from the desirable, etc. It is therefore clear that one who pursues pleasure does in reality pursue pain, or in other words, pleasure is a synonym for pain.

मृणक्लेशप्रवृत्त्यनुबन्धादपवर्गाभावः ॥ ४ । १ । ५६ ॥

59. There is, some say, no opportunity for us to attain release because of the continual association of our debts, troubles and activities.—59.

The objection stands thus :—The scripture declares that as soon as we are born we incur three debts which we must go on clearing off until the time of our decay and death ; and troubles are our constant companions, while activities pursue us throughout our life. There is then no opportunity for us to attain release.

The three debts are :—

Debt to sages (Rishi-riṇa)—which can be cleared off only by undergoing a course of student life.

Debt to gods (Deva-riṇa)—from which we can be freed only by performing sacrifices.

Debt to our progenitors (Pitṛi-riṇa)—which cannot be cleared off except by begetting children.

Activity has been defined in 1-1-17 and 1-1-18.

प्रधानशब्दानुपपत्तेर्गुणशब्देनानुवादो निन्दाप्रशंसोपपत्तेः ॥
४ । १ । ६०

60. If an expression is inadmissible in its literal sense we are to accept it in its secondary meaning to suit blame or praise.—60.

"As soon as a person is born he incurs three debts"—this expression, inadmissible as it is in its literal sense, is to be taken in its secondary meaning, viz., " as soon as a person enters the life of a householder, he incurs three debts the clearing off of which brings him credit." The expression " until the time of our decay and death " signifies that " as long as we do not arrive at the fourth stage when we are to adopt the life of a mendicant." If the scriptural texts are interpreted in this way, it becomes clear that our whole life does not pass away in the mere clearing off of our debts.

अधिकाराच्च विधानं विद्यान्तरवत् ॥ ४ । १ । ६१ ॥

61. An injunction must be appropriate to its occasion just as a topic must be appropriate to the treatise which deals with it.—61.

A treatise on Logic which is to deal with its own special problems cannot be expected to treat of etymology and syntax which form the subject of a separate treatise. A sacred book which professes to deal with the life of a householder can appropriately bestow every encomium on him. A certain Vedic text extols *karma* by saying that immortality is attained by the force of one's own acts, while another text lays down as a compliment to asceticism that immortality cannot be attained except through renunciation. Some text declares emphatically that it is by the knowledge of Brahma alone that one can attain immortality, there is no other way to it. There are again certain texts which attach an equal importance to study, sacrifice and charity each of which is to be performed by us at the different stages of our life. Hence a text which aims at extolling the life of a householder can, without creating any misapprehension in us, lay down that as soon as we are born we incur ·three debts which we must go on clearing off until the time of our decay and death.

समारोपणादात्मन्यप्रतिषेधः ॥ ४ । १ । ६२ ॥

62. There is no lack of opportunity for our release because the sacrifices (to be performed for clearing off our debts) are trusted to the soul.—62.

A Brahman, while old, should refrain from all searches after sons, wealth and retinue. Sruti (Veda) instructs him to retire from the world when he has trusted to his soul the sacrifices which he used to perform to clear off his debts. By so doing he will imagine that his soul is the sacrificial fire in which his physical actions are offered as oblations. Freed from all debts, he will live on alms and find an ample opportunity for effecting his own release.

As regards the division of life into four stages, there is the authority of Itihâsa, Purâna and Dharma Sâstra.

सुषुप्तस्य स्वप्नादर्शने क्लेशाभाववदपवर्गः ॥ ४ । १ । ६३ ॥

63. As there is no distress in a person who is sound asleep and sees no dream, so there is no association of troubles in one who attains release.—63.

A person who has, through the knowledge of Brahma, attained release, is freed from all bonds of lust, pleasure, pain, etc.

[The word *kleśa* (here rendered as trouble) is a technical term very extensively used in the Buddhist Sanskrit and Pâli literature to signify depravity, defilement, corruption or passion. *Kleśa*, called in Pali *kileso*, is the cause of all sinful actions and consequently of re-births. Arhatship consists in the annihilation of *kleśa*. The Pâli Piṭakas enumerate ten *kileśas*, of which five are prominent. The ten *kileśas* are :—

लोभो (greed), दोसो (hatred), मोहो (stupidity), मानो (pride), दिट्ठि (heretical view), विचिकिच्छा (doubt), थीनम् (sloth), उद्धच्चम् (arrogance), अहिरिका (shamelessness) and अनोत्तप्पम् (recklessness).

The Buddhist Sanskrit books enumerate six *kleśas* and twenty-four *upakleśas*.

षट्क्लेशाः ॥

रागः प्रतिघो मानोऽविद्या कुदृष्टिर्विचिकित्सा चेति ॥

(Dharmasaṁgraha LXVII.)

चतुर्विंशतिरुपक्लेशाः । तद्यथा ॥

क्रोध उपनाहो म्रक्षः प्रदाश ईर्ष्या मात्सर्यं शाठ्यं माया मदो विहिंसाह्रीरन-पत्रपा स्त्यानमश्राद्धं कौसीद्यं प्रमादो मुषितस्मृतिर्विक्षेपोऽसंप्रजन्यं कौकृत्यं मिद्धं वितर्को विचारश्चेति ॥

(Dharmasaṁgraha LXIX.)

The word *kleśa* used in the Nyâya Sûtra 4-1-59, 4-1-63, 4-1-64 and 4-1-65 evidently conveys the meaning of moral depravity. *Hina-kleśa* (हीनक्लेश) used in 4-1-64 rings in my ears as a phrase borrowed from the Buddhist philosophy.]

न प्रवृत्तिः प्रतिसन्धानाय हीनक्लेशस्य ॥ ४ । १ । ६४ ॥

64. The activity of one who has got rid of the troubles does not tend to obstruction.—64.

Activity does not present any obstacle to release (apavarga) in respect of a person who is freed from the troubles of lust, hatred and stupidity. In his case activity produces neither merit nor demerit, and consequently no re-birth.

न क्लेशसन्ततेः स्वाभाविकत्वात् ॥ ४ । १ । ६५ ॥

65. There is, some say, no end of troubles because these are natural.—65.

The objection raised here is this:—None can attain release because it is impossible to get rid of troubles which are natural (beginningless).

प्रागुत्पत्तेरभावानित्यत्ववत्स्वाभाविकेऽप्यनित्यत्वम् ॥४॥१॥६६॥

66. Even the natural, says some one, are non-eternal like the non-existence that was antecedent to production.—66.

The objection raised in the previous aphorism is answered by some one as follows :—

A non-existence antecedent to production is natural (beginningless) but it disappears as soon as the production takes place. Similarly the troubles are natural (beginningless) but they terminate as soon as release is attained.

A jar before it is produced is non-existent. This non-existence is called antecedent non-existence. It has no beginning but it has an end for it disappears as soon as the jar is produced. The troubles like the antecedent non-existence are beginningless but not endless.

[It is only an existence, that is, an existent thing that can be called eternal or non-eternal. We cannot apply the epithets " eternal " and " non-eternal " to non-existence except in a figurative sense.]

अणुश्यामताऽनित्यत्ववद्वा ॥ ४ । १ । ६७ ॥

67. Or non-eternal like the blackness of an atom.—67.

An earthy atom, which is naturally black, changes its colour when it is baked red in the kiln. Likewise the troubles which are natural disappear as soon as release is attained.

न सङ्कल्पनिमित्तत्वाच्च रागादीनाम् ॥ ४ । १ । ६८ ॥

68. It is, we reply, not so because affection etc. are caused by misapprehension.—68.

The Naiyâyika says :—There is no necessity for us here to admit that a thing which is natural (beginningless) may not be endless. The troubles are not in fact natural (beginningless) because they are caused by activity which springs from our affection, aversion and stupidity. These last are generated by our misapprehension. The troubles not being natural, there is no lack of opportunity for us to attain release.

BOOK IV —CHAPTFR II.

दोषनिमित्तानां तत्त्वज्ञानादहङ्कारनिवृत्तिः ॥ ४ । २ । १ ॥

69. Through knowledge about the true nature of the causes of faults, there is cessation of egotism—1.

Egotism is a stupidity of the form "I am." It consists of the notion "I am," entertained by a person who is devoid of self. It disappears as soon as we attain knowledge about the true nature of the faults which are caused by all objects such as body etc. enumerated in aphorism 1—1—9.

दोषनिमित्तं रूपादयो विषयाः सङ्कल्पकृताः ॥ ४।२।२ ॥

70. The colour and other objects, when regarded as good, become the causes of faults—2.

It is only when we look upon colour or any other object as a source of enjoyment that it becomes a cause of our affection, aversion or stupidity.

तन्निमित्तान्त्ववयव्यभिमानः ॥ ४ । २ । ३ ॥

71. The faults are caused through a conception of the *whole* apart from its *parts.*—3.

The faults are produced if a man or woman looks upon each other as a *whole, viz.,* as a male or female with all his or her paraphernalia of teeth, lips, eyes, nose, etc., together with their secondary marks ; and they are shunned if he or she looks upon each other by *parts* only, *viz.,* upon his or her hair, flesh, blood, bone, nerve, head, phlegm, bile, excrement etc., all of which are frail. The notion of the *whole* engenders lust while that of the *parts* produces equanimity. We must regard every thing from the standpoint of evil *e. g.* the rice boiled with poison is looked upon by a wordly man as rice and by an ascetic as poison.

विद्याऽविद्याद्वैविध्यात् संशयः ॥ ४ । २ । ४ ॥

72. Owing to the apprehension and non-apprehension being each of two kinds, there arises a doubt as to the existence of a whole apart from its parts. —4.

There are two kinds of apprehension, *viz.,* real and unreal. The apprehension of water in a tank is real while that of mirage as a mass of water is unreal. The non-apprehension is also of two kinds, *viz.,* real and unreal. The non-apprehension of a hare's horn (which is non-existent) is a real non-apprehension while that of the ether (which is existent) is an unreal non-apprehension. The apprehension and non-apprehension being both real and unreal there arises a doubt as to whether there is really a whole apart from its parts. If we apprehend a whole apart from its parts, our apprehension may be unreal. If we do not apprehend a whole, our non-apprehension too may be unreal.

तदसंशयः पूर्वहेतुप्रसिद्धत्वात् ॥ ४ । २ । ५ ॥

73. There is no room for doubt with regard to the existence of a whole already established through arguments. —5.

No one has yet set aside the arguments employed in aphorism 2—1—34 to establish a whole apart from its parts.

वृत्त्यनुपपत्तेरपि तर्हि न संशयः ॥ ४ । २ । ६ ॥

74. There is, says some one, no room for doubt even with regard to the non-existence of a whole on account of the impossibility of the whole residing any where.—6.

In the preceding aphorism the Naiyâyika has said that there is no doubt as to the existence of a whole apart from its parts as demonstrated in aphorism 2—1—34. In the present aphorism his opponent says that there is no doubt as to the non-existence of a whole apart from its parts because neither the whole can reside in its parts nor the latter in the former. One affirms that there is a whole while the other affirms that there is no whole. In either case there is no room for doubt.

कृत्स्नैकदेशावृत्तित्वादवयवानामवयव्यभावः ॥ ४ । २ । ७ ॥

75. There is, says the objector, no whole because its parts reside in it neither totally nor partially.—7.

A part does not occupy the whole in its totality owing to the difference of their dimensions; neither does it occupy the whole partially because the part can reside neither in itself nor in another part.

तेषु चावृत्तेरवयव्यभावः ॥ ४ । २ । ८ ॥

76. Also because the whole does not, continues the objector, reside in its parts.—8.

The whole does not reside in each of its parts separately on account of the difference of their dimensions. Neither does it reside in some of its parts collectively because in that case it loses its connection with the other parts.

पृथक् चावयवेभ्योऽवृत्तेः ॥ ४ । २ । ९ ॥

77. Owing to the lack of residence, affirms the objector, there is no whole apart from its parts.—9.

The *whole* does not exist as the relation between it and its parts is not that of the container and the contained.

न चावयव्ययवाः ॥ ४ । २ । १० ॥

78. And the parts are not the whole.—10.

The objector says that the relation between the whole and its parts is not that of identity. No one says that the thread is the web or the pillar is the house.

एकस्मिन् भेदाभावाच्चेदशब्दप्रयोगानुपपत्तेरप्रश्नः ४ । २ । ११ ॥

79. There is, we reply, no room for the question owing to the impropriety in the use of the term "variety" in reference to what is *one*.—11.

In aphorism 4—2—7 an opponent raised the question as to whether the whole occupied its parts totally or partially. The Naiyâyika disposes of the question by saying that there is no room for it because the terms "totally" and "partially" cannot be applied to "*one*." The term "totally" is employed only in the case of several things of which no one has been left out while the word "partially" refers to an aggregate of which some parts have been left out. Now, neither the term "totally" nor the term "partially" is applicable to what is "one", that is, to a "whole." In the case of a whole the employment of language implying variety is unjustifiable.

अवयवान्तरभावेप्यवृत्तेरहेतुः ॥ ४ । २ । १२ ॥

80. The question, we further reply, is unreasonable because even if one part could be the residence of another part, it would not be the residence of the *whole*.—12.

When we speak of a whole residing in its parts we must not understand that the term residence refers to any space, in fact it refers to the relation of refuge and refugee. A refuge is that with which the refugee is inseparably, connected and without which it can never exist. Hence there is no impossibility of the whole residing in its parts.

केशसमूहे तैमिरिकोपलब्धिवत्तदुपलब्धिः ॥ ४ । २ । १३ ॥

81. The perception of a "whole" bears analogy to that of a collection of hairs by a person affected with a dimness of sight.—13.

Just as a person of dim sight cannot perceive hairs separately but can perceive them in a mass, so we cannot perceive the atoms separately but can perceive them in a mass in the form of a jar or the like.

स्वविषयानतिक्रमेणेन्द्रियस्य पटुमन्दभावाद्विषयग्रहणस्य
तथाभावो नाविषये प्रवृत्तिः ॥ ४ । २ । १४ ॥

82.　A sense is inoperative in reference to what is not its object because its acuteness or dullness of apprehension is restricted to its own object which it cannot transcend.—14.

The eye, whether it is acute or dim, cannot apprehend a sound. Similarly the ear, sharp or dull, cannot see a colour. All senses have their special objects to which their operation is restricted. An atom which is supersensuous, cannot be apprehended by any of our senses—no matter whether these are acute or dim. Each hair being perceptible, its collection also is capable of being perceived whereas the atoms being imperceptible their collection cannot be perceived. As we can perceive the collection of atoms in the shape of a jar or the like, we must admit that the collection or the whole is a reality independent of its parts (the atoms).

अवयवावयविप्रसङ्गश्चैवमाप्रलयात् ॥ ४ । २ । १५ ॥

83.　The whole and its parts should in that case be supposed to continue up to the time of annihilation.—15.

Even if we admit the existence of a whole and its parts, we cannot suppose them to continue for ever because they are subject to destruction at the time of annihilation. A whole has got its parts and the parts again have their parts which do not cease until they become non-existent at the time of annihilation.

न प्रलयोऽणुसद्भावात् ॥ ४ । २ । १६ ॥

84.　There is, we reply, no annihilation because there are atoms.—16.

There will never come a time when there will be an utter annihilation, for things will even then continue to exist in the state of atoms. An atom is a thing of the smallest dimension, that is, a thing which is not capable of being of smaller dimension,

परं वा त्रुटेः ॥ ४ । २ । १७ ॥

85. An atom is that which is not capable of being divided.—17.

An atom is not divisible into further parts.

[Two atoms make a *dvyaṇuka* (dyad) and three *dvyaṇukas* make a *tryasareṇu* (triad). All things which we perceive are composed of *tryasreṇus*. An atom (aṇu) is finer than a *dvyaṇuka* and the latter finer than a *tryasareṇu*.]

आकाशव्यतिभेदात् तदनुपपत्तिः ॥ ४ । २ । १८ ॥

86. There is, says some one, an impossibility of such a thing, as it is divided throughout by ether.—18.

The Naiyâyika defines the atom as a whole which has no parts, that is, a thing which is not divisible into further parts. Some one controverts the definition by saying that an atom is not devoid of parts because it is intersected by ether *within* and *without*.

आकाशासर्व्वगतत्वं वा ॥ ४ । २ । १६ ॥

87. Else there would not be the omnipresence of the ether.—19.

The ether would not be called omnipresent if it could not reside within the atoms.

अन्तर्बहिश्च कार्य्यद्रव्यस्य कारणान्तरवचनादकार्य्ये तदभावः ॥ ४ । २ । २० ॥

88. There is no "within" or "without" of an eternal thing. The terms are applicable only to factitious things inasmuch as they imply constituents other than those which are seen.—20.

The word "within" refers to that constituent of a thing which is enclosed by another constituent thereof while the word "without" refers to that constituent which encloses another constituent, but is not enclosed by it. These terms cannot be applied to eternal things such as atoms which do not possess constituents some of which may enclose the rest.

सर्व्वसंयोगशब्दविभवाच्च सर्व्वगतम् ॥ ४ । २ । २१ ॥

89. The ether is omnipresent because of the universality of its conjunction which is a cause of sound.—21.

Owing to sound being produced everywhere it is inferred that the ether is omnipresent. If a certain place were devoid of contact with ether there would be no sound there. There is in fact a conjunction of ether everywhere.

अव्यूहाविष्टम्भविभुत्वानि चाकाशधर्माः ॥ ४ । २ । २२ ॥

90. The ether possesses three properties; *viz.* that it is not repelled, that it does not obstruct and that it is all-pervading.—22.

The ether is not repelled because it does not possess any form, it does not obstruct because it is intangible, and it is all-pervading because it is omnipresent.

मूर्तिमताश्च संस्थानोपपत्तेरवयवसद्भावः ॥ ४ । २ । २३ ॥

91. There are, says some one, parts in an atom because a thing that is endowed with a form must also possess a collocation of parts.—23.

The objection stands thus :—

An atom is divisible into parts because it possesses a form, that is, it is of a limited dimension.

The ether, soul, space and time being of unlimited dimensions are not divisible into parts.]

संयोगोपपत्तेश्च ॥ ४ । २ । २४ ॥

92. An atom, continues the objector, must possess parts because it is capable of being conjoined with another atom.—24.

The objection is this :—

The fact that atoms possess the quality of conjunction proves that they have parts, because an atom can come in conjunction with another only in some of its parts.

अनवस्थाकारित्वादनवस्थानुपपत्तेश्चाप्रतिषेधः ॥ ४ । २ । २५ ॥

93. The doctrine of the indivisibility of atoms cannot, we reply, be refuted because such a refutation would give rise to a *regressus ad infinitum* which is not proper.—25.

If you say that an atom is divisible into parts, you will have to admit that those parts again are divisible into further parts. This would give rise to a *regressus ad infinitum* which should, if possible, be avoided. If all things were indefinitely divisible we should find a large thing and a small one to be of equal dimensions as both possess an infinite number of parts. A thing although indefinitely divided should not lose itself. There must remain a particle, *viz*, an atom which should not perish even at the time of annihilation.

बुद्ध्या विवेचनात्तु भावानां याथात्म्यानुपलब्धिस्तन्त्वपकर्षणे पटसद्भावानुपलब्धिवत् तदनुपलब्धिः ॥ ४ । २ । २६ ॥

94. Things, some say, do not possess a reality if they are separated from our thoughts, just as there is no reality in a web separated from its threads.—22.

The objection is this :—

Things do not possess a reality independent of our thoughts just as a web does not possess a reality independent of its threads. Hence it is our thoughts alone that are real, the external things are all unreal [This aphorism refers to the doctrine of the Yogâcâra Buddhist philosophy explained in the Laṅkâvatâra Sûtra].*

व्याहतत्वादहेतुः ॥ ४ । २ । २७ ॥

95. The reason, we reply, is not good as it hurts itself.—27.

The Naiyâyika says that his opponent's reason, *viz*, that things do not possess a reality if they are separated from our thoughts, is self-destructive because if things are capable of being separated from our thoughts they cannot be said to be unreal, and on the other hand if things are unreal they are incapable of being separated from our thoughts. The opponent commits a contradiction by saying that things are unreal and at the same time by going to separate them from our thoughts.

तदाश्रयत्वादपृथग्ग्रहणम् ॥ ४ । २ । २८ ॥

96. There is, we reply, no separate perception of a refuge and its refugee.—28.

*बुद्ध्या विविच्यमानानां स्वभावो नावधार्य्यते ।
यस्मात् तस्माद् अनभिलाप्यास्ते निःस्वभावाश्च देशिताः ।
(लंकावतार सूत्र, २ परिवर्त्ते, पृष्ठ ५०)
बुद्ध्या विविच्यमानानां स्वभावो नावधार्य्यते ।
यस्मादनभिलाप्यास्ते निःस्वभावाश्च देशिताः ॥
लंकावतार सूत्र १० परिवर्त्ते, पृ० ११५ ॥

A web being the refuge of its threads, the perception of the former includes that of the latter so that there are no separate perceptions of them. If our thoughts were the refuge of external things, then there would be no separate perceptions of them. But the opponent's argument *viz.*, that "if things are separated from our thoughts," makes it manifest that our thoughts are not the refuge of external things.

प्रमाणतश्चार्थप्रतिपत्तेः ॥ ४ । २ । २९ ॥

97.   And things are established by evidences.—29.

The reality of things is proved by evidences such as perception. Every thing requires an evidence for its establishment. The very assertion that "things are not real if they cannot be separated from our thoughts" must be based on an evidence if it is to commend itself to our acceptance. Hence we cannot deny things if they are established by evidences.

प्रमाणानुपपत्त्युपपत्तिभ्याम् ॥ ४ । २ । ३० ॥

98.   The non-reality of things is demonstrated neither by evidences nor without them.—30.

The proposition that "there is nothing" cannot be proved in any way. If you say that there is an evidence to prove it, you hurt your own proposition, *viz*, that, there is nothing. If again you say that there is no evidence, how do you then establish your proposition?

स्वप्नविषयाभिमानवदयं प्रमाणप्रमेयाभिमानः ॥ ४ । २ । ३१ ॥

99.   The concept of the means and the objects of knowledge, says some one, bears analogy to that of things in a dream.—31.

The means and the objects of knowledge are as delusive as things appearing in a dream.

[The aphorisms 4-2-31 and 4-2-32 evidently refer to the Buddhist doctrine of "non-reality" expounded in the Ârya-Upâli-pricchâ, Samâdhi-râja-sûtra, Ârya-gagana-gañja-sûtra, Mâdhyamika-sûtra, Ârya-ratnâvalî, Lalitavistara-sûtra and other Mahâyâna works.*]

---

* यथा माया यथा स्वप्नो गन्धर्ब्बनगरं यथा ।
तथोत्पादस्तथा स्थानं तथा भङ्ग उदाहृतम् ॥ (Mâdhyamika-Sûtra, Chap. VII.)
यथैव गन्धर्ब्बपुरं मरीचिका यथैव माया सुपिनं यथैव ।
स्वभावशून्या तु निमित्तभावना तथोपमान् जानत सर्व्वधर्म्मान् ।
                          (Quoted in Mâdhyamikâ Vritti, p. 57).
माया मरीचि समो हि विकल्पः । (Ârya-Upâlipriccha, quoted in M. V. 63)
मायोपमा गगनविद्युसमोदकचन्द्रसन्निभमरीचिसमाः । (Ârya-Samâdhirâja-Bhat-
                          târaka quoted in Mâdhyamikâ Vritti, Chap. XXI.)

मायागन्धर्व्वनगरमृगतृष्णिकावद्धा ॥ ४ । २ । ३२ ॥

100. It may, continues the objector, be likened to jugglery, the city of the celestial quiristers or a mirage.—32.

The means and the objects of knowledge are as unreal as things exhibited in jugglery, etc.

हेत्वभावादसिद्धिः ॥ ४ । २ । ३३ ॥

101. This cannot, we reply, be proved, as there is no reason for it.—33.

There is no reason that the concept of the means and the objects of knowledge should bear an analogy to the concept of things in a dream but not to that of things in our wakeful state. If you, to prove the unreality of things in a dream, adduce the reason that these are not perceived in our wakeful state, we would, to prove the reality of the means and the objects of knowledge, adduce the reason that these are perceived in our wakeful state.

स्मृतिसङ्कल्पवच्च स्वप्नविषयाभिमानः ॥ ४ । २ । ३४ ॥

102. The concept of things in a dream arises in the same way as remembrance and imagination.—34.

The things that appear in a dream are not unreal. We can conceive of them in a dream just as we can do in our wakeful state. Our concept of things in the dream is due to our memory and imagination.

It is by a reference to the knowledge in our wakeful condition, that we ascertain our knowledge in the dream to be unreal. But in the event of there being only one condition, viz., that of wakefulness, the analogy to the dream would not be appropriate.

मिथ्योपलब्धिविनाशस्तत्त्वज्ञानात् स्वप्नविषयाभिमानप्रणाश-
वत् प्रतिबोधे ॥ ४ । २ । ३५ ॥

103. Our false apprehension is destroyed by a knowledge of the truth, just as our concept of objects in a dream comes to an end on our awaking.—35.

In the case of jugglery, the city of the celestial quiristers and the mirage, our apprehension, if it is false, consists of our imputing "that" to what is "not that" just as when we mistake a post for a man. The objects of the apprehension are, however, not unreal, inasmuch as they arise from our memory and imagination.

18

Jugglery (mâyâ) consists of a false apprehension produced in others by an artificer through the use of materials similar to those originally announced by him.

Just as our concept of objects in a dream passes away as soon as we are awake, so also our false apprehension of objects disappears as soon as we attain a true knowledge of those objects.

बुद्धेश्चैवं निमित्तसद्भावोपलम्भात् ॥ ४ । २ । ३६ ॥

104. There is therefore no denial of false knowledge, inasmuch as we perceive that there is a cause for that knowledge.—36.

It has already been shown that our *concept* of objects in a dream is unreal, inasmuch as we do not actually perceive them at that time, but that the *objects* of the dream are not unreal, inasmuch as they arise from our memory and imagination. In fact, the objects that give rise to false knowledge are never unreal, although the knowledge itself may be false.

तत्त्वप्रधानभेदाच्च मिथ्याबुद्धेर्द्वैविध्योपपत्तिः ॥ ४ । २ । ३७ ॥

105. And false knowledge involves a two-fold character on account of the distinction between the essence and appearance of its object.—37.

When we mistake a post for a man, our knowledge assumes the form "that is man." Our knowledge of the post, in so far as it is called "that" is a true knowledge, but in so far as it is described as "man" is a false knowledge. This falsity of knowledge is due to our recognition of certain properties common to the post and the man.

समाधिविशेषाभ्यासात् ॥ ४ । २ । ३८ ॥

106. The knowledge of truth is rendered habitual by a special practice of meditation.—38.

Meditation is the soul's union with the mind abstracted from the senses whose contact with objects does not produce any perception. The knowledge of the truth is rendered habitual by the repeated practice of this meditation.

नार्थविशेषप्राबल्यात् ॥ ४ । २ । ३६ ॥

107. Meditation, some say, is not practicable by reason of the predominance of certain external objects.—39.

There are innumerable obstacles to meditation, *e. g.*, hearing the thundering noise of a cloud, one is prevented from practising meditation,

नुधादिभिः प्रवर्त्तनाच्च ॥ ४ । २ । ४० ॥

108. And by reason of our being impelled to action by hunger, etc.—40.

Hunger and thirst, heat and cold, disease, etc., sometimes prevent us from practising meditation.

पूर्वकृतफलानुबन्धात् तदुत्पत्तिः ॥ ४ । २ । ४१ ॥

109. It arises, we reply, through possession of the fruits of our former works.—41.

We acquire a habit of practising meditation in consequence of our good deeds of a previous life.

अरएयगुहापुलिनादिषु योगाभ्यासोपदेशः ॥ ४ । २ । ४२ ॥

110. We are instructed to practise meditation in such places as a forest, a cave or a sand-bank.—42.

The meditation practised in these places is not seriously disturbed by any obstacle.

अपवर्गेऽ प्येवं प्रसङ्गः ॥ ४ । २ । ४३ ॥

111. Such possibilities may occur even in release. —43.

Even a person who has attained release may be disturbed by the violence of an external object.

न निष्पन्नावश्यम्भावित्वात् ॥ ४ । २ । ४४ ॥

112. It is, we reply, not so, because knowledge must spring up only in a body already in the state of formation. —44.

A violent external object produces knowledge only in a body which has been formed, in consequence of our previous deeds and which is endowed with senses, etc.

तदभावश्चापवर्गे ॥ ४ । २ । ४५ ॥

113. And there is absence of a body in our release. —45.

Our merits and demerits having already been exhausted, we cannot get a body after we have attained release. Release is the perfect freedom from all sufferings : it consists in a complete destruction of all the seeds and seats of suffering.

तदर्थं यमनियमाभ्यामात्मसंस्कारो योगाच्चाध्यात्मविध्यु-
पायैः ॥ ४ । २ । ४६ ॥

114.   For that purpose there should be a purifying of
our soul by abstinence from evil and observance of certain
duties as well as by following the spiritual injunctions
gleaned from the Yoga institute.—46.

In order to attain release we must practise meditation after our soul
has been purified by our abstinence, etc. The injunctions gleaned from
the Yoga institute refer to penances, the controlling of our breaths, the
fixing of our mind, etc.

ज्ञानग्रहणाभ्यासस्तद्विद्यैश्च सह संवादः ॥ ४ । २ । ४७ ॥

115.   To secure release, it is necessary to study and
follow this treatise on knowledge as well as to hold discussions with those learned in that treatise.—47.

The spiritual injunctions furnished by the Yoga institute cannot be
properly assimilated unless we have already acquired a true knowledge
of the categories explained in the Nyâya Sâstra. It is therefore very
useful to study the Nyâya Sâstra and to hold discussions with persons
learned in the Sâstra.

तं   शिष्यगुरुसब्रह्मचारिविशिष्टश्रेयोर्थिभिरनसूयिभिर-
भ्युपेयात् ॥ ४ । २ । ४८ ॥

116.   One should enter upon discussions with unenvious persons, such as disciples, preceptors, fellow-students
and seekers of the *summum bonum.*—48.

The epithet " unenvious " excludes those who do not seek truth but
desire victory. Discussion has been defined in aphorism 1—2—1.

प्रतिपत्तिहीनमपि वा प्रयोजनार्थमर्थित्वे ॥ ४ । २ । ४९ ॥

117.   In case of a necessity for the search of truth,
discussion may be held even without an opposing side.—49.

A person desirous of knowledge may submit his views for examination by simply expressing his curiosity for truth without an attempt
to establish the views.

तत्त्वाध्यवसायसंरचणार्थं जल्पवितरडे वीजप्ररोहसंरच-
णार्थं करटकशाखावरणवत् ॥ ४ । २ । ५० ॥

118. Wranglings and cavils may be employed to keep up our zeal for truth just as fences of thorny boughs are used to safe-guard the growth of seeds.—50.

Certain talkative people propound philosophies which are mutually opposed, while others violate all sense of rectitude out of a bias for their own side. Seeing that these people have not attained true knowledge and are not freed from faults, we may, in our disputation against them, employ wranglings and cavils which do not in themselves deserve any profit or encomium.

BOOK V, CHAPTER I.

साधर्म्यवैधर्म्योत्कर्षापकर्षवर्ण्यावर्ण्य विकल्पसाध्यप्राप्त्य-
प्राप्तिप्रसङ्ग प्रतिदृष्टान्तानुत्पत्ति संशयप्रकरणाहेत्वर्थापत्यविशेषो-
पपत्त्युपलब्ध्यनुपलब्धिनित्यानित्य कार्य्यसमाः ॥ ५ । १ । १ ॥

1. Futilities are as follows :—(1) Balancing the homogeneity, (2) balancing the heterogeneity, (3) balancing an addition, (4) balancing a subtraction, (5) balancing the questionable, (6) balancing the unquestionable, (7) balancing the alternative, (8) balancing the reciprocity, (9) balancing the co-presence, (10) balancing the mutual absence, (11) balancing the infinite regression, (12) balancing the counter-example, (13) balancing the non-produced, (14) balancing the doubt, (15) balancing the controversy, (16) balancing the non-reason, (17) balancing the presumption, (18) balancing the non-difference, (19) balancing the demonstration, (20) balancing the perception, (21) balancing the non-perception, (22) balancing the non-eternality, (23) balancing the eternality and (24) balancing the effect.—1.

Futility, which is a fallacious argument, has been in general terms defined in aphorism 1-2-18. The twenty four kinds of futility enunciated here will each be defined in due course. The fallacious characters of the twenty four kinds will also be exposed in separate aphorisms.

साधर्म्यवैधर्म्याभ्यामुपसंहारे तद्धर्माविपर्य्ययोपपत्तेः
साधर्म्यं वैधर्म्यसमौ ॥ ५ । १ । २ ॥

2. If against an argument based on a homogeneous or heterogeneous example one offers an opposition based on the same kind of example, the opposition will be called "balancing the homogeneity" or "balancing the heterogeneity."—2.

Balancing the homogeneity. A certain person, to prove the non-eternality of sound, argues as follows :—

> Sound is non-eternal,
> because it is a product,
> like a pot.

A certain other person offers the following futile opposition :—

> Sound is eternal,
> because it is incorporeal,
> like the sky.

The argument, *viz.*, sound is non-eternal, is based on the homogeneity of sound with the non-eternal pot on the ground of both being products. The opposition, *viz.*, sound is eternal, is said to be based on the homogeneity of sound with the eternal sky on the alleged ground of both being incorporeal. This sort of opposition, futile as it is, is called " balancing the homogeneity" which aims at showing an equality of the arguments of two sides in respect of the homogeneity of examples employed by them.

Balancing the heterogeneity.—A certain person, to prove the non-eternality of sound, argues as follows :—

> Sound is non-eternal,
> because it is a product,
> whatever is not non-eternal is not a product,
> as the sky.

A certain other person offers a futile opposition thus :—

> Sound is eternal,
> because it is incorporeal,
> whatever is not eternal is not incorporeal,
> as a pot.

The argument, *viz.*, sound is non-eternal, is based on the heterogeneity of sound from the not-non-eternal sky which are mutually incompatible. The opposition, *viz.*, sound is eternal, is said to be based on the heterogeneity of sound from the not-incorporeal pot which are alleged to be incompatible with each other. This sort of opposition, futile as it is, is called " balancing the heterogeneity" which aims at showing an equality of the arguments of two sides in respect of the heterogeneity of examples employed by them.

गोत्वाद्गोसिद्धिवत्तत्सिद्धिः ॥ ५ ॥ १ ॥ ३ ॥

3. That is, we say, to be established like a cow through cowhood (or cow-type).—3.

The Naiyâyika says :--If the opposition referred to in the previous aphorism is to be valid it must be based on the example, homogeneous or heterogeneous, exhibiting a universal connection between the reason and the predicate such as we discern between a cow and cowhood or a universal disconnection between the reason and the absence of the predicate such as we discern between a cow and absence of cowhood. In the argument— " sound is non-eternal, because it is a product, like a pot" the homogeneous example " pot " exhibits a universal connection between productivity and non-eternality, all products being non-eternal ; but in the opposition —" sound is eternal, because it is incorporeal, like the sky"—the homogeneous example sky does not exhibit a universal connection between incorporeality and eternality because there are things, such as intellect or knowledge, which are incorporeal but not eternal. A similar obser-vation is to be made with regard to the opposition called " balancing the heterogeneity." In the opposition " sound is eternal, because it is incor-poreal, whatever is not eternal is not incorporeal, as a pot" the heterogeneous example pot does not exhibit a universal disconnection between incorporeality and absence of eternality because there are things, such as intellect or knowledge, which are incorporeal but not eternal.

साध्यदृष्टान्तयोर्धर्म्मविकल्पादुभयसाध्यत्वाच्चोत्कर्षापक-
र्षवर्ण्यावर्ण्यविकल्पसाध्यसमाः ॥ ५ । १ । ४ ॥

4. The subject and example alternating their charac-ters or both standing in need of proof, there occur (futilities called) " balancing an addition" " balancing a subtraction" " balancing the questionable," " balancing the unquestionable" " balancing the alternative" and " balancing the reciprocity."—4.

Balancing an addition.—If against an argument based on a certain character of the example one offers an opposition based on an additional character thereof, the opposition will be called " balancing an addition."

A certain person, to prove the non-eternality of sound, argues as follows :—

Sound is non-eternal,

because it is a product,

like a pot,

A certain other person offers a futile opposition thus :—

> Sound is non-eternal (and corporeal),
> because it is a product,
> like a pot (which is non-eternal as well as corporeal).

The opponent alleges that if sound is non-eternal like a pot, it must also be corporeal like it : if it is not corporeal let it be also not non-eternal. This sort of futile opposition is called " balancing an addition " which aims at showing an equality of the arguments of two sides in respect of an additional character (possessed by the example and attributed to the subject).

Balancing a subtraction.—If against an argument based on a certain character of the example one offers an opposition based on another character wanting in it, the opposition will be called " balancing a subtraction."

A certain person, to prove the non-eternality of sound, argues as follows :—

> Sound is non-eternal,
> because it is a product,
> like a pot. ·

A certain other person offers the following futile opposition :—

> Sound is non-eternal (but not audible),
> because it is a product,
> like a pot (which is non-eternal but not audible.)

The opponent alleges that if sound is non-eternal like a pot, it cannot be audible, for a pot is not audible ; and if sound is still held to be audible, let it be also not non-eternal. This sort of futile opposition is called " balancing a subtraction " which aims at showing an equality of the arguments of two sides in respect of a certain character wanting in the example (and consequently also in the subject),

Balancing the questionable.—If one opposes an argument by maintaining that the character of the example is as questionable as that of the subject, the opposition will be called " balancing the questionable."

A certain person, to prove the non-eternality of sound, argues as follows :—

> Sound is non-eternal,
> because it is a product,
> like a pot.

19

A certain other person offers a futile opposition thus :—

> A pot is non-eternal,
> because it is a product,
> like sound.

The opponent alleges that if the non-eternality of sound is called in question, why is not that of the pot too called in question, as the pot and sound are both products ? His object is to set aside the argument on the ground of its example being of a questionable character. This sort of futile opposition is called "balancing the questionable" which aims at showing an equality of the arguments of two sides in respect of the questionable character of the subject as well as of the example.

Balancing the unquestionable.—If one opposes an argument by alleging that the character of the subject is as unquestionable as that of the example, the opposition will be called "balancing the unquestionable."

A certain person, to prove the non-eternality of sound, argues as follows : —

> Sound is non-eternal,
> because it is a product,
> like a pot.

A certain other person offers a futile opposition thus :—

> A pot is non-eternal,
> because it is a product,
> like sound.

The opponent alleges that if the non-eternality of a pot is held to be unquestionable, why is not that of sound too held to be so, as the pot and sound are both products ? His object is to render the argument unnecessary on the ground of its subject being of an unquestionable character. This sort of futile opposition is called "balancing the unquestionable" which aims at showing the equality of the arguments of two sides in respect of the unquestionable character of the example as well as of the subject.

Balancing the alternative.—If one opposes an argument by attributing alternative characters to the subject and the example, the opposition will be called "balancing the alternative."

A certain person, to prove the non-eternality of sound, argues as follows :—

> Sound is non-eternal,
> because it is a product,
> like a pot.

A certain other person offers a futile opposition thus :—

Sound is eternal and formless,
because it is a product,
like a pot (which is non-eternal and has forms).

The opponent alleges that the pot and sound are both products, yet one has form and the other is formless : why on the same principle is not one (the pot) non-eternal and the other (sound) eternal? This sort of futile opposition is called "balancing the alternative" which aims at showing an equality of the arguments of two sides in respect of the alternative characters attributed to the subject and example.

Balancing the reciprocity.—If one opposes an argument by alleging a reciprocity of the subject and the example, the opposition will be called "balancing the reciprocity."

A certain person, to prove the non-eternality of sound, argues as follows :—

Sound is non-eternal,
because it is a product,
like a pot.

A certain other person offers a futile opposition thus : —

A pot is non-eternal,
because it is a product,
like sound.

The opponent alleges that the pot and sound being both products, one requires proof for its non-eternality as much as the other does. Sound is to be proved non-eternal by the example of a pot and the pot is to be proved non-eternal by the examples of sound. This leads to a reciprocity of the pot (example) and sound (subject) resulting in no definite conclusion as to the eternality or non-eternality of sound. This sort of futile opposition is called "balancing the reciprocity" which brings an argument to a stand-still by alleging the reciprocity of the subject and the example.

किंचित्साधम्म्यादुपसंहारसिद्धेर्वैधम्म्यादप्रतिषेधः ॥ ५ । १ । ५ ॥

5. This is, we say, no opposition because there is a difference between the subject and the example although the conclusion is drawn from a certain equality of their characters.—5.

The Naiyâyika says :—The futilities called "balancing an addition," "balancing a subtraction," "balancing the questionable," "balancing the unquestionable" and "balancing the alternative" are all based on the false supposition of a complete equality of the subject and the example. Though there is no denial of an equality of the subject and the example in certain characters, there is indeed a great difference between them in other characters.

Sound is non-eternal,

because it is a product,

like a pot.

In this argument although there is an equality of "sound" and "pot" in respect of their being both products, there is a great difference between them in other respects. A cow possesses some characters in common with a *bos gavaeus* but there is no complete identity between them. No body can commit the futilities mentioned above if he bears in mind the equality of the subject and the example only in those characters which are warranted by the reason (middle term). In the case of the futility called "balancing an addition" it is clear that the equality supposed to exist between the pot and sound in respect of corporeality is not warranted by the reason (*viz.* being a product), because there are things, such as intellect or knowledge, which are products but not corporeal. Similarly with regard to the futility called "balancing a subtraction," the reason (*viz.* being a product) does not justify an equality of sound and pot in respect of their being not audible. As regards the futilities called "balancing the questionable" and "balancing the unquestionable," we cannot ignore the difference between the subject and the example without putting an end to all kinds of inference. The futility called "balancing the alternative" introduces an equality between the pot and sound in respect of a character (*viz.* being eternal) which is not warranted by the reason *viz.* being a product.

साध्यातिदेशाच्च दृष्टान्तोपपत्तेः ॥ ५ । १ । ६ ॥

6.   And because the example happens to surpass the subject.—6

The futility called "balancing the reciprocity" is based on the false supposition that the example stands exactly on the same footing as the subject. But that one surpasses the other is evident from aphorism 1-1-25 which states that the example does not stand in need of proof as to its characters.

Sound is non-eternal,

because it is a product,

like a pot.

In this argument sound (the subject) may not be known by some to be non-eternal but a pot (the example) is known by all to be a product as well as non-eternal. "Balancing the reciprocity" is therefore a fallacious argument.

प्राप्य साध्यमप्राप्य वा हेतोः प्राप्त्या अविशिष्टत्वादप्राप्त्या असाधकत्वाच्च प्राप्त्यप्राप्तिसमौ ॥ ५ । १ । ७ ॥

7. If against an argument based on the co-presence of the reason and the predicate or on the mutual absence of them one offers an opposition based on the same kind of co-presence or mutual absence, the opposition will, on account of the reason being non-distinguished from or being non-conducive to the predicate, be called "balancing the co-presence" or "balancing the mutual absence."—7.

Balancing the co-presence.—If against an argument based on the co-presence of the reason and the predicate, one offers an opposition based on the same kind of co-presence, the opposition will, on account of the reason being non-distinguished from the predicate, be called "balancing the co-presence."

A certain person, to prove that there is fire in the hill, argues as follows :—

> The hill has fire,
> because it has smoke,
> like a kitchen.

A certain other person offers a futile opposition thus :—

> The hill has smoke,
> because it has fire,
> like a kitchen.

The arguer has taken the smoke to be the reason and the fire to be the predicate. The opponent raises a question as to whether the smoke is present at the same site which is occupied by the fire or is absent from that site. If the smoke is present with fire at the same site, there remains, according to the opponent, no criterion to distinguish the reason from the predicate. The smoke is, in his opinion, as much a reason for the fire as the fire for the smoke. This sort of futile opposition is called "balancing the co-presence" which aims at stopping an argument on the alleged ground of the co-presence of the reason and the predicate.

Balancing the mutual absence.—If against an argument based on the mutual absence of the reason and the predicate, one offers an opposition based on the same kind of mutual absence, the opposition will, on account of the reason being non-conducive to the predicate, be called " balancing the mutual absence."

A certain person, to prove that there is fire in the hill, argues as follows :—

> The hill has fire,
> because it has smoke,
> like a kitchen.

A certain other person offers a futile opposition thus :—

> The hill has smoke,
> because it has fire,
> like a kitchen.

The opponent asks : "Is the smoke to be regarded as the reason because it is absent from the site of the fire ?" "Such a supposition is indeed absurd." The reason cannot establish the predicate without being connected with it, just as a lamp cannot exhibit a thing which is not within its reach. If a reason unconnected with the predicate could establish the latter, then the fire could be as much the reason for the smoke as the smoke for the fire. This sort of futile opposition is called " balancing the mutual absence " which aims at bringing an argument to a close on the alleged ground of the mutual absence of the reason and the predicate.

घटादिनिष्पत्तिदर्शनात् पीडने चाभिचारादप्रतिषेधः ॥ ५ । १ । ८ ॥

8.   This is, we say, no opposition because we find the production of pots by means of clay as well as the oppression of persons by spells.—8.

A potter cannot produce a pot without getting clay within his reach but an exorcist can destroy persons by administering spells from a distance. Hence it is clear that a thing is accomplished sometimes by the cause being present at its site and sometimes by being absent from it. "Balancing the co-presence " and "balancing the mutual absence " which attach an undue importance to the proximity or remoteness of sites, are therefore totally fallacious arguments.

दृष्टान्तस्य करणानपदेशात् प्रत्यवस्थानाच्च प्रतिदृष्टान्तेन

प्रसङ्गप्रतिदृष्टान्तसमौ ॥ ५ । १ । ९ ॥

9. If one opposes an argument on the ground of the example not having been established by a series of reasons or on the ground of the existence of a mere counter-example, the opposition will be called "balancing the infinite regression" or "balancing the counter-example."—9.

Balancing the infinite regression.—A certain person, to prove the non-eternality of sound, argues as follows :—

Sound is non-eternal,
because it is a product,
like a pot.

A certain other person offers a futile opposition thus :—

If sound is proved to be non-eternal by the example of a pot, how is the pot again to be proved as non-eternal? The reason which proves the non-eternality of the pot is to be proved by further reasons. This gives rise to an infinite regression which injures the proposition "sound is non-eternal" not less than the proposition "sound is eternal." This sort of futile opposition is called "balancing the infinite regression" which aims at stopping an argument by introducing an infinite regression which is said to beset the example.

Balancing the counter-example.—A certain person, to prove the non-eternality of sound, argues as follows :—

Sound is non-eternal,
because it is a product,
like a pot.

A certain other person offers a futile opposition thus :—

Sound is eternal,
like the sky.

The opponent alleges that if sound is held to be non-eternal by the example of a pot, why it should not be held to be eternal by the example of the sky? If the example of the sky is set aside, let the example of the pot too be set aside. This sort of futile opposition is called "balancing the counter-example" which aims at setting aside an argument by the introduction of a counter-example.

प्रदापादानप्रसङ्गनिवृत्तिवत्तद्विनिवृत्तिः ॥ ५ । १ । १० ॥

10. The example does not, we say, require a series of reasons for its establishment just as a lamp does not require a series of lamps to be brought in for its illumination.—10.

The Naiyâyika says :—

An example is a thing the characters of which are well-known to an ordinary man as well as to an expert. It does not require a series of reasons to reveal its own character or to reveal the character of the subject with which it stands in the relation of homogeneity or heterogeneity. In this respect it resembles a lamp which illumines itself as well as the things lying within its reach.

> Sound is non-eternal,
> > because it is a product,
> > > like a pot.

In this argument the pot is the example which is so well-known that it requires no proof as to its being a product or being non-eternal.

Hence the opposition called "balancing the infinite regression" is not founded on a sound basis.

प्रतिदृष्टान्तहेतुत्वे च नाहेतुर्दृष्टान्तः ॥ ५ ॥ १ ॥ ११ ॥

11. The example, we say, cannot be set aside as unreasonable only because a counter-example is advanced as the reason.—11.

The Naiyáyika says :—

The opponent must give a special reason why the counter-example should be taken as specially fitted to lead to a conclusion, and the example should not be taken as such. Until such a special reason is given, the counter-example cannot be accepted as leading to a definite conclusion. In fact a mere counter-example without a reason (middle term) attending it cannot be conducive to any conclusion. Hence we must rely on an example attended by reason but not on a counter-example unattended by reason.

> Sound is eternal,
> > like the sky.

This opposition which is founded on a mere counter-example is therefore to be rejected as unreasonable.

प्रागुत्पत्तेः कारणाभावादनुत्पत्तिसमः ॥ ५ ॥ १ ॥ १२ ॥

12. If one opposes an argument on the ground of the property connoted by the reason being absent from the thing denoted by the subject while it is not yet produced, the opposition will be called "balancing the non-produced."

A certain person, to prove that sound is non-eternal, argues as follows : —

> Sound is non-eternal,
>> because it is an effect of effort,
>> like a pot.

A certain other person offers a futile opposition thus : —

> Sound is eternal,
>> because it is a non-effect of effort,
>> like the sky.

The opponent alleges that the property connoted by the reason, viz., being an effect of effort, is not predicable of the subject, viz., sound (while it is not yet produced). Consequently sound is not non-eternal, it must then be eternal. There is, according to the opponent, an apparent agreement between the two sides as to the sound being non-eternal on account of its being a non-effect-of-effort. This sort of futile opposition is called "balancing the non-produced" which pretends to show an equality of the arguments of two sides assuming the thing denoted by the subject to be as yet non-produced.

तथाभावादुत्पन्नस्य कारणोपपत्तेन कारणप्रतिषेधः ॥५॥१॥१३॥

13. This is, we say, no opposition against our reason so well predicable of the subject which becomes as such only when it is produced.—13.

The Naiyâyika disposes of the futile opposition called "balancing the non-produced" by stating that the subject can become as such only when it is produced, and that there is then no obstacle to the property of the reason being predicated of it. The opposition, viz., "sound (while non-produced) is eternal, because it is not then an effect of effort," carries no weight with it, since we do not take the sound to be the subject before it is produced. Sound, while it is produced, is certainly an effect of effort and as such is non-eternal.

सामान्यदृष्टान्तयोरैन्द्रियकत्वे समाने नित्यानित्यसाधम्यात्
संशयसमः ॥ ५ ॥ १ ॥ १४ ॥

14. If one opposes an argument on the ground of a doubt arising from the homogeneity of the eternal and the non-eternal consequent on the example and its genus (or

type) being equally objects of perception, the opposition will be called " balancing the doubt."—14.

A certain person, to prove the non-eternality of sound, argues as follows :—

> Sound is non-eternal,
>> because it is a product,
>> like a pot.

A certain other person offers a futile opposition thus :—

> Sound is non-eternal or eternal (?)
>> because it is an object of perception,
>> like a pot or pot-ness.

The opponent alleges that sound is homogeneous with a pot as well as pot-ness inasmuch as both are objects of perception ; but the pot being non-eternal and pot-ness (the genus of pots or pot-type) being eternal there arises a doubt as to whether the sound is non-eternal or eternal. This sort of futile opposition is called "balancing the doubt" which aims at rejecting an argument in consequence of a doubt arising from the homogeneity of the eternal and the non-eternal.

साधम्र्यात्संशये न संशयो वैधम्र्यादुभयथा वा संशयेऽ त्यन्तसंशयो नित्यत्वानभ्युपगमाच्च ⁕सामान्यस्याप्रतिषेधः

॥ ५ । १ । १५ ॥

15. This is, we say, no opposition because we do not admit that eternality can be established by the homogeneity with the genus : a doubt that arises from a knowledge of the homogeneity vanishes from that of the heterogeneity, and that which arises in both ways never ends.—15.

The Naiyâyika says :—

Sound cannot be said to be eternal on the mere ground of its homogeneity with pot-ness (the genus of pots or pot-type) but it must be pronounced to be non-eternal on the ground of its heterogeneity from the same in respect of being a product. Though on the score of homogeneity we may entertain doubt as to whether sound is eternal or non-eternal, but on the score of heterogeneity we can pronounce it undoubtedly to be non-eternal. In this case we must bear in mind that we cannot ascertain the true nature of a thing unless we weigh it in

---

* The term *sâmânya* in the sense of "general notion, genus or type" was evidently taken from the Vaiśeṣika philosophy.

respect of its homogeneity with as well as heterogeneity from other things. If even then there remains any doubt as to its true nature, that doubt will never end.

उभयसाधम्म्यात् प्रक्रियासिद्धेः प्रकरणसमः ॥ ५ । १ । १६ ॥

16. " Balancing the controversy " is an opposition which is conducted on the ground of homogeneity with (or heterogeneity from) both sides.—16.

A certain person, to prove the non-eternality of sound, argues as follows :—

Sound is non-eternal,
because it is a product,
like a pot.

A certain other person offers a futile opposition thus :—
Sound is eternal,
because it is audible.
like soundness.

The opponent alleges that the proposition, viz. sound is non-eternal, cannot be proved because the reason, viz., audibility which is homogeneous with both sound (which is non-eternal) and soundness (which is eternal), provokes the very controversy for the settlement of which it was employed. This sort of futile opposition is called " balancing the controversy " which hurts an argument by giving rise to the very controversy which was to be settled.

प्रतिपत्तात् प्रकरणसिद्धेः प्रतिषेधानुपपत्तिः प्रतिपत्तोपपत्तेः ॥ ५ । १ । १७ ॥

17. This is, we say, no opposition because it provokes a controversy which has an opposing side.—17.

The Naiyâyika says :—The opposition called " balancing the controversy " cannot set aside the main argument because it leads to a controversy which supports one side quite as strongly as it is opposed by the other side.

त्रैकाल्यासिद्धेर्हेतोरहेतुसमः ॥ ५ । १ । १८ ॥

18. " Balancing the non-reason " is an opposition which is based on the reason being shown to be impossible at all the three times.—18.

A certain person, to prove the non-eternality of sound, argues as follows : —

Sound is non-eternal,

because it is a product,

like a pot.

Here "being a product" is the reason or sign for "being non-eternal" which is the predicate or significate.

A certain other person offers a futile opposition thus :—

The reason or sign is impossible at all the three times because it cannot precede, succeed, or be simultaneous with the predicate or significate.

(a) The reason (or sign) does not precede the predicate (or significate) because the former gets its name only when it establishes the latter. It is impossible for the reason to be called as such before the establishment of the predicate.

(b) The reason (or sign) does not succeed the predicate (or significate) because what would be the use of the former if it latter existed already.

(c) The reason (or sign) and the predicate (or significate) cannot exist simultaneously for they will then be reciprocally connected like the right and left horns of a cow.

This sort of futile opposition is called "balancing the non-reason" which aims at setting aside an argument by showing that the reason is impossible at all the three times.

न हेतुतः साध्यसिद्धेस्त्रैकाल्यासिद्धिः ॥ ५ । १ । १६ ॥

19. There is, we say, no impossibility at the three times because the predicate or significate is established by the reason or sign.—19.

The Naiyayika says :—The knowledge of the knowable and the establishment of that which is to be established take place from reason which must precede that which is to be known and that which is to be established.

प्रतिषेधानुपपत्तेः प्रतिषेद्धव्याप्रतिषेधः ॥ ५ । १ । २० ॥

20. There is, we further say, no opposition of that which is to be opposed, because the opposition itself is impossible at all the three times.—20.

It being impossible for the opposition to precede, succeed or be simultaneous with that which is to be opposed, the opposition itself is invalid and consequently the original argument holds good.

अर्थापत्तिः प्रतिपचसिद्धेरर्थापत्तिसमः ॥ ५ । १ । २१ ॥

21. If one advances an opposition on the basis of a presumption, the opposition will be called " balancing the presumption."—21.

A certain person, to prove the non-eternality of sound, argues as follows :—

> Sound is non-eternal,
>> because it is a product,
>>> like a pot.

A certain other person offers a futile opposition thus :—
> Sound is presumed to be eternal,
>> because it is incorporeal,
>>> like the sky.

The opponent alleges that if sound is non-eternal on account of its homogeneity with non-eternal things (e.g. in respect of its being a product), it may be concluded by presumption that sound is eternal on account of its homogeneity with eternal things (e.g. in respect of its being incorporeal). This sort of futile opposition is called "balancing the presumption" which aims at stopping an argument by setting presumption as a balance against it.

अनुक्तस्यार्थापत्तेः पचहानेरुपपत्तिरनुक्तत्वादनैकान्तिकत्वाचा-
र्थापत्तेः ॥ ५ । १ । २२ ॥

22 If things unsaid could come by presumption, there would, we say, arise a possibility of the opposition itself being hurt on account of the presumption being erratic and conducive to an unsaid conclusion.—22.

> Sound is eternal,
>> because it is incorporeal,
>>> like the sky.

If by presumption we could draw a conclusion unwarranted by the reason, we could from the opposition cited above draw the following conclusion :—

> Sound is presumed to be non-eternal,
>> because it is a product,
>>> like a pot.

This would hurt the opposition itself. In fact the presumption as adduced by the opponent is erratic. If one says that "sound is non-eternal because of its homogeneity with non-eternal things", the presumption that naturally follows is that "sound is eternal because of its homogeneity with eternal things" and *vice versa*. There is no rule that presumption should be made in one case and not in the case opposed to it ; and in the event of two mutually opposed presumptions no definite conclusion would follow. Hence the opposition called "balancing the presumption" is untenable.

एकधर्मोपपत्तेरविशेषे सर्व्वाविशेषप्रसङ्गात् सद्भावोपपत्ते-
रविशेषसमः ॥ ५ । १ । २३ ॥

23. If the subject and example are treated as non-different in respect of the possession of a certain property on account of their possessing in common the property connoted by the reason, it follows as a conclusion that all things are mutually non-different in respect of the possession of every property on account of their being existent : this sort of opposition is called "balancing the non-difference."—23.

A certain person, to prove the non-eternality of sound, argues as follows :—

> Sound is non-eternal,
> > because it is a product,
> > > like a pot.

A certain other person offers a futile opposition thus :—

If the pot and sound are treated as non-different in respect of non-eternality in consequence of their both being products, it follows as a conclusion that all things are mutually non-different in respect of the possession of every property in consequence of their being existent. Therefore, no difference existing between the eternal and the non-eternal, sound may be treated as eternal. This sort of opposition is called "balancing the non-difference" which aims at hurting an argument by assuming all things to be mutually non-different.

कचिद्धर्म्मानुपपत्तेः कचिच्चोपपत्तेः प्रतिषेधाभावः ॥ ५।१। २४ ॥

24. This is, we say, no opposition because the property possessed in common by the subject and the example

happens in certain instances to abide in the reason while in other instances not to abide in it.—24.

> Sound is non-eternal,
>> because it is a product,
>>> like a pot.

Here the pot and sound possessing in common the property of being a product are treated as non-different in respect of the possession of non-eternality. On the same principle if all things are treated as non-different in consequence of their being existent, we would like to know in what respect they are non-different. If they are treated as non-different in respect of non-eternality, then the argument would stand thus :—

> All things are non-eternal,
>> because they are existent,
>>> like (?)

In this argument " all things" being the subject, there is nothing left which may serve as an example. A part of the subject cannot be cited as the example because the example must be a well-established thing while the subject is a thing which is yet to be established. The argument, for want of an example, leads to no conclusion. In fact all things are not non-eternal since some at least are eternal. In other words, non-eternality abides in some existent things and does not abide in other existent things. Hence all things are not mutually non-different and the opposition called " balancing the non-difference" is unreasonable.

उभयकारणोपपत्तेरुपपत्तिसमः ॥ ५ ॥ १ ॥ २५ ॥

25. If an opposition is offered by showing that both the demonstrations are justified by reasons, the opposition will be called " balancing the demonstration."—25.

A certain person demonstrates the non-eternality of sound as follows :—

> Sound is non-eternal,
>> because it is a product,
>>> like a pot.

A certain other person offers an opposition by the alleged demonstration of the eternality of sound as follows :—

> Sound is eternal,
>> because it is incorporeal,
>>> like the sky.

The reason in the first demonstration supports the non-eternality of sound while that in the second demonstration supports the eternality of sound, yet both the demonstrations are alleged to be right. The opponent advanced the second apparent demonstration as a balance against the first to create a dead lock. This sort of opposition is called " balancing the demonstration."

उपपत्तिकारणाभ्यनुज्ञानादप्रतिषेधः ॥ ५ । १ । २६ ॥

26. This is, we say, no opposition because there is an admission of the first demonstration.—26.

The Naiyáyika says :—

The opponent having asserted that both the demonstrations are justified by reasons, has admitted the reasonableness of the first demonstration which supports the non-eternality of sound. If to avoid the incompatibility that exists between the two demonstrations, he now denies the reason which supports non-eternality we would ask why does he not deny the other reason which supports the eternality of sound, for he can avoid incompatibility by denying either of the reasons. Hence the opposition called " balancing the demonstration " is not well-founded.

निर्दिष्टकारणाभावेऽप्युपलम्भादुपलब्धिसमः ॥ ५ । १ । २७ ॥

27. If an opposition is offered on the ground that we perceive the character of the subject even without the intervention of the reason, the opposition will be called "balancing the perception."—27.

A certain person, to prove the non-eternality of sound, argues as follows :—

> Sound is non-eternal,
> because it is a product,
> like a pot.

A certain other person offers a futile opposition thus :—

Sound can be ascertained to be non-eternal even without the reason that it is a product, for we *perceive* that sound is produced by the branches of trees broken by wind. This sort of opposition is called " balancing the perception " which aims at demolishing an argument by setting up an act of perception as a balance against it.

कारणान्तरादपि तद्धर्मोपपत्तेरप्रतिषेधः ॥ ५ । १ । २८ ॥

28. This is, we say, no opposition because that character can be ascertained by other means as well.—28.

The Naiyáyika says that the argument, *viz.*, " sound is non-eternal, because it is a product, like a pot," implies that sound is proved to be non-eternal through the reason that it is a product. It does not deny other means, such as perception etc., which also may prove sound to be non-eternal. Hence the opposition called "balancing the perception" does not set aside the main argument.

तदनुपलब्धेरनुपलम्भादभावसिद्धौ तद्विपरीतोपपत्तेरनुप-लब्धिसमः ॥ ५ । १ । २९ ॥

29. If against an argument proving the non-existence of a thing by the non-perception thereof, one offers an opposition aiming at proving the contrary by the non-perception of the non-perception, the opposition will be called "balancing the non-perception."—29.

In aphorism 2-2-19 the Naiyâyika has stated that there is no veil which covers sound for we do not perceive such a veil   In aphorism 2-2-20 his opponent has stated that there is a veil because we do not perceive the non-perception thereof.   If the non-perception of a thing proves its non-existence, the non-perception of the non-perception must, in the opinion of the opponent, prove the existence of the thing.   This sort of opposition is called "balancing the non-perception" which aims at counteracting an argument by setting up non-perception as a balance against it.

अनुपलम्भात्मकत्वादनुपलब्धेरहेतुः ॥ ५ । १ । ३० ॥

30. The reasoning through non-perception is not, we say, sound, because non-perception is merely the negation of perception.—30.

The Naiyâyika says :—Perception refers to that which is existent while non-perception to that which is non-existent.   The non-perception of non-perception which signifies a mere negation of non-perception cannot be interpreted as referring to an existent thing.   Hence the opposition called "balancing the non-perception" is not well-founded.

ज्ञानविकल्पानाञ्च भावाभावसंवेदनादध्यात्मम् ॥ ५ । १ । ३१ ॥

31. There is, moreover, an internal perception of the existence as well as of the non-existence of the various kinds of knowledge.—31.

There are internal perceptions of such forms as " I am sure," " I am not sure," " I have doubt," " I have no doubt" etc., which prove that we can perceive the non-existence of knowledge as well as the existence

21

thereof. Hence the non-perception itself is perceptible, and as there is no non-perception of non-perception, the opposition called " balancing the non-perception" falls to the ground.

साधम्म्यांत्तुल्यधम्मोंपपत्तेः सर्व्वांनित्यत्वप्रसङ्गादनित्यसमः ॥

५ । १ । ३२ ॥

32. If one finding that things which are homogeneous possess equal characters, opposes an argument by attributing non-eternality to all things, the opposition will be called " balancing the non-eternality.'—32.'

A certain person, to prove the non-eternality of sound, argues as follows :—

> Sound is non-eternal,
>> because it is a product,
>>> like a pot.

A certain other person offers a futile opposition thus :—

If sound is non-eternal on account of its being homogeneous with a pot which is non-eternal, it will follow as a consequence that all things are non-eternal because they are in some one or other respect homogeneous with the pot—a consequence which will render all inferences impossible for want of heterogeneous examples. This sort of opposition is called " balancing the non-eternal" which seeks to counteract an argument on the alleged ground that all things are non-eternal.

साधम्म्यांदसिद्धेः प्रतिषेधासिद्धिः प्रतिषेध्यसाधम्म्यांच्च ॥

५ । १ । ३३ ॥

33. The opposition, we say, is unfounded because nothing can be established from a mere homogeneity and because there is homogeneity even with that which is opposed.—33.

The Naiyâyika says :—

We cannot ascertain the character of a thing from its mere homogeneity with another thing : in doing so we must consider the logical connection between the reason and the predicate. Sound, for instance, is non-eternal not merely because it is homogeneous with a non-eternal pot but because there is a universal connection between " being a product" and " being non-eternal." Hence it will be unreasonable to conclude that all things are non-eternal simply because they are homogeneous with a non-eternal pot in some one or other respect. Similarly a mere homogeneity of all things with the eternal sky in some one or other respect, does not prove all things to be eternal. The opposition called "balancing the non-eternal" is therefore not founded on a sound basis.

दृष्टान्ते च साध्यसाधनभावेन प्रज्ञातस्य धर्मस्य हेतुत्वा-त्तस्य चोभयथाभावान्नाविशेषः ॥ ५ । १ । ३४ ॥

34.   There is, we say, no non-distinction, because the reason is known to be the character which abides in the example as conducive to the establishment of the predicate and because it is applied in bôth ways.—34.

The Naiyâyika says that we are not justified in concluding that all things are non-eternal because there is no character in respect of which "all things" may be homogeneous with a pot. In order to arrive at a correct conclusion we must consider the reason as being that character of the example (and consequently of the subject) which bears a universal connection with the character of the predicate. The pot possesses no such character in common with "all things." The reason moreover is applied in the homogeneous as well as in the heterogeneous ways. We cannot draw a conclusion from a mere homogeneity of the subject with the example in a certain respect. The opposition called " balancing the non-eternal " is therefore unreasonable.

नित्यमनित्यभावादनित्ये नित्यत्वोपपत्तेर्नित्यसमः ॥ ५ । १ । ३५ ॥

35.   If one opposes an argument by attributing eternality to all non-eternal things on the ground of these being eternally non-eternal, the opposition will be called "balancing the eternal."—35.

A certain person, to prove the non-eternality of sound, argues as follows :—

> Sound is non-eternal,
>   because it is a product,
>   like a pot.

A certain other person offers a futile opposition thus :—You say that sound is non-eternal. Does this non-eternality exist in sound always or only sometimes ? If the non-eternality exists *always*, the sound must also be always existent, or in other words, sound is eternal. If the non-eternality exists only *sometimes*, then too the sound must in the absence of non-eternality be pronounced to be eternal. This sort of opposition is called "balancing the eternal" which counteracts an argument by setting up eternality as a balance against it.

प्रतिषेध्ये   नित्यमनित्यभावादनित्ये   नित्यत्वोपपत्तेः प्रतिषेधाभावः ॥ ५ । १ । ३६ ॥

36.   This is, we say, no opposition because the thing opposed is always non-eternal on account of the eternality of the non-eternal.—36.

The Naiyâyika says :—

By speaking of eternality of the non-eternal you have admitted sound to be *always* non-eternal and cannot now deny its non-eternality. The eternal and non-eternal are incompatible with each other : by admitting that sound is non-eternal you are precluded from asserting that it is also eternal.   Hence "balancing the eternal " is not a sound opposition.

प्रयत्नकार्य्यानेकत्वात्कार्य्यसमः ॥ ५ । १ । ३७ ॥

37.   If one opposes an argument by showing the diversity of the effects of effort, the opposition will be called " balancing the effect."—37.

A certain person to prove the non-eternality of sound, argues as follows :—

          Sound is non-eternal,
             because it is an effect of effort.

A certain other person offers a futile opposition thus :—

The effect of effort is found to be of two kinds, *viz.* (1) the production of something which was previously non-existent, *e.g.* a pot, and (2) the revelation of something already existent, *e.g.* water in a well. Is sound an effect of the first kind or of the second kind ? If sound is an effect of the first kind it will be non-eternal but if it is of the second kind it will be eternal. Owing to this diversity of the effects of effort, it is not possible to conclude that sound is non-eternal. This sort of opposition is called " balancing the effect."

कार्य्यान्यत्वे प्रयत्नाहेतुत्वमनुपलब्धिकारणोपपत्तेः ॥ ५ । १ । ३८ ॥

38.   Effort did not give rise to the second kind of effect, because there was no cause of non-perception.—38.

The Naiyâyika answers the opposition called "balancing the effect" as follows :—

We cannot say that sound is revealed by our effort because we are unable to prove that it existed already. That sound did not exist previously is proved by our non-perception of the same at the time. You cannot say that our non-perception was caused by a veil because no veil covered sound. Hence sound is an effect which is not revealed but produced.

प्रतिषेधेऽपि समानो दोष: ॥ ५ ॥ १ ॥ ३९ ॥

39. The same defect, we say, attaches to the opposition too.—39.

A certain person argued :—
Sound is non-eternal,
because it is an effect of effort.

A certain other person opposed it saying that sound would not be non-eternal if "effect" meant a thing revealed.

The Naiyâyika observes that if an argument is to be set aside owing to an ambiguous meaning of the word "effect", why is not the opposition too set aside on the same ground? The reason in the argument is as erratic as that in the opposition. Just as there is no special ground to suppose that the "effect" in the argument signified "a thing produced and not revealed," so also there is no special ground to suppose that the word in the opposition signified "a thing revealed and not produced." Hence the opposition called "balancing the effect" is self-destructive.

सर्वत्रैवम् ॥ ५ ॥ १ ॥ ४० ॥

40. Thus everywhere.—40.

If a special meaning is to be attached to the opposition, the same meaning will have to be attached to the original argument. In this respect there will be an equality of the two sides in the case of all kinds of opposition such as "balancing the homogeneity" etc.

प्रतिषेधविप्रतिषेधे प्रतिषेधदोषवद्दोष: ॥ ५ ॥ १ ॥ ४१ ॥

41. Defect attaches to the opposition of the opposition just as it attaches to the opposition.—41.

A certain person to prove the non-eternality of sound, argues as follows :—
Sound is non-external,
because it is an effect of effort.

A certain other person, seeing that the effect is of diverse kinds
offers an opposition thus :—

Sound is eternal,

because it is an effect of effort.

(Here " effect " may mean " a thing revealed by effort.")

The arguer replies that sound cannot be concluded to be eternal
because the reason " effect " is erratic (which may mean " a thing produced by effort.")

The opponent rises again to say that sound cannot also be concluded to be non-eternal because the reason " effect " is erratic (which may
mean a thing revealed by effort). So the defect which is pointed out in
the case of the opposition, may also be pointed out in the case of the
opposition of the opposition.

प्रतिषेधं सदोषमभ्युपेत्य प्रतिषेधविप्रतिषेधे समानो दोष-
प्रसङ्गो मतानुज्ञा ॥ ५ । १ । ४२ ॥

42. If one admits the defect of his opposition in
consequence of his statement that an equal defect attaches
to the opposition of the opposition, it will be called " admission of an opinion."—52.

A certain person lays down a proposition which is opposed by a certain other person. The first person, viz. the disputant charges the opposition
made by the second person, viz. the opponent, with a defect, e.g. that the
reason is erratic. The opponent instead of rescuing his opposition from the
defect with which it has been charged by the disputant, goes on charging the disputant's opposition of the opposition with the same defect.
The counter-charge which the opponent brings in this way is interpreted
by the disputant to be an admission of the defect pointed out by him.
The disputant's reply consisting of this kind of interpretation is called
"admission of an opinion."

स्वपक्षलक्षणापेक्षोपपत्त्युपसंहारे हेतुनिर्देशे परपक्षदोषाभ्यु-
पगमात्समानो दोष इति ॥ ५ । १ । ४३ ॥

43. " Admission of an opinion " also occurs when the
disputant instead of employing reasons to rescue his side from
the defect with which it has been charged, proceeds to admit
the defect in consequence of his statement that the same
defect belongs to his opponent's side as well.

Six-winged disputation (Ṣaṭpakṣî kathâ).

Disputant—to prove the non-eternality of sound says :—

> Sound is non-eternal,
>> because it is an effect of effort.

This is the first wing.

Opponent—seeing that the effect is of diverse kinds, offers an opposition thus :—

> Sound is eternal,
>> because it is an effect of effort.

(Here "effect" means a thing which already existed and is now revealed by effort).

This is the second wing.

Disputant—seeing that the reason "effect" is erratic, charges the opposition with a defect thus :—

> Sound is *not* eternal,
>> because it is an effect of effort.

(Here the reason "effect" is erratic meaning (1) either a thing that did not previously exist and is now produced (2) or a thing that already existed and is now revealed by effort).

This is the third wing.

Opponent—finding that the reason "effect," which is erratic, proves neither the eternality nor the non-eternality of sound, brings a counter-charge against the disputant thus :—

> Sound is also *not* non-eternal,
>> because it is an effect of effort.

He alleges that the defect (*viz.* the erraticity of the reason) with which his opposition (*viz.* sound is eternal) is charged, also attaches to the opposition of the opposition made by the disputant (*viz.* sound is *not* eternal or non-eternal).

This is the fourth wing.

Disputant—finding that the counter-charge brought against him amounts to his opponent's admission of self-defect says :—

The opponent by saying that "sound is also not non-eternal" has admitted that it is also not eternal. In other words the counter-charge has proved the charge, that is, it has indicated that the opponent admits the disputant's opinion.

This is the fifth wing.

Opponent—finding that the disputant instead of rescuing his argument from the counter-charge has taken shelter under his opponent's admission of the charge says :—

The disputant by saying that "sound is also not eternal" has admitted that it is also not non-eternal. In other words, if the counter-charge proves the charge, the reply to the counter-charge proves the counter-charge itself.

This is the sixth wing.

The first, third and fifth wings belong to the disputant while the second, fourth and sixth to the opponent. The sixth wing is a repetition of the fourth while the fifth wing is a repetition of the third. The sixth wing is also a repetition of the meaning of the fifth wing. The third and fourth wings involve the defect of "admission of an opinion." All the wings except the first three are unessential.

The disputation would have come to a fair close at the third wing if the disputant had pointed out that the word "effect" had a special meaning, viz., a thing which did not previously exist but was produced.

The disputant and the opponent instead of stopping at the proper limit has carried on their disputation through six wings beyond which no further wing is possible. After the six-winged disputation has been carried on, it becomes patent that neither the disputant nor the opponent is a fit person to be argued with.

BOOK V.—CHAPTER II.

प्रतिज्ञाहानिः प्रतिज्ञान्तरं प्रतिज्ञाविरोधः प्रतिज्ञासन्न्यासो
हेत्वन्तरमर्थान्तरं निरर्थकमविज्ञातार्थमपार्थकमप्राप्तकालं न्यून-
मधिकं पुनरुक्तमननुभाषणमज्ञानमप्रतिभा विक्षेपो मतानुज्ञा
पर्य्यनुयोज्योपेक्षणं निरनुयोज्यानुयोगोऽपसिद्धान्तो हेत्वाभा-
साश्च निग्रहस्थानानि ॥ ५ । २ । १ ॥

1. The occasions for rebuke are the following :—

1. Hurting the proposition, 2. Shifting the proposition, 3. Opposing the proposition, 4. Renouncing the proposition, 5.. Shifting the reason, 6. Shifting the topic,
7. The meaningless, 8. The unintelligible, 9. The incoherent,
10. The inopportune, 11. Saying too little, 12. Saying
too much, 13. Repetition, 14. Silence, 15. Ignorance,
16. Non-ingenuity, 17. Evasion, 18. Admission of an
opinion, 19. Overlooking the censurable, 20. Censuring
the non-censurable, 21. Deviating from a tenet, and
22. The semblance of a reason.—44.

The definition of "an occasion for rebuke" has been given in aphorism 1-2-19. "An occasion for rebuke" which is the same as "a ground
of defeat", "a place of humiliation" or "a point of disgrace" arises generally
in connection with the proposition or any other part of an argument and
may implicate any disputant whether he is a discutient, wrangler or
caviller.

प्रतिदृष्टान्तधर्म्माभ्यनुज्ञा स्वदृष्टान्ते प्रतिज्ञाहानिः ॥ ५ । २ । २ ॥

2. "Hurting the proposition" occurs when one admits
in one's own example the character of a counter-example.
—45.

A disputant argues as follows :—

   Sound is non-eternal,
   Because it is cognisable by sense,
   Whatever is cognisable by sense is non-eternal
         as a pot,
   Sound is cognisable by sense,
   Therefore sound is non-eternal.

A certain other person offers an opposition thus :—

A genus (*e.g.*, potness or pot-type), which is cognisable by sense, is found to be eternal, why cannot then the sound which is also cognisable by sense, be eternal ?

The disputant being thus opposed says :—

<blockquote>
Whatever is cognisable by sense is eternal

as a pot,

Sound is cognisable by sense,

Therefore sound is eternal.
</blockquote>

By thus admitting in his example (pot) the character of a counter-example (genus or type), he has hurt his own proposition (*viz.* sound is non-eternal). A person who hurts his proposition in this way deserves nothing but rebuke.

प्रतिज्ञातार्थप्रतिषेधे धर्म्मविकल्पात्तदर्थनिर्देशः प्रतिज्ञा-

न्तरम् ॥ ५ । २ । ३ ॥

3. " Shifting the proposition " arises when a proposition being opposed one defends it by importing a new character to one's example and counter-example.—46.

A certain person argues as follows :—

<blockquote>
Sound is non-eternal,

because it is cognisable by sense

like a pot.
</blockquote>

A certain other person offers an opposition thus :—

<blockquote>
Sound is eternal,

because it is cognisable by sense like a genus (or type).
</blockquote>

The first person in order to defend himself says that a genus (or type) and a pot are both cognisable by sense, yet one is all-pervasive and the other is not so : hence the sound which is likened to a pot is non-all-pervasively non-eternal.

The defence thus made involves a change of proposition. The proposition originally laid down was :—

<blockquote>
Sound is non-eternal,
</blockquote>

while the proposition now defended is :

<blockquote>
Sound is non-all-pervasively non-eternal.
</blockquote>

A person who shifts his proposition in this way is to be rebuked in as much as he has not relied upon his original reason and example.

प्रतिज्ञाहेत्वोर्विरोधः प्रतिज्ञाविरोधः ॥ ५ । २ । ४ ॥

4. "Opposing the proposition" occurs when the proposition and its reason are opposed to each other.—47.

> Substance is distinct from quality,
>> because it is perceived to be non-distinct from colour etc.

In this argument it is to be observed that if substance is distinct from quality, it must also be distinct from colour etc. which constitute the quality. The reason viz. substance is non-distinct from colour etc., is opposed to the proposition, viz. substance is distinct from quality A person who thus employs a reason whtch opposes his proposition is to be rebuked as a fool.

पक्षप्रतिषेधे प्रतिज्ञातार्थापनयनं प्रतिज्ञासन्न्यासः ॥ ५ । २ । ५ ॥

5. A proposition being opposed if one disclaims its import, it will be called "renouncing the proposition."—48.

A certain person argues as follows :—

> Sound is non-eternal,
>> because it is cognisable by sense,

A certain other person offers an opposition thus :—

Just as a genus (or type) is cognisable by sense and is not yet non-eternal, so a sound is cognisable by sense and is not yet non-eternal. The first person, as a defence against the opposition, disclaims the meaning of his proposition thus :—

"Who says that sound is non-eternal ?

This sort of denial of the import of one's own proposition is called "renouncing the proposition" which rightly furnishes an occasion for rebuke.

अविशेषोक्ते हेतौ प्रतिषिद्धे विशेषमिच्छतो हेत्वन्तरम् ॥

५ । २ । ६ ॥

6. "Shifting the reason" occurs when the reason of a general character being opposed one attaches a special character to it.—49.

A certain person, to prove the non-eternality of sound, argues as follows :—

> Sound is non-eternal,
>> because it is cognisable by sense.

A certain other person says that sound cannot be proved to be non-eternal through the mere reason of its being cognisable by sense, just as a genus (or type) such as pot-ness (or pot-type) is cognisable by sense and is not yet non-eternal.

The first person defends himself by saying that the reason, *viz.* being cognisable by sense, is to be understood as signifying that which comes under a genus (or type) and is as such cognisable by sense. Sound comes under the genus (or type) "soundness" and is at the same time cognisable by sense ; but a genus or type such as pot-ness or pot-type does not come under another genus or type (such as pot-ness-ness or pot-type-type) though it is cognisable by sense. Such a defence, which consists in shifting one's reason, rightly furnishes an occasion for rebuke.

प्रकृतादर्थादप्रतिसम्बद्धार्थमर्थान्तरम् ॥ ५ । २ । ७ ॥

7. "Shifting the topic" is an argument which setting aside the real topic introduces one which is irrelevant.—50.

A certain person, to prove the eternality of sound. argues as follows :—

Sound is eternal (proposition),
 because it is intangible (reason).

Being opposed by a certain other person he attempts, in the absence of any other resource, to defend his position as follows :—

Hetu, which is the sanskrit equivalent for "reason," is a word derived from the root "hi" with the suffix "tu". A word, as a part of a speech, may be a noun, a verb, a prefix or an indeclinable. A noun is defined as etc. etc.

The defence made in this way furnishes an instance of defeat through non-relevancy. The person who makes it deserves rebuke.

वर्णक्रमनिर्देशवन्निरर्थकम् ॥ ५ । २ । ८ ॥

8. "The meaningless" is an argument which is based on a non-sensical combination of letters into a series.—51.

A certain person, to prove the eternality of sound, argues as follows :—

Sound is eternal,
 because k, c, ṭ, t and p are j, v, g, ḍ and d,
  like jh, bh, gh, ḍh and dh.

As the letters k, c, ṭ etc. convey no meaning, the person who employs them in his argument deserves rebuke.

परिषत्प्रतिवादिभ्यां त्रिरभिहितमप्यविज्ञातमविज्ञातार्थम् ॥
५ । २ । ६ ॥

9. "The unintelligible" is an argument, which although repeated three times, is understood neither by the audience nor by the opponent.—52.

A certain person being opposed by another person and finding no means of self-defence, attempts to hide his inability in disputation by using words of double entendre or words not in ordinary use or words very quickly uttered which as such are understood neither by his opponent nor by the audience although they are repeated three times. This sort of defence is called "the unintelligible" which rightly furnishes an occasion for rebuke.

पौर्व्वापर्य्यायोगादप्रतिसम्बद्धार्थमपार्थकम् ॥ ५ । २ । १० ॥

10. "The incoherent" is an argument which conveys no connected meaning on account of the words being strung together without any syntactical order.—53.

A certain person being opposed by another person and finding no other means of self-defence, argues as follows :—

Ten pomegranates, six cakes, a bowl, goat's skin and a lump of sweets.

This sort of argument, which consist of a series of unconnected words, is called "the incoherent" which rightly presents on occasion for rebuke.

अवयवविपर्य्यासवचनमप्राप्तकालम् ॥ ५ । २ । ११ ॥

11. "The inopportune" is an argument the parts of which are mentioned without any order of precedence.—54.

A certain person, to prove that the hill has fire, argues as follows :—

The hill has fire (proposition .

Whatever has smoke has fire, as a kitchen (example).

Because it has smoke (reason).

The hill has fire (conclusion).

The hill has smoke (application).

This sort of argument is called "the inopportune" which rightly presents an occasion for rebuke. Since the meaning of an argument is affected by the order in which its parts are arranged, the person who overlooks the order cannot establish his conclusion and is therefore rebuked.

हीनमन्यतमेनाप्यवयवेन न्यूनम् ॥ ५ । २ । १२ ॥

12. If an argument lacks even one of its parts, it is called " saying too little."—55.

The following is an argument which contains all its five parts :—

1. The hill has fire (proposition),
2. Because it has smoke (reason),
3. All that has smoke has fire, as a kitchen (example),
4. The hill has smoke (application),
5. Therefore the hill has fire (conclusion).

As all the five parts or members are essential, a person who omits even one of them should be scolded as " saying too little."

हेतूदाहरणाधिकमधिकम् ॥ ५ । २ । १३ ॥

13. "Saying too much " is an argument which consists of more than one reason or example.—56.

A certain person, to prove that the hill has fire, argues as follows :—

The hill has fire (proposition),

Because it has smoke (reason),

And because it has light (reason),

like a kitchen (example),

and like a furnace (example),

In this argument the second reason and the second example are redundant.

A person, who having promised to argue in the proper way (according to the established usage), employs more than one reason or example is to be rebuked as " saying too much."

शब्दार्थयोः पुनर्वचनं पुनरुक्तमन्यत्रानुवादात् ॥ ५ । २ । १४ ॥

14. " Repetition " is an argument in which (except in the case of reinculcation) the word or the meaning is said over again.—57.

Repetition of the word—Sound is non-eternal,

sound is non-eternal.

Repetition of the meaning—Sound is non-eternal,

echo is perishable, what is heard is impermanent, etc.

A person who unnecessarily commits repetition is to be rebuked as a fool.

Reinculcation has been explained in aphorism 2-1-66.

अनुवादे त्वपुनरुक्तं शब्दाभ्यासादर्थविशेषोपपत्तेः ॥ ५ । २ । १५ ॥

15. In reinculcation there is no repetition in as much as a special meaning is deduced from the word which is repeated.—58.

> The hill has fire (proposition),
> Because it has smoke (reason),
> All that has smoke has fire
>   as a kitchen (example),
> The hill has smoke (application),
> Therefore the hill has fire (conclusion).

In this argument the "conclusion" is a mere repetition of the "proposition" and yet it serves a special purpose.

अर्थादापन्नस्य स्वशब्देन पुनर्वचनम् ॥ ५ । २ । १६ ॥

16. "Repetition" consists also in mentioning a thing by name although the thing has been indicated through presumption.—59.

"A thing possessing the character of a product is non-eternal" —this is a mere repetition of the following :—

"A thing not possessing the character of a product is not non-eternal."

विज्ञातस्य परिषदा त्रिरभिहितस्याप्यनुच्चारणमननुभाष णम् ॥ ५ । २ । १७ ॥

17. "Silence" is an occasion for rebuke which arises when the opponent makes no reply to a proposition although it has been repeated three times by the disputant within the knowledge of the audience.—60.

How can a disputant carry on his argument if his opponent maintains an attitude of stolid silence? The opponent is therefore to be rebuked.

अविज्ञातञ्चाज्ञानम् ॥ ५ । २ । १८ ॥

18. "Ignorance" is the non-understanding of a proposition.—61.

Ignorance is betrayed by the opponent who does not understand a proposition although it has been repeated three times within the knowledge of the audience. How can an opponent refute a proposition the meaning of which he cannot understand? He is to be rebuked for his ignorance.

उत्तरस्याप्रतिपत्तिरप्रतिभा ॥ ५ । २ । १६ ॥

19. "Non-ingenuity" consists in one's inability to hit upon a reply.—62.

A certain person lays down a proposition. If his opponent understands it and yet cannot hit upon a reply, he is to be scolded as wanting in ingenuity.

कार्य्ये व्यासङ्गात् कथाविच्छेदो विक्षेपः ॥ ५ । २ । २० ॥

20. "Evasion" arises if one stops an argument in the pretext of going away to attend another business.—63.

A certain person having commenced a disputation in which he finds it impossible to establish his side, stops its further progress by saying that he has to go away on a very urgent business. He who stops the disputation in this way courts defeat and humiliation through evasion.

स्वपक्षदोषाभ्युपगमात् परपक्षदोषप्रसङ्गो मतानुज्ञा ॥ ५।२।२१ ॥

21. "The admission of an opinion" consists in charging the opposite side with a defect by admitting that the same defect exists in one's own side.—64.

A certain person addressing another person says :—"You are a thief."

The other person replies :—"You too are a thief."

This person, instead of removing the charge brought against him, throws the same charge on the opposite side whereby he admits that the charge against himself is true. This sort of counter-charge or reply is an instance of "admission of an opinion" which brings disgrace on the person who makes it.

निग्रहस्थानप्राप्तस्यानिग्रहः पर्य्यनुयोज्योपेक्षणम् ॥ ५। २।२२ ॥

22. "Overlooking the censurable" consists in not rebuking a person who deserves rebuke.—65.

It is not at all unfair to censure a person who argues in a way which furnishes an occasion for censure. Seeing that the person himself does not confess his short-coming, it is the duty of the audience to pass a vote of censure on him. If the audience failed to do their duty they would earn rebuke for themselves on account of their "over-looking the censurable."

अनिग्रहस्थाने निग्रहस्थानाभियोगो निरनुयोज्यानुयोगः ॥

५ । २ । २३ ॥

23. "Censuring the non-censurable" consists in rebuking a person who does not deserve rebuke.—66.

A person brings discredit on himself if he rebukes a person who does not deserve rebuke.

सिद्धान्तमभ्युपेत्यानियमात्कथाप्रसङ्गोऽपसिद्धान्तः ॥ ५ । २ । २४ ॥

24. A person who after accepting a tenet departs from it in the course of his disputation, is guilty of "deviating from a tenet."—67.

A certain person promises to carry on his argument in consonance with the Sânkhya philosophy which lays down that (1) what is existent never becomes non-existent, and (2) what is non-existent never comes into existence etc. A certain other person opposes him by saying that all human activity would be impossible if the thing now non-existent could not come into existence in the course of time and that no activity would cease if what is existent now could continue for ever. If the first person being thus opposed admits that existence springs from non-existence and non-existence from existence, then he will rightly deserve rebuke for his deviation from the accepted tenet.

हेत्वाभासाश्च यथोक्ताः ॥ ५ । २ । २५ ॥

25. "The fallacies of a reason" already explained do also furnish occasions for rebuke.—68.

From aphorism 1-2-4 it is evident that the fallacies are mere semblances of a reason. A person who employs them in a disputation do certainly deserve rebuke.

There are infinite occasions for rebuke of which only twenty-two have been enumerated here.

Alphabetical Index to the Sutras.

अ.

				PAGE
अणुश्यामतानित्यत्ववदेतत्स्यात्	iii	2	77	106
अणुश्यामतानित्यत्ववद्धा ...	iv	1	67	126
अत्यन्तप्रायैकदेशसाधर्म्यादुपमाना-				
सिद्धिः ...	ii	1	44	35
अथ तत्पूर्वकं त्रिविधमनुभानं पूर्ववच्छेषवत्सा-				
मान्यतो दृष्टं च ...	i	1	5	3
अधिकाराच्च विधानं दिद्धान्तरवत्	iv	1	61	124
अध्यापनादप्रतिषेध ...	ii	2	28	50
अनर्थापत्तावर्थाभ्यप्रत्यभिमानात् ...	ii	2	4	44
अनवस्थाकारित्वादनवस्थानुपपत्तेश्चा-				
प्रतिषेधः ...	iv	2	25	132
अनवस्थायित्वे च वर्णोपलब्धिवत्तद्विकारोप-				
पत्तिः ...	ii	2	54	57
अनिग्रहस्थाने निग्रहस्थानाभियोगो निरनुयो-				
ज्यानुयोगः	v	2	23	175
अनित्यत्वग्रहाद्बुद्धे बुद्धयन्तराद्विनाशः शब्द-				
वत् ...	iii	2	25	90
अनिमित्ततो भावोत्पत्तिः कण्टकतैक्ष्ण्यादिद-				
र्शनात्	iv	1	22	112
अनिमित्तनिमित्तत्वान्नानिमित्तः	iv	1	23	113
अनियमे नियमान्नानियमः ...	ii	2	57	58
अनुक्तस्यार्थापत्तेः पञ्चहानेरुपपत्तिरनुक्तत्वाद्-				
नैकान्तिकत्वाच्चार्थापत्तेः ...	v	1	22	155
अनुपलम्भात्मकत्वादनुपलब्धेर्हेतुः	ii	1	22	49
अनुपलम्भात्मकत्वादनुपलब्धेर्हेतुः	v	1	30	159
अनुपलम्भाद्प्यनुपलब्धिसद्भावाद्भावरणानुपपत्ति-				
रनुपलम्भात्	ii	2	21	49
अनुवादे रवपुनरुक्तं शब्दाभ्यासार्थ्य				
विशेषोपपत्तेः ...	v	2	15	173
अनुवादोपपत्तेश्च ...	ii	1	61	40
अनेकद्रव्यसमवायादूपविशेषाच्च				
रूपोपलब्धिः ...	iii	1	36	71
अनैकान्तिकः सव्यभिचारः ...	i	2	5	15
अन्तर्बहिश्च कार्यद्रव्यस्य कारणान्तरवचनाद्-				
कार्ये तद्भावः	iv	2	20	131

				PAGE
अन्यादन्यस्मादनन्यत्वादनन्यदित्यन्य-				
ताभावः	ii	2	32	51
अपरिसंख्यानाच्च स्मृतिविषयस्य ...	iii	1	15	66
अपरीन्दिताभ्युपगमात् तद्विशेषपरीक्षणमभ्युप-				
गमसिद्धान्तः ...	i	1	31	10
अपवर्गेऽप्येवं प्रसङ्ग ...	iv	2	43	137
अप्रतेजीवायूनां पूर्वे पूर्वमपोह्या-				
काशस्योत्तर ...	iii	1	64	78
अप्रतीचातात्सन्निकर्षोपपत्तिः ...	iii	1	46	74
अप्रत्यभिज्ञानं च विषयान्तरव्या-				
सङ्गात् ...	iii	2	7	85
अप्रत्यभिज्ञाने च विनाशप्रसङ्गः	iii	2	5	84
अप्राप्य ग्रहणं काचाभ्रपटलस्फटिकान्तरितोप-				
लब्धेः ...	iii	1	44	73
अभावाद्भावोत्पत्तिर्नानुपमृदप्रादु-				
र्भावात् ...	iv	1	14	110
अभिव्यक्तौ चाभिभवात्	iii	1	42	73
अभ्यासात्	ii	2	30	51
अभ्युपेत्य कालभेदे दोषवचनात् ...	ii	1	60	40
अयसो ऽयस्यकान्तामिगमनवत्तदुप-				
सर्पणम्	iii	1	23	69
अरण्यगुहापुलिनादिषु योगाभ्यासो-				
पदेश	iv	2	42	137
अर्थादापन्नस्य स्वशब्देन पुनर्वचनम्	v	2	16	173
अर्थापत्तिः प्रतिपन्नसिद्धे र्थ-				
पत्तिसम् ...	v	1	21	155
अर्थापत्तिप्रमाणमनैकान्तिकत्वात्	ii	2	3	44
अलातचक्रदर्शनवत्तदुपलब्धिरासु-				
संचारात् ...	iii	2	62	102
अवयवनाशे प्ययवयवयुपलब्धेर्हेतुः	iii	1	10	65
अवयवविपर्यासवचनमप्राप्तकालम्	v	2	11	171
अवयवान्तराभावे प्यक्तरहेतुः	iv	2	12	129
अवयवावयविप्रसङ्गश्चैवमाप्रलयात्	v	2	15	130
अविज्ञाततत्त्वे र्थे कारणोपपत्तितस्त्वज्ञाना-				
र्थमूहस्तर्कः	i	1	40	13
अविज्ञातं चाज्ञानम्	v	2	18	173

PAGE

अविशेषाभिहितेर्ऽयं वक्तुरभिप्रायादर्थान्तरकल्प-
ना वाक्छलम्... ... i 2 12 18

अविशेषे वा किंचित्साधर्म्यादेकच्छल-
प्रसङ्गः ... i 2 17 19

अविशेषोक्तौ हेतौ प्रतिषिद्धे विशेषमिच्छतो
हेत्वन्तरम् ... v 2 6 169

अव्यक्तग्रहणमनवस्थायित्वाद्विसु त्सम्पाते रूपा-
द्रव्यत्तग्रहणवत् ... iii 2 47 98

अव्यभिचाराञ्च प्रति घातो
भौतिकधर्मे ... iii 1 38 72

अव्यवस्थात्मनि व्यवस्थितत्वाञ्चाव्य
वस्थायाः ... ii 1 4 23

अव्यूह्नाविष्टर्कभविभूत्वानि चाकाश-
धर्माः ... iv 2 22 132

अश्रवणकारणानुपलब्धे सततश्रवण-
प्रसङ्गः ... ii 2 35 52

असत्यर्थे नाभाव इति चेद् नान्यलक्षणो-
पपत्तेः ... ii 2 9 45

अस्पर्शत्वात् ... ii 2 23 50

अस्पर्शत्वादप्रतिषेधः ... ii 2 39 53

आ.

आकाशव्यतिभेदात्तदनुपपत्तिः ... iv 2 18 131

आकाशासर्वगतत्वं वा ... iv 2 19 131

आकृतिर्जातिलिङ्गाख्या ... ii 2 70 61

आकृतिस्तदपेक्षत्वात् सत्यव्यवस्थान-
सिद्धिः ... ii 2 65 60

आत्मनित्यत्वे प्रत्यभावसिद्धिः ... iv 1 10 109

आत्मेश्वरणयटृच्छाज्ञातामिश्च न
संयोगविशेषः ... iii 2 32 92

आत्मशरीरेन्द्रियार्थबुद्धिमनःप्रवृत्तिदोषप्रेत्यभा-
वफलदुःखापवर्गास्तु प्रमेयम् i 1 9 4

आर्शीदकयोः प्रसादस्वाभाव्याद्रूपोपलब्धिवत्त-
दुपलब्धिः ... ... iii 1 49 74

आदित्यरश्मेः स्फटिकान्तरितेऽपि दाह्ये
अविघातात् ... iii 1 47 74

आदिमते वादैरिन्द्रियकत्वात्कृतकवदु-
पचाराञ्च ... ii 2 14 47

आप्तोपदेशः शब्दः ... i 1 7 4

आप्तोपदेशसामर्थ्याच्छब्दादर्थ-
संप्रत्ययः ... ii 1 52 37

आश्रयव्यतिरेकाद्वृद्धफलोत्पत्तिव-
दित्यहेतुः ... iv 1 51 121

PAGE

इ.

इच्छाद्वेषप्रयत्नसुखदुःखज्ञानान्यात्मनो लिङ्ग-
मिति ... i 1 10 5

इन्द्रियान्तरविकारात् ... iii 1 12 66

इन्द्रियार्थेपञ्चत्वात् ... iii 1 58 77

इन्द्रियार्थसन्निकर्षोत्पन्नं ज्ञानमव्यपदेश्यमव्य-
भिचारि व्यवसायात्मकं
प्रत्यक्षम् ... i 1 4 2

इन्द्रियैर्मनसः सन्निकर्षाभावात्तद्-
नुत्पत्तिः ... iii 2 22 89

ई.

ईश्वरः कारणं पुरुषकर्माफल्य-
दर्शनात् ... iv 1 19 112

उ

उत्तरस्याप्रतिपत्तिप्रतिभा ... v 2 19 174

उत्पाद्यव्ययदर्शनात् ... iv 1 46 120

उदाहरणसाधर्म्यात्साध्यसाधनं
हेतुः ... i 1 34 11

उदाहरणापेक्षस्तथेत्युपसंहारे न तथेति वा
साध्यस्योपनयः ... i 1 38 12

उपपत्तिकारणाभ्युनुज्ञानाद्-
प्रतिषेधः ... v 1 26 158

उपपन्नश्च तद्वियोगः कर्मदेया-
पपत्तेः ... iii 2 72 105

उपलब्धेरद्विप्रवृत्तित्वात् ... ii 1 50 37

उपलभ्यमाने चानुपलब्धेरसत्वाद्-
नपदेश ... ii 2 36 52

उभयकारणोपपत्तेरूपपत्तिसमः ... v 1 25 157

उभयसाधर्म्यात् प्रक्रियाप्रसिद्धिः
प्रकरणसम ... v 1 16 153

उभयोः पक्षयोरन्यतरस्याध्यापनाद्-
प्रतिषेधः ... ii 2 29 51

ऋ.

ऋणक्लेशप्रवृत्त्यनुबन्धादप
वर्गाभावः ... iv 1 59 123

ए.

एकधर्मोपपत्तेरविशेषे सर्वाविशेषप्रसङ्गात्सद्धा-
वोपपत्तेरविशेषसमः ... v 1 23 156

एकविनाशे द्वितीयाविनाशा-
न्नित्यत्वम् ... iii 1 9 65

PAGE

एकस्मिन् भेदाभावादभेदशब्दप्रयोगानुपपत्तेर-
प्रश्नः ... ... iv 2 11 129
एकीकरणेनोत्तरोत्तरगुणसद्भावादुत्तरेषां तदनु-
पलब्धिः ... iii 1 66 79
एतेनानियमः प्रयुक्तः ... iii 2 71 104

ऐ.

ऐन्द्रियकत्वाद्रूपादीनामप्रतिषेधः iii 2 59 102

क.

कर्मकारितश्चेन्द्रियाणां व्यूहः पुरुषार्थ-
तन्त्रः ... iii 1 37 72
कर्माकाशसाधर्म्यात्संशयः iii 2 1 83
कर्मानवस्थायिग्रहणात् ... iii 2 45 98
कारणद्रव्यस्य प्रदेशशब्देनाभिधाना(न्त्रित्येष्वप्य-
व्यभिचार इति) ... ii 2 18 48
कारणान्तरादपि तद्धर्मोपपत्तेरप्रतिषेधः v 1 28 158
कार्यव्यासङ्गात्कथाविच्छेदो विक्षेपः v 2 20 174
कार्यान्यत्वे प्रयत्नाहेतुत्वमनुपलब्धिकारणो-
पपत्तेः ... ... v 1 38 162
कालात्ययापदिष्टः कालातीतः ... i 2 9 17
कालान्तरेणानिष्पत्तिर्हेतुविनाशात् iv 1 46 119
किञ्चित्साधर्म्यादुपसंहारसिद्धेर्वैधर्म्यादप्रति-
षेधः ... ... v 1 5 145
कुम्भादिष्वनुपलब्धेर्हेतुः ... iii 2 39 95
कृतताकर्तव्यतोपपत्तेस्तूभयथा ग्रहणम् ii 1 43 35
कुत्रचिन्नैकदेशवृत्तित्वादवयवानामवयव्य-
भावः ... ...iv 2 7 128
कृष्णसारे सत्युपलम्भाद् व्यतिरिच्य चो-
पलम्भात् संशयः ... iii 1 30 70
केशनखादिष्वनुपलब्धे ... iii 2 55 100
केशसमूहे तैमिरिकोपलब्धिवत्तदुप-
लब्धिः ... iv 2 13 129
क्रमनिर्देशादप्रतिषेधः ... iv 1 18 110
क्रमवृत्तित्वाद्युगपद्ग्रहणम् ... iii 2 6 84
क्वचित्तद्धर्मानुपपत्तेः क्वचिद्योपपत्तेः
प्रतिषेधाभावः ... v 1 24 156
क्वचिन्निनाशकारणानुपलब्धेः क्वचिच्चो-
पलब्धेरनेकान्त ... iii 2 18 88
क्षीरविनाशे कारणानुपलब्धिवद्व्युद्-
त्पत्तिः ... ... iii 2 14 87
क्षुदादिभिः प्रवर्तनाच्च ... iv 2 40 137

ग.

गन्धत्वाद्रव्यव्यतिरेकादगन्धादीनामप्रति-
षेधः ... ... iii 1 60 77
गन्धरसरूपस्पर्शशब्दानां स्पर्शपर्यन्ता
पृथिव्याः ... ... iii 1 64 78
गन्धरसरूपस्पर्शशब्दाः पृथिव्यादिगुणा-
स्तदर्थाः ... i 1 14 5
गुणान्तरापत्युपमर्दान्ह्रासवृद्धिलेशश्लेषे-
भ्यस्तु विकारोपपत्तेर्वर्णविकाराः ii 2 59 58
गोत्वाद्गोसिद्धिवत्तत्सिद्धिः ... v 1 3 141

घ.

घटादिनिष्पत्तिदर्शनात्पीडने चाभिचारा-
द्प्रतिषेधः ... v 1 8 148
घ्राणरसनचक्षुस्त्वक्श्रोत्राणीन्द्रियाणि
भूतेभ्यः ... i 1 12 5

च.

चेष्टेन्द्रियार्थाश्रयः शरीरम् i 1 11 5

ज.

जातिविशेषे चानियमात् ... ii 1 57 39
जन्मेच्छाद्वेषनिमित्तत्वादारम्भ-
निवृत्त्योः ... iii 2 36 94
ज्ञातुर्ज्ञानसाधनोपपत्तेः संज्ञाभेदमात्रंii 1 17 67
ज्ञानग्रहणाभ्यासस्तद्विद्दिश्च सह
संवादः ... ...iv 2 47 138
ज्ञानलिङ्गत्वादात्मनो नानवरोधः ii 1 23 29
ज्ञानविकल्पानां च भावाभावसंवेद-
नाद्ध्यात्मम् ... v 1 31 159
ज्ञानसमवेदात्मप्रदेशसन्निकर्षान्मनसः
स्मृत्युत्पत्तिर्न युगपदुत्पत्तिः iii 2 26 91
ज्ञानायौगपद्यादेकं मनः ... iii 2 60 102

त.

तत्कारितत्वाद्धेतुः ... iv 1 21 112
तद्विरुद्धं वाक्छलं सामान्यच्छलमुपचार-
च्छलंचेति ... i 2 11 18
तत्त्वे रागद्वेषमोहार्थान्तरभावात् iv 1 3 108
तत्त्वप्रधानभेदाच्च मिथ्याबुद्धेर्द्वे विधो-
पपत्तिः ... iv 2 37 136
तत्त्वभाक्तयोर्नानाखविभागाद्व्यभिचार ii 2 16 48
तत्त्वाध्यवसायसंरक्षणार्थं जल्पवितण्डे
बीजप्ररोहसंरक्षणार्थं कण्टकशा-
खावरणवत् ... iv 2 50 139

		PAGE		
तत्प्रामाण्ये वा न सर्वप्रमाणवि-				
प्रतिषेध:	ii	1	14	26
तत्प्रामाण्ये वा नार्थापत्त्यप्रामाण्यम्	ii	2	6	45
तत्सम्बन्धात् फलनिष्पत्तेस्तेषु फल-				
वदुपचार:	iv	1	54	122
तत्सिद्धे रत्नचितेष्वहेतु: ...	ii	2	10	46
तथात्यंतसंशयस्तद्धर्मसातत्यौपपत्ते:	ii	1	5	23
तथा दोषा:	iv	1	2	108
तथा भावादुत्पन्नस्य कारणोपपत्तेर्न				
कारणप्रतिषेध:	v	1	13	151
तथा वैधर्म्यात् ...	i	1	35	11
तथाऽल्हारस्य ...	iii	2	68	104
तयैत्युपसंहारादुपमानसिद्धिर्नाविशेष:	ii	1	48	36
तदत्यन्तविमोदोऽपवर्ग: ...	i	1	22	7
तदृष्टृकारितमिति चेत्पुनस्तत्प्रसङ्गो-				
ऽपवर्गे ...	iii	2	73	105
तदनित्यत्वमग्रे द्रोह्यं विनाश्यानु-				
विनाश्यवत् ...	iv	1	27	113
तदनुपलब्धेरनुपलम्भादभावसिद्धि				
तद्विपरीतोपपत्तेरनुपलब्धिसम:	v	1	29	159
तदनुपलब्धेरनुपलम्भादावरणोपपत्ति:	ii	2	20	49
तदनुपलब्धेर्हेतु: ...	iii	1	33	71
तदन्तरालानुपलब्धेर्हेतु: ...	ii	2	27	50
तदप्रामाण्यमनृतव्याघातपुनरुक्त-				
दोषेभ्य:	ii	1	58	39
तदभावश्चापवर्गे	iv	2	45	137
रुदभाव: सात्मकप्रदाहेऽपि तन्नि-				
त्यत्वात्	iii	1	5	64
तदभावे नास्त्यनन्यता तयोरितरेत-				
रापेक्षसिद्धि: ..	ii	2	33	52
तदयौगपद्यलिङ्गत्वाच्च न मनस: ...	ii	1	24	29
तदर्थं यमनियमाभ्यामात्मसंस्कारो योगाच्चा-				
ध्यात्मविध्युपायी: ...	iv	2	46	138
तदर्थे व्यक्ताकृतिजातिस्त्रिष्विधावुपचा-				
रात्संशय: ...	ii	2	61	59
तदसंशय: पूर्ववैहेतुप्रसिद्धत्वात्	iv	2	5	128
तदात्मगुणत्वेऽपि तुल्यम्	iii	2	21	89
तदात्मगुणसद्भावाद्प्रतिषेध:	iii	1	14	66
तदाश्रयत्वाद्पृथग्ग्रहणम्	iv	2	28	133
तदुपलब्धिरितरेतरद्रव्यगुणवैधर्म्यात्	iii	1	75	81
तद्विकल्पाज्जातिग्रहणस्त्यानबहुत्वम्	i	2	20	21
तद्विकाराणां सुखभावाव्यतिरेकात्	ii	2	49	56
			PAGE	
तद्विवृत्तेर्वा प्रमाणसिद्धिवत्प्रमेय-				
सिद्धि: ...	ii	1	18	27
तद्विपर्ययाद्धा विपरीतम् ...	i	1	37	12
तद्व्यवस्थानं तु भूयस्त्वात्	iii	1	71	81
तद्व्यवस्थानादेवात्मसद्भावादप्र-				
तिषेध: ...	iii	1	3	63
तन्त्राधिकरणाभ्युपगमसंस्थिति:				
सिद्धान्त: ...	i	1	26	8
तन्निमित्तं त्ववयव्यभिमान: ...	iv	2	3	127
तयोरप्यभावो वर्तमानाभावे तदपे-				
क्षत्वात् ...	ii	1	40	34
तल्लक्षणावरोधादप्रतिषेध: ...	iv	1	31	114
तल्लिङ्गत्वादिच्छाद्वेषये: पार्थिवा-				
द्रव्यप्रतिषेध: ...	iii	2	37	94
तं शिष्यगुरुसब्रह्मचारिविशिष्टश्रेयेायि-				
भिरनसूयुभिरुपेयात्	iv	2	48	138
तेनैव तस्याग्रहणाच्च	iii	1	73	81
ते विभक्तान्त: पदम्	ii	2	60	59
तेषां मोक्ष: पापीयाऽऽश्रमूढस्येतरो-				
त्पत्ते: ...	iv	1	6	109
तेषु चाद्युत्तेरवयवभाव:	iv	2	8	128
तैश्चापदेशो ज्ञानविशेषाणाम्	ii	1	27	30
त्वं काल्याप्रतिषेधश्च शब्दादातोद्सि-				
द्विवत्तसिद्धे: ...	ii	1	15	27
त्वं काल्यासिद्धे: प्रतिषेधानुपपत्ति:	ii	1	12	26
त्वं काल्यासिद्धे हेतोरहेतुसम:	v	1	18	153
त्वक्पर्यन्तत्वाच्छरीरस्य केशनखादि-				
ष्वप्रसङ्ग: ...	iii	2	56	101
त्वगवयवविशेषेण धूमोपलब्धिवत्त-				
दुपलब्धि:	iii	1	54	76
त्वग्व्यतिरेकात् ...	iii	1	52	75

द.

दर्शनस्पर्शनाभ्यामेकार्थग्रहणात् ...	iii	1	1	63
दिग्देशकालाकाशेष्वप्येवं प्रसङ्ग:	ii	1	22	29
दु:खजन्मप्रवृत्तिदोषमिथ्याज्ञानानामुत्तरोत्त-				
रापाये तदनन्तराभावादपवर्ग:	i	1	2	2
दुख: विकल्पे सुखवभिमानाच्च	iv	1	58	122
दृश्यानुमितानां नियोगप्रतिषेध-				
नुपपत्ति: ...	iii	1	50	75
दृष्टान्तविरोधादप्रतिषेध:	iii	1	11	65

PAGE

दृष्टान्तस्य कारणानपदेशात् प्रत्यवस्थानाच्च
प्रतिदृष्टान्तेन प्रसङ्गप्रतिदृष्टान्त-
समौ ... v 1 9 148

दृष्टान्ते च साध्यसाधनभावेन धर्मस्य हेतु-
त्वात्तस्य चोभयथाभावाच्चा-
विशेष: ... v 1 34 161

दोषनिमित्तं रूपादयो विषया: सङ्-
रूपकृता: ... iv 2 2 127

दोषनिमित्तानां तत्त्वज्ञानादहङ्कार-
निवृत्ति: ... iv 2 1 127

द्रव्यगुणधर्मभेदाज्ञोपलब्धिनियम:... iii 1 35 71

द्रव्यविकारे वैषम्यवद् वर्णविकार-
विकल्प: ... ii 2 45 55

द्रव्ये स्वगुणपरगुणोपलब्धे:
संशय: ... iii 2 50 99

ध.

धर्मविकल्पनिर्देशे येषद्भावप्रतिषेध उपचार-
च्छलम् ... i 2 14 19

धारणाकर्षणोपपत्ते श्च ... ii 1 35 33

न.

न करणाकरणयो रारम्भदर्शनात् iii 2 74 105

न कर्मकत्वं साधनवैगुण्यात् ... ii 1 59 39

न कर्मानित्यत्वात्... ... ii 2 24 50

न कारणावयवभावात् ... iv 1 42 118

न कार्याश्रयकर्त्वधात् ... iii 1 6 64

न कुड्यान्तरितानुपलब्धेरप्रतिषेध: iii 1 45 74

नक्त चरनयनरश्मिदर्शनाज्ञ ... iii 1 43 73

न क्ले शसन्तते: स्वभाविकत्वात् iv 1 65 125

न गत्यभावात् ... iii 2 8 85

न घटाद् घटानिष्पत्ते: ... iv 1 12 110

न घटाभावसामान्यानित्यत्वाच्चानित्येष्वप्यनित्य-
वदुपचाराञ्च ... ii 2 15 47

न चतुर्ष्वसैतिद्यार्थापत्तिसंभवाभावप्रामा-
ण्यात् ... ii 2 1 43

न चाव्यव्यवया: ... ... iv 2 10 129

न चैकदेशोपलब्धिर्वर्यसिद्धभावात् ii 1 32 32

न तदनवस्थानात् ... ii 2 63 60

न तदर्थबहुत्वात् ... iii 1 59 77

न तदर्थान्तरभावात् ... i 2 16 19

न तदाशुगतित्वान्मनस: ... iii 2 30 92

न दोषलक्षणावरोधान्मोहस्य ... iv 1 8 109

न निष्पन्नावश्यंभावित्वात् ... iv 2 44 137

न पयस: परिणामगुणान्तरप्रा-
दुर्भावात् ... iii 2 16 88

न पाकजगुणान्तरोत्पत्ते: ... iii 2 52 100

न पार्थिं वाप्ययो: प्रत्यक्षत्वात्... iii 1 69 80

न पुरुषकर्मभावे फलानिष्पत्ते: iv 1 20 112

न प्रत्यद्ण यावत्तावदप्युपलम्भात् ii 1 31 32

न प्रदीपप्रकाशवत्तत्सिद्धे: ii 1 19 28

न प्रलयो अणुसद्भावात् ... iv 2 16 130

न प्रवृत्ति: प्रतिसन्धानाय
हीनक्ले शस्य ... iv 1 64 125

न बुद्धिलक्षणाधिष्ठानगत्याकृतिजातिपञ्च-
त्वेभ्य: ... iii 1 62 78

न युगपद्ग्रहणात् ... iii 2 4 84

न युगपदनेकक्रियोपलब्धे: ... iii 2 61 102

न युगपदर्थानुपलब्धे: ... iii 1 53 76

न रात्रावप्यनुपलब्धे: ... iii 1 40 72

न रूपादीनामितरेतरवैधर्म्यात् iii 2 58 101

न लक्षणावस्थितापेक्षासिद्धि: ... ii 2 11 46

न विकारधर्मानुपपत्ते: ... ii 2 46 55

न विनष्टेभ्योऽनिष्पत्ते: ... iv 1 17 111

न विषयव्यवस्थानात् ... iii 1 2 63

न व्यवस्थानुपपत्ते: ... iv 1 33 115

न शब्दगुणोपलब्धे: ... iii 1 74 81

न सद्य: कालान्तरोपभोग्यत्वात् iv 1 45 119

न सर्वगुणानुपलब्धे: ... iii 1 65 79

न सङ्कल्पनिमित्तत्वाञ्च रागादीनाम् iv 1 68 126

न सङ्कल्पनिमित्तत्वाद्रागादीनाम् iii 1 27 69

न साध्यसमत्वात् ... iii 2 66 103

न सामयिकत्वाच्छब्दार्थे सम्प्रत्ययस्य ii 1 56 39

न सुखस्यान्तरालनिष्पत्ते: ... iv 1 56 122

न स्मरणकालानियमात् ... iii 2 31 92

न स्मृते: स्मतिव्यविषयत्वात् . iii 1 13 66

न स्वभावसिद्धिरपेक्षिकत्वात् ... iv 1 39 117

न स्वभावसिद्धे र्भावानाम् ... iv 1 38 117

न हेतुत: कार्यसिद्धि स्लैकाल्यासिद्धि: v 1 19 154

न हेत्वभावात् ... ... ii 2 10 85

नाकृताभ्यागमप्रसङ्गात् ... iii 2 78 106

नाकृतिव्यत्यपेदत्वाज्ज्ञात्यभिव्यक्ते: ii 2 67 61

नाशुगतित्वात् ... ... ii 2 25 50

नातीतानागतयोरितरेतरापेक्षासिद्धि: ii 1 41 34

				PAGE
नातीतानागतया: कारकशब्दप्रयोगात्	iv	1	16	111
नातुल्यप्रकृतीनां विकारविकल्पात्	ii	2	44	55
नात्मप्रतिपत्तिहेतूनां मनसि सम्भवात्	iii	1	16	67
नात्समनसो: सन्निकर्षाभावे प्रत्यक्षो-				
त्पत्ति: ...	ii	1	21	29
नानित्यतानित्यत्वात् ...	iv	1	26	113
नानुमीयमानस्य प्रत्यक्षतोऽनुपलब्धिर-				
भावहेतु: ...	iii	1	34	71
नानुवादपुनरुक्तयोरविशेष: शब्दाभा-				
सोपपत्ते: ...	ii	1	67	42
नानेकलद्धैरेकभावनिष्पत्ते:	iv	1	35	116
नान्त:शरीरवृत्तित्वान्मनस: ...	iii	2	27	91
नान्यत्व प्रवृत्त्यभावात् ...	iii	1	24	69
नान्यत्वे प्यभ्यासस्योपचारात् ...	ii	2	31	51
नाप्रत्यक्षे गवये प्रमाणार्थमुपमानस्य पश्याम				
इति ...	ii	1	47	36
नाभावप्रामाण्यं प्रमेयासिद्धि: ...	ii	2	7	45
नार्थविशेषप्राबल्यात् ...	ii	1	29	31
नार्थविशेषप्राबल्यात् ...	iv	2	39	136
नासन्न सन्न सदसत् सदसतोर्वैधर्म्यात्	iv	1	48	120
निग्रहस्थानप्रासस्यानिग्रहा पर्यनुयोज्यो-				
पेक्षणम् ...	v	2	22	174
नित्यत्वप्रसङ्गश्च प्रायणानुपपत्ते:	iii	2	76	106
नित्यत्वे विकारादनित्यत्वे चानव-				
स्थानात् ...	ii	2	52	56
नित्यनैमित्तिकोपपत्तेश्च तुल्यजातीयानामप्रति-				
षेध: ...	iv	1	9	109
नित्यमनित्यभावादनित्ये नित्यत्वोपपत्तेनि-				
त्यसम: ...	v	1	35	161
नित्यास्याप्रत्याख्यानं यथोपलब्धिव्यव-				
स्थानात् ...	iv	1	28	114
नित्यानामतीन्द्रियत्वात्तद्धर्मविकल्पाच्च वर्णवि-				
कारणामप्रतिषेध:	ii	2	53	57
निमित्तनैमित्तिकोपपत्तेश्च तुल्यजातीया-				
नामप्रतिषेध: ...	iv	1	9	109
निमित्तनैमित्तिकयोरर्थान्तरभावाद-				
प्रतिषेध:	iv	1	24	113
नियमानियमौ तु तद्विशेषकौ	iii	2	40	95
नियमश्च निरनुमान:	iii	1	18	67
नियमहेत्वभावादऽदोषदर्शनाभ्यनुज्ञा	iii	2	12	86
नियमानियमविरोधादनियमे नियमाद्वाप्रति-				
षेध:	ii	2	58	58

				PAGE
निरवयवत्वादहेतु:	iv	1	43	118
निर्दिष्टकारणाभावेऽप्युपलम्भादुपल-				
ब्धिसम	v	1	27	158
नेतरेतरधर्मप्रसङ्गात्	iii	1	48	74
नेन्द्रियान्तराद्यौनुपलब्धे:	iii	1	53	76
नेन्द्रियार्थयोस्सन्निद्विनाशेऽपि				
ज्ञानावस्थानात्	iii	2	19	89
नैकदेशत्वाससादृश्येभ्यो				
र्थान्तरभावात्	ii	1	38	33
नैकप्रत्यनीकभावात्	iv	1	4	108
नैकस्मिन्नासास्त्वित्व्यवहिते				
द्वित्वाभिमानात्	iii	1	8	65
नोत्पत्तिकारणापदेशात्	iii	2	23	90
नोत्पत्तिकारणोपलब्धे:	iv	1	32	114
नोत्पत्तिनिमित्तत्वान्मातापितो:	ii	2	67	103
नोत्पत्तिविनाशकारणोपलब्धे:	iii	2	13	87
नोत्पत्तिविनाशकारणोपलब्धे:	iv	1	30	114
नोष्णगीतवर्षकालनिमित्तत्वात्पञ्चात्मकविका-				
राणाम्	iii	1	21	68
न्यूनसमाधिकोपलब्धे विकाराणा-				
महेतु:	ii	2	43	54
प				
पक्षप्रतिषेधे प्रतिज्ञातार्थापनयनं				
प्रतिज्ञासंन्यास: ...	v	2	5	169
पद्मादिषु प्रबोधसंमीलनविकारव-				
त्तद्विकार: ...	iii	1	20	68
परश्वादावारम्भनिवृत्तिदर्शनात्	iii	2	38	94
परं वा त्रुटे:	iv	2	17	131
परिशेषादप्युक्तहेतूपपत्तेश्च	iii	2	42	96
परिषत्प्रतिवादिभ्यां तिरभिहितमप्यविज्ञातम-				
विज्ञातार्थम् ...	v	2	9	171
पक्षत्रासिद्धौ न प्रमाणेभ्य: प्रमे-				
यसिद्धि: ...	ii	1	10	25
पाणिनिमित्तप्रश्लेषाच्छब्दाभावे				
नानुपलब्धि:	ii	2	37	53
पार्थिवं गुणान्तरोपलब्धे:	iii	1	28	70
पुत्रपशुस्त्री परिच्छदहिरण्याद्रादिफल-				
निर्देशात्	iv	1	53	121
पुनरुत्पत्ति: प्रेत्यभाव:	i	1	19	7
पूरणप्रदाहपाटनान्नुपलब्धेश्च				
सम्बन्धाभाव: ...	ii	1	54	38
पूर्वकृतफलानुबन्धात्तदुत्पत्ति:	iii	2	64	103

		PAGE
पूर्वैकृतफलानुबन्धात्तदुत्पत्तिः ... iv	2 41	137
पूर्वेपूर्वैगुणोत्कर्षात्तत्तत्प्रधानम् ... iii	1 70	80
पूर्वे हि प्रमाणसिद्धौ नेन्द्रियार्थस-		
द्विकर्षात् प्रत्यक्षोत्पत्तिः ... ii	1 9	25
पूर्वाभ्यस्तस्मृत्यनुबन्धाज्जातस्य		
हर्षभयशोककसम्प्रतिपत्तेः ... iii	1 19	68
पृथक्चावयवेभ्यो ऽवृत्तेः ... iv	2 9	128
पृथिव्याप्सतेजो वायुराकाशमितिभूतानि i	1 13	5
पैर्वापर्यायोगादप्रतिसम्बद्धार्थमपार्थकम् v	2 10	171
प्रकृतादर्थादप्रतिसम्बद्धार्थमर्थान्तरम् v	2 7	170
प्रकृतिविवृद्धौ विकारविवृद्धेः ... ii	2 42	54
प्रकृत्यनियमाद्वर्णविकाराणाम् ... ii	2 56	58
प्रणिधाननिबन्धाभ्यासलिङ्गलक्षणसा-		
दृश्यपरिग्रहाश्रयाश्रितसम्बन्धान-		
न्तर्द्वियोगैकार्यविरोधातिशय-		
प्राप्तिव्यवधानसुखदुःखेच्छाद्वेषप्रभ-		
र्यार्थित्वक्रियारागधर्माधर्मनिमि-		
त्तेभ्यः ... iii	2 44	96
प्रणिधानलिङ्गादिज्ञानानामयुग-		
पद्भावाद्युगपत्स्मरणम् ... iii	2 34	93
प्रतिज्ञाहेतूदाहरणोपनयनिगमनान्य-		
न्यवयवा: ... i	1 32	10
प्रतिज्ञातार्थप्रतिषेधे धर्मविकल्पात्तदर्थनि-		
र्देशः प्रतिज्ञान्तरम् ... v	2 3	168
प्रतिज्ञाहानिः प्रतिज्ञान्तरं प्रतिज्ञा-		
विरोधः प्रतिज्ञासंन्यासोहेत्वन्तर-		
मर्थान्तरं निरर्थकमविज्ञातार्थमपा-		
र्थकमप्राप्तकालं न्यूनमधिकं पुन-		
रुक्तमननुभाषणमज्ञानमप्रतिभा		
विक्षेपो मतानुज्ञा पर्यनुयोज्योपेक्षणं		
निरनुयोज्यानुयोगो ऽपसिद्धान्तोहेत्वा-		
भासाश्च निग्रहस्थानानि ... v	5 1	167
प्रतिज्ञाहेतुर्वोर्विरोधः प्रतिज्ञाविरोधः v	2 4	169
प्रतिदृष्टान्तधर्माभ्यनुज्ञा स्वदृष्टान्ते		
प्रतिज्ञाहानिः ... v	2 2	167
प्रतिदृष्टान्तधर्माभ्यनुज्ञा स्वदृष्टान्ते प्रति-		
ज्ञाहानिः प्रतिदृष्टान्तहेतुत्वे च नाहे-		
तुर्दृष्टान्तः ... v	1 11	150
प्रतिद्वन्द्विसिद्धिः पाकजानाम-		
प्रतिषेधः ... iii	2 53	100
प्रतिषद्वहीनमपि वा प्रयोजनार्य-		
मर्थित्वे ... iv	2 49	138

		PAGE
प्रतिषद्धात् प्रकरणप्रसिद्धेः प्रतिषे-		
धानुपपत्तिः ... v	1 17	153
प्रतिषेधविप्रतिषेधे प्रतिषेधदोषवद्दोष: v	1 41	163
प्रतिषेधं सदोषमभ्युपेत्य प्रतिषेधविप्रतिषेधे		
समाने दोषप्रसङ्गो मतानुज्ञा v	1 42	164
प्रतिषेधानुपपत्तेः प्रतिषेद्धव्याप्रतिषेध: v	1 20	154
प्रतिषेधाप्रामाण्यं चानैकान्तिकत्वात् ii	2 5	44
प्रतिषेधेऽपि समानो दोष: v	1 39	163
प्रतिषेध्ये नित्यमनित्यभावादनित्ये नित्य-		
त्वविपत्ति:प्रतिषेधाभाव: ... v	1 36	162
प्रत्यक्षनिमित्तत्वाच्चे न्द्रियार्थयो: सन्निक-		
र्षस्य पृथक् वचनम् ... ii	1 25	30
प्रत्यक्षमनु.नमेकदेशग्रहणादुपलब्धे: ii	1 30	31
प्रत्यक्षलक्षणानुपपत्तिरसमग्रवचनात् ii	1 20	28
प्रत्यक्षादीनामप्रामाण्यं त्रैकाल्यासिद्धि: ii	1 8	24
प्रत्यक्षानुमानोपमानशब्दा: प्रमाणानि i	1 3	2
प्रत्यक्षेणाप्रत्यक्षसिद्धि: ... ii	1 46	36
प्रदीपार्चि:सन्तत्यभिव्यक्तग्रहणवत्त-		
द्ग्रहणम् ... iii	2 49	99
प्रदीपोपादानप्रसङ्गनिवृत्तिवत्तद्वि-		
निवृत्ति: ... v	1 10	149
प्रधानशब्दानुपपत्तेर्गुणशब्देनानुवादो		
निन्दाप्रशंसोपपत्ते: ... iv	1 60	123
प्रभाणतर्कसाधनोपालम्भ: सिद्धान्ताविरुद्ध:		
पञ्चावयवोपपन्न: पक्षप्रतिपक्षपरि-		
ग्रहोवाद: ... i	2 1	14
प्रमाणश्चार्थप्रतिपत्ते: ... iv	2 29	134
प्रमाणत: सिद्धे: प्रमाणानां प्रमाणान्तर-		
सिद्धिप्रसङ्ग: ... ii	1 17	27
प्रमाणतोऽनुलब्धे ... ii	1 53	28
प्रमाणप्रमेयसंशयप्रयोजनदृष्टान्तसिद्धान्ता-		
वयवतर्कनिर्णयवादजल्पवितण्डाहे-		
त्वाभासश्छलजातिनिग्रहस्थानानां		
तत्त्वज्ञानान्नि:श्रेयसाधिगम: ... i	1 1	1
प्रमाणानुपपत्त्युपपत्तिभ्याम् ... iv	2 30	134
प्रमेयता च तुलाप्रामाण्यवत् ... ii	1 16	27
प्रयत्नकार्योनेकत्वात् कार्यसम: ... v	1 37	162
प्रवर्तनालक्षणा दोषा: ... i	1 18	7
प्रवृत्तिदोषजनिता अर्थे: फलम् ... i	1 20	7
प्रवृत्तिरर्थोक्ता ... iv	1 1	108
प्रवृत्तिर्बुद्धिशरीरारारम्भ इति i	1 17	6

PAGE

प्रसिद्धिसाधर्म्यात्साध्यसाधनमुपमानम् i 1 6 3

प्रसिद्धिसाधर्म्यादुपमानसिद्धे यथोक्त दोषानु-
पपत्ति: ... ... ii 1 45 35

प्रागुत्पत्तेरभावानित्यत्ववत्स्वभाविकि-
ष्यनित्यत्वम् iv 1 66 126

प्रागुच्चारणादनुपलब्धेरावरणादनुप-
लब्धेश्च ... ... ii 2 19 49

प्रागुत्पत्तेरभावेपपत्तेश्च ii 2 12 46

प्रागुत्पत्ते: कारणाभावादनुत्पत्तिसम v 1 11 150

प्रागुत्पत्तेर्वैधर्म्यफलवत्तत्स्यात् iv 1 47 119

प्रातिभवत्तु प्रणिधानादनपेक्षे स्मार्ते
योगपद्यप्रसङ्ग: ... iii 2 35 93

प्रास्तरिहि निमित्तनैमित्तिकभावादर्था-
न्तरभावो दोषेय: iv 1 7 109

प्राप्सी चानियमात् iii 2 69 104

प्राप्य साध्यमप्राप्य वा हेतो:प्राप्त्या
ऽविशिष्टत्वाद्प्राप्त्या ऽसाधकत्वाच्च-
प्राप्त्यप्राभिमौ v 1 7 147

प्रीतिरात्मा श्रयत्वाद्प्रतिषेध: iv 1 52 121

प्रेत्याहाराभ्यासकृतात्स्तन्याभिलाषात् iii 1 22 68

ब.

बाधनानिवृत्तेर्वेदयत: पर्येषणादो-
षादुप्रतिषेध: ... ... iv 1 57 122

बाधनालदणं दु:खमिति ... i 1 21 7

बाह्यप्रकाशानुग्रहाद् विषयोपलब्धेर-
नभिव्यक्ति तो ऽनुपलब्धि: ... iv 1 41 73

बुद्धिरुपलब्धिर्ज्ञानमित्यनर्थान्तरम् i 1 15 6

बुद्धिसिद्धिन्तु तदसत् .. iv 1 50 121

बुद्धे श्चैवं निमित्तसद्वावोपलम्भात् iv 2 36 136

बुद्धवस्थानात् प्रत्यवरेस्मृत्यभाव: iii 2 46 98

बुद्ध्या विवेचनात् भावानां याथात्म्यानु-
पलब्धिस्तन्त्वपकर्षणे पटसद्वावानु-
पलब्धिवत्तदनुपलब्धि: ... iv 2 26 133

भ.

भूतगुणविशेषोपलब्धेस्तादात्म्यम् iii 1 63 78

भूतेभ्यो मूर्त्युपादानवत्तदुपादानम् iii 2 65 103

म.

मध्यन्दिनोल्कापुकाशानुपलब्धिव-
त्तदुपलब्धि:... iii 1 39 72

मन:कर्मनिमित्तत्वाच्च संयोगानुच्छेद: iii 2 75 106

मन्त्रायुर्वेदप्रामाण्यवञ्च तत्प्रामाण्यमाप

प्रामाण्यात् ... ... ii 1 69 42

महदनुग्रहणात् ... iii 1 31 70

मायागन्धर्वनगरमृगतृष्णिकावद्वा iv 2 32 135

मिथ्योपलब्धिविनाशस्तत्वज्ञानात्स्वम
विषयाभिमानपूणाषवत्प्रतिबोधे iv 2 35 135

मूर्तिं सतां च संस्थानोपपत्तेरवयव-
सद्वाव: ... iv 2 23 132

य.

यत्र संशयस्तत्र वमुत्तरोत्तरप्रसङ्ग: ii 1 7 24

यत्सिद्धावन्यप्रकरणसिद्धि: सो अधिकरण
सिद्धान्त: ... i 1 30 9

यथोक्तहेतुत्वाज्ज्ञानु... iii 2 63 103

यथोक्तहेतुत्वादपारतन्त्र्याद्कृताभ्या-
गमाज्ञ न मनस: iii 2 41 95

यथोक्ताध्यवसायादेव तद्विशेषापेक्षा-
त्संशये नासंशये नात्यन्तसंशये वा ii 1 6 23

यथोक्तोपपन्नछलजातिनिग्रहस्थानसाधनोपाल-
म्भो जल्प: ... i 2 2 15

यमर्थमधिकृत्य प्रवर्तते तत्प्रयोजनम् i 1 24 8

यस्मात् पूकरणचिन्ता स निर्णयार्थमपदिष्ट:
पूकरणसम: ... i 2 7 16

यावच्छरीरभावित्वाद्रूपादीनाम् ... iii 2 51 99

याशब्दसमूहत्यागपरिग्रहसंख्याबृद्ध्युपचयवर्ण-
समासानुबन्धानां व्यक्तावुपचाराद्-
व्यक्ति: ... ii 2 62 59

युगपज्ज्ञानानुत्पत्तिर्मनसो लिङ्गम् i 1 16 6

युगपज्ज्ञेयानुपलब्धेश्च न मनस: iii 2 20 89

युगपत्सिद्धौ प्रत्ययनियतत्वात् क्रमवृत्तित्वाभावो
बुद्धीनाम् ... ii 1 11 25

र.

रश्म्यर्थसन्निकर्षविशेषात्तद्ग्रहणम् iii 1 32 71

रोगोपघातसाट्दृश्येभ्यो व्यभिचारादनुमानम-
पूमाणम् ... ii 1 37 33

ल.

लक्षणव्यवस्थानादेवप्रतिषेध: iv 1 36 116

लद्धितेष्वलद्मणलद्मितत्वाद्लद्मितानां
तत्पूमेयसिद्धि: ... ii 2 8 45

लिङ्गतो ग्रहणाम्मनुपलब्धि: iii 2 15 87

लौकिकपरीद्मकाणां यस्मिन्नर्थे बुद्धिसाम्यं स
टृशन्त: ... i 1 25 8

व.

		PAGE
वचनविघातोऽर्थविकल्पोपपत्त्या छलम्	i 2 10	17
वर्णक्रमनिर्देशवन्निरर्थकम् ...	v 2 8	170
वर्णत्वाव्यतिरेकाद्वर्णविकाराणाम- प्रतिषेधः ...	ii 2 5)	56
वर्तमानाभावः पतितपतितव्य कालो- पपत्तेः ...	ii 1 39	34
वर्तमानाभावे सर्वाग्रहणं प्रत्यक्षा- नुपपत्तेः ...	ii 1 42	35
वाक्छलमेवोपचारच्छलं तद्विशेषात्	i 2 15	19
वाक्यविभागस्य चार्थग्रहणात् ...	ii 1 62	40
विकारधर्मित्वे नित्यत्वाभावात् कालान्तरे		
विकारोपपत्तेश्चाप्रतिषेधः ...	ii 2 55	57
विकारप्रासानमपुनरावृत्तेः ...	ii 2 47	55
विकारादेशेपदेशात्संशयः ...	ii 2 41	54
विज्ञातस्य परिषदा तिरभिहितस्याप्यपूर्त्युच्चार- णमननुभाषणम् ..	v 2 17	173
विद्याविद्याद्वैविध्यात् संशयः ...	iv 2 4	127
विधिर्विधायकः ...	ii 1 64	41
विधिविहितस्यानुबचनमनुवादः ...	ii 1 66	41
विध्यैवादानुवादवचनविनियोगात्	ii 1 63	40
विनाशकारणानुपलब्धेश्चावस्थाने तन्नित्यत्वप्रसङ्ग ...	ii 2 38	53
विनाशकारणानुपलपलब्धेश्चावस्थाने तन्नित्य- त्वप्रसङ्ग ...	iii 2 24	90
विनाशकारणानुपलब्धे ...	ii 2 34	52
विप्रतिपत्तिर्प्रतिपत्तिश्च निग्रहस्थानम् ...	i 2 19	20
विप्रतिपत्ती च संप्रतिपत्तेः ...	ii 1 3	22
विप्रतिपत्तिव्यवस्थाध्यवसायाज्ञ ...	ii 1 2	22
विप्रतिषेधाञ्च न त्वनेका ...	iii 1 57	76
विभक्त्यन्तरोपपत्तेश्च समासे ...	ii 2 40	54
विमशेर्हेत्वनुयोगे च विप्रतिपत्तेः संशयः ...	ii 2 13	46
विसृज्य पक्षप्रतिपक्षाभ्यामर्थावधारणं निर्णयः ...	i 1 41	13
विविधबाधनायोगाद्दुःखस्येव जन्मोत्पत्तिः ...	iv 1 55	122
विषयत्वाव्यतिरेकादेकत्वम् ...	iii 1 61	77
विषयप्रत्यभिज्ञानात् ...	iii 2 2	83
विष्टं ह्यपरं परेण ...	iii 1 68	80
वीतरागजन्मादर्शनात् ...	iii 1 25	69

		PAGE
वृत्त्यनुपपत्तेरपि तर्हि न संशयः...	iv 2 6	128
व्यक्ताद्दृष्टनिष्पत्तेःप्रतिषेधः ...	iv 1 13	110
व्यक्ताव्यक्तानां प्रत्यक्षप्रामाण्यात्	iv 1 11	110
व्यक्तिगुणविशेषाश्रयो मूर्तिः ...	ii 2 69	61
व्यक्त्याकृतिजातयस्तु पदार्थः ...	ii 2 68	61
व्यक्त्याकृतियुक्त ऽप्यपसृङ्गात् प्रोक्षणादीनां सृद्रव्यके जातिः ...	ii 2 66	61
व्यभिचारादहेतुः ...	iv 1 5	108
व्याघातादप्रयोग ...	iv 1 15	110
व्यासक्तमनसः पादव्यथनेन संयोगविशेषेण समानम् ...	iii 2 33	93
व्याहतत्वयुक्तम् ...	iv 1 40	117
व्याहतत्वाद्धेतुः ...	ii 1 28	31
,, ,, ...	iii 1 55	76
व्याहतत्वाद्धेतुः ...	iv 2 27	133
व्यूहान्तरादुद्रव्यान्तरोत्पत्तिदर्शनं पूर्वेद्रव्यनि- वृत्तिरनुमानात् ...	iii 2 17	88

श.

		PAGE
शब्द इतिह्यार्थान्तरभावादनुमानेऽर्थापत्तिसम्भवा- भावानर्थान्तरभावाञ्चाप्रतिषेध ...	ii 2 2	43
शब्दार्थयोः पुनर्वचनं पुनरुक्तमन्यता- नुवादात् ...	v 2 14	172
शब्दार्थव्यवस्थानादप्रतिषेध ...	ii 1 55	38
शब्दोऽनुमानमर्थस्यानुपलब्धेरनुमेय- त्वात् ...	ii 1 49	36
शरीरगुणवैधर्म्यात् ...	iii 2 57	101
शरीरदाहे पातकाभावात् ...	iii 1 4	63
शरीरव्यापित्वात् ...	iii 2 54	100
शरीरोत्पत्तिनिमित्तवत्संयोगोत्पत्ति निमित्तं कर्म ...	iii 2 70	104
शीघ्रतरगमनोपदेशवदभ्यासात्स्ना- विशेष ...	ii 1 68	42
श्रुतिप्रामाण्याञ्च ...	iii 1 29	70

स.

		PAGE
सगुणद्रव्योत्पत्तिवत्तदुत्पत्तिः ...	iii 1 26	69
सगुणानामिन्द्रियभावात् ...	iii 1 72	81
सद्यः कालान्तरे च निष्पत्तेः संशय ...	iv 1 44	119
स द्विविधो दृष्टादृष्टार्थत्वात् ...	i 1 8	4
स प्रतिपक्षस्थापनाहीनो वितण्डा ...	i 2 3	15
समाधिविशेषाभ्यासात् ...	iv 2 38	136

	PAGE

समानतन्त्रसिद्धिः परतन्त्रसिद्धिः प्रतितन्त्र-
सिद्धान्तः ... i 1 29 9
समानप्रसवात्मिका जातिः ... ii 2 71 62
समानानेकधर्माध्यवसायाद्न्यतरधर्माध्यवसाया-
द्वा न संशयः ... ii 1 1 22
समानानेकधर्मोपपत्तेर्विप्रतिपत्तेरुपलब्ध्यनुपल-
ब्ध्यव्यवस्थातश्च विशेषापेक्षो विमर्शः
संशयः ... i 1 23 7
समारोपणादात्मन्यप्रतिषेधः ... iv 1 62 124
सर्वतन्त्रप्रतितन्त्राधिकरणाभ्युपगमसं-
स्थितेर्थान्तरभावात् ... i 1 27 9
सर्वतन्त्राविरुद्धस्तन्त्रेऽधिकृतोऽर्थः सर्वतन्त्र-
सिद्धान्तः ... i 1 28 9
सर्वेत्वेवम् ... v 1 40 163
सर्वं नित्यं पञ्चभूतनित्यत्वात् ... iv 1 29 114
सर्वं पृथग्भावलक्षणपृथक्त्वात् ... iv 1 34 115
सर्वप्रमाणप्रतिषेधाच्च प्रतिषेध-
नुपपत्तिः ... ii 1 13 26
सर्वैर्नित्यमुत्पत्तिविनाशधर्मैकत्वात् iv 1 25 113
सर्वमभावो भावेष्वितरेतराभाव-
सिद्धेः ... iv 1 37 117
सर्वसंयोगशब्दविभवाच्च सर्वगतम् ... iv 2 21 131
सर्वग्रहणमवयवसिद्धिः ... ii 1 34 32
सव्यदृष्ट्स्य तरेण प्रत्यभिज्ञानात् iii 1 7 64
सव्यभिचारविरुद्धप्रकरणसमसाध्यसमकाला-
हेत्वाभासाः ... i 2 4 15
सहचरणस्थानताद्यर्थवृत्तमानधारणसामीप्ययोग-
साधनाधिपत्येभ्यो ब्राह्मणमञ्चकटराजसक्तु-
चन्दनगङ्गाशाटकान्नपुरुषेष्वतद्भावेऽपि तदु-
पचारः ... ii 2 64 60
संख्यैकान्तासिद्धिः कारणानुपपत्युप-
पत्तिभ्याम् ... iv 1 41 118
सन्तानानुमानविशेषणात् ... ii 2 17 48
सम्प्रदानात् ... ii 2 26 50
सम्बन्धाच्च ... ii 1 51 37
सम्भवतोऽर्थस्याप्रतिसामान्ययोगादसम्भूतार्थकल्प-
ना सामान्यच्छलम् ... i 2 13 18
संयोगोपपत्तेश्च ... iv 2 24 132
संसर्गेऽप्यनेकगुणग्रहणम् ... iii 1 67 79
साधर्म्यवैधर्म्याभ्यामुपसंहारे तद्धर्मे विपर्ययो-
पपत्तेः साधर्म्यवैधर्म्यसमौ .. v 1 2 140

साधर्म्यावैधर्म्याभ्यां प्रत्यवस्थानं
जातिः ... i 2 18 19
साधर्म्यवैधर्म्योत्कर्षापकर्षवर्ण्यावर्ण्यविकल्पसा-
ध्यप्राप्त्यप्राप्तिप्रसङ्गट्टष्टान्तानुत्पत्तिसंशय-
प्रकरणहेत्वर्थापत्त्यविशेषोपपत्त्युपलब्ध्यनुप-
लब्ध्यनित्यानित्यकार्यसमाः v 1 1 140
साधर्म्यात्तुल्यधर्मोपपत्तेः सर्पानित्यत्व प्रसङ्-
गादनित्यसमः ... v 1 32 160
साधर्म्यात्संशये न संशयो वैधर्म्यादुभयथा वा
संशये अत्यन्तसंशयप्रसङ्गोनित्यत्ववानभ्युपग-
माच्च सामान्यस्याप्रतिषेधः ... v 1 15 152
साधर्म्यादसिद्धिः प्रतिषेधासिद्धिः प्रतिषेध्य-
साधर्म्याच्च ... v 1 33 160
साध्यवादवयविनि संदेहः ... ii 1 33 32
साध्यसमत्वादहेतुः ... iii 2 3 83
साध्यत्वादहेतुः ... iii 2 28 91
साध्यदृष्टान्तयोर्धर्मविकल्पादुभय-
साध्यत्वाच्चोत्कर्षापकर्षवर्ण्यावर्ण्यां-
वर्ण्यविकल्पसाध्यसमाः ... v 1 4 142
साध्यनिर्देशः प्रतिज्ञा ... i 1 33 10
साध्यसमत्वादहेतुः ... iii 2 3 83
साध्यसाधर्म्यात्तद्धर्मभावी दृष्टान्त
उदाहरणम् ... i 1 36 11
साध्यातिदेशाच्च दृष्टान्तोपपत्तेः v 1 6 146
साध्याविशिष्टः साध्यत्वात्साध्यसमः i 2 8 16
सामान्यदृष्टान्तयोरैन्द्रियकत्वे समाने
नित्यानित्यसाधर्म्यात्संशयसमः ... v 1 14 151
सामान्यवतो धर्मयोगो न सामान्यस्य ii 2 51 56
सिद्धान्तमभ्युपेत्य तद्विरोधी
विरुद्धः ... i 2 6 16
सिद्धान्तमभ्युपेत्यानियमात्
कथाप्रसंगो ण्सिद्धान्तः ... v 2 24 175
सुव्यासक्तमनसां चेन्द्रियार्थः
संनिकर्षनिमित्तत्वात् ... ii 1 26 30
सुवर्णादीनां पुनरुत्पत्तेरहेतुः ... ii 2 48 56
सुषुप्तस्य स्वप्नादर्शने क्लेशाभावा-
दपवर्गः ... iv 1 63 124
सेनावनवद्ग्रहणमिति चेन्नातीन्द्रियत्वा-
दणूनाम् ... ii 1 36 33
स्तुतिनिन्दा परकृतिः पुराकल्प
इत्यर्थवादः ... ii 1 65 41

		PAGE	
स्थानान्यत्वे नानाखाद्वयाविना-			
नास्यानत्वाच्च संशय: ...	iii	1 51	75
स्फटिकान्यत्वाभिमानवत्तद्न्यत्वा-			
भिमान: ...	iii	2 9	85
स्फटिके ध्यपरापरोत्पत्ते: त्वाणि-			
कत्वाद् व्यक्तीनामहेतु: ...	iii	2 10	86
स्मरणं खात्मनो च्वस्वाभाव्यात्	iii	2 43	96
स्मरत: शरीरभारणोपपत्तेर-			
प्रतिषेध: ...	iii	2 29	92
स्मृतिसंकल्पवच्च स्वम्विषयाभि-			
मान: ...	iv	2 34	135
स्वपच्चदोषाभ्युपगमात्परपच्चे दोष-			
प्रसंगो मतानुज्ञा ...	v	2 21	174
स्वपच्चलक्षणापेच्चोपपरयुपसंहारे			
हेतुर्निर्देशे परपच्चदोषाभ्यु-			
पगमात्स्वमानो दोष इति ...	v	1 43	164

		PAGE	
स्वपूतिपच्चस्थापनाहीनो वितण्डा	i	2 3	15
स्वप्रविषयाभिमानवद्यं			
प्रमाणप्रमेयाभिमान: ...	iv	2 31	134
स्वविषयानत्क्रिमेशेन्द्रियस्य पटु-			
मन्दभावाद्वि षयग्रहणस्य			
तथाभावो नाविषये प्रवृत्ति:	iv	2 14	130

ह्.

हीनमन्यतमेनाप्यवयवेन न्यूनम् ...	v	2 12	172
हेतूदाहरणाधिकमधिकम् ...	v	2 13	172
हेतूपादानारत्प्रतिषेद्व्याभ्यनुज्ञा ...	iii	2 48	98
हेत्वपदेशात्प्रतिज्ञाया: पुनर्वचनं			
निगमनम् ...	i	1 39	12
हेत्वभावादसिद्धि: ...	iv	2 33	135
हेत्वाभासाश्च यथोक्ता: ...	v	2 25	175

इति ।

Index of Words in English.

A

Page.

Abhâva 2, 117
Abode 9
Abode of particular qualities 61
Absence ... 112, 137
Absence of link ... 87
Absence of perception ... 49
Abstinence 138
Absurd 76, 86
Absurdities 89
Absurdity 13
Acceptance 9
Act 8, 39
Act force 81
Action 5, 6, 32, 41, 50, 83, 96
Activities 123
Activity 2, 5, 6, 7, 94, 108, 123, 125
Act of knowledge ... 118
Acts 112
Acuteness 130
Acuteness or dullness of ap-
prehension 130
Admission of an opinion 164, 167, 174
Adoption 13
Adultery 6
Advantage 40
Affection 2, 3, 7, 96, 108, 126
Affirmative ... 11, 12
Affirmative application ... 12
Affirmative example ... 11
Affix 59
Âgama 2
Agent of knowledge ... 118
Aggregates 115
Air 9, 79
Airy 70
Aitihya 2

Page.

Akritâbhyâgama 110
All-pervading ... 20, 70, 132
Alteration 40
Alteration of time ... 40
Alternating character ... 142
Alternative 17
Analogy ... 17, 113, 119, 121
Annihilation 2, 130
Ant hill 87
Antecedent ... 46, 126
Anumâna 2, 3
Apavarga 7, 125
A posteriori 3, 34,
Apparently 79
Apparent modification ... 59
Appearance 136
Appearances 116
Appearance of difference ... 85
Application ... 10, 12
Apprehension 6, 71, 79, 98, 127, 130
A priori 3
A priori inference ... 34
Appropriate 124
Approach 69
Aprâpta kâla 17
Arbitrariness 92
Arbuda 104
Argument 47, 50, 52, 147, 150
Argumentation 1
Arguments ... 20, 67, 96, 128
Arrogance 125
Arthâ-patti ... 2, 43, 44
Artificial 47, 48
Ârya 2
Ârya desa ... 115, 120
Âryas... 39
Ascertainment 1, 13

9

Page.

Âdhaka 43
Asleep 124
Asolute rule 86
Assumption 17
Assent 86
Assertion 3, 4
Association ... 60, 123
Association of troubles ... 124
Assumption 88
Atom 50, 103, 106, 126, 131
Atomic dimension ... 95
Atomic mind 89
Atomic substance ... 6, 29
Atoms ... 8, 15, 130
Attach 15
Attainment of supreme felicity 1
Attendants 121
Attention ... 93, 96
Audience 24
Auditory ... 20, 78
Auditory perception 20, 30, 31
Augmentation 59
Authority ... 9, 15, 70
Authors 42
Avayava ... 1, 10, 129
Aversion .. 2, 3, 5, 7, 94, 108
Awaking 135
Awanting 121

● B

Balancing the addition ...140, 142
Balancing the alternative ...140, 144
Balancing in co-presence ...140, 147
Balancing the counter-exam-
ple 140, 149
Balancing the controversy 140, 153
Balancing the demonstration 140, 157
Balancing the doubt ...140, 152
Balancing the effect ...140, 162
Balancing the eternal ... 161
Balancing the eternality ··· 140
Balancing the heterogeneity 140, 141

Page.

Balancing the homogeneity 140, 141
Balancing the infinite re-
gression 140, 149
Balancing the mutual
absence 140, 148
Balancing the non-difference 140, 156
Balancing the non-eternality 140, 160
Balancing the non-perception 140, 159
Balancing the non-produced 150, 170
Balancing the non-reason ...140, 153
Balancing the perception ...140, 158
Balancing the presumption 140, 155
Balancing the questionable 140, 143
Balancing the reciprocity ...140, 145
Balancing the subtraction ...140, 143
Balancing the unquestionable 140, 144
Beginning 47
Beginningless 126
Bhâṣya-commentary ... 31
Bhâṭṭas 2
Birth 27, 122
Blackness 126
Blame 41, 123
Blanket 18
Block-head 20
Bodily actions 6
Body 5, 63, 64. 70, 100, 101, 137
Bone 65
Bosgavaeus 4, 36
Bragging 15
Brâhmaṇa ... ···3, 18, 60
Breast 69
Buddhas 2
Buddhi 6
Buddhist ... 15, 22, 86
Buddhist Sanskrit and Pali
Literature 125
Bulk 54
Burning 38

C

Capacity 10, 83

	Page.
Carelessness	112
Carping	15
Cârvâkas	2
Categories	1, 24
Cattle	121
Cause 3, 23, 104, 112, 114, 127	
Cause and effect ...	109
Cause of destruction ..	90
Cause of growth and decay...	87
Cause of in-audition ...	52
Cause of production ...103, 113	
Causes of faults ...	127
Cave	157
Cavil ... 1, 14, 15, 139	
Caviller	15
Censuring the non-censur- able 167, 175	
Cessation 106, 127	
Cessation of egotism ...	127
Cessation of recognition ...	84
Cessation of the intellect ...	84
Chala	1, 17
Channels	9
Character 7, 11, 12, 13, 23, 54, 71, 75, 78, 96, 101, 113, 136	
Characterised	80
Character of an object ...	77
Character of a modification	55
Character of perception ...	114
Character of transparency ...	75
Charaka	41
Change	88
Circle of fire brand ...	102
City of the celestial quiris- ters	135
Classification of Vedic speech	40
Clay	148
Clay statue	104
Co-abide	54
Cognisable 76, 87	
Cognised	47
Cognitions ... 25, 26, 90, 93, 102	

	Page.
Collocation of parts ...	132
Colour 5, 9, 17, 30, 59, 71, 78, 98, 101 102, 127	
Combustibles	113
Command	42
Commixture	79
Common	22
" Commonly seen " ...	3,34
Comparison 2, 3, 4, 25, 35, 36	
Common properties ...	22
Compendious expression ...	36
Complete destruction ...	2
Compound	59
Compassion	6
Conceit ... 65, 85, 122	
Conceit of difference ...	85
Conceit of duality ...	65
Conceit of pleasure ...	122
Concept	135
Concept of means ...	134
Conception ... 62, 127	
Conciousness	6
Concentration	112
Conclusion 10, 12, 13, 15, 20, 67, 88, 145	
Concomitant	10
Conditions	10
Conduct	18
Confirmation	13
Conflicting	22
Conflicting judgment ...	7
Conflicting testimony ...	22
Conflicting opinions ...	46
Conflicting reasons ...	46
Confutation ... 1, 13, 35	
Conjointly	22
Conjunction 6, 29, 31, 60, 90, 92, 93, 104, 106, 122, 131	
Connection ... 3, 20, 37, 38, 39	
Connoted	150
Consciousness	14
Consequence ... 78, 73	

	Page.
Constant audition	82
Constituents	131
Contact	3, 25, 30, 71, 73, 81, 89
Contentious	23
Context	96
Continuity	23
Contingency	84, 90
Contradiction	39, 40, 76
Contradictory	15, 16, 58
Contradictory reason	16
Contrary	13, 22
Controversy	153
Convention	39
Conviction	22
Copresence	147
Corresponding element	80
Corresponding substrata	81
Corruption	125
Countenance	68
Counter argument	53
Counter example	149, 150
Course	2
Covetousness	6
Cow	4
Cowhood	141
Critical examination	1
Crystal	73, 74, 85, 86
Curd	87
Cuticle	101

D

Dadhi	54
Deaths	7
Debt to Gods	123
Debt to progenitors	123
Debt to sages	123
Debts	123
Decay	83, 87
Declaration	4
Deeds	95, 103
Defect	39, 40
Defence	15

	Page.
Defilement	2, 125
Definite form	61
Definition	1, 24
Deliverance	7
Demarcate	95
Demerits	72, 125
Demonstration	157
Denial	114, 136
Depravity	125
Desert	104, 105, 106
Design	60
Desire	5, 68, 69, 94
Desire and aversion	96
Destruction	2, 9, 19, 48, 57, 65, 88, 89, 90, 106, 110, 111, 114, 120
Determinate	3
Determination	10, 13
Deva-riṇa	123
Devotion	6
Dharma Sastra	124
Dialogue	14
Diminution	59
Dimness	129
Direct	19
Direction	29
Disappearance	106
Disconnection	20
Disciples	138
Discussion	1, 10, 14, 138
Disjoined	88
Disputant	20, 22, 24
Disputation	14
Dissimilarity	20
Dissolution	70
Distinct	110
Distress	122, 124
Distribution	116
Divisible	108
Doctrine	14, 132
Dogma	9, 10
Doubt	1, 7, 22, 23, 32, 54, 59, 119, 125, 127, 151, 152

		Page.
Dream	...	124, 134, 135
Dṛṣṭânta	...	... 1
Drum	...	...17, 27
Duality	...	... 65
Dullness	...	... 130
Durable	...	... 17
Duration	...	... 92
Dust ...	...	... 3
Duties	...	... 138
Dvyaṇuka	...	... 131

E

Ear ...	...	... 5, 81
Earth	...	... 5, 9
Earthenware	...	... 61
Earthy	..	...70, 80
Effect	...	3, 109, 162
Efforts of attention	...	93
Egotism	...	... 127
Element		5, 9, 78, 79, 80, 103
Emancipation	...	105, 106
Endless doubt	...	... 23
Enjoyable	...	... 117
Entity 28, 60, 110, 111, 112, 116, 117		
Entreaty	...	... 96
Enunciation	...	... 1, 24
Epithet	...	... 3, 12
Equal to the question	...	16
Erratic	...	15, 108
Essence and appearance	...	136
Established tenet	...	1, 9
Establishment	...	... 118
Eternal 8, 10, 13, 15, 47, 50, 51, 53,		
57, 64, 69, 90, 106, 109, 113, 114,		
		131, 157, 161
Eternalness	...	... 57
Eternality	...	12, 16, 152
Eternity	...	... 9
Ether 83, 5, 9, 20, 29, 53, 79, 129,		
		132
Ethereal	...	... 70
Evasion	...	167, 174

		Page.
Evidence	...	110, 134
Examination	...	1, 10, 24
Example	10, 12, 13, 142, 145	
Excess	...	... 96
Excitement	...	... 66
Exclusion	...	... 96
Exercise	...	... 96
Existence	...	49, 63, 109, 127
Existent	...	... 120
Extension	...	... 48
Expanding	...	... 68
Experience	...	... 4
Expert	...	... 4, 8
Expression	...	... 110
Expressive of action	..	111
External light	...	... 73
External objects	...	136
Eye	...	... 5, 8
Eye ball	...	... 70
Eye knowledge	...	... 30

F

Factitious	...	.. 131
Fallacies	...	... 15
Fallacies of a reason		15, 175
Fallacious argument		... 147
Fallacy	...	... 1
False apprehension		... 135
False knowledge ...		... 136
Familiar instance		... 1
Fault	...	... 5
Faults	...	2, 7, 108, 127
Faults of untruth ...		... 39
Fear	...	...68, 96
Felicity	...	... 1, 2
Fences	...	... 139
Fiery	...	...10, 70
Figuratively	...	... 60
Filling	...	... 38
Five	...	8, 38, 79, 113
Fire brand	...	... 102
Fineness	...	... 81

	Page.
Fire sacrifice	41
Five elements	114
Five objects	77
Five senses	77
Fixation	60
Fixed character	75
Fixed connection	38
Fixed relation	63
Fixity	58
Fixity of number	118
Food ...	38, 121
Forbearance	94
Forbearance from activity ...	94
Forest 4,	137
Forester	4
Form ... 59, 61, 62,	78
Formation	137
Fortuitous effects	112
Fruit ... 5, 7, 13, 95, 103, 112, 119,	
	137
Fruit of previous deeds ...	103
Fulfilment	105
Function ... 60, 76,	91
Futile	20
Futilities ... 15, 21,	140
Futility ... 1, 20,	146
Future ... 34,	111

G

	Page.
Ganges	60
General nation	152
Generality 5,	32
Genus ... 18, 47, 59, 61,	
	62, 170
Gesture	5
Glass	73
God	112
Gold ... 56,	121
Good	127
Greed	125
Grief	68
Ground	90

	Page.
Growth	87
Gustatory	78
Gustatory perception ...	30

H

	Page.
Habitual	136
Hatchet	38
Hair	100
Happiness	121
Horse sacrifices	4
Hatred	125
Heat	68
Heretical view	125
Heterogeneous ...	11, 12
Heterogeneous example	12, 140
Heterogeneity ...	152, 153
Hetvâbhâsa	1, 15
Hîna kleśa	125
Hunger	137
Homogeneity ...151, 152, 153, 160	
Homogeneous	11
Homogeneous example ...	140
Homogeneous things ...	109
Hurting the proposition ...	167
Hypothesis	9
Hypothetical	9
Hypothetical dogma ..	9
Hypothetical reasoning ...	1

I

	Page.
Ideas	69
Identical ...	78, 84
Ignorance ... 20, 167, 173	
Illumination ...	28, 149
Illusion	28
Imagination	135
Immediate	119
Immediate subsequency ...	96
Immolation	61
Impelling	92
Impermanent	56
Implication	9

	Page.
Implied dogma ...	... 9, 10
Impossibility ...	18, 128, 131
Impressions ...	... 93
Impropriety ...	... 129
Inactive ...	... 20
Inadmissible ...	... 123
Inanimate ...	19, 68
Inaudition ...	... 52
Incapacity ...	.. 95
Inconsistency ...	... 111
Incoherent ...	167, 17
Incompatible ...	... 50
Incongruous ...	... 120
Inconsistent ...	... 110
Indifference ...	... 10
Indirect ...	... 19
Indeterminate ...	... 3
Individual ...	59, 60, 61, 86
Individuality ...	... 61
Indivisibility ...	... 132
Indivisibility of atoms	... 132
Inequality ...	... 104
Inexperience ...	... 105
Inference ...	2, 3, 25, 28, 31, 33, 67, 71
Infinite regression	140, 149
Injunction ...	40, 41, 75, 124
Innumerable ...	... 67
Inopportune ...	17, 130, 157 171
Inquiry ...	... 10
Instance ...	1, 8, 12
Instructive assertion ...	4
Instrument ...	... 67
Instrument of knowledge ...	67
Intangible ...	15, 16, 50, 53
Intellect ...	5, 6, 7, 16, 83, 84, 85
Intelligence ...	... 5
Internal-perception ...	... 159
Interpenetrated ...	... 80
Interrelation ...	... 109
Interrelation of cause and effect	109

	Page.
Interval ...	50, 122
Intervention ...	... 96
Intimate relation ...	... 5, 32
Intimately ...	... 71
Invalid ...	... 45
Invariable ...	... 10
Investigator ...	... 8
Investigation ...	... 13
Invisibility ...	... 73
Iron ...	... 69
Ironball ...	... 10
Irregularities ...	... 22
Irregularity ...	23, 24, 95
Irregularity of perception ...	7
Itihâsa ...	... 124

J

Jalpa ...	... 1
Jar ...	17, 47, 110
Jâti ...	1, 62, 140
Jijñâsâ ...	... 10
Jñâna ...	.. 6
Judgment ...	... 7
Jugglery ...	... 135
Jyotiṣṭoma ...	... 41

K

Kalala ...	... 104
Kandara ...	... 104
Karma ...	81, 124
Kathâ ...	... 14
Kileso ...	... 125
Killing ...	... 6
Kitchen ...	8, 10
Kleśa ...	... 125
Knave ...	... 20
Knower ...	67, 96
Knowledge 1, 2, 3, 6, 9, 24, 29, 35, 67, 78, 84, 89, 90, 91, 96, 97, 101, 127, 136, 137	
Knowledge of truth ...	135
Kritahâni ...	... 110

L

	Page.
Lalitavistara Sûtra	... 134
Lamp	... 17, 28, 99, 149
Laṅkâvatâra Sûtra	... 133
Light	5, 9, 72, 73
Likeness	 96
Link	 87
Letter	... 55, 56
Loadstone	 69
Locomotion	 22
Lotus	 68

M

Mâdhyamika Buddhist philo- sophy	 120
Mâdyamika Sûtra	... 134
Magnitude	 71
Mahâyâna works ...	 134
Mâṃsa peśî	 104
Malice	 6
Manifestation	17, 61, 73, 110, 111
Mark	6, 45, 87, 96, 115, 116
Mat	 60
Material	... 39, 54, 70, 78
Material substance	...70, 72
Matter	... 4, 6, 95
Maturation	 100
Mâyâ	 136
Meaningless	... 167, 170
Means of knowledge	... 118
Means of right knowledge	1, 2, 26
Measure	 60
Medical Science ...	 42
Meditation	... 136, 137
Members	... ... 1, 10
Membrane	 73
Memory	... 68, 96
Merit	... 74, 112, 125
Merit and demerit	... 96
Metaphor	... 17, 19
Metaphorically	 19
Meteor	 72

	Page.
Mica	 73
Milk	 87
Mimâm Śakas	 9
Mind	5, 6, 10, 29, 67, 90, 92
Mirage	... 8, 135
Mirror	 75
Misapprehension ...	2, 112, 126
Mistimed	... 15, 17
Mistimed reason ...	... 17
Mleccha	... ... 4, 39
Modification	... 54, 55, 57, 58
Modification and substitute ...	54
Momentary	... 86, 99
Mother	 163
Motion	... 17, 85
Magical power	 89
Multiplicity	 21
Mutual absence ...	140, 147
Mutual difference...	... 101

N

Nâgârjuna	... 115, 120
Nails	 100
Naiyâyika	... 2, 22, 80, 83, 94
Natural	 125
Natural connection	... 38
Natural quality ...	... 99
Nature	... 1, 6, 77
Nature of sound ...	... 46
Navakambala	 18
Necessity	 138
Negative	... ...4, 12
Negative application	... 12
Newborn	 69
Night	 73
Nigraha sthâna ...	... 1, 17
Nirṇaya	 1
Nirvikalpaka	 3
No-cause	 113
Non-difference	... 36, 157
Non-distinction ...	... 161
Non-distinguished	... 147

Page.

Non erratic 3
Non entity ... 110, 111, 117
Non eternal 8, 10, 11, 12, 13, 16, 48,
50, 90, 113, 126, 151, 162
Non eternalness 113
Non eternality ... 11, 158
Non-existence 2, 43, 45, 47, 48, 71,
126, 128, 159
Non existent ... 117, 120
Nonfulfilment 105
Non ingenuity ... 167, 174
Non-material 72
Non perception 22, 28, 29, 32, 49,
52, 87, 159, 162
Nonperception of knowledge in
pots 95
Non-produced 150
Non production 89
Non reality 134
Non simultaneous ... 84
Non simultaneousness 93, 102
Non simultaneousness of cog-
nitions 102
Non simultaneity... ... 29
Non transparent 75
Nose 5, 65
" Not commonly seen " ... 3
Nyâya Sûtra ... 2, 10, 17, 138

O

Object 3, 5, 7, 8, 9, 30, 66, 76,
81, 83, 85, 89, 136
Objection 23, 35
Object of knowledge 118, 134
Object of right knowledge ... 1
Objects of sense ... 5, 76, 77,
Obscurity 73
Observance 138
Observation 112
Obstruction ... 72, 125
Obviousness ... 71, 72, 73
Occasion for rebuke 1, 20, 167

Page.

Occurrence 86
Odour 77, 78
Olfactory 78
Olfactory perception ... 30
Omnipresence 131
One 129
Operation ... 64, 66, 93
Operations of stimuli ... 93
Operations of the Soul ... 64
Operator 39
Opponent ... 14, 20, 22
Oppression of persons by spells 48
Opportunity 124
Opposing the proposition 167, 169
Opposition 17, 20, 48, 51, 63, 96, 114,
145
Organ of vision 65
Origination 83
" Other " 51
Otherness 51
Overlooking the censurable 167, 174

P

Pâda 104
Pain 2, 5, 7, 122
Paradise 41
Part 32, 127, 128
Partially 128
Partially eternal 48
Partial similarity ... 35
Particularity 5, 32
Parts ... 127, 128, 129
Parts in an atom 132
Past 34, 111
Paurânikas 2
Perception 2, 3, 4, 6, 8, 13, 22, 24, 25,
28, 30, 32, 38, 57, 70, 71, 74, 76,
81, 110, 114, 133, 158, 159
Perception of sound ... 81
Perfect tranquillity ... 2
Perishable 50
Permanency 83

	Page.
Persistent ...	53, 83, 98
Permanent intellect	... 84
Person ...	... 122
Persuasion ...	40, 41
Pervades ...	... 100
Philosophy ...	... 8
Physician ...	... 4
Pitṛi ṛiṇa ...	... 123
Pleasure ...	5, 7, 122
Pleasure and pain...	... 96
Ploughing ...	... 119
Possession	75, 78, 95, 96, 137
Pot ...	16, 95, 198
Prâbhâkaras ...	... 2
Practice ...	... 68
Practicable ...	... 136
Praise ...	41, 123
Prakriti ...	... 6
Pramâṇa ...	... 1
Prameya ...	... 1
Pratyakṣa ...	2, 6, 74
Prayojana ...	... 1, 10
Preceptors ...	... 138
Predicable ...	... 151
Predicate ...	147, 154
Predominance ...	80, 136
Predominant quality	... 81
Pre-eminence ...	... 31
Prescription ...	... 41
Present time ...	... 34
Presumption ...	2, 43, 44, 155
Previous life ...	68, 69
Pride	... 125
Primordial matter	... 6, 70
Principle ...	... 96
Principle of injunction	... 40
Probability ...	... 2, 43
Processes ...	... 78
Produced ...	113, 119
Product ...	... 20
Production	46, 90, 103, 104, 110, 111, 112, 113, 114, 120, 126, 148

	Page.
Prohibition ...	75, 110
Promiscuously ...	... 120
Pronunciation ...	... 49
Proof	16, 83, 85
Propagation ...	... 59
Proper ...	... 132
Properties ...	7, 8, 22, 23
Property ...	8, 11, 150
Proposition	8, 10, 11, 12, 13, 15, 16, 167
Purâṇa ...	... 124
Purifying ...	... 138
Purpose ...	1, 8, 10, 72
Puruṣa ...	... 6, 94

Q

Qualities	5, 9, 54, 69, 70, 71, 79, 99, 102, 112
Qualities of earth ...	... 70
Quality	5, 32, 59, 66, 79, 99, 145
Quality of soul ...	... 89
Quality of sound ...	... 81
Question ...	... 8
Questioning ...	... 10
Quibble ...	1, 15, 17, 18

R

Radish ...	... 8
Rain	... 68
Rapt in mind ...	... 93
Ray	70, 71, 72
Reality ...	... 133
Really eternal ...	... 48
Reason	10, 11, 12, 13, 16, 83, 91, 118, 135, 147, 154
Reason ...	46, 118
Reasoning ...	... 1
Rebirth ...	... 125
Rebuke ...	1, 15, 17, 20, 21
Receipt ...	... 96
Receptacle ...	... 121

	Page.
Receptacle of happiness ...	121
Reception	84
Recognition 7, 8, 22, 23, 83, 84, 85	
Recognition of objects ...	83
Recollection ...30, 91, 92, 93, 98	
Recklessness	125
Reductio ad absurdum ...	1, 35
Reflection	6
Refuge ...	129, 133
Refuge ad refugee ...	97
Refutation	114
Regressus ad infinitum ...	132
Regularity ...	23, 95
Regulation ...	114, 115
Reinculcation ... 40, 41, 42, 172	
Relation	109
Relation of refuge ad refugee ...	96
Release 2, 5, 7, 63, 123, 124, 137	
Reliable	42
Reliable person	4
Reliability	42
Reliance	37
Remembrance ...	66, 135
Renouncing the proposition	167, 169
Repelled	132
Repetition 41, 51, 167, 172, 173	
Residence ...	128, 129
Right knowledge 1, 2, 13, 26, 27, 43	
Riṣi	4, 39
Riṣi ṛiṇa ...	123
River	33
Rumour ...	2, 43
S	
Śabda	2
Sacred books	6
Sacrifice ...	39, 124
Sâdhya ...	118
Śakya prâpti ...	10
Samâdhirâja Sûtra ...	134
Sambhava	2
Sameness	52

	Page.
Sânkhya Philosophy ...	6
Sânkhyas ...	2, 9, 83, 94
Samśaya ...	1, 10
Samśaya vyudâsa	10
Samskâra ...	81
Sarvajit sacrifice	41
Satisfaction ...	8
Ṣaṭpakṣî kathâ ...	164
Savikalpaka ...	3
Savour ...	78
Saying too little ...	167, 172
Saying too much ...	167, 172
Scaffolds ...	18, 60
Scepticism ...	6
School ...	9
Screened ...	73
Scriptures ...	13, 14, 15, 70
Search of truth ...	138
Season ...	68
Seat of knowledge	95
Secondary meaning	123
Sacred fire ...	121
Seeds ...	139
Self existent ...	117
Sense 3, 5, 9, 30, 47, 51, 63, 65, 66, 70, 72, 75, 76, 77, 78, 80, 85, 89, 130	
Sense organ ...	6, 7, 10, 89
Sense perception ...	35
Sensuous bodies ...	89
Sentiments ...	5, 7
Separately ...	22
Separation ...	7, 97, 105
Sivaḥ ...	104
Series ...	7
Series of reasons ...	149
Several marks ...	115
Shadow ...	17
Shamelessness ...	125
Shifting the proposition	167, 168
Shifting the reason	167, 169
Shifting the topic	167, 170

	Page.			Page.
Siddhânta	1	Statue of stone		103
Significate	154	Stealing		6
Sight	63	Step		111
Sign	96, 154	Study		8
Silence	167, 173	Stupidity	2, 7, 108, 109, 125	
Similarity	3, 19, 20, 33, 35	Subject	2, 142, 145, 146	
Simultaneous	24, 93	Subject in dispute		83
Simultaneous cognitions	89	Subservient		72, 112
Simultaneously	84	Substance	3, 5, 9, 10, 32, 55, 59, 71	
Simultaneous productions	91	Substitute		54
Sin	63, 64	Substrata		81
Single entity	116	Substratum		53
Single thing	108	Succession		84
Site of operations of the soul	64	Successive annihilation		2
Sites	78	Summer		3
Sixteen categories	1	Summum bonum		138
Six-winged disputation	164, 166	Sun		3
Skin	5	Supersensuous		71
Sloth	125	Supreme felicity		1, 2
Smell	5, 9, 70	Supremacy		60
Smoke	3, 8, 76	Sustaining		92
Smoky	10	Sustenance		60
Solution	16	Syllogism		10
Son	121	System		8
Soul	3, 5, 8, 11, 20, 22, 29, 63, 66, 67, 69, 91, 92, 95, 96, 104, 109, 121, 124, 138,		**T**	
Soul is receptacle of happiness	121	Tactual		78
		Tactual perception		30
Sound	5, 8, 9, 10, 11, 12, 17, 27, 46, 50, 51, 53, 78, 81, 90, 131	Taking		59
Soundness	8, 53	Tallness		8
Space	29	Tangibility		28
Speech	40	Tank		8
Special qualities	78	Tarka		1
Special part of touch	76	Taste		5, 9
Special practice of meditation,	136	Tautology		39, 40, 42
Spell	42, 148	Teaching		50, 51
Spiritual injunction	138	Technicalities		5
Splitting	38	Tenet		1, 9, 10
Statements	22	Term		17, 19
State of formation	137	Termination		105
		Termination of deserts		105
		Testimony		2, 4, 8, 22

	Page.
" That " ...	... 59
Thing ...	...75, 88
Thing denoted ...	... 150
Thorn ...	... 112
Thoughts ...	... 133
Time	... 29
Tongue ...	... 5
Touch	5, 26, 63, 75, 76, 101
Touching ...	... 9
Total absence ...	... 73
Totally ...	... 128
Tranquillity ...	... 2
Transcend ...	... 130
Transitory ...	83, 98, 99
Transmigration ...	2, 5, 7, 13, 109
Transparency ...	... 75
Transparent consciousness ...	6
Treatise ...	... 124
Treatise on knowledge	... 138
Tree	... 119
Trick	... 67
Troubles ...	123, 124, 125
True knowledge ...	... 2
True nature ...	...1, 127
Trusted to the soul	... 124
Tryasarenu ...	... 131
Twilight ...	... 8, 22
Type	... 170

U

Udyotakara ...	... 30
Umpire ...	... 24
Unassailable ...	... 57
Unattended ...	... 112
Uncertainty ...	...44, 88
Uncommon properties	... 22
Undemonstrable ...	... 106
Understanding ...	... 121
Uneasiness ...	... 7
Unenvious persons	... 138
Uniformity ...	... 39
Unintelligible ...	167, 171

	Page.
Uninterrupted course	... 2
Union ...	...17, 20
Universal ...	... 20
Universality ...	... 131
Universal uniformity	... 39
Unlimited dimensions	... 132
Unmarked ...	... 45
Unnameable ...	... 3
Unobviousness ...	... 73
Unperceived ...	... 36
Unproved ...	... 16
Unreasonable	...117, 121, 129, 150
Unsaid ...	... 155
Unsaid conclusion	... 155
Untenable ...	... 90
Untruth ...	... 39
Upakleśa ...	... 125
Upalabdhi ...	... 6
Upamâna ...	... 2
Uttara Kurus ...	... 37

V

Vâcaspati ...	... 30
Vacuum ...	... 53
Vâda	... 1
Vaiśeṣikas ...	... 2
Vaiśeṣika Philosophy	... 5
Valid	43, 83, 118
Validity ...	... 26
Vanquisher ...	... 22
Vapour ...	... 10
Varieties ...	... 54
Variety ...	... 129
Vâtsayana	1, 3, 17, 27, 30, 31
Veda	...39, 42
Vedântin ...	... 2
Verbal ...	... 2
Verbal testimony ...	2, 4, 25, 38
Verbal trick ...	... 67
Vicinity ...	... 60
Veil	... 49
Vision... ...	... 65

	Page.
Visual	... 78
Visual perception	...31, 80
Viśvanatha	... 30
Vitaṇdâ	... 1
Vividness	... 93
Vocal actions	... 6
Voice ...	... 6
Volition	... 5

W

Warning	... 41
Water...	... 3, 5, 8, 9, 75, 79
Watery	...70, 80
Waxing	... 59
Web ...	... 133
Whole	... 32, 127, 128, 129

	Page.
" Within "	... 131
Wife ...	... 121
" Without "	... 131
Word ...	4, 38, 59
World	... 2
Wrangler	... 15
Wrangling	... 1, 14, 15, 139

Y

Yoga institute	... 138
Yogacara Buddhist philosophy	133
Yogi ...	... 89
" Yava "	... 39

Z

Zeal for truth	... 139

WORD INDEX TO THE NYÂYA SÛTRA.

अ

					Page.
अकरणयोः iii. 2. 74.	...	...	...	...	105
अकर्तव्यता ii. 1. 43. ...	...	...	...	...	35
अकार्ये iv. 2. 20.	...	...	...	...	131
अकृत iii. 2. 78.	...	...	...	...	106
अकृताभ्यागमात् iii. 2. 41.	...	...	...	...	94
अग्नेः iv. 1. 27.	...	...	...	...	113
अग्रहणं ii. 1. 12., iii. 2. 6.	...	...	...	35, 84
अग्रहणात् iii. 1. 73., iii. 2. 4.	...	...	...	81, 84
अज्ञताभिः iii. 2. 32. ...	...	...	...	...	92
अज्ञानं v. 2. 1., v. 2. 18.	...	...	...	167, 173
अणु ii. 2. 25., iii. 1. 31., iii. 2. 63., iii. 2. 77., iv. 1. 67., iv. 2. 16.					
			50, 70, 103, 106, 126, 130
अणूनाम् ii. 1. 36. ...	...	...	...	...	33
अतन्द्रावे ii. 2. 64. ...	...	...	...	...	60
अतः ii. 1. 15., ii. 1. 17.	...	...	...	...27, 27
अत्यन्त i. 1. 22., ii. 1. 5., ii. 1. 6., ii. 1. 44., v. 1. 15.,	... 7, 23, 23, 35, 152
अत्यन्तसंशयः ii. 1. 5.	...	...	...	...	23
अस्यय i. 2. 9.	...	...	...	...	17
अतिदेशात् v. 1. 6. ...	...	...	...	...	146
अतिशय iii. 2. 44. ...	...	...	...	...	96
अतिसामान्य i. 2. 13.	...	...	...	...	18
अतिसामान्ययोगात् i. 2. 13.	...	...	...	...	18
अतीत ii. 1. 41., iv. 1. 16.	...	...	...	34, 111
अतीतकाला i. 2. 4. ...	...	...	...	...	15
अतीन्द्रियत्वात् ii. 1. 36., ii. 2. 53. ...	...	...	...33, 57
अतुल्यप्रकृतीनां ii. 2. 44.	...	...	...	...	55
अथ i. 1. 5.	...	...	...	...	3
अदर्शनात् iii. 1. 25. ...	...	...	...	...	69
अदर्शने iv. 1. 63. ...	...	...	...	...	124
अदृष्टान्ते v. 2. 2. ...	...	...	...	...	167
अदृष्टार्थत्वात् i. 1. 8. ...	...	...	...	...	4

		Page.
अथ ii. 1. 15.	...	27
अद्विप्रवृत्तित्वात् ii. 1. 50.	...	37
अधर्मे iii. 2. 44.	...	96
अधिकं v. 2. 1., v. 2. 13.	...	167, 172
अधिकरण i. 1. 26., i. 1. 27., i. 1. 30.	...	8, 9, 9
अधिकारात् iv. 1. 61.	...	124
अधिकृत्य i. 1. 24.	...	8
अधिकृतः i. 1. 28.	...	9
अधिगमः i. 1. 1.	...	1
अधिष्ठान iii. 1. 62.	...	78
अध्यवसाय iv. 2. 50.	...	139
अध्यवसायात् ii. 1. 1., ii. 1. 2., ii. 1. 6.	...	22, 22, 23
अध्यात्म iv. 2. 46.	...	138
अध्यात्मम् v. 1. 31.	...	159
अध्यापनात् ii. 2. 28., ii. 2. 29.	...	50, 51
अध्युत्पत्तिवत् iii. 2. 14.	...	87
अनतिक्रमेण iv. 2. 14.	...	130
अनन्यता ii. 2. 33.	...	52
अनन्यत्वात् ii. 2. 32.	...	51
अननुभाषणं v. 2. 1.	...	167
अनपदेशः ii. 2. 36.	...	52
अनपदेशात् iii. 2. 23., v. 1. 9.	...	90, 148
अनपेक्षे iii. 2. 35.	...	93
अनप्राप्तस्य v. 2. 22.	...	174
अनभिव्यक्तिः iii. 1. 41.	...	73
अनभ्युपगमात् v. 1. 15.	...	152
अनर्थे i. 1. 15.	...	6
अनर्थान्तरम् i. 1. 15.	...	6
अनर्थापत्तौ ii. 2. 4.	...	44
अनवरोधः ii. 1. 23.	...	29
अनवस्था iv. 2. 25.	...	132
अनवस्थानात् ii. 2. 52., ii. 2. 63.	...	56, 60
अनवस्थायि iii. 2. 45.	...	98
अनवस्थायित्वात् iii. 2. 47.	...	98
अनवस्थायित्वे ii. 2. 54.	...	57
अनागतयोः ii. 1. 41., iv. 1. 16.	...	34, 111
अनिग्रहः v. 2. 22.	...	174

		Page.
अनिग्रहस्थाने v. 2. 23. …	… … …	… 175
अनित्य v. 1. 1., v. 1. 14.	… … …	140, 151
अनित्यं iv. 1. 25.	… … … …	… 113
अनित्यत्व iii. 2. 25., v. 1 32.	… … …	90, 160
अनित्यत्वं iv. 1. 27., iv. 1. 66.	… … …	113, 126
अनित्यता iv. 1. 26.	… … … …	… 113
अनित्यत्वात् ii. 2. 24., iv. 1. 26.	… … …	50, 113
अनित्यभावात् v. 1. 35., v. 1. 36. …	… …	161, 162
अनित्ये v. 1. 35., v. 1. 36.	… … …	161, 162
अनित्यत्वे ii. 2. 52.	… … … …	… 56
अनित्यवत् ii. 2. 15., iii. 2. 77., iv. 1. 66.	… …	47, 106, 126
अनित्यसमः v. 1. 32. …	… … …	… 160
अनिमित्त iv. 1. 23.	… … … …	… 113
अनिमित्तः iv. 1. 22., iv. 1. 23.	… … …	112, 113
अनिमित्तयोः iv. 1. 24.	… … … …	… 113
अनियम ii. 2. 58.	… … … …	… 58
अनियमः ii. 2. 57., iii. 2. 77.	… … …	58, 194
अनियमात् ii. 1. 57., ii. 2. 56., iii. 2. 31., iii. 2. 69., v. 2. 24.,		…39, 58,
		92, 104, 175
अनियमे ii. 2. 57.	… … …	… 58
अनियमौ iii. 2. 40.	… … …	… 95
अनिवृत्तेः iv. 1. 57.	… … …	… 122
अनिष्पत्तिः iv. 1. 46. …	… … …	… 119
अनिष्पत्तेः iv. 1. 17.	… … …	… 111
अनुकस्य iii. 1. 22.	… … …	… 155
अनुकृतवात् v. 1. 22. …	… … …	… 155
अनुग्रहात् iii. 1. 41. …	… … …	… 73
अनुच्चारणं v. 2 17. …	… … …	… 173
अनुच्छेदः iii. 2. 75. …	… … …	… 106
अनुत्पत्ति v. 1. 1.	… … …	… 140
अनुत्पत्ति i. 1. 16., ii. 1. 20., iii. 2. 22.	… …	6, 28, 89
अनुपपत्ति ii. 2. 21., iv. 1. 41., iv. 2. 30.	… …	49, 118, 134
अनुपपत्तिः ii. 1. 45., iii. 1. 50., iv. 2. 18., v. 1. 17.	… 35, 75, 131, 153
अनुपपत्तेः ii. 1. 42., ii. 2. 46., iii. 2. 76., iv. 1. 33., iv. 1. 60., iv. 2.		
6., iv. 2. 11., iv. 2. 25., v. 1. 20., v. 1. 24. … 35, 55, 106, 115, 123, 128,		
		129, 132, 154, 156
अनुपपत्तिसमः v. 1. 12.	… … …	… 150

		Page.
अनुपलंभ v. 1. 30. … … … … …		159
अनुपलंभात् ii. 2. 20., ii. 2. 21., v. 1. 29. … …		49, 49, 159
अनुपलब्धि i. 1. 23., ii. 2. 21., v. 1. 38. … …		7, 49, 102
अनुपलब्धिः ii. 2. 37., iii. 1. 34., iii. 1. 41., iii. 1. 66., iii. 2. 15., iv. 2. 26. … … …		53, 71, 73, 79, 87, 133
अनुपलब्धिवत् iii. 1. 39., iv. 2. 26. … …		72, 133
अनुपलब्धिसमः v. 1. 29. … … … .. …		159
अनुपलब्धेः ii. 1. 49., ii. 1. 53., ii. 1. 54., ii. 2. 19., ii. 2. 20., ii. 2. 22., ii. 2. 27., ii. 2. 34., ii. 2. 35., ii. 2. 36., ii. 2. 38., iii. 1. 40., iii. 1. 45., iii. 1. 65., iii. 2. 18., iii. 2. 20., iii. 2. 24., iii. 2. 39., iii. 2. 55.. v. 1. 29., v. 1. 30. … 36, 38, 38, 49, 49, 49, 50, 52, 52, 52, 53, 72, 74, 79, 88, 89, 90, 95, 100, 159, 159		
अनुपदृद्य iv. 1. 4. … … … … …		110
अनुवचनम् ii. 1. 66. … … … …		41
अनुबन्धात् iii. 1. 19., iii. 2. 64., iv. 1. 59., iv. 2. 41. … 68, 103, 123, 137		
अनुबन्धानां ii. 2. 62. … … … …		59
अनुभाषणं v. 2. 17. … … … …		173
अनुमान i. 1. 3. … … … … …		2
अनुसानं i. 1. 5., ii. 1. 30., ii. 1. 37., ii. 1. 49., ii. 2. 17., iii. 2. 17. … 3, 31, 33, 36, 48, 88		
अनुमाने ii. 2. 2. … … … … …		43
अनुमतानां iii. 1. 50. … … … …		75
अनुमीयमानस्य iii. 1. 34. … … … …		71
अनुमेयत्वात् ii. 1. 49. … … … …		36
अनुयोगः v. 2. 1., v. 2. 23. … … …		167, 175
अनुयोगे ii. 2. 13. … … … …		49
अनुविनाशवत् iv. 1. 27. … … …		113
अनुवाद ii. 1. 61., ii. 1. 63., ii. 1. 67. … …		40, 40, 42
अनुवादः ii. 1. 66., iv. 1. 60. … …		41, 123
अनुवादात् v. 2. 14. … … … …		172
अनुवादे v. 2. 15. … … … …		175
अनुसूयिभिः iv. 2. 48. … … … …		138
अनेक i. 1. 23., ii. 1. 1., iii. 1. 36., iii. 1. 67., iv. 1. 35. …7, 22, 71, 79, 116		
अनेकत्वात् v. 1. 37. … … … …		167
अनेकधर्मे ii. 1. 1. … … … …		22
अनेकान्तः iii. 2. 18. … … … .. …		88
अनैकान्तिकः i. 2. 5. … … … …		15

		Page.
अनैकान्तिकत्वात् ii. 2. 3., ii. 2. 5., v. 1. 22. ...	...	44, 44, 155
अनृत ii. 1. 58. ...	... ...	... 39
अन्तः iii. 2. 27. ...	... ...	... 91
अन्तर i. 1. 2., i. 2. 16., ii. 2. 40., iii. 1. 12., 3. 2. 52., iv. 2. 12., iv. 2. 20. ...	.. ... 2, 19, 54, 66, 100,	129, 131
अन्तरम् i. 1. 15., v. 2. 1., v. 2. 3., v. 2. 6. ...	... 6, 167,	168, 169
अन्तरभावात् ii. 2. 2. ...	... ...	... 43
अन्तरवत् iv. 1. 16. ...	... ...	124
अन्तरविकारात् iii. 1. 12. ...	... ...	... 66
अन्तरात् v. 1. 28. ...	... ...	... 158
अन्तराल ii. 2. 27., iv. 1. 56. ...	... ...	50, 122
अन्तरित iii. 1. 44., iii. 1. 45. ...	... ...	73, 74
अन्तरे iv. 1. 44. ...	... ...	... 119
अन्यतमेन v. 2. 12. ...	... ...	... 172
अन्यतर ii. 1. 1. ...	... ...	... 22
अन्यतरधर्मे ii. 1. 1. ...	... ...	... 22
अन्यतरस्य ii. 2. 29. ...	... ...	... 51
अन्यता ii. 2. 32. ...	... ...	... 51
अन्यत्व iii. 2. 9. ...	... ...	... 85
अन्यत्वे ii. 2. 31., v. 1. 38. ...	... ...	51, 162
अन्यत्र iii. 1. 24., v. 2. 14. ...	... ...	69, 172
अन्यप्रकरण i. 1. 30. ...	... ...	... 9
अन्यस्मात् ii. 2. 32. ...	... ...	... 51
अन्यलक्षणा ii. 2. 9. ...	... ...	... 45
अन्यात् ii. 2. 32. ...	... ...	... 51
अप iii. 1. 64. ...	... ...	... 78
अपकर्ष v. 1. 1., v. 1. 4. ...	... ...	140, 142
अपकर्षेण iv. 2. 26. ...	... ...	... 133
अप्तेजोवायूनां iii. 1. 64. ...	... ...	... 78
अपदिष्टः i. 2. 7., i. 2. 9. ...	... ...	16, 17
अपदेशः ii. 1. 27. ...	... ...	... 30
अपदेशात् i. 1. 39. ...	... ...	... 12
अपनयनं v. 2. 5. ...	... ...	... 169
अपरस्परेण iii. 1. 68. ...	... ...	... 80
अपरापर iii. 2. 11. ...	... ...	... 86
अपरिसंख्यानात् iii. 1. 15. ...	... ...	... 66
अपरीक्षित i. 1. 31. ...	... ...	... 16

	Page.
अपसिद्धान्तः v. 2. 1.	167
अपसिद्धान्तः v. 2. 24.	175
अपवर्गे iv. 1. 59.	123
अपवर्गः i. 1. 2., i. 1. 22., iv. 1. 63.	2, 7, 124
अपवर्गाः i. 1. 9.	4
अपवर्गे iii. 2. 13., iv. 2. 43., iv. 2. 45.	105, 137, 137
अपायात् i. 1. 2.	2
अपाये i. 1. 2.	2
अपार्थं v. 2. 1.	167
अपार्थकम् v. 2. 10.	171
अपि ii. 1. 22., ii. 1. 31., ii. 1. 40., ii. 2. 15., ii. 2. 18., ii. 2. 21., ii. 2. 31., ii. 2. 64., ii. 2. 66., iii. 1. 5., iii. 1. 10., iii. 1. 40., iii. 7. 47., iii. 2. 11., iii. 3. 19., iii. 2. 21., iv. 1. 66., iv. 2. 6., iv. 2. 12., iv. 2. 43., iv. 2. 49., v. 1. 27., v. 1. 28., v. 1. 39., v. 2. 9., v. 2. 12., v. 2. 17. ... 29, 32, 34, 47, 48, 49, 51, 60, 61, 64, 65, 72, 74, 86, 89, 89, 126, 128, 129, 137, 138, 158, 158, 163, 171, 172, 173	
अपुनर् ii. 2. 47.	55
अपुनः v. 2. 15.	173
अपेक्ष v. 1. 43.	164
अपेक्षः i. 1. 23., i. 1. 38.	7, 12
अपेक्षत्वात् ii. 1. 40., ii. 2. 67.	34, 61
अपेक्षसिद्धेः ii. 2. 33.	52
अपेक्षा ii. 1. 41., ii. 2. 11.	34, 16
अपेक्षात् ii. 1. 6.	23
अपृथक् iv 2. 28.	133
अपोहय iii 1. 64.	78
अप्रतिषेध ii. 1. 15., ii. 1. 55., ii. 2. 2., ii. 2. 28., ii. 2. 29., ii. 2. 39., ii. 2. 50., ii. 2. 53., ii. 2. 55., ii. 2. 58., iii. 1. 3., iii. 1. 11., iii. 1. 14., iii. 1. 45., iii. 1. 60., iii. 2. 29., iii. 2. 37., iii. 2. 53., iii. 2. 59., iv. 1. 13., iv. 118. iv. 1. 24., iv. 1. 31., iv. 1. 36., iv. 1. 52., iv. 1. 57., iv. 1. 62., v. 1. 28., iv. 2. 25., v. 1. 5., v. 1. 8., v. 1. 15., v. 1. 20., v. 1. 26., ... 27, 38, 43, 50, 51, 53, 56, 57, 57, 58, 63, 65, 66, 74, 77, 92, 94, 100, 102, 110, 111, 113, 114, 116, 121, 122, 124, 128, 132, 145, 148, 152, 154, 158	
अप्रतिघातात् iii. 1. 46.	74

					Page.
अप्रतिपत्तिः i. 2. 19., v. 2. 19.	...	...	...		20, 174
अप्रतिभा v. 2. 1., v. 2, 19.	...	...	...		167, 173
अप्रतिसंबद्धार्थे v. 2. 7., v. 2. 10,		...	...		170, 171
अप्रत्यक्ष ii. 1. 46.	...	...	...		36
अप्रत्यक्षसिद्धेः ii. 1. 46.		...	...		36
अप्रत्यक्षे ii. 1. 47.	...	...	...		36
अप्रत्यभिज्ञानं iii. 2. 7	...	...	...		85
अप्रत्यभिज्ञाने iii. 2. 5.		...	...		84
अप्रत्याख्यानं iv. 1. 28.	...	...	...		114
अप्रमाणम् ii. 1. 37., ii. 2. 3.	...	...	...		33, 44
अप्रयोगः iv. 1. 15.,	...		...		110
अप्रश्नः iv. 2. 11.	...	...	...		129
अप्रसंगः iii 2. 56.	...	...	...		101
अप्रसंगात् ii. 2. 66.	...	...	...		61
अप्राप्ति v. 1. 1.	...	...	...		140
अप्राप्तिसमौ v 1. 7.	...	...	...		147
अप्राप्तकालं v. 2. 1., v. 2. 11.	...	...	...		167, 177
अप्राप्य iii. 1. 44., v. 1. 7.	...	...	...		73, 147
अप्रामाण्यं ii. 1. 8., ii. 1. 58., ii. 2. 5.		...	...		24, 39, 44
अभाव ii. 2. 1., ii 2. 9., iv. 1. 37., iv. 1. 66., v. 1. 29., v. 1. 31.					43, 45,
			117, 126, 159, 159		

अभावः ii. 1. 11., ii. 1. 39., ii. 1. 40., ii. 1. 54., ii. 2. 32., iii. 2. 46., iv.
1. 59.. iv. 2. 7., iv. 2. 8. iv. 2. 14., iv. 2. 20., iv. 2. 45., v. 1. 24.,
v. 1. 36.   ...   .   25, 34,
              34, 38, 51, 98, 123, 128, 128, 130, 131, 137, 156, 162

| अभावप्रामाण्यं ii. 2. 7., | | ... | ... | ... | 45 |
| अभावहेतुः iii. 1 34., ... | ... | ... | ... | | 71 |

अभावात् ii. 2. 55., iii. 1. 4., iii. 1. 24., iii. 2. 8., iii. 2. 10., iii. 2. 12.,
iv. 1. 14., iv. 1. 63., iv. 2. 11., iv. 2. 33., v. 1. 12., v. 1. 13.,
v. 1. 34.   57, 63, 69, 85, 85, 86, 110, 124, 129, 155, 150, 151, 161

अभावानां ii. 2. 2.	...	...	...		43
अभावे ii. 1. 40., ii. 1. 42., ii. 2, 33., iv. 1. 20., iv. 2. 12., v. 1. 27.				...	34
			35, 52, 112, 129, 158		
अभावोपपत्तेः ii. 2. 12.	...	...	...		46
अभिगमनवत् iii. 1 23.	...	...	...		69
अभिचारात् v. 1. 8.	...	...	...		148
अभिधानात् ii. 2. 18. ...	...	...	...		48

4

	Page.
अभिप्रायात् i. 2. 12. ...	18
अभिभवात् iii. 1. 42.	73
अभिमानः iii. 2. 9., iv. 2. 3., iv. 2. 31., iv. 2. 35., iv. 2. 34.	85
	127, 134, 135, 135
अभिमानवत् iii. 2. 9., iv. 2. 31.	85, 134
अभिमानात् iv. 1. 58.	122
अभियोग v. 2. 23.	175
अभिव्यक्त iii. 2. 49.	99
अभिव्यक्तेः ii. 2. 67.	61
अभिव्यक्तौ iii. 1. 42.	73
अभिलाषात् iii. 1. 22.	68
अभिहितं v. 2. 9.	171
अभिहितस्य v. 2. 17.	173
अभिहिते i. 2. 12.	18
अभ्यनुज्ञा iii. 2. 12., iii. 2. 48.	86, 98
अभ्यनुज्ञानात् v. 1. 26.	158
अभ्यनुज्ञासु v. 2. 2.	167
अभ्यागम, iii. 2. 78.	106
अभ्यास ii. 1. 67., iii. 2. 44., iv. 2. 46., iv. 2. 47.,	42, 96, 138, 138
अभ्यासकृतात् iii. 1 22.	68
अभ्यासस्य ii. 2. 31.	51
अभ्यासात् iii. 1. 68., ii. 2. 30., iv. 2. 38., v. 2. 15.	42, 51, 136, 173
अभ्युपगम i. 1. 26., i. 1. 27.	8, 9
अभ्युपगमसिद्धान्तः i. 1. 31.	10
अभ्युपगमात् i. 1. 31., v. 1. 43., v. 2. 21.	10, 164, 174
अभ्युपेत्य i. 2. 6., ii. 1. 60., v. 1. 42., v. 2. 24.	16, 40, 164, 175
अभ्युपेयात् iv. 2. 48.	138
अमूढस्य iv. 1. 6.	109
अयं iv. 2. 31.	138
अयसः iii. 1. 23.	69
अयस्कान्तः iii. 1. 23.	69
अयुक्तम् iv. 1. 40.	117
अयुगपत् iii. 2. 6., iii. 2. 34.	84, 93
अयोगात् v. 2. 10.	171
अयौगपद्य ii. 1. 24.	29
अयौगपद्यात् iii. 2. 60.	102
अर्चिः iii. 2. 49.	99

Page.

अर्थ i. 1. 4., i. 1. 28., i 2. 10., i 1. 41., i. 2. 14., i. 2. 16., iv. 2. 29., iv. 2.
    39., v. 2. 5., v. 2. 3., v. 2. 15.   ...   . 2, 9,
                    13, 17, 19, 19, 134, 136, 169, 168, 173

अर्थ॑ i. 1. 24., i. 1. 40., i. 2. 7., ii 1. 47., iv. 2. 46., iv. 2. 49., v. 2. 9., 8, 13,
                            16, 36, 138, 138, 171

अर्थः i. 1. 20.   7
अर्थकल्पना i. 2. 13. 18
अर्थग्रहणात् ii. 1. 62. 40
अर्थपति v. 1. 1.   140
अर्थयेाः v. 2. 14.   172
अर्थवादः ii. 1. 65. 41
अर्थविशेष ii. 1. 29. 31
अर्थसंनिकर्ष iii. 1. 32.   71
अर्थस्य i. 2. 13., ii. 1. 49. ...   ...   18, 36
अर्थाः i. 1 14.   5
अर्थात् v. 2. 7., v. 2. 16.   ...   ...   170, 173
अर्थान्तर i. 1. 27., i. 2. 12., i. 2. 16., ii. 1. 38., iv. 1. 3., iv. 1. 7., iv.
    1. 24.   ...   . 9, 18, 19, 33, 108, 109, 113
अर्थान्तरं v. 2. 1., v. 2. 7.   ...   . 167, 170
अर्थान्तरकल्पना i. 2. 12.   18
अर्थान्तराभावात् i. 2. 16., ii. 1. 38.   ...   ... 19, 33
अर्थानुपलब्धेः iii. 1. 53., iii. 1. 56.   ...   ... 76, 76
अर्थापत्यप्रामाण्यं ii. 2. 6.   45
अर्थापत्यभिमानात् ii. 2. 4. 44
अर्थापत्ति ii. 2. 2. 43
अर्थापत्तिः ii. 2. 3. 44
अर्थापत्तितः v. 1. 21. 155
अर्थापत्तिसमः v. 1. 21.   155
अर्थापत्तेः v. 1. 22. 155
अर्थित्व iii. 2. 44. 96
अर्थित्वे iv. 2. 49 138
अर्थिभिः iv. 2. 48. 138
अर्थे i. 1. 25., i. 1. 40., i 2. 12., ii. 1. 52. ...   ... 8, 13, 18, 37
अरण्य iv. 2 42. 137
अलक्षण ii. 2. 8. 45
अलक्षितानां ii. 2. 8. 45
अलक्षितेषु ii. 2. 10. 46

Page.

अवधारणं i. 1. 41. 13

अवयव i. 1. 1., i. 3. 1., iii. 1. 10., iii. 1 54., iv. 1. 42., iv. 2. 12., iv. 2.
15., iv. 2. 23., v. 2. 11. ... 1, 14, 65, 76, 118, 129, 130, 132, 171

अवयवनाशे iii. 1. 10. 65

अवयवानां iv. 2. 7. 128

अवयवाः i 1. 32., iv. 2. 10. ... ... 10, 129

अवयवि iv. 2. 15 130

अवयविनि ii. 1. 33 32

अवयविसत् ii, 1. 32. 32

अवयवी ii. 1. 34., iii. 1. 10., iv. 2. 3., iv. 2. 7., iv. 2. 8., iv. 2. 10. ... 32
64, 127, 128, 128, ... 129

अवयवेन v. 2. 12. 172

अवयवेभ्यः iv. 2 9. 128

अवरणवत् iv. 2. 50. 139

अवरोधात् iv. 1. 8., iv. 1. 31. ... ... 109, 114

अवर्ण्ये v. 1. 1. 140

अवर्णो v. 1. 4. 142

अवश्यं iv. 2. 44. 137

अवस्थानात् iii. 2. 19., ii. 3. 46. ... ... 89, 98

अवस्थाने ii. 2. 38., iii. 2. 24. ... ... 53, 90

अवस्थित ii, 2. 11. 46

अविच्छेद v. 2. 20. 174

अविज्ञात i. 1. 40., v. 2. 9. ... ... 13, 171

अविज्ञातं v. 2. 9., v. ii. 18. ... ... 171, 173

अविज्ञातत्वे i. 1. 40, ... 13

अविज्ञातार्थे v. 2. 1. 167

अविघातात् iii. 1. 47. 77

अविद्या iv. 2. 4. 127

अविरुद्धः i. 1 28. 9

अविशिष्ट i. 2. 8. 16

अविशिष्टत्वात् v. 1. 7. 147

अविशेषः i. 2. 12., v. 1. 7., v. 1. 23., v. 2. 6. ... 18, 140, 156, 169

अविशेष ii. 1. 45., ii. 1. 68., v. 1. 34. ... ... 36, 42, 161

अविशेषसमः v. 1 23. 153

अविशेषात् i. 2. 15. 19

अविशेषे i. 2. 17., v. 1. 23. ... ... 19 156

अविषये iv. 2 14 30

					Page.
अविष्टंभ iv. 2. 22.	...	...	...	...	... 132
अवृत्तित्वात् iv. 2. 7.	...	...	...	...	... 128
अवृत्ते: iv. 2. 8., iv. 2. 9., iv. 2. 12.		...	...	128, 128, 129
अव्यक iii. 2. 47.	...	...	...	...	... 98
अव्यतिरेकात् ii. 2. 40, ii 2. 50., iii. 1. 60., iii. 1. 61.		...	56, 56, 77, 77
अव्यपदेश्यं i. 1. 4.	...	...	...	...	... 2
अव्यभिचार: ii. 2. 16, ii. 2. 18.	...	...	...	48, 48
अव्यभिचारात् iii. 1. 38.	...	...	...	...	... 72
अव्यभिचारि i. 1. 4.	...	...	...	...	... 2
अव्यवस्थ ii. i. 2.	...	...	...	...	... 22
अव्यवस्था ii. 1 4.	...	..	...	...	... 23
अव्यवस्थायाः ii. 1. 4.	...	...	...	...	... 23
अव्यवस्थात्मनि ii. 1. 4.	...	...	...	...	... 23
अव्यूह iv. 2. 22.	...	...	...	...	... 132
अश्रवण ii. 2. 35.	...	...	...	...	... 52
असत् iv. 1. 50.	...	...	...	...	... 121
असत्यर्थे ii. 2. 9.	...	...	...	...	... 45
असद् iv. 1 48.	...	...	...	...	... 120
असमग्र ii. 1. 20.	...	...	...	...	... 28
असंभूत i. 2. 13.	...	...	...	...	... 18
असंशय: ii. 1. 6., iv. 2. 5.	...	...	...	23, 128
अस्ति ii. 2. 33.	...	...	...	...	... 52
अस्पर्शत्वात् ii. 2. 23., ii. 2. 39.	...	...	...	50, 53
अस्य ii. 2. 16.	...	...	...	...	... 48
असाधकत्वात् v. 1. 7.	...	...	...	...	... 147
असिद्धि: ii. 1. 10., ii. 1. 12., ii. 1. 41., ii. 1. 44., iv. 1. 41., iv. 2. 33, v. 1. 19., v. 1. 33.		...	25, 26, 34, 35, 118, 135, 154, 160
असिद्धे: ii. 1. 8., ii 1. 12., ii. 1. 34., ii. 2. 7., ii. 2. 11., v. 1. 18., v. 1. 33.	...	...	... 24, 26, 32, 45, 46, 153, 160
अहेतु: ii. 1. 28., ii. 2. 10., ii. 2. 22., ii. 2. 27., ii. 2. 43., ii. 2. 48., iii. 1. 10., iii. 1. 33., iii. 1. 55., iii. 2. 3., iii. 2. 11., iii. 2. 28., iii. 2. 39., iv. 1. 5., iv. 1. 21., iv. 1. 43., iv. 1. 51., iv. 2. 12., iv. 2 27., v. 1. 11., v. 1. 30.	...	31, 46, 49, 50, 54, 56, 65, 71, 76, 83, 86, 91, 95, 108, 112, 118, 121. 129, 133, 150, 159
अहेतुसम: v. 1 18.	...	...	...	...	... 153
अहंकार iv. 2. 1.	...	...	...	...	... 127

आ

		Page.
आकर्षण ii. 1. 35.	... ...	33
आकल्पदर्शनात् iv. 1. 19.	... ...	112
आकारस्य iii. 1. 64. ...	... ...	78
आकाश iii. 2. 1., iv. 2. 18., iv. 2. 19., iv. 2. 22	...	83, 131, 131, 132
आकाशम् i. 1. 13. ...	... ...	5
आकाशेषु ii. 1. 22. ...	... ...	29
आकृति ii. 2. 61., ii. 2. 66., ii. 2. 67., ii. 2. 68., iii. 2. 62.	...	59, 61, 61, 61, 78
आकृतिः ii. 2. 65, ii. 2. 70.	... ...	60, 61
आत्म i. 1. 9., iii. 2. 32., iv. 1. 10.	... ..	4, 92, 109
आत्मकत्वात् v. 1 30.	... ...	159
आत्मकं i. 1. 4. ...	... ...	2
आत्मगुण iii. 1. 14. ...	... ...	66
आत्मगुणत्वे iii. 2. 21.	... ...	81
आत्मनि ii. 1. 4., iv. 1. 62.	... ...	23, 124
आत्मनो iii. 2. 43. ...	... ...	96
आत्मनः i. 1. 10., ii. 1. 23.	... ...	5, 29
आत्मप्रतिपत्तिः iii. 1. 16.	... ...	67
आत्ममनसः ii. 1. 21. ...	... ...	29
आत्मसन्द्रावात् iii. 1. 3.	.. ..	63
आत्मसंस्कार iv. 2. 46.	... ...	138
आत्मा iv. 1. 52. ...	... ...	121
आदर्श iii. 1. 49. ...	... ...	74
आदि i. 1. 14., ii. 2. 19., iii. 1. 60., iv. 1. 22., iv. 1. 53.	...	5, 49, 77, 112, 121
आदित्यरश्मे iii. 1. 47.	... ...	74
आदिमत्वात् ii. 2. 74. ...	... ...	47
आदिषु iii. 2. 55., iii. 2. 56., iv. 2. 42.	...	100, 101, 137
आदीनां ii. 1. 8., iii. 2. 51., iii. 2. 58., iii. 2. 59.	...	24, 99, 101, 102
आदेश ii. 2. 41.	... ...	54
आद्येषु iii. 2. 37.	... ...	94
आधिपत्येभ्यः ii. 2. 64.	... ...	60
आनन्त्य्थ iii. 2. 44 ...	... ...	96
आनर्थ ii. 2. 27.	... ...	43
आनिष्पत्तेः iv. 1. 12., iv. 1. 20. ...	... ...	110, 112
आपः i. 1. 13.	... ...	5
आपत्ति ii. 2. 1.	... ...	43
आपत्तेः ii. 2. 48.	... ...	56

					Page.
आपन्नस्य v. 2. 16.	...	...	...	...	173
आपुलिन iv. 2. 42.	...	...	...	...	137
आपेक्षिकत्वात् iv. 1. 39.	...	...	...	...	117
आप्त i. 1. 7., ii. 1. 52., ii. 1. 68.	...	...	...	4, 37, 42
आप्रलयात् iv. 2. 15.	...	...	...	...	130
आप्तप्रामाण्यात् ii. 1. 69.	...	...	...	...	42
आम्र iii. 1. 44.	...	...	...	...	73
आयुर्वेद ii. 1. 69.	..	...	...	...	42
आरंभ i. 1. 17., iii. 2. 36., iii. 2. 38., iii. 2. 74.		...	6, 94, 94, 105
आवरण ii. 2. 19., ii. 2. 20., ii. 2. 21.	...	...	...	7
आवृत्तेः ii. 2. 47.	...	...	...	...	55
आशु iii. 2. 30., iii. 2. 62.	...	...	...	92, 102
आश्रय iii. 2. 44., iv. 1. 51.	...	...	...	96, 121
आश्रयः i. 1. 11.	...	...	...	...	5
आश्रयत्वात् iv. 1. 52., iv. 2. 28.	...		...	121, 133
आश्रित iii. 2. 44.	...	...	...	...	96
आसन्न iv. 1. 48.	...	...	...	...	120
आहारस्य iii. 2. 68.	...	...	...	...	104
आहाराः iii. 1. 22.	...	...	...	...	68

इ

इच्छतः v. 2. 6.	...	...	...	...	169
इच्छा i. 1. 10., iii. 2. 32., iii. 2. 36., iii. 2. 37., iii. 2. 44.	...	5, 92, 94, 94, 96
इतर iv. 1. 6.	...	...	...	...	109
इतरेण iii. 1. 7.	...	...	...	...	64
इतरेतर ii. 1. 41., ii. 2. 33., iii. 1. 48., iii. 1. 75., iii. 2. 58., iv. 1. 37.			
			34, 52, 74, 81, 101, 117
इति i. 1. 10., i. 1. 13., i. 1. 15., i. 1. 17., i. 1. 21. i. 1. 38., i. 2. 11.,			
ii. 1. 36., ii. 1. 47., ii. 1. 48., ii. 1. 65., ii. 2. 9., ii. 2. 18., ii. 2. 32.			
iii. 2. 73., iv. 1. 51., v. 1. 43. 5, 5, 6, 6, 7, 12, 18, 33, 36, 36,			
			41, 45, 48, 51, 105, 121, 164
इन्द्रिय i. 1. 4., iii. 1. 12.	...	...	...	2, 66
इन्द्रियभावात् iii. 1. 72.	...	...	...	81
इन्द्रियस्य iv. 2. 14.	...	...	...	...	130
इन्द्रियाणां iii. 1. 37.	...	...	...	...	72
इन्द्रियाणि i. 1. 12.	...	...	...	...	5
इन्द्रियान्तर iii. 1. 53.	...	...	...	...	76

	Page.
इन्द्रियार्थे i. 1. 4., i. 1. 9., i. 1. 11., ii. 1. 9., iii. 1. 58. ...	2, 4, 5, 25, 77
इन्द्रियार्थेः ii. 1. 26. ...	30
इन्द्रियार्थयोः ii. 1. 25., iii. 2. 19. ...	30, 89
इन्द्रियैः iii. 2. 22. ...	89

ई

| ईश्वरः iv. 1. 19. ... | 112 |

उ

उक्त i. 2. 2., ii. 1. 6., ii. 1. 45., ii. 1. 58., iii. 2. 41., iii. 2. 42., iii. 2. 63.	
	15, 23, 35, 39, 95, 96, 103
उक्तम् v. 2. 1., v. 2. 14., v. 2. 15.	167, 172, 173
उक्तयोः ii. 1. 67. ...	42
उक्ता iv. 1. 1. ...	108
उक्ताः v. 2. 25. ...	175
उक्ते v. 2. 6. ...	169
उच्चारणात् ii. 2. 19. ...	49
उत्कर्ष v. 1. 1., v. 1. 4. ...	140, 142
उत्कर्षात् iii. 1. 70. ...	80
उत्तर i. 1. 2., ii. 1. 6. ...	2, 24
उत्तरः iii. 1. 64. ...	78
उत्तरप्रसंगः ii. 1. 7. ...	24
उत्तरस्य v. 2. 19. ...	174
उत्तरापाये i. 1. 2. ...	2
उत्तरोत्तर ii. 1. 7., iii. 1. 66. ...	24, 79
उत्तरोत्तराणां iii. 1. 66. ...	79
उत्पत्तिः iii. 2. 13., iii. 2. 17., iii. 2. 23., iii. 2. 67., iii. 2. 70., iv. 1. 25.,	
iv. 1. 30., iv. 1. 32., v. 1. 1. ... 87, 88, 90, 103, 104, 113, 114, 114, 140	
उत्पत्तिः i. 1. 19., ii. 1. 9., ii. 1. 21., iii. 1. 26., iii. 2. 26., iii. 2. 64.,	
iv. 1. 14., iv. 1. 22., iv. 1. 55., iv. 2. 41. ... 7, 25, 29, 69, 91, 103, 110,	
	112, 122, 137
उत्पत्तिवत् iii. 1. 26., iv. 1. 51. ...	69, 121
उत्पत्तेः ii. 2. 12., iii. 2. 11., iii. 2. 26., iii. 2. 52., iv. 1. 6., iv. 1. 66.,	
v. 1. 12. ... 46, 86, 91, 10, 109, 126, 150	
उत्पन्नं i. 1. 4. ...	2
उत्पन्नस्य v. 1. 13. ...	151
उत्पाद iv. 1. 40. ...	120

		Page.
उदकयोः iii. 1. 49.		74
उदाहरणं i. 1. 32., i. 1. 34., i. 1. 38., v. 2. 13. ...		10, 11, 12, 172
उदाहरणं i. 1. 36.		11
उपघात ii. 1. 37.		33
उपचय ii. 2. 62.		59
उपचार i. 2. 11.		18
उपचारः iv. 1. 54.		122
उपचारात् i. 2. 14., ii. 2. 14., ii. 2. 15., ii. 2. 31., ii. 2. 61., ii. 2. 62.		
		19, 47, 47, 51, 59, 59
उपदेश ii. 1. 52.		37
उपदेशः i. 1. 7., iv. 2. 42.		...4, 137
उपदेशवत् ii. 9. 68.		42
उपदेशात् ii. 2. 21.		54
उपनय i. 1. 32.		10
उपनयः i. 1. 38.		12
उपपत्यां i. 2. 10.		17
उपपत्ति v. 1. 26., v. 1. 43.		158, 164
उपपत्तिः ii. 2. 5., iv. 2. 37., v. 1. 22.		57, 126, 155
उपपत्तितः i. 1. 40.		13
उपपत्तिसमः v. 1. 25.		157
उपपत्तेः i. 1 23., ii. 1. 5., ii. 1. 35., ii. 1 39., ii. 1. 43., ii. 1. 61., ii. 1. 67., ii. 2. 9., ii. 2. 40., iii. 1. 17., iii. 2. 29., iii. 2. 42., iii. 2. 72., iv. 1. 9., iv. 1. 60., v. 1. 28., iii. 2. 23., iv. 2. 24., v. 1. 3., v. 1. 6, v. 1 13., v. 1. 17., v. 1. 23., v. 1. 24., v. 1. 25., v. 1. 23., v. 1. 29., v. 1. 32., v. 1. 35, v. 1. 36., v. 1. 38., v. 2. 15. ... 7, 23, 33, 34, 35, 40, 42, 45, 54, 67, 92, 96, 105, 109, 123, 128, 132, 132, 140, 146, 151, 153, 156, 156, 157, 158, 159, 160, 161, 162, 162, 173		
उपपन्नः i. 2. 1., i. 2. 2., iii. 2. 12.		14, 15, 105
उपपतिभ्यां iv. 1. 4., 1. 2. 30.		118, 134
उपभोग्यत्वात् iv. 1. 45.		119
उपमर्दे ii. 2 59		58
उपमान i. 1. 3., ii. 1. 44., ii. 1. 45., ii. 1. 48.		2, 35, 35, 36
उपमानं i. 1. 6.		3
उपमानशब्दाः i. 1. 3.		2
उपमानस्य ii. 1. 47.		36
उपमानासिद्धिः ii. 1. 44		35

Page.

उपलब्धि i. 1. 23., iv. 1. 28., iv. 2, 35., v. 1. 1. ...   7, 114, 135, 140

उपलब्धिः i. 1. 5., ii. 1. 32., ii. 2. 20., iii. 1. 75., iii. 2. 62., iv. 2. ... 73, 6, 32, 49, 70, 73, 78, 81, 102, 129

उपलब्धिनियमः iii. 1. 35.   71

उपलब्धिवत् ii. 2. 54., iii. 1. 54., iii. 2. 14., v. 2 13.   57, 54, 76, 87, 129

उपलब्धिसमः v. 1. 27.   158

उपलब्धेः ii. 1. 10., ii. 1. 50., ii. 2. 43., iii. 1. 10., iii. 1. 28., iii. 1. 44., iii. 1. 63., iii. 1. 74., iii. 2. 13., iii. 2. 50., iii. 2. 61., iv. 1. 30., iv. 1. 32.   ...   ...31, 37, 54, 65, 81, 87, 99, 162, 114, 114

उपलभ्यमाने ii. 2. 36.   52

उपलंभात् ii. 1. 31., iii. 1. 30., iv. 2. 36., v. 1. 27.   32, 70, 136, 158

उपसर्पणम् iii. 1. 23.   69

उपसंहार v. 1. 5.   145

उपसंहारात् ii. 1. 48.   36

उपसंहारे v. 1. 2., v. 1. 43.   ...   ...   140, 164

उपसंहारः i. 1. 38.   12

उपादानम् iii. 2. 65.   103

उपादानवत् iii. 2. 65.   103

उपादानात् iii. 2. 48.   98

उपायैः iv. 2. 46.   138

उपालंभः i. 2. 1., i. 2. 2.   ...   .   14, 15

उपेक्षणं v. 2. 1., v. 2. 22.   ...   ...   167, 174

उभय v. 1. 4., v. 1. 16., v. 1. 25.   ...   ... 142, 153, 157

उभयथा ii. 1. 43., v. 1. 15., v. 1. 34.   ...   ... 35, 152, 161

उभयोः ii. 2. 29.   51

उल्काप्रकाश iii. 1. 39.   72

उष्ण iii. 1. 21.   68

ऊ

ऊहः i. 1. 40.   13

ऋ

ऋण iv. 1. 59.   123

ए

एक i, 2. 17., iii. 2. 44., iii. 2. 61. iv. 1. 4., v. 1. 23. 19, 96, 102, 108, 156

एकत्वं iii. 1. 9., iii. 1. 61.   ...   ...   65, 77

Page.

एकदेश ii. 1. 32., ii. 1. 38., ii. 1. 44., iv. 2. 7. ... 32, 33, 35, 128

एकदेशग्रहात् ii. 1. 30. 31

एकभाव iv. 1. 35. 116

एकविनाशा iii. 1. 9. 65

एकस्मिन् iii. 1. 8., iv. 2. 11. ... ... 65, 129

एका iii. 1. 57. 76

एकान्त iv. 1. 41. 118

एकार्थग्रहणात् iii. 1. 1. 63

एकैकस्य iii. 1. 66. 79

एकं iii. 2. 60. 102

एतत् iii. 2. 77. 106

एति ii. 2. 7. 43

एतेन iii. 2. 71. 104

एव ii. 1. 6., iii. 1. 3., iii. 1. 66., iii. 1 73., iv. 1. 36., iv. 1. 55. ... 23

63, 79, 81, 116, 122

एवं ii. 1. 7., ii. 1. 22., iv. 2. 15., iv. 2. 36., iv. 2. 43., v. 1. 40.

24, 29, 130, 136, 137, 163

ऐ

ऐति ii. 2. 2. 43

ऐन्द्रियकत्वात् ii. 2. 14., iii. 2. 59. ... ... 47, 102

ऐन्द्रियकत्वे v. 1. 14. 151

क

कट ii. 2. 64. 60

कंटक iv. 1. 22., iv. 2. 50. ... ... 112, 139

कथा v. 2. 20., v. 2. 24. ... ... 174, 175

करण iii. 2. 74., v. 1. 9. ... ... 105, 148

कर्तृ ii. 1. 59. 39

कर्तृबधात् iii. 1. 6. 64

कर्म ii. 1. 59., ii 2. 24., iii. 2. 1., iii. 2. 45., iii. 2. 70., iii. 2. 72., iii.

2. 75., iv. 1. 19., iv. 1. 20. ... 39, 50, 83, 98, 104, 105, 106, 112, 112

कर्मकारितः iii. 1. 37. 72

कल्पना i. 2. 12. 18

काच iii. 1. 44. 73

कारक iv. 1. 16. 111

Page.

कारण i. 1. 40., ii. 2. 18., ii. 2. 35., iii. 2. 14., iii. 2. 18., iii. 2. 23.,
    iii. 2. 24., iv. 1. 19., iv. 1. 30., iv. 1. 32., iv. 1. 41., iv. 1. 42.,
    iv. 2. 20., v. 1. 12., v. 1. 13., v. 1. 25., v. 1. 26., v. 1. 27., v. 1. 28.,
    v. 1. 38.   ...   13, 48, 52, 87, 88, 90, 90, 112, 114, 114, 118, 118,
                131, 150, 151, 157, 158, 158, 158, 162

कारितत्वात् iv. 1. 21.   112

कारितं iii. 2. 73.   105

कारित्व iv. 2. 25.   132

कार्ये iii. 2. 44., iv. 2. 20., v. 1. 38., v. 1. 37., v. 2. 20.   ...   96, 131, 162,
                167, 174

कार्यसमः v. 1. 37.   167

कार्यसमाः v. 1. 1.   140

कार्याश्रय iii. 1. 6.   64

काल i. 2. 9., ii. 1. 22., ii. 1. 39., iii. 2. 31., iv. 1. 44.   ...   17, 29, 34, 92,
                119

कालभेदे ii. 1. 60.   40

कालातीतः i. 2. 9.   17

कालान्तर iv. 1. 45.   119

कालान्तरे ii. 2. 55.   57

कालान्तरेण iv. 1. 46.   119

किंचित् i. 2. 17., v. 1. 5.   ...   .   19, 145

कुड्य iii. 1. 45.   74

कुड्यान्तरित iii. 1. 45.   74

कुं'भादिषु iii. 2. 39.   95

कृतकवत् ii. 2. 14.   47

कृतता ii. 1. 43.   35

कृत्स्न iv. 2. 17.   28

कृष्णसारे iii. 1. 30.   70

केश iii. 2. 55., iii. 2. 56., iv. 2. 13.   ...   ...   100, 101, 129

क्रम iv. 1. 18., v. 2. 8.   ...   .   111, 170

क्रमवृत्तित्व ii. 1. 11.   25

क्रमवृत्तित्वात् iii. 2. 6.   84

क्रिया iii. 2. 44., iii. 2. 61.   ...   .   96, 102

क्लेश iv. 1. 59., iv. 1. 63., iv. 1. 65.   ...   ...   123, 124, 125

क्लेशास्य iv. 1. 64.   125

क्वचित् iii. 2. 18., v. 1. 24.   ...   .   88, 156

क्षणिकत्वात् iii. 2. 11.   86

		Page.
क्षय iii. 2. 72.	... ...	... 105
क्षोर iii. 2. 14.	... ...	87
क्षुधादिभिः iv. 2. 40. ...	... ...	... 137

ग

गंगा ii. 2. 64.	... ...	... 60
गतम् iv. 2. 21.	... ...	... 131
गति iii. 1. 62., iii. 2. 8.	... ...	...78, 85
गतित्वात् iii. 2. 30. ...	... ...	... 92
गन्ध i. 1. 14:, iii. 1. 64.	... ...	... 5, 78
गन्धत्व iii. 1. 60.	... ...	... 77
गन्धर्वे iv. 2. 32.	... ...	... 135
गन्धादीनां iii. 1. 60. ...	... ...	... 77
गमन ii. 1. 68.	... ...	... 42
गवये ii. 1. 47.	... ...	... 36
गुण ii. 2. 69., iii. 1. 66., iii. 1. 67., iii. 1. 74., iii. 1. 75., iii. 2 50., iii. 2. 52., iii. 2. 57., iv. 1. 60. ...	61, 79, 79, 81, 81, 99, 100, 101, 123	
गुणाः i. 1. 14.	... ...	... 5
गुणान्तर iii. 1. 28., iii. 2. 16.	... ...	...70, 88
गुणान्तरापत्ति ii. 2. 59.	... ...	... 58
गुह iv. 2. 42.	... ...	... 137
गौत्वात् v. 1. 3.	... ...	... 141
गोसिद्धिवत् v. 1. 3. ...	... ...	... 141
ग्रहण iii. 2. 49., iv. 2. 47.	... ...	99, 138
ग्रहणं ii. 1. 43., iii. 1. 44., iii. 1. 67., iii. 2. 47., iv. 2. 28.	...35, 73, 79, 98, 133	
ग्रहणवत् iii. 2. 47., iii. 2. 49.	... ...	...98, 99
ग्रहणस्य iv. 2. 14.	... ...	... 130
ग्रहणात् iii. 1. 31., iii. 2. 15., iii. 2. 45.	... ...	70, 87, 98
ग्रहात् iii. 2. 25.	... ...	... 90

घ

घट iv. 1. 12., iv. 1. 13.	... ...	110, 110
घटात् iv. 1. 12.	... ...	... 110
घटादि v. 1. 18.	... ...	... 148
घटाभाव ii. 2. 15.	... ...	... 47
घ्राण i. 1. 12.	... ...	... 5

च

च i. 1. 5., i. 1. 23., i. 2. 11., i. 2. 19., ii. 1. 2., ii. 1. 3., ii. 1. 4., ii. 1.
15., ii. 1. 16., ii. 1. 25., ii. 1. 26., ii. 1. 27., ii. 1. 32., ii. 1. 35., ii.
1. 51., ii. I. 54., ii. 1. 51., ii. 1. 61., ii. 1. 62., ii. 1. 69., ii. 2. 2.,
ii. 2. 5., ii. 2. 12., ii. 2. 13., ii. 2. 14., ii. 2. 15., ii. 2. 36., ii. 2. 38.,
ii. 2. 40., ii. 2. 52., ii. 2. 53., ii. 2. 54., ii. 2. 55., ii. 2. 58., ii. 2.
64., iii. 1. 15., iii. 1. 18., iii. 1. 29., iii. 1. 30., iii. 1. 35., iii. 1. 37.,
iii. 1. 38., iii. 1. 42., iii. 1. 43., iii. 1. 51., iii. 1. 57., iii. 1. 67., iii.
1. 73., iii. 2. 5., iii. 2. 7., iii. 2. 14., iii. 2. 20., iii. 2. 24., iii. 2.
32., iii. 2. 42., iii. 2. 63., iii 2. 69., iii. 2. 72., iii. 2. 75., iii. 2.
76., iv. 1. 9., iv. 1. 44., iv. 1. 58., iv. 1. 61., iv. 1. 68., iv. 2. 8., iv.
2. 9., iv. 2. 10., iv. 2. 15., iv. 2. 20., iv. 2. 21., iv. 2. 22., iv. 2.
23., iv. 2. 24., iv. 2. 24., iv. 2. 29., iv. 2. 34., iv. 2. 36., iv. 2. 37.,
iv. 2. 40., iv. 2. 45., iv. 2. 46., iv. 2. 47., v. 1. 4., v. 1. 6., v. 1., 7.,
v. 1. 8., v. 1. 9., v. 1. 11., v. 1. 15., v. 1. 22., v. 1. 34., v. 1. 31.,
v. 1. 33., v. 1. 34., v. 2. 1., v. 2. 18., v. 2. 25.   ... 3, 7, 18, 20, 23,
23, 27, 27, 30, 30., 30, 32, 33, 37, 38, 39, 40, 40, 42, 43, 44, 46, 46,
47, 47, 52, 53, 54, 56, 57, 57, 57, 58, 60, 66, 67, 70, 70, 71, 72, 72, 73,
73, 75, 76, 79, 81, 84, 85, 87, 89, 90, 92, 96, 103, 104, 105, 106, 106,
109, 119, 122, 124, 126, 128, 128, 129, 130, 131, 131, 132, 132, 132,
132, 134, 135, 136, 136, 137, 137, 138, 138, 142, 146, 147, 148, 148,
150, 152, 155, 156, 159, 160, 161, 167, 173, 175

चक्र iii. 2. 62.   102
चक्षुः i. 1. 12.   5
चतुष्ट्वम् ii. 2. 1.   43
चतुष्ट्वमैति ii. 2. 1.   43
चन्दन ii. 2. 64.   60
चरण ii. 2. 64.   60
चिन्ता i. 2. 7.   16
चेत् ii. 1. 36., iii. 2. 73.   ...   .   33, 105
चेतन ii. 2. 9.   45
चेष्टा i. 1. 4.   5

छ

छल i. 1. 1., i. 2. 2., i. 2. 17.   ...   .   1, 15, 19
छलं i. 2. 10., i. 2. 11., i. 2. 12., i. 2. 15.   ...   ... 17, 18, 18, 19

ज

जन्म i. 1. 2., iii. 1. 25., iv. 1. 55.   ...   ...   2, 69, 122

					Page.
जन्मदर्शनात् iii. 1. 25.	...	...	...	...	69
जनितः i. 1. 20.	...	...	...	...	7
जल्प i. 1. 1., iv. 2. 50.	...	...	...	1, 139	
जल्पः i. 2. 2.	...	...	...	...	15
जातयः ii. 2. 68.	...	...	...	...	61
जातस्य iii. 1. 19.	...	...	...	...	68
जाति i. 1. 1., i. 2. 2., i. 2, 20., ii. 2. 61., ii. 2. 67., iii. 1. 62.				... 1, 15, 21, 59, 61, 78	
जातिः i. 2. 18., ii. 2. 66., ii. 2. 71.			...	19, 61, 62	
जातिविशेषे ii. 1. 57. ...	...	...	...	...	39
जातिलिंगाख्या ii. 2. 70.	...	...	...	...	61
ज्ञस्य iii. 2. 36.	...	...	...	...	94
ज्ञातुः iii. 1. 17.	...	...	...	...	67
ज्ञान i. 1. 16., ii. 1. 23., 2. 1. 27., iii. 1. 17., iii. 2. 19., iii. 2. 26., iii. 2. 60., iv. 2. 47., v. 1. 31.		...	6, 29, 30, 67, 89, 91, 102, 138, 159		
ज्ञानं i. 1. 4., i. 1. 15.	...	...	...	... 2, 6	
ज्ञानानां i. 1. 2., iii. 2. 34.	...	...	...	... 2, 93	
ज्ञानानि i. 1. 10.	...	...	...	...	5
ज्ञेय iii. 2. 20.	...	...	...	...	89

त

तत् i. 1. 2., i. 1. 5., i. 1. 14., i. 1. 22., i. 1. 24., i. 1. 31., i. 1. 36., i. 1. 37., i. 2. 6., i. 2. 11., i. 2. 15., i. 2. 16., i. 2. 20., ii. 1. 6., ii. 1. 14., ii. 1. 15., ii. 1. 18., ii. 1. 19., ii. 1. 24., ii. 1. 40., ii. 1. 58., ii. 1. 69., ii. 2. 6., ii. 2. 10., ii. 2. 20., ii. 2. 27., ii. 2. 33., ii. 2. 38., ii. 2. 49., ii. 2. 53., ii. 2. 63., iii. 1. 3., iii. 1. 5., iii. 1. 23., iii. 1. 66., iii. 1. 70., iii. 1. 71., iii. 1. 75., iii. 2. 9., iii. 2. 19., iii. 2. 21., iii. 2. 22., iii. 2. 24., iii. 2. 30., iii. 2. 37., iii. 2. 40., iii. 2. 49., iii. 2. 62., iii. 2. 64., iii. 2. 65., iii. 2. 72., iii. 2. 73., iv. 1. 3., iv. 1. 21., iv. 1. 27., iv. 1. 31., iv. 1. 32., iv. 1. 47., iv. 1. 50., iv. 1. 54., iv. 2. 3., iv. 2. 5., v. 1. 28., iv. 2. 13., iv. 2. 18., iv. 2. 20., iv. 2. 26., iv. 2. 41., iv. 2. 45., iv. 2. 46., v. 1. 2., v. 1. 3., v. 1. 10., v. 1. 29., v. 2. 3. ... 2, 3, 5, 7, 8, 10, 11, 12, 16, 18, 19, 19, 11, 23, 26, 27, 27, 28, 29, 34, 39, 42, 45, 46, 49, 50, 52, 53, 56, 57, 60, 63, 64, 69, 79, 80, 81, 81, 85, 89, 89, 89, 90, 92, 94, 95, 99, 102, 103, 103, 105, 105, 108, 112, 113, 114, 114, 119, 121, 122, 127, 128, 128, 129, 131, 131, 133, 137, 137, 138, 140, 141, 149, 159, 168

तत्पूर्वकं i. 1. 5. 3

	Page.
तत्त्वप्रमेयसिद्धौ ii. 2. 8.	45
तच्च ii. 1. 7.	24
तत्त्व iv. 2. 37., iv. 2. 50.	136, 139
तत्त्वज्ञान i. 1. 40.	13
तत्त्वज्ञानात् i. 1. 1., iv. 2. 1., iv. 2. 35.	1, 127, 135
तात्त्वभाक्तयोः ii. 2. 16.	48
तत्त्वे i. 1. 40.	13
तत्सिद्धिः ii. 1. 18.	27
तथा i. 1. 35., i. 1. 38., ii. 1. 5., ii. 1. 48., iii. 2. 68., iv. 1. 2., iv. 2 14.,	
v. 1. 13. ... ... 11, 12, 23, 36, 104, 108, 130, 151	
तदनुपलब्धि iii. 1. 39.	72
तदनुपलब्धेः iii. 1. 33.	71
तदपेक्षत्वात् ii. 2. 64.	60
तदभावः iii. 1. 5.	64
तदर्थेबहुत्वात् iii. 1. 59.	77
तदर्थाः i. 1. 14.	5
तदर्थे ii. 2. 61.	59
तद्ग्रहणम् iii. 1. 32.	71
तद्विकारः iii. 1. 20.	68
तद्विचैः iv. 2. 47.	138
तदा iii. 1. 14., iv. 2. 22.	66, 130
तदुपचारः ii. 2. 64.	60
तदुपपत्तिः iii. 2. 14.	87
तदुपलब्धिः iii. 1. 49., iii. 1. 54.	74, 16
तं iv. 2. 48.	138
तंतु iv. ii. 26.	133
तंत्र i. 1. 26., i. 1. 27., i. 1. 28., i. 1. 29., iii. 1. 37. ...	8, 9, 9, 9, 72
तंत्रे i. 1. 28.	9
तयोः ii. 1. 40., ii. 2. 33.	34, 52
तर्क i. 1. 1., i. 2. 1.	1, 14
तर्के i. 1. 40.	13
तर्कः i. 1. 40.	109, 128
तर्हि iv. 1, 7., iv. 2. 6.	81, 161
तस्य iii. 1. 73., v. 1. 34.	60
तादर्थ्य ii. 2. 64.	78
तादात्म्यम् iii. 1. 63.	5
तानि i. 1. 13.	32
तावत् ii. 1. 31.	

Page.

तु i. 1. 9., ii. 2. 16., ii. 2. 59., ii. 2. 68., iii. 1. 71., iii. 2. 35., iii. 2. 40.,
    iii. 2. 43., iv. 1. 50., iv. 2. 3., iv. 2. 26., v. ii. 15.   ...   4, 48, 56, 61,
                                     81, 93, 95, 96, 121, 127, 133, 173

तुला ii. 1. 16.   27
तुलाप्रामाण्यवत् ii. 1. 16   27
तुल्यजातीयानां iv. 1. 9.   109
तुल्यधर्मे v. 1 32.   160
तुल्यं iii. 2. 21.   89
ते ii. 2. 60.   59
तेज iii. 1. 64.   78
तेजः i. 1. 13.   5
तेन iii. 1. 73.   81
तेषां iv. 1. 6.   169
तेषु iv. 1 54., iv. 2. 8.   ...   ...   122, 128
तैः ii. 1. 27.   50
तैक्ष्ण्य iv. 1. 22.   112
तैमिरिक iv. 2. 13.   129
त्वक् i, 1. 12., iii. 1. 54., iii. 1. 57., iii. 2. 56.   ..   5, 76, 76, 101
त्वगव्यतिरेकात् iii. 1. 52.   75
त्याग ii. 2 62.   59
त्रास ii. 1. 38.   33
त्रि v. 2. 9., v. 2. 17. ...   .   171, 173
त्रिविधम् i. 1. 5., i. 2. 11.   ...   . 3, 18,
त्रुटे iv. 7. 19.   131
त्रैलोक्य ii. 1. 8., ii. 1. 12., ii. 1. 15., v. 1. 18., v. 1. 19. 24, 26, 27, 153, 154
त्रैराश्यं iv. 1. 3.   108

द

दर्शनं iii. 2. 12., iii. 2. 17.   ...   .   86, 88
दर्शनवत् iii. 2. 66. 102
दर्शनस्पर्शनाभ्यां iii. 1. 1.   63
दर्शनात् iii. 2. 38., iii. 2. 74., iv. 1. 22., iv. 1. 49., v. 1. 8.   ... 94,
                              105, 112, 120, 148
दाहे iii. 1. 4.   63
दाह्य iv. 1. 27.   113
दाह्ये iii. 1. 47.   74

		Page.
दुःख i. 1. 2., i. 1. 9., i. 1. 10., iii. 2. 44., iv. 1. 58.		2, 4, 5, 96, 122
दुःखं i. 1. 21., iv. 1. 55.		7, 122
दृष्ट i. 1. 8., iii. 1. 50., iii. 2. 73.		4, 75, 105
दृष्टं i. 1. 5.		3
दृष्टान्त i. 1. 1., 1. 1. 36., iii. 1. 11., v. 1. 6.		1, 11, 65, 146
दृष्टान्तः i. 1. 25., v. 1. 11.		8, 150
दृष्टान्तयोः v. 1. 4., v. 1. 14.		142, 151
दृष्टान्तविरोधात् iii. 1. 11.		65
दृष्टान्तस्य v. 1. 9.		148
दृष्टान्ते v. 1. 34.		161
देश ii. 1. 22.		29
दोष i. 1. 2., i. 1. 9., i. 1. 20., ii. 1. 45., ii. 1. 60., iv. 1. 8., iv. 2. 1., iv. 2. 2., v. 1 42., v. 1. 43., v. 2. 21.		2, 4, 7, 35, 40, 109, 127, 127, 164, 174, 174
दोषः v. 1. 39., v. 1. 41.		163, 163
दोषवचनात् ii. 1. 60.		40
दोषवत् v. 1. 41.		163
दोषात् iv. 1. 57.		122
दोषाः i. 1. 18., iv 1. 2.		7, 108
दोषेभ्यः iv. 7. 7., ii. 1. 58.		109, 39
द्रव्य iii. 1. 26., iii. 1. 75., iii. 2. 17.		69, 81, 88
द्रव्यविकारे ii. 2. 45.		55
द्रव्यस्य ii. 2. 18., iv. 2. 20.		48, 131
द्रव्यसमवायात् iii. 1. 36.		71
द्रव्यान्तर iii. 2. 17.		88
द्रव्ये iii. 2. 50.		99
द्वित्वाभिमानात् iii. 1. 8		65
द्वितीयाविनाशात् iii. 1. 9.		65
द्विविधः i. 1. 8.		4
द्वेष i. 1. 10., iii. 2. 36., iii. 2. 44., iv. 1. 3.		5, 94, 96, 108
द्वेषयोः iii. 2. 34.		94

ध

| धर्म i. 1. 23., i. 1. 36., i. 2. 14., ii. 1. 1., ii. 2. 46., ii. 2. 53., iii. 2. 44., v. 1. 28., v 1. 4., v. 1. 23., v. 1. 24., v. 2. 2., v. 2. 3. | | 7, 11, 19, 22, 55, 57, 96, 128, 142, 156, 167, 168 |
| धर्माः iv. 2. 22. | | 132 |

	Page.
धर्मेकत्वात् iv. 1. 25.	113
धर्मप्रसंगात् iii. 1. 48.	74
धर्मभावी i. 1. 36.	11
धर्मयोगः ii. 2. 51.	56
धर्मस्य v. 1. 34.	161
धर्मित्वे ii. 2. 55.	57
धर्मोपपत्तेः i. 1. 23.	7
धारण ii. 1 35., ii. 2. 64.	...33, 60
धूम iii. 1. 5—4.	76

न

न i. 1. 38., i. 2. 16., ii. 1. 1., ii. 1. 6., ii. 1. 9., ii. 1. 10., ii. 1. 14., ii. 1. 19.,
ii. 1. 21., ii. 1. 23., ii. 1. 24., ii. 1. 29., ii. 1. 31., ii. 1. 32.,
ii. 1. 36., ii. 1. 38., ii. 1. 41., ii. 1. 47., ii. 1. 48., ii. 1. 56.,
ii. 1. 59., ii. 1. 67., ii 1. 68., ii. 2. 15., ii. 2. 16., ii. 2. 6., ii. 2. 7.,
ii. 2. 9., ii. 2. 11., ii. 2. 24., ii. 2. 25., ii. 2. 31., ii. 2. 33., ii. 2. 37.,
ii. 2. 44., ii. 2. 46., ii. 2. 51., ii. 2. 57., ii. 2. 63., ii. 2. 64.,
ii. 2. 67., iii. 1. 2., iii. 1. 6., iii. 1. 8., iii. 1. 13., iii. 1. 16.,
iii. 1. 21., iii. 1. 24., iii. 1. 27., iii. 1. 34., iii. 1. 40., iii. 1. 45.,
iii. 1. 48., iii. 1. 53., iii. 1. 56., iii. 1. 57., iii. 1. 59., iii. 1. 62.,
iii. 1. 65., iii. 1. 69., iii. 1. 74., iii. 2. 4., iii. 2. 8., iii. 2. 10.,
iii. 2. 13., iii. 2. 15., iii. 2. 16., iii. 2. 19., iii. 2. 20., iii. 2. 23.,
iii. 2. 26., iii. 2. 27., iii. 2. 30., iii. 2. 31., iii. 2. 32., iii. 2. 41.,
iii. 2. 52., iii. 2. 58., iii. 2. 61., iii. 2. 65., iii. 2. 67., iii. 2. 74.,
iii. 2. 78., iv. 1. 3., iv. 1. 6., iv. 1. 8., iv. 1. 12., iv. 1. 16., iv. 1. 17.,
iv. 1. 20., iv. 1. 23., iv. 1. 26., iv. 1. 29., iv. 1. 32., iv. 1. 33.,
iv. 1. 35., iv. 1. 38., iv. 1. 39., iv. 1. 42., iv. 1, 45., iv. 1. 48., iv. 1. 53.,
iv. 1. 56., iv. 1. 64., iv. 1. 65., iv. 1. 68., iv. 2. 6., iv. 2. 10.,
iv. 2. 14., iv. 2. 16., iv. 2. 39., iv. 9. 44., v. 1. 11., v. 1. 15.,
v. 1. 19., v. 1. 13., v. 1. 34. ... 12, 19, 22, 23, 25, 25, 26, 28, 29, 29,
29, 31, 32, **32**, 33, 33, 34, 36, 36, 39, 39, 42, 42, 42, 43, 45, 45,
45, 46, 50, 50, 51, 52, 53, 55, 55, 56, 58, 60, 60, 60, 63, 64, 65,
66, 67, 68, 69, 69, 71, 72, 74, 74, 76, **76**, 76, 77, 78, 79, 80, 81,
84, 85, 85, 87, 87, 88, 89, 89, 90, 91, 91, 92, 92, 92, 95, 100,
101, 102, **103**, 103, 105, 106, 108, 109, 110, 111, 111, 112, 113,
113, 114, **114**, 115, 116, 117, 117, 118, 119, 120, 121, 122, 125,
125, 126, **128**, 129, 130, 130, 136, 137, 150, 152, 154, 157, 161

Page.

नक्तांचर iii. 1. 43. 73

नख iii. 2. 55., iii. 2. 56. ... ... 100, 101

नगर iv. 2. 32. 135

नयन iii. 1. 43. 73

नाना ii. 2. 16. 48

नानात्वात् iii. 1. 5. 1. 75

नाशो iii. 1. 10. 65

निगमनं i. 1. 39. 12

निगमानि i. 1. 32. 10

निग्रह i. 1. 1., i. 2. 2., i. 2. 19., i. 9. 20., v. 2. 1. ... 1. 15, 20, 21, 167

निग्रहस्थान v. 2. 23. 175

निग्रहस्थानम् i. 2. 19. 20

निग्रहस्य v. 2. 2. 174

नित्य v. 1. 1., v. 1. 14. ... ... 140, 151

नित्यं iv. 1. 29., v. 1. 35., v. 1. 36. ... 114, 161, 162

नित्यत्व ii. 2. 38., ii. 2. 55., iii. 2. 24., iii. 2. 76., v. 1. 15., v. 1. 35.,
v. 1. 36. ... ... 53, 57, 90, 106, 152, 161, 162

नित्यत्वात् ii. 2. 15., ii. 2. 25., iii. 1. 5., iv. 1. 29. ... 47, 50, 64, 114

नित्यत्वे ii. 2. 52, iv. 1. 10. ... ... 56, 109

नित्यस्य iv. 1. 28. 114

नित्यसमः v. 1. 35. 161

नित्यानां ii. 2. 53. 57

नित्येषु ii. 2. 15., ii. 2. 18. ... ...47, 48

निन्दा ii. 1. 65., iv. 1. 60. ... ... 41, 123

अनिबन्ध iii. 2. 44. 96

निमित्त ii. 2. 37., iv. 1. 7., iv. 1. 9., iv. 1. 24., iv. 2. 36. ... 53, 109, 109,
113, 136

निमित्तं iii. 2. 70., iv. 2. 2., iv. 2. 3. ... ... 104, 127, 127

निमित्तवत् iii. 2. 70. 104

निमित्तत्वात् ii. 1. 25., ii. 1. 26., iii. 1. 21., iii. 1. 27., iii. 2. 36.,
iii. 2. 67., iii. 2. 75., iv. 1. 23., iv. 1. 68.... 30, 30, 68, 94, 103,
106, 113, 126

निमित्तानां iv. 2. 1. 127

निमित्तभ्यः iii. 2. 44. 96

नियतत्वात् ii. 1. 11. 25

नियम ii. 2. 58., iii. 2. 40., iv. 2. 46. ... ... 58, 95, 138

नियमः iii. 1. 18. 67

				Page.
नियमात् ii. 2. 57., ii. 2. 58.	...	...	...	...58, 58
नियमे ii. 2. 58.	..	...	...	... 58
नियमहेतु iii. 2. 12.	...	...	...	... 80
नियोग iii. 1. 50.	...	...	...	... 75
निरर्थकं v. 2. 1., v. 2. 8.	...	...	..	167, 170
निरनुमानः iii. 7. 18.	...	...	...	... 67
निरनुयोज्य v. 2. 23.	...	...	...	... 175
निरवयवत्वात् iv. 1. 43.	...	...	...	118
निर्णय i. 1. 1., 1. 2. 7.	...	...	...	... 1, 16
निर्णयः i. 1. 41.	...	...	...	... 13
निर्दिष्ट v. 1. 27.	...	...	...	... 158
निर्देशः v. 2. 3.	...	...	...	... 168
निर्देशवत् v. 2. 8.	...	...	...	... 170
निर्देशात् iv. 1. 18., iv. 1. 53.	...	...	...	111, 121
निर्देशे i. 2. 14., v. 1. 43.	...	...	...	10, 164
निवृत्ति iii. 2. 38.	...	...	..	... 94
निवृत्तिः iv. 2. 1., v. 1. 10.	...	...	...	127, 149
निवृत्तिवत् v. 1. 10.	...	...	...	... 149
निवृत्तेः iii. 2. 17.	...	...	...	... 88
निवृत्त्योः iii. 2. 36.	...	...	...	... 94
निःश्रेयस i. 1. 1.	...	...	...	... 1
निष्पत्ति v. 1. 8.	...	...	...	... 148
निष्पत्तेः iv. 1. 13., iv. 1. 35., iv. 1. 44., iv. 1. 47., iv. 1. 54., iv. 1. 56.				
		110, 116, 119, 119, 122, 122		
निष्पन्न iv 2. 44.	..	...	...	... 137
नैमित्तिक iv. 1. 7., iv. 1. 9.	..	...	...	109, 109
न्यून ii. 2. 43.	...	...	...	... 54
न्यूने v. 2. 1., v. 2. 12.	...	...	...	167, 172

प

पक्ष i. 1. 41., i. 2 1., v. 2. 5.	...	...	...	13, 14, 169
पक्षप्रतिपक्षाभ्यां i. 1. 41.	...	...	...	13
पक्षयोः ii. 2. 29.	...	...	...	... 51
पक्षहानेः v. 1. 22.	...	...	...	... 155
पंच i. 2. 1.	...	...	...	... 14
पंचत्वात् iii. 1. 58.	...	...	...	.. 77
पंचत्वेभ्यः iii. 1. 62.	...	,,,	,,,	... 78

					Page.
पंचभूत iv. 1. 29.	...	...	...	...	... 114
पंचात्मक iii. 1. 21.	...	...	...	...	... 68
पट iv. 2. 26.	...	...	...	...	... 133
पटल iii. 1. 44.	...	...	...	...	... 73
पटु iv. 2. 14.	...	...	...	...	... 130
पततः ii. 1. 39.	...	...	...	...	... 34
पतितव्य ii. 1. 39.	...	...	...	...	... 34
पदार्थे ii. 2. 68.	...	...	...	...	... 61
पदं ii. 2. 60.	...	...	...	...	... 59
पद्मादिषु iii. 1. 20.	...	...	...	...	... 68
पयसः iii. 2. 10.	...	...	...	...	... 88
पर i. 1. 29.	...	...	...	...	... 9
परऋति: ii. 1. 65.	...	...	...	...	... 41
परगुण iii. 2. 50.	...	...	...	...	... 99
परतंत्र i. 1. 29.	...	...	...	...	... 9
परतंत्रसिद्धः i. 1. 29.	...	...	...	...	... 9
परपक्ष v. i. 43., v. 2. 21.	...	...	...	164, 174
परश्वादिषु iii. 2. 38.	...	...	...	...	... 94
परं iv. 2. 17.	...	...	...	...	... 131
पर्यनुयोज्य v. 2. 1., v. 2. 22.	...	...	...	167, 174
पर्यंतत्वात् iii. 2. 56.	...	...	...	...	... 101
पर्येषण iv. 1. 57.	...	...	...	...	... 122
परिग्रह ii. 2. 62., iii. 2. 44.	...	...	...	59, 96
परिग्रहः i. 2. 1.	...	...	...	...	... 14
परिच्छद iv. 1. 53.	...	...	...	...	... 121
परिणाम iii. 2. 16.	...	...	...	...	... 88
परिशेषात् iii. 2. 42.	...	...	...	...	... 96
परिषत् v. 2. 9.	...	...	...	...	... 171
परिषदा v. 2. 17.	...	...	...	...	... 173
परीक्षकाणां i. 1. 25.	...	...	...	...	... 8
परीक्षणम् i. 1. 31.	...	...	...	...	... 10
पश्चात् ii. 1. 10.	...	...	...	...	... 25
पश्याम ii. 1. 47.	...	...	...	...	... 36
पशु iv. 1. 53.	...	...	...	...	... 121
पाकज iii. 2. 52.	...	...	...	...	... 100
पाकजानां iii. 2. 53.	...	...	...	...	... 100
पातक iii. 1. 4.	...	...	...	...	... 63

	Page.
पातकाभावात् iii. 1. 4.	63
पाद iii. 2. 33.	93
पाटना ii. 1. 54.	38
पाणि ii. 2. 37.	53
पापीयान् iv. 1. 6.	109
पारतंत्र्यात् iii. 2. 41.	95
पार्थिव iii. 2. 37.	94
पार्थिवं iii. 1. 28.	70
पार्थिवाप्पयोः iii. 1. 69.	80
पीडने v. 1. 8.	148
पुत्र iv. 1. 53.	121
पुनः i. 1. 19., ii. 1. 58., ii. 1. 67., iii. 2. 73., v. 2. 1., v. 2. 14., v. 2. 16.	
	7, 39, 42, 105, 167, 172, 173
पुनर् i. 1. 39., ii. 2. 48.	12, 56
पुनरुक्तयोः ii. 1. 67.	42
पुराकल्प ii. 1. 65.	41
पुरुष iv. 1. 19., iv. 1. 20.	112, 112
पुरुषार्थतंत्रः iii. 1. 37.	72
पुरुषेषु ii. 2. 64.	60
पूर्ण ii. 1. 54.	38
पूर्व ii. 1. 9., iii. 1. 64., iii. 1. 70., iii. 2. 17.	25, 78, 80, 88
पूर्वं i. 1. 5.	3
पूर्वकृत iii. 1. 64., iv. 2. 41.	103, 137
पूर्वगण iii. 1. 70.	80
पूर्ववत् i. 1. 5.	3
पूर्वहेतुः iv. 2. 5.	128
पूर्वाभ्यस्त iii. 1. 19.	68
पृथक् ii. 1. 25., iv. 1. 34., iv. 2. 9.	30, 115, 128
पृथक्त्वात् iv. 1. 34.	115
पृथिवी i. 1. 13., i. 1. 14.	5, 5
पृथिव्याः iii. 1. 64	78
पैर्वापय v. 2. 10.	171
प्रकरण i. 1. 30., i. 2. 4., i. 2. 7., v. 1. 1.	9, 15, 16, 140
प्रकरणसम i. 2. 4.	15
प्रकरणसमः i. 2. 7., v. 1. 16.	16, 153
प्रकरणसिद्धेः v. 1. 17.	153
प्रकाशवत् ii. 1. 19.	28

Page.

प्रकृतात् v. 2. 7. 170

प्रकृति ii. 2. 42., ii. 2. 56. ... ...54, 58

प्रक्रिया v. 1. 16. 153

प्रज्ञातस्य v. 1. 34. 161

प्रणिधान iii. 2. 34. 93

प्रणिधानादि iii 2. 35.... 93

प्रत्यक्ष i. 1. 3., ii. 1. 8., ii. 1. 9., ii. 1. 20., ii. 1. 21., ii. 1. 25., ii. 1. 42.,
iv. 1. 11. ... ... 2, 24, 25, 28, 29, 30, 35, 110

प्रत्यक्षम् i. 1. 4., ii. 1. 30. ... ... 2, 31

प्रत्यक्षतः iii. 1. 34. 71

प्रत्यक्षत्वात् iii. 1. 69. 80

प्रत्यक्षत्वे iii. 2. 46. 98

प्रत्यक्षेण ii. 1. 31., ii. 1. 46. ... ...32, 36

प्रत्यनीक iv. 1. 4. 108

प्रत्यभिज्ञानात् iii. 1. 7., iii. 2. 20. 64,83

प्रत्यर्थे ii. 1. 11. 25

प्रत्यवस्थानं i. 2. 18. 19

प्रत्यवस्थानात् v. 1. 9. 148

प्रत्युक्तः iii. 2. 71. 104

प्रतिज्ञा i. 1.32., i. 1. 33., v. 2. 1., v. 2. 2., v. 2. 4., v. 2. 5.... 10, 10, 167, 167,
169, 169

प्रतिज्ञां v. 2. 3. 168

प्रतिज्ञाता v. 2. 5. 169

प्रतिज्ञायाः i. 1. 39. 12

प्रतितंत्र i. 1. 27. 9

प्रतितंत्रसिद्धान्तः i. 1. 29. 9

प्रतिदृष्टान्त v. 1. 1., v. 1. 11., v. 2. 2. ... 140, 150, 167

प्रतिदृष्टान्तसमौ v. 1. 9. 148

प्रतिदृष्टान्तेन v. 1. 9. 148

प्रतिद्वन्द्वि iii. 2. 53. 100

प्रतिपक्ष i. 2. 1., i. 2. 3., iv. 2. 49., v. 1. 17., v. 1. 21. 14, 15, 138, 153, 155

प्रतिपक्षात् v. 1.17. 153

प्रतिपक्षाभ्यां i. 1. 41. 13

प्रतिपत्तेः iv. 2. 29. 134

प्रतिबोधे iv. 2. 35. 135

प्रतिवादिभ्यां v. 2. 9. 171

प्रतिषिद्धे v. 2. 6. 169

Page.

प्रतिषेध i. 2. 14., ii. 1. 12., ii. 2. 5., iii. 1. 50., v. 1. 17., v. 1. 20.,
    v. 1. 24., v. 1. 33., v. 1. 36., v. 1. 41., v. 1 42. 19,26,
        44, 75, 153, 154, 156, 160, 162, 163, 164

प्रतिषेधे v. 1. 39 , v. 2. 3., v. 2. 5.   ..   ...   163, 168, 169

प्रतिषेधं v. 1. 42.   164

प्रतिषेधः ii. 1. 14., iv. 1. 9., v. 1. 13.   ...   ...   26, 109, 151

प्रतिषेद्द्रव्य iii. 2. 48., v. 1. 20.   ...   .   98, 154

प्रतिषेध्य v. 1. 33.   160

प्रतिषेध्ये v. 1. 36.   162

प्रतिसंबन्धनाय iv. 1. 64.   125

प्रतीघातः iii. 1 38.   72

प्रदायात् v. 1. 10.   149

प्रदाह ii. 1. 54.   38

प्रदाहे iii. 1. 5.   64

प्रदीप ii. 1. 19., iii. 2. 49.   ...   .28, 99

प्रदेश ii. 2. 18., iii. 2. 26.   ...   .48, 91

प्रधान iv. 1. 60., iv. 2. 37.   ...   .   123, 136

प्रधानं iii. 1. 70.   80

प्रबोध iii. 1. 20.   68

प्रमाण i. 1. 1., i. 2. 1., ii. 1. 9., ii. 1. 14., ii. 1. 17., ii. 1. 18., ii. 1 47.,
    iv. 2. 30., iv. 2. 31.   ...   1, 14, 25, 26, 27, 27, 36, 134, 134

प्रमाणतः ii. 1. 53., iv. 2. 29.   ...   ...   38, 134

प्रमाणसिद्धौ ii. 1. 9.   25

प्रमाणान्तर ii. 1. 17.   27

प्रमाणानां ii. 1. 17.   27

प्रमाणानि i. 1. 3.   2

प्रमाणार्थं ii. 1. 47.   36

प्रमाणेभ्यः ii. 1. 10.   25

प्रमेय i. 1. 1., ii. 1. 10., ii. 2. 7., iv. 2. 31.   ...   ...   1, 25, 45, 134

प्रमेयम् i. 1. 9.   4

प्रमेयता ii. 1. 16.   27

प्रमेयासिद्धेः ii. 2. 7.   45

प्रयत्न i. 1. 10., v. 1. 37., v. 1. 38.   ...   ...   5, 162, 162

प्रयोग iv. 2. 11.   129

प्रयोगात् iv. 1. 16.   111

प्रयोजन i. 1. 1., iv. 2. 49.   ...   ...   1, 138

प्रयोजनं i. 1. 24.   8

	Page.
प्रवर्चेते i. 1. 24.	8
प्रवर्तन i. 1. 18.	7
प्रवर्तनात् iv. 2. 40	137
प्रवृत्ति i. 1. 2., i. 1. 9., i. 1, 20., iii. 1. 24., iv. 1. 59. ...	2, 4, 7, 69, 123
प्रवृत्तिः i. 1. 17., iv. 1. 64., iv. 1. 1., iv. 2. 14. ...	6, 25, 108, 130
प्ररोह iv. 1. 50.	139
प्रलयः iv. 2. 16.	130
प्रशंसा iv. 1. 60.	123
प्रश्लेषात् ii. 2. 37.	53
प्रसवात्मिका ii. 2. 71.	62
प्रसाद iii. 1. 49.	74
प्रसिद्ध i. 1. 6., ii. 1. 45.	3, 35
प्रसिद्धत्वात् iv. 2, 5.	128
प्रसंग v. 1. 1., v. 1. 9.	140, 148
प्रसंगात् iii. 1. 48., iii. 2. 78., v. 1. 23., v. 1. 32. ... 74, 106, 156, 160
प्रसंगः i. 2. 77., ii. 1. 7., ii. 1. 17., ii. 1. 22., ii. 2. 35., ii. 2. 38., iii. 2. 5.,
iii. 2. 24., iii. 2. 35., iii. 2. 73., iii. 2. 76., iv. 2. 15., iv. 2. 43,
v. 1. 42., v. 2. 21., v. 2. 24. ... 19, 24, 27, 29, 52, 53, 84, 90, 93, 105,
106, 136, 137, 164, 174, 175
प्राक् ii. 2. 12., ii. 2. 19., iv. 1. 47., iv. 1. 66., v. 1. 12. ... 46, 49, 119, 126,
150
प्रातिभवत् iii. 2. 35.	93
प्रादुर्भावात् iii. 2. 16., iv. 1. 14.	88, 110
प्राप्य v. 1. 7.	147
प्राप्नः iv. 1. 7.	109
प्राप्यता v. 1. 7.	147
प्रासानां ii. 2. 47.	55
प्राप्ति iii. 2. 44., v. 1. 1., v. 1. 7.	96, 140, 147
प्राप्तौ iii. 2. 69.	104
प्राबल्यात् iv. 2. 39.	136
प्रामाण्यवत् ii. 1. 16., ii. 1. 69.	27, 42
प्रामाण्यात् ii. 2. 1., iii. 2. 29., iv. 1. 11. ...	43, 70, 116
प्रामाण्ये ii. 1. 14., ii. 2. 6.	26, 45
प्रमाण्यं ii. 1. 69.	42
प्रायः ii 1. 44.	35
प्रायश iii. 2. 76.	106
प्राबल्यात् ii. 7. 29.	31

	Page.
प्रीतेः vi. 1. 52.	121
प्रेत्य i. 1. 9., iii. 1. 22., iv. 1. 10.	4, 68, 109
प्रेत्यभावः i. 1. 19.	7
प्रेरण iii. 2. 32.	92
प्रोक्षणादीनां ii. 2. 66.	61

फ

फल i. 1. 9., iii. 2. 64., iv. 1. 20., iv. 1. 44., iv. 1.51., iv. 1. 53., iv. 1. 54., iv. 2. 44. ... 4, 103, 112, 119, 121, 121, 122, 137	
फलम् i. 1. 20.	7
फलवत् iv. 1. 47., iv. 1. 54.	119, 122

ब

बधात् iii. 1. 6.	64
बहिः iv. 2. 20.	131
बहुत्वम् i. 2. 20.	21
बाधना i. 1. 21., iv. 1. 55., iv. 1. 57.	7, 122, 122
बाह्यप्रकाश iii. 1. 41.	73
बुद्धि i. 1. 9., i. 1. 17., i. 1. 25., iv. 1. 50.	4, 6, 8, 121
बुद्धिः i. 1. 15.	6
बुद्धिसाम्यं i. 1. 25.	8
बुद्धीनाम् ii. 1. 11.	25
बुद्धेः iv. 2. 36.	136
बुद्ध्यन्तरात् iii. 2. 25.	90
ब्राह्मणं ii. 2. 64.	60

भ

भय iii. 1. 19., iii. 2. 44.	...68, 96
भाव i. 1. 9., ii. 2. 49., iv. 1. 10., iv. 1. 14., iv. 1. 22., iv. 1. 34., v. 1. 31. ... ... 4, 56, 109, 110, 112, 115, 159	
भावः iv. 1. 7.	7
भावात् i. 1. 27., i. 2. 16., ii. 1. 32., ii. 1. 38., iii. 1. 34., iv. 1. 3., iv. 1. 4., iv. 1. 7., iv. 1. 24., iv. 1. 42. ... 9, 19, 32, 33, 93, 108, 108, 109, 113, 118	
भावानां iv. 1. 38., iv. 2. 26.	117, 133
भावित्वात् iii. 2. 51., iv. 2. 44.	99, 137
भावी i. 1. 36.	11

		Page.
भावेन v. 1. 34.	... ...	161
भावेषु iv. 1. 51.	... ...	117
भूतगुण iii. 1. 63.	... ...	78
भूतेभ्यः i. 1. 12., iii. 2. 65.	... ...	5, 103
भूयस्त्वात् iii. 1. 71.	... ...	81
भेद iv. 2. 11.	... ...	129
भेदमात्रं iii. 1. 17.	... ...	67
भेदात् iv. 2. 37.	... ...	136
भौतिक iii 1. 38.	... ...	72
भौतिकधर्मः iii. 1. 38.	... ...	72

म

मतानुज्ञा v. 1. 42., v. 2. 1., v. 2. 21.	... ...	164, 167, 174
मध्यन्दिन 3. 1. 39.	... ...	72
मनः i. 1. 9., iii. 2. 60., iii. 2. 75. ...	... ...	4, 102, 106
मनसः i. 1. 16., ii. 1. 24., iii. 2. 20., iii. 2. 22., iii. 2. 26., iii. 2. 27., iii. 2. 30., iii. 2. 33., iii. 2. 41. 6, 29, 89, 89, 91, 91, 92, 93,		95
मन्दभावात् iv. 2. 14.	... ...	130
मनसां ii. 1. 26.	... ...	30
मनसि iii. 1. 16.	... ...	67
महत् iii. 1. 31.	... ...	70
महदणु iii. 1. 31.	... ...	70
मातापित्रोः iii. 2. 67.	... ...	103
माया iv. 2. 32.	... ...	135
मिथ्या i. 1. 2., iv. 2. 35., iv. 2. 37.	... ...	2. 135, 136
मिथ्याज्ञानानां i. 1. 2.	... ...	2
मूर्ति iii. 2. 65.	... ...	103
मूर्तिः ii. 2. 69.	... ...	61
मूर्तिमतां iv. 2. 23.	... ...	132
मृगतृष्णिकावत् iv. 2. 32.	... ...	135
मृदुगवके ii. 2. 66.	... ...	61
मोह iv. 1. 3.	... ...	108
मोहः iv. 1. 6.	... ...	109
मोहस्य iv. 1. 8.	... ...	109
मंत्र ii. 1. 69.	... ...	42

य

यत् i. 1. 30., iii. 2. 32.	... ...	9, 92

Page.

यन्त्र ii. 1. 7. 24

यथा i. 2. 2., ii. 1. 6., ii. 1. 45., iii. 2. 12., iii. 2. 41., iii. 2. 42., iii. 2. 63.,
iv. 1. 1., iv. 1. 28. v. 2. 25., 15, 23, 35, 86, 95, 96, 103, 108, 114, 175

यम iv. 2. 41. 138

यस्मात् i. 2. 7. 16

यस्मिन् i. 1. 25. 8

या ii. 2. 62. 59

याथात्म्य iv. 2. 26. 133

यावत् ii. 1. 31., iii. 2. 51. ... ...32, 99

युक्तेः ii. 2. 66. 61

युगपत् i. 1. 16., ii. 1 11., iii. 1. 56., iii. 2. 4., iii. 2. 20., iii. 2. 26.,
iii. 2. 61. ... ... 6, 25, 76, 84, 89, 91, 102

योगसाधन ii. 2. 64. 60

योगात् i. 2. 73., iv. 1. 55., iv. 2. 46. ... ... 18, 122, 138

योगाभ्यास iv. 2. 42. 137

यौगपद्य iii. 2. 35. 93

र

रश्मि iii. 1. 32. 71

रश्मिदर्शनात् iii. 1. 43. 73

रस i. 1. 14., iii. 1. 64. ... ... 5, 78

रसन i. 1. 12. 5

राग iii. 2. 44., iv. 1. 3. .. .. 96, 108

रागादीनां iii. 1. 27., iv. 1. 68. ... ... 69, 126

राज्ञ ii. 2. 64. 60

रात्रौ iii. 1. 40. 72

रूप i. 1. 14., iii. 1. 64., iii. 2. 47., iii. 2. 51., iii. 2. 58., iii. 2. 59. ... 5,
78, 98, 99, 101, 102

रूपविशेषात् iii. 1. 36. 71

रूपादयः iv. 2. 2. 127

रूपोपलब्धिः iii. 1. 36. 71

रूपोपलब्धिवत् iii. 1. 49. 74

रोध ii 1. 37. 33

ल

लक्षण ii. 1. 20., iii. 1. 62., iii. 2. 44., iv. 1. 8., iv. 1. 31., iv. 1. 34.,
iv. 1. 36., v. 1. 43. ... ... 28, 78, 96, 109, 114, 115,
116, 164

	Page.
लक्षणा i. 1. 21.	7
लक्षणा ii. 2. 11.	46
लक्षणैः iv. 1. 35.	116
लक्षितेष ii. 2. 8.	45
लक्षितत्वात् ii. 2. 8.	45
लिंग iii. 2. 44.	96
लिंगं i. 1. 10., i. 1. 16.	5, 6
लिंगतः iii. 2. 15.	87
लिंगत्वात् ii. 1. 23., ii. 1. 24., iii. 2. 37.	29, 29, 94
लिंगादि iii. 2. 34.	93
लेश ii. 2. 59.	58
लौकिक i. 1. 25.	8

व

	Page.
वक्तुः i. 2. 12.	18
वचन ii. 1. 63.	40
वचन i. 2. 10.	17
वचनं i. 1. 39., ii. 1. 25., v. 2. 11., v. 2. 16., v. 2. 14., v. 2. 16. ... 12, 30, 171, 172, 173	
वचनात् ii. 1. 20., ii. 1. 60., iv. 2. 20. ... ... 28, 40, 131	
वनवत् ii. 1. 36.	33
वर्ण ii. 2. 45., ii. 2. 50., ii. 2. 54., ii. 2. 62., v. 2. 8. ... 55, 56, 57, 59, 170	
वर्णत्व ii. 2. 50.	56
वर्णविकार ii. 2. 45.	55
वर्णविकारः ii. 2. 59.	58
वर्णविकाराणां ii. 2. 53., ii. 2. 56.	57, 58
वर्णी v. 1. 1., v. 1. 4.	140, 142
वर्तमान ii. 1. 39., ii. 1. 40., ii. 1. 42. ... ... 34, 34, 35	
वर्षकाल iii. 1. 21.	68
वा i. 1. 37., i. 1. 38., i. 2. 17., ii. 1. 1., ii. 1. 6., ii. 1. 14., ii. 1. 18., ii. 2. 6., iv. 1. 67., iv. 2. 17., iv. 2. 19., iv. 2. 32., iv 2. 49., v. 1. 7., v. 1. 15. ... 12, 12, 19, 22, 23, 26, 27, 45, 126, 131, 131, 135, 138, 147, 152	
वाक् i. 1 17, i. 2. 12.	6, 18
वाक्छलं i. 2. 11., i. 2. 12.	18, 18
वाक्य ii. 1. 62.	40
वाद i. 1. 1.	1

			Page.
वादः i. 2. 1.	... ...	...	14
वायुः i. 1. 13.	... ...	...	5
वायूनां iii. 1. 64.	... ...	...	78
विकल्प i. 2. 10, i. 2. 14., v. 1. 1., v. 1. 4.	...	...	17, 19, 140, 142
विकल्पः ii. 2. 45.	... ...	...	55
विकल्पात् i. 2. 20., ii. 2. 44., ii. 2. 53., v. 1. 4, v. 2. 3.		21, 55, 57, 142, 168
विकल्पानां v. 1. 31.	... ...	...	159
विकल्पे iv. 1. 58.	... ...	...	22
विकार ii. 2. 41., ii. 2. 42., ii. 2. 44., ii. 2. 45., ii. 2. 46, ii. 2. 47., ii. 2. 54.,		
		54, 54, 55, 55, 55, 55, 57
विकारवत् iii. 1. 20. ...	... ...	...	68
विकारात् ii. 2. 52., iii. 1. 12.	... ...	...	56, 66
विकाराणां ii. 2. 43., ii. 2. 49, ii. 2. 50., iii. 1. 21.	...	54, 56, 56, 68
विकारोपपत्तेः ii. 2. 55., ii. 2. 59. ...	...	...	...57, 58
विक्षेपः v. 2. 1, v. 2. 20.	...	...	167, 174
विघातः i. 2. 10.	...	...	17
विज्ञातस्य v. 2. 17. ...	... ...	...	173
वितंड i. 2. 3.	... ...	...	15
वितंडा i. 1. 1.	... ...	...	1
वितंडे iv. 2. 50.	... ...	...	139
विद्या iv. 1 61., iv. 2. 4.	... ...	...	124, 127
विद्युत् iii. 2. 47.	... ...	...	98
विधानं iv. 1. 61.	... ...	...	124
विधायकः ii. 1. 64.	... ...	...	41
विधिः ii. 1. 64., ii. 1. 66., iv. 2. 46.	... ...	41, 41, 138
विध्यर्थवाद ii. 1. 63. ...	... ...	...	40
विनष्टेभ्यः iv. 1. 17. ...	... ...	...	111
विनाश iii. 2. 5., iii. 2. 18., iii. 2. 24., iv. 1. 25., iv. 1. 30.		84, 88,
		90, 113, 114
विनाशः iii. 2. 35., iv. 2. 35.	... ...	...	90, 135
विनाशकारण ii. 2. 34., ii. 2. 38., iii. 2. 13.	...	...	52, 53, 87
विनाश्य iv. 1. 27. ...	... ...	...	113
विनाशात् iv. 1. 46.	... ...	...	119
विनाशे iii. 2. 14., iii. 2. 19.	... ...	...	...87, 89
विनियोगात् ii. 1. 63.	... ...	...	40
विनिवृत्ते ii. 1. 18. ...	... ...	...	27
विपरीत v. 1. 29.	... ...	...	159

					Page.
विपरीतम् i. 1. 37.	...	...	...	...	12
विपर्यय v. 1. 2.	...	...	...	...	140
विपर्ययात् i. 1. 37.	...	...	...	...	12
विपर्य्यास v. 2. 11.	...	...	...	...	171
विप्रतिपत्ति ii. 1 2.	...	...	...	...	22
विप्रतिपत्तिः i. 2. 19.	...	...	...	...	20
विप्रतिपत्ते ः i. 1. 23., ii. 2. 13.	...	...	...	... 7, 46
विप्रतिपत्तौ ii. 1. 3.	...	...	...	...	22
विप्रतिषेधात् iii. 1. 57.	...	...	...	...	76
विप्रतिषेधे v. 1. 41., v. 1. 42.	...	...	...	163, 164
विभक्ति ii. 2. 40.	...	...	...	...	54
विभागात् ii. 2. 16., iv. 2. 21.	...	..	...	48, 131
विभागस्य ii. 1. 62.	...	...	...	...	40
विभुत्वानि iv. 2. 22.	...	...	...	...	137
विमर्श ii. 2. 13.	...	...	...	...	46
विमर्शः i. 1. 23.	...	...	...	...	7
विमृश्य i. 1. 41.	...	...	...	...	13
विमोक्षः i. 1. 22.	...	...	...	...	7
वियोग iii. 2. 44.	...	...	...	...	96
वियोगः iii. 2. 72.	...	...	...	...	105
विरुद्ध i. 2. 4.	...	...	...	...	15
विरुद्धः i. 2. 1., i. 2. 6.	...	...	...	...14, 16
विरोध iii 2. 44.	...	...	...	...	96
विरोधः v. 2. 1., v. 2. 4.	...	...	...	167, 169
विरोधात् ii. 2. 58.	...	...	...	...	58
विरोधात् iii. 1. 11.	...	...	...	...	65
विरोधी i. 2. 6.	...	...	...	...	16
विविध iv. 1. 55.	...	...	...	...	122
विवृद्धः ii. 2. 42.	...	...	...	...	54
विवृद्धौ ii. 2. 42.	...	...	...	...	54
विवेचनात् iv. 2. 26. ...	...	...	...	...	133
विशिष्ट iv. 2. 48.	...	...	...	...	7
विशेष i. 1. 23., i. 1. 31., ii. 1. 61., iii. 1. 63., iv. 2. 38., iv. 2. 39.,					
v. 2. 15.	...	...	7, 10, 23, 78, 136, 136, 173
विशेषं v. 2. 6.	...	...	...	...	169
विशेषः ii. 1. 67i., iii. 2. 32.	...	...	...	...42, 92
विशेषकौ iii. 2. 40.	...	...	...	...	95

Page.

विशेषणात् ii. 2. 17. 48

विशेषपरीक्षणं i. 1. 31. 10

विशेषात् iii. 1. 32. 71

विशेषाणां ii. 1. 27. 30

विशेषेण iii. 1. 54., iii. 2. 33. ... ...76, 93

विष्वं iii. 1. 68. 80

विषय iii. 1. 2., iii. 2. 1., iv. 2. 14., iv. 2. 31., iv. 2. 34., iv. 2. 35.,
63, 83, 130, 134, 135, 135

विषयत्व iii. 1. 61. 77

विषयत्वात् iii. 1. 13. 66

विषयस्य iii 1. 15. 66

विषयाः iv. 2. 2. 127

विषयान्तर iii. 2. 7. 85

विषयोपलब्धेः iii. 2. 41. 73

विहितस्य ii. 1. 66. 41

वीज iv. 2. 50. 139

वीतराग iii. 1. 25. 69

बुद्धि iii. 1. 62., iii. 2. 46. ... ... 78, 98

बुद्धेः iii. 2. 25., iv. 2. 37. ... ... 90, 136

बुद्ध्या iv 2. 26. 133

वृक्ष iv. 1. 47., iv. 1. 51 ... ... 119, 121

वृत्ति iv. 2. 6. 128

वृद्धि ii. 2. 59., ii. 2. 62. ... ...58, 59

वेदयतः iv, 1. 57. 122

वै iv. 2. 4. 127

वैगुण्यात् ii. 1. 59. 39

वैधर्म्ये v. 1. 1. 140

वैधर्म्यात् i. 1. 35., iii. 1. 75., iii 2. 57., iii. 2. 58., iv. 1. 48., v. 1. 5.,
v. 1 15. ... ... 11, 81, 101, 101, 120, 145, 152
... ... 140

वैधर्म्यसमौ v. 1 2. 140

वैधर्म्याभ्यां v. 1 2. 19

वैधर्म्यायां i. 2. 18. 136

वैविध्य iv. 2. 37. 55

वैषम्यवत् ii. 2. 45 ... ... 110, 110

व्यक्तात् iv. 1. 11., iv. 1. 13. 110

व्यक्तानां iv. 1. 11. ... ... 59, 61, 61, 61

व्यक्ति ii. 2. 61., ii. 2. 66., ii. 2. 67., ii. 2. 68.

8

Page.

व्यक्तिः ii. 2. 62., ii. 2. 69. ... ...59, 61

व्यक्तीनां iii. 2. 11. 86

व्यक्तौ ii. 2. 62. 59

व्यतिभेदात् iv. 2. 18. 131

व्यतिरिच्य iii. 1. 30. 70

व्यतिरेकात् iv. 1. 51. 121

व्यथनेन iii. 2. 33. 93

व्यभिचारात् ii. 1. 37., iv. 1. 5. ... ... 33, 108

व्यय iv. 1. 49. 120

व्यवधान iii. 2. 44. 96

व्यवस्थातः i. 1. 23. 7

व्यवस्थान ii. 2. 65., iv. 1. 33. ... ... 60, 115

व्यवस्थानं iii. 1. 71. 81

व्यवस्थानात् ii. 1. 55., iii. 1. 2., iii. 1. 3., iv. 1. 28., iv. 1. 36., ... 38, 63, 63, 114, 116

व्यवस्थितत्वात् ii. 1. 4. 23

व्यवसाय i. 1. 4. 2

व्यवसायात्मकं i. 1. 4. 2

व्यवहिते iii. 1. 8. 6

व्याघात ii. 1. 58. 39

व्याघातात् iv. 1. 15. 110

व्यायित्वात् iii. 2. 54. 100

व्यासक्त ii. 1. 26., iii. 2. 33. ... ...30, 93

व्यासक्तमनसः iii. 2. 33. 93

व्यासंगात् iii. 2. 7., v. 2. 20. ... ... 85, 174

व्याहतत्वात् iii. 1. 55., iv. 1. 40., iv. 2. 27. ... ... 76, 117, 133

व्याहृतत्वात् ii. 1. 28. 31

व्यूहः iii, 1. 37. 72

व्यूहान्तरात् iii. 2. 17. ... ...

श

शक्तु ii. 2. 64. 60

शब्द ii. 1. 67., ii. 2. 2., iii. 1. 74., iv. 1. 16., iv. 1. 60., iv. 2. 11., iv. 2. 21., v. 2. 14., v. 2. 15. ... 42, 43, 81, 111, 123, 129, 131, 172, 173

शब्दः i. 1. 7., ii. 1. 49. ... ... 4, 36

शब्दवत् iii. 2. 25. 90

शब्दसमूहः ii. 1. 62. 59

Page.

शब्दाः i. 1. 3., i. 1. 14. ... ... 2, 5

शब्दात् ii. 1. 15., ii. 1. 52. ... ...27, 37

शब्दानां iii. 1. 64. 78

शब्दाभावे ii. 2. 37. 53

शब्दार्थे ii. 1. 55., ii. 1. 56. ... ...38, 39

शब्देन ii. 2. 18., iv. 1. 60., v. 2. 16. ... ... 48, 123, 173

शरीर i. 1. 9., i. 1. 17., iii 2. 27., iii. 2. 51., iii. 2. 54., iii. 2. 57.,

    iii. 2. 70. ... ... 4, 6, 91, 99, 100, 101, 104

शरीरम् i. 1. 11. 5

शरीरदाहे iii. 1. 4. 63

शरीरधारण iii. 2. 29. 92

शरीरवृत्तित्वात् iii, 2. 27. 91

शरीरस्य iii. 2. 56. 101

शाखा iv. 2. 50. 139

शाकटात् ii. 2. 64. 60

शिष्य iv. 2. 48. 138

शीघ्रतर ii. 1. 68. 42

शीत iii. 1. 21. 68

शेषवत् i. 1. 5. 3

शोक iii. 1. 19. 68

श्यामता iii. 2. 27., iv. 1. 67. ... ... 106, 126

श्रवण ii. 2. 35. 52

श्रुति iii. 1. 29. 70

श्रोत्राणि i. 1. 12. 5

श्लेषेभ्यः ii. 2. 59. 58

स

संकल्प iii. 1. 27., iv. 1. 68. ... ... 69, 126

संकल्पकृताः iv. 2. 2. 127

संकल्पवत् iv. 2. 34. 135

संख्या ii. 2. 62., iv. 1. 41. ... ... 59, 118

सगुण iii. 1. 26. 69

सगुणानां iii. 1. 72 81

संचारात् iii. 2. 62. 102

संज्ञा iii. 1. 17. 67

संज्ञाभेदमात्रं iii. 1. 17. 67

सतत ii. 2. 35. 52

					Page.
सति iii. 1. 30.	...	...	...	...	... 70
सत्व ii. 2. 65.	...	...	...	...	... 60
सत्वात् ii. 2. 36.	...	...	...	...	... 52
सदोषं v. 1 42.	...	...	...	...	... 164
सद् iv. 1. 48.	...	...	...	...	... 120
सद्भाव i. 2. 14., iv. 2 26., iv. 2 36, v. 1. 1. 23.			... 19, 133, 136, 156
सद्भावता ii. 2. 21.	...	...	...	...	... 49
सद्भावात् iii. 1 14., iii. 1. 66., iv. 2. 16.		...	...	66, 79, 130
सद्भाव: iv. 2 23.	...	...	...	...	... 132
सद्य: iv. 1. 44., iv. 1. 45.	...	...	...	119, 119
सद्म iv. 1. 48.	...	...	...	...	... 120
सन्तति iii. 2. 49.	...	...	...	...	... 99
सन्ततै: iv 1. 65.	...	...	...	...	... 125
सन्तान ii. 2 17.	...	...	...	...	... 48
सन्देह: ii. 1. 33.	...	...	...	...	... 32
संन्यास: v. 2 1., v. 2. 5.	...	...	...	167, 169
सन्निकर्ष i 1. 4., ii. 1. 26.	...	...	...	... 2, 30
सन्निकर्ष स्य ii. 1. 23.	...	...	...	...	... 30
सन्निकर्षात् ii. 1. 9., iii. 2. 26.	...	...	...	25, 91
सन्निकर्षाभावे ii. 1. 21.	...	...	...	...	...
सन्निधौ ii. 2. 61.	...	...	...	...	... 59
संप्रत्यय: ii. 1. 52	...	...	...	...	... 37
संप्रतिपत्ते: iii. 1. 19.	...	...	...	...	... 68
सब्रह्मचारि iv. 2. 48.	...	...	...	...	... 138
सम्बन्ध ii. 1. 54., iii. 2. 44.	...	...	...	38, 96
संबन्धात् ii. 1. 51., iv. 1. 54	...	...	...	37, 122
संभव ii. 2. 1., ii. 2. 2	...	...	...	43, 43
संभवत: i. 2. 13.	...	...	...	...	... 18
समवेत iii. 2. 26.	...	...	...	...	... 91
समाधि iv. 2. 38.	...	...	...	...	... 136
समान i. 1. 23., i. 1. 29., ii. 1. 1.	...	...	7, 9, 22
समाने v. i. 14.	...	...	...	...	... 151
समानम् iii. 2. 33	...	...	...	...	... 93
समान: v. 1. 39, v. 1. 42., v. 1. 43.	...	...	163, 164, 164
समारोपणात् iv. 1. 62.	...	...	...	...	... 124
समास ii. 2. 62.	...	...	...	...	... 59
समासे ii. 2. 40.	...	...	...	...	... 54

			Page.
सम्प्राते iii. 2. 47.			98
सम्प्रत्ययस्य ii 1 56.			39
सम्प्रतिपत्ते ii. 1. 3.			22
सम्प्रदानात् ii. 2. 26			50
समूहे iv. 2. 13.			129
संयोग iii. 2. 32., iii. 2. 33., iii. 2 70., iii. 2. 75., iv. 21., iv. 2 24., ...			92,
93, 104, 106, 131, 132			
सर्वे i. 1. 27., i. 1. 28., ii. 1. 14., ii. 1. 42., iv. 1. 34., iv. 2. 21., v. 1. 23.,			
v. 1. 32.		9, 9, 26, 35, 115, 131, 156, 160	
सर्वगुण iii. 1 65.			311
सर्वगतत्वं iv. 2. 19.			79
सर्वतंत्र i. 1. 28.			9
सर्वत्र v. 1. 40.			163
सर्वोग्रहणं ii. 1. 34.			32
सर्वं iv. 1. 25., iv. 1. 29., iv. 1. 37. ...		113, 114, 117	
संरक्षणार्थे iv. 2. 50.			139
सव्यभिचारः i 2. 5., i. 2. 4		75, 15	
सव्यहृष्टस्य iii. 1. 7.			64
संवादः iv. 2. 47.			138
संवेदनात् v. 1. 31.			159
संशय i. 1. 1., i. 1. 23., iii. 1. 51., v. 1. 1. ...		1, 7, 75, 140	
संशयसमः v. 1. 14.			151
संशये v. 1. 15.			152
संशयेन ii. 1. 6.			23
संशयः ii. 1. 1., ii. 1. 5., ii. 1. 6., ii. 1. 7., ii. 2. 23., ii. 2. 41., ii. 2. 61.,			
iii. 1. 30., iii. 2. 1., iii. 2. 50., iv. 1. 44., iv. 2. 4., iv. 2. 6., v. 1. 15.,			
v. 1. 15. ...	22, 23, 23, 24, 46, 54, 59, 70, 83, 99, 119, 127,		
128, 151, 152			
संसर्गात् iii. 1. 67.			79
संस्थान iv. 2. 23.			132
संस्थिति i. 1. 27., 1. 1. 26.			9, 8
सह ii. 2. 64., iv. 2. 47.		60, 138	
साहृश्य iii. 2. 44			96
साहृश्येभ्यः ii. 1 37., ii. 1, 38.		33, 33	
साधन i. 2. 1., i. 2. 2., ii. 1. 59., iii. 1. 17., v. 1. 34. ...		14, 15, 39, 67, 161	
साधनं i. 1. 6., i. 1. 34.		3, 11	
साधर्म्ये i. 2. 18., v. 1. 1., iii. 1. 2. ...		.. 19, 140, 140	

Page.

साधर्म्यात् i. 1. 6., i. 1. 34., i. 2. 17., ii. 1. 44., ii 1 45 , iii. 2. 1,
v. 1. 5:, v. 1. 14., v. 1. 15., v. 1. 16., v. 1. 32., v. 1. 33 ...   3, 11, 19, 34,
35, 83, 145, 151, 152, 153, 160, 160

साध्य i. 1 6., 1. 1. 36., 1. 2. 4, i. 2. 8., v 1. 1., v. 1. 4., v. 1. 6., v. 1. 7.,
v. 1. 19., v. 1 34.   3, 11, 15, 16, 140, 142, 146, 147, 154, 161

साध्यत्वात् i 2. 8, ii 1. 33., iii 2 28., v. 1. 4   16, 32, 91, 142

साध्यस्य i. 1. 38.   12

साध्यसम i. 2. 4., i. 2. 8.   ...   .   15, 16

साध्यसमत्वात् iii. 2. 3., iii. 2. 66.   ...   ...   83, 103

साध्यसमाः v. 1. 4.   142

साध्यसाधनं i. 1. 6, 1. 1. 34.   ...   . 3, 11

सामर्थ्यात् ii 1. 52. 37

सामयिकत्वात् ii. 1. 56.   39

साम्यं i. 1. 25   8

सामान्य i. 2. 11., ii. 2. 15., v. 1. 14.   ...   ... 18, 47, 151

सामान्यच्छलम् i. 2. 13.   18

सामान्यतः i. 1. 5.   3

सामान्यवतः ii. 2. 51.   56

सामान्यस्य ii. 2. 51., v 1 15.   ...   . 56, 152

सामीप्य ii. 2. 64.   60

सिद्धः i. 2. 29.   9

सिद्धं iv 1. 50.   121

सिद्धान्त i. 1. 1., i. 2. 1.   ...   . 1, 14

सिद्धान्तं i. 2 6., v. 2 24.   ...   .   16, 175

सिद्धान्तः i 1. 76., i. 1. 28., i. 1. 29., i 1. 30. ...   ...   8, 9, 9, 9

सिद्धि ii. 1. 17.   27

सिद्धिः i. 1. 30., iv. 1. 10., iv. 1 39., v. 1 3 ...   ... 9, 109, 117, 141

सिद्धिप्रसंगः ii. 1. 17 27

सिद्धिवत् ii. 1. 15, ii. 1. 18.   ...   .   27, 27

सिद्धेः ii. 1. 15., ii. 1. 17., ii. 1. 19., ii. 1. 45., ii. 1. 48., ii. 2. 10, ii. 2 65,
iii. 2. 53., iv. 1. 37., iv. 1. 38., v. 1. 5., v. 1 16., v. 1. 19., v. 1. 21. ...   27,
27, 28, 35, 36, 46, 60, 100, 117, 117, 145, 153, 154, 155

सिद्धौ i. 1. 30., ii. 1. 9., ii. 1. 10., ii 1. 11., v. 1. 29.   ... 9, 25, 25, 25, 159

सुख i. 1. 10., iii. 2. 44., iv. 1. 58.   ...   ...   5, 96, 122

सुखस्य iv. 1. 56.   122

सुत ii. 1. 26.   30

सुवर्ण ii. 2. 49.   56

					Page.
सुवर्णादीनां ii. 2. 48.	...	...	...	...	56
सुषुसस्य iv, 1 63	...	...	...	...	124
सेना ii. 1. 36.	...	...	...	...	33
सेनावनवत् ii. 1. 36.	...	...	...	...	33
स्तन्य iii 1. 22	...	...	...	...	68
स्त्री iv. 1. 53.	...	...	...	...	121
स्तुत ii 1. 65.	...	...	...	...	41
स्थान i. 2. 20., i. 2. 2, ii. 2 64.	...	...	...	21, 15, 60	
स्थानम् ii 2 19.	...	...	...	...	20
स्थानान्यत्वे iii. 1. 51.	...	...	...	...	75
स्थानानां i. 1. 1.	...	...	...	...	1
स्थानानि v 2. 1.	...	...	...	...	167
स्थापना i. 2. 3.	...	...	...	...	15
स्पर्श i. 1. 14., iii 1. 64.	...	...	...	5, 78	
स्पर्शपर्य्यन्ताः iii. 1. 64.	...	...	...	...	78
स्फटिक iii. 1. 44., iii. 2 9	...	...	...	73, 85	
स्फटिकान्तरे iii. 1 47.	...	...	...	...	74
स्फटिके iii. 2 11.	...	...	...	...	86
स्मरण iii. 2. 31.	...	...	...	...	92
स्मरणं iii. 2. 34., iii. 2. 43.	...	...	...	93, 96	
स्मरतः iii. 2. 29.	...	...	...	...	92
स्मर्तव्य ii 1. 13.	...	...	...	...	66
स्मार्तं iii. 2. 35.	...	...	...	...	93
स्मृति iii. 2. 15., iii. 1. 19., iii 2 46., iii. 2. 26., iv. 2. 34.	...	...	...	66,	
				68, 98, 91, 135	
स्मृतिविषयस्य iii. 1. 15.	...	...	...	...	60
स्मृतेः iii. 1. 13.	...	...	...	...	66
स्व i 2. 3, iii. 2. 50., v. 2. 16.	...	...	...	15, 99, 173	
स्वपक्ष v. 1. 43., v. 2. 21.	...	...	...	164, 174	
स्वप्न iv. 1. 63, iv. 2. 31., iv. 2. 34, iv. 2. 35.		...	...	124, 134, 135, 135	
स्वभाव iv. 1. 38., iv. 1. 39.	...	...	...	117, 117	
स्वविषयस्य iv. 2. 14	...	...	...	...	130
स्वाभाविकत्वात् iv. 1. 65.	...	...	...	...	125
स्वाभाविके iv. 1. 60.	...	...	...	...	126
स्वाभाव्यात् iii. 1. 49., iii. 2. 43.	...	...	...	74, 96	

ह

	Page.
हर्ष iii. 1. 19.	68
हानिः v. 2. 1., v 2. 2.	167, 167
हि ii. 1. 9., ii. 2. 1., ii. 2 2., iii. 1. 68.	25, 43, 43, 80
हिरण्यात् iv. 1. 53.	... 121
हीन iv. 1 64.	... 125
हीन iv. 2. 49., v. 2. 12.	138, 172
हीनः i. 2. 3.	... 15
हेतु i. 1. 32., i. 1. 39., ii. 2. 13., iii. 2. 10., iii. 2. 42., iii. 2 48., iv. 1. 46., iv. 2. 33., v. 1. 1., v. 2. 1., v. 2. 6., v. 2. 13. ...	10, 12, 46, 85, 96, 98, 119, 135, 140, 167, 169, 172
हेतुः i. 1. 34., v. 1. 43.	11, 164
हेतुत्वम् v. 1. 38.	... 162
हेतुत्वे v. 1. 11.	... 150
हेतुतः v. 1. 19.	... 154
हेतुत्वात् iii. 2. 41., iii. 2. 63., v. 1. 34.	95, 103, 101
हेतूना iii. 1. 16.	... 67
हेतौः v. 1. 7., v. 1. 18.	147, 153
हेतौ v. 2. 6.	... 169
हेत्वभावात् iii. 2. 10	... 85
हेत्वाभास i. 1. 1.	... 1
हेत्वाभासः v. 2. 1.	... 167
हेत्वाभासाः i. 2. 4., v. 2. 25.	15, 175
हेत्वोः iii. 2. 4.	... 169
ह्रास ii. 2, 59.	... 58